For Doris Diebald,
   With very best regards,

   Peggy Anderson

July 2, 1975

The Daughters

The Daughters

An Unconventional Look at America's Fan Club—The DAR

PEGGY ANDERSON

St. Martin's Press   New York

For Kay, Pete, and Pam
with love.

ACKNOWLEDGEMENTS

I have many people to thank. The idea for this book originated with Jay Acton, now an editor at T.Y. Crowell, whose
willingness to entrust the project to an unknown provided me
with two fascinating years and invaluable journalistic experience. Jean Byrne, Michael Pakenham, and Olaf Saugen gave me
editorial assistance; Maureen Carroll gave me editorial assistance, a key to her Washington apartment, and limitless hospitality. For timely pushes in a direction I wasn't sure I could go, I am
especially grateful to Charles Caldwell, Russell Chappell, Leslie
Hanscom, David Hapgood, Charles Peters, and Carroll Stoner
Burgezyn. Other friends who encouraged me were too helpful
to go unmentioned, among them Lis Chappell, Shyrlee Dallard,
Don Drake, Alvia Golden, Pat Brown Kelly, Pat McBroom,
Robert Rice, Robert Shogan, Elaine Tait, and Barbara Wilson.
The fun could all have been ruined by a cavalier editor, but I
was lucky enough to draw Leslie Pockell.

My understanding of the DAR was greatly enriched by Margaret Gibbs' history, *The DAR*, and by Wallace Evan Davies'
study, *Patriotism on Parade*. The assistance given me by Eleanor
Gilman at Hampton Institute and by theater librarians
Geraldine Duclow (Free Library of Philadelphia), Marilyn
Mahanand (Howard University), and Dorothy Swerdlove (Lincoln Center) served to clear up mysteries about Washington
theater policies in the 1930s I had begun to think were insoluble.
My stay at Tamassee DAR School was delightful as well as useful,
thanks to Lincoln Jones, Willard Johnson, and the staff and
children of Tamassee.

While nothing in this book was cleared by the Daughters, I undertook the project with their cooperation. Many Daughters contributed to the final product. Among those who went out of their way to give me assistance I requested were president general Eleanor Spicer, Chick Anderson, Sue Barr, Edna Burns, Carolyn Donohue, Ada Helmbreck, Estelle Irwin, Aileen Jordan, Sarah King, Karen Kiser, Jean Paulus, Janet Shay, Jean Walter, and Lois Wilson. They are not responsible for my conclusions, and I hope my gratitude will not embarrass them.

Last but far from least, I owe very special thanks to the women of Independence Hall chapter. Regent Dorothy Irwin took a chance when she let a stranger with a notebook "join" Independence Hall for a year, and she and the other members submitted to scrutiny with uncommon graciousness.

CONTENTS

CHAPTER I

The DAR Reconsidered

A sure way to carbonate dull moments at certain American gatherings is to mention the DAR. The very thought of the Daughters of the American Revolution makes some people laugh. If these people were to compare notes, they would probably discover that the characteristics of the DAR residing in their respective heads are remarkably similar. Many Americans picture the Daughters wearing outlandish hats upon heads that are gray or white on the outside and muddled inside. The faces are stony. The lips are pressed together. The women each have a million dollars, earned by their forebears, which is quietly and steadily appreciating in value, but while the money is evident in the Daughters' attitudes, it is not noticeable in their appearance. They all buy dresses in half sizes tending toward the enormous, especially on top. Their stockings sag.

The Daughters in this image love antiques—ideological antiques in particular. They care more about their ancestors than about the living poor. They are most at home in cemetaries, where they hobble around in their tennis shoes scrutinizing headstones and making little notes on the backs of their church programs. When they are not checking out graves, they are marching in parades or standing on the curb to take down the name of every spectator who does not have his hand on his heart when the American flag goes by. According to popular notion, the Daughters of the American Revolution stopped turning the pages on their calendars somewhere back in the first third of the century, and they resent anyone who hasn't done likewise.

Not only is it possible to get a laugh by mentioning the DAR, but it is also possible to establish credentials as a modern and right-thinking American by poking fun at the organization. "I'm eligible for the DAR, because my relatives were in it," a young teacher told a liberal political cartoonist at a recent party. "I got a letter from them asking me to become a member, but I wrote back and said, 'Dear DAR, Thank you very much, but I don't agree with your politics and I would never become a member, so fuck you.' " She smiled expectantly. Everybody agreed it was a good party.

In short, to many Americans the Daughters of the American Revolution are a laughingstock. When the DAR Continental Congress meets in Washington in April, the town buzzes with jokes about the women's hats, although most Daughters are no longer wearing them. As provided in its charter the DAR reports annually to the U.S. Congress, and the U.S. Congress routinely votes to bear the cost of printing the report (about $4,000), but the decision to do so is usually made after a mini-row between opposing factions and a few broad winks: One year Pennsylvania Senator Joseph S. Clark offered a substitute resolution that would have authorized the printing, at government expense, of the annual reports of the John Birch Society, the Americans for Democratic Action, and the National Association for the Advancement of Colored People, among others. When the Daughters issue their resolutions each spring, they succeed only in entertaining some Americans, who sit with newspapers quivering as they read with considerable enjoyment what those crazy fool women are up to now.

The subject of all this amusement is the largest women's hereditary patriotic organization in the country. The Daughters number nearly 200,000. Their headquarters covers a block of prime land in Washington, D.C., across from the Washington Monument. Much of the space is taken up by Constitution Hall, the biggest auditorium in the nation's capital. The largest auditorium in the Kennedy Center seats approximately 2,700; Constitution Hall seats 3,752. The DAR complex is the largest in the world owned and operated by women. Most of the Daughters are housewives who believe that by their membership they are serving their country, and over the years they have served it in many ways.

While outsiders enjoy a good laugh at the DAR's expense, the Daughters today are involved in many activities their critics might well approve of. They contribute at least $50,000 a year to the support of two schools for American Indians. Each year they pay for the planting of thousands of trees and shrubs on public land, feed tons of seed to birds and wild animals, give scholarships in conservation, and contribute money and time to local conservation and anti-pollution efforts all over the country. Over the years the Daughters have restored several hundred of America's oldest structures, buildings significant because of their age or the people associated with them or both—the Connecticut birthplace of Revolutionary War artist John Trumbull; "Rosalie" in Mississippi, federal headquarters in 1862; a log cabin in Oregon; a schoolhouse in Wisconsin; and many more. Some are maintained as museums. The DAR Museum of Decorative Arts in Washington, D.C., unknown to most local residents, contains twenty-eight period rooms full to overflowing with items of daily life in early America.

The Daughters built the bell tower at Valley Forge. They planted a rose garden in Independence National Park with fifty-four varieties of roses of the kind that flourished when the nation was born. Right now they are working to refurnish two of the three rooms on the second floor of Independence Hall in Philadelphia with authentic period pieces. Until DAR president general* Eleanor Spicer cut the ribbon across the Hall staircase on July 4, 1972, the second floor had been closed to the public for twenty years. The National Park Service renovated the rooms but couldn't afford to furnish them. The Daughters undertook their project as a "Gift to the Nation" for the U.S. Bicentennial. It is costing them a little more than a dollar per member. Independence Hall curator Charles Dorman swears that without the DAR he would have committed hara-kiri. "If it hadn't been for the Gift to the Nation," Dorman says, "we would probably have had to settle for some pretty miserable reproductions."

The laughter of their fellow citizens does not roll easily off the Daughters' backs. It hurts, and it is very perplexing to them. The Daughters believe deeply in America. As they see it, theirs is an organization chartered by the United States Congress for purposes that are unassailably worthwhile. Their job is to preserve, perpetuate, and maintain the things of traditional value in America. Buildings. Human and natural resources. Freedoms. The lessons of the past. As formulated by the founding Daughters, their objectives are historical, educational and patriotic in scope: To "perpetuate the memory and spirit of the men and women who achieved American Independence," "to promote . . . institutions for the general diffusion of knowledge . . ."; and to "foster true patriotism and love of country, and to aid in securing for mankind, all the blessings of liberty."

The ideals espoused here are probably embraced by most Americans. Since the Daughters organized in 1890, they have raised and spent millions of dollars to support what they consider to be American causes. They have done, and they continue to do, everything they can think of to get other Americans to support those causes. Yet as a result of their actions and attitudes they are toyed with by the press, taken to task by congressmen, and ridiculed by ordinary citizens. It is one of the curiosities of American history that this organization, which set itself up as a

---

*"General" refers to a national officer, of which the DAR has twelve. Unless otherwise noted, all national, state, and chapter DAR officers and committee chairmen are referred to by the titles they held at the time this book was being researched in 1972-3.

fan club for America, has become one of the most unpopular groups ever to take root in the nation's soil.

The DAR has not always been unpopular. For several decades after its founding in 1890 it was held in rather high regard by a considerable number of Americans, including individuals at the highest levels of government. One reason for this was that in the early years of its life the DAR was headed by some very prominent women. Determined that their organization would be large and important, the DAR's founders decided that the logical person to run the new Society was the First Lady of the land. President Benjamin Harrison's wife, Caroline, agreed to serve the Society as president general.

Mrs. Harrison was followed in the post by Mrs. Adlai E. Stevenson, wife of Grover Cleveland's Vice-President. The next three women to lead the DAR were Mrs. John W. Foster (the grandmother of John Foster Dulles), whose husband was Secretary of State under Harrison; Mrs. Daniel Manning, wife of Cleveland's Treasury Secretary; and Mrs. Charles W. Fairbanks, whose husband was Senator from Indiana and later served as Teddy Roosevelt's Vice-President. Without these figures at its helm, the DAR might have been no more noticeable than any of the dozens of other hereditary patriotic societies forming about the same time. With such leaders, however, the DAR enjoyed both the cachet of "name" leadership and direct connections to charmed circles of society. Whether Benjamin Harrison would have given the Daughters two evening White House receptions had his wife not been president general is a moot point, but his official recognition cast an impressive glow around the DAR that graced none of the other societies. The press covered these events in minute detail. When Presidents Cleveland and McKinley proved as cordial as Harrison, the Daughters' impressive good image was virtually guaranteed.

Friends in high places helped, but the organization's activities in its formative years also contributed to the esteem in which the Daughters were held. The DAR was scarcely a week old when leaders decided to construct a museum for Revolutionary War memorabilia. George Washington had expressed a desire for such a museum, but nobody did anything about it until 1902. In that year the Daughters broke ground for Memorial Continental Hall, the first of the three buildings, now attached, which constitute their present headquarters. The location of the lovely pillared hall a few blocks from the White House and opposite the

Washington Monument made the DAR uniquely conspicuous.

When the Spanish-American War broke out in 1898, the Daughters instantly offered their services to President McKinley. McKinley designated the DAR as the official screening agency for Army nurses. The Daughters delivered up a thousand qualified nurses in very short order. The DAR consequently credits itself today with having established the nucleus of the Army Nurse Corps. For this and other contributions to the war effort the Daughters won considerable acclaim in the press. In gratitude for the DAR's help, Mrs. McKinley appointed wartime president general Mary Manning as the official American representative at the Paris Exposition in 1900. There Mrs. Manning bestowed upon France a statue of George Washington, bought by the DAR and given on behalf of all American women.

In suceeding years, the DAR took a distinctly progressive part in the social reform of the early twentieth century. It formed a Committee on Legislation Pending in the United States Congress, intended to encourage DAR support for a few important bills a year, such as conservation regulations and restrictive child-labor laws. Leaders also encouraged members to join the National Child Labor Committee, which was urging the establishment of a Children's Bureau in the Department of Commerce.

Once the Bureau was established, the efforts of the Daughters' Child Labor Committee were extended to women. As Margaret Gibbs wrote in her history of the organization*, "As late as 1916, the DAR agenda bristled with a series of liberal recommendations favoring regulation of women's work hours, universal marriage and divorce laws, a ban on new tenements lacking proper facilities, the improvement of sanitary conditions in stores and factories, tuberculosis control, compulsory education, work-hour limitation and work permits for anyone under sixteen, federal control of child labor, juvenile courts, and the prohibition of the sale of cigarettes, drugs, and liquor to minors." The Daughters claim credit for some of the social legislation that passed Congress during that period.

Despite a difference of opinion with Woodrow Wilson, the DAR emerged from the World War I era with its good reputation intact. Americans became vitally interested in the promo-

*The DAR, by Margaret Gibbs (New York: Holt, Rinehart and Winston), 1969.

tion of the world peace after the Spanish-American War, and the DAR shared that interest. In 1911, a few years after Andrew Carnegie announced that he would pay for the construction of the Palace of Peace at the Hague, a year after he had founded the Endowment for International Peace, the Daughters set up a Committee on International Peace Arbitration.

But then the war began to change the Daughters' minds about pacifism. In 1914, after President Wilson urged the U.S. to remain an "island of sanity," the DAR had pledged itself to neutrality. When Theodore Roosevelt and General Leonard Wood began warning that American military strength was insufficient to protect American shores, however, the Daughters' feelings of nationalism began to assert themselves. The DAR offered its services to the War Department. At the Department's direction, the women collected books for servicemen and did some grass-roots promotion for a strong military force. Finally, at a time when the concept of American neutrality was beginning to deteriorate, the DAR, under president general Daisy Story (who was also an officer of the National Society of Patriotic Women, which favored military procedures), repudiated pacifism.

President Wilson did not take kindly to the Daughters' stand. When war was finally declared, and the president general suggested that the DAR run a refugee relief program, Wilson gave the job to the Red Cross.

If the Daughters were unhappy about the rebuff they didn't say so. They worked with the Red Cross. They invited soldiers and sailors to their homes for home-cooked meals. Again in World War II, the Daughters contributed large amounts of money to the war effort (several million dollars for both wars) and purchased Liberty Bonds with a value of $130,000,000. The Daughters were important enough to Wilson that he actively sought their support for his League of Nations in 1919. The Daughters gave that support.

In 1921, although the Daughters had cast their lot with the militarists during the war, the DAR offered the use of Memorial Continental Hall for the International Conference on the Limitation of Armament. For their kind hospitality the Daughters were warmly praised by *The Washington Post*, which said the whole country owed them a vote of thanks. The same year the Daughters began their work with immigrants. Like other hereditary patriotic organizations they opposed unrestricted immigration, but they also felt a responsibility to assist the new-

comers to become part of America. At the DAR's instigation,
Congress had established the Americanization School in
Washington, D.C., in 1919. (Operated by the District of Columbia schoool system, the only public school in the country today
devoting full time to the foreign-born, the Americanization
School gives English instruction to nearly 1,300 foreign nation-
als a year and prepares another forty or fifty for U.S. citizenship.) Now the DAR began to issue and distribute a *Manual for
Citizenship*, a study guide for the men and women preparing to
become naturalized citizens. (In the intervening years they have
given away nearly ten million of these manuals.) With their
own money and the sanction of the federal government, they
also set up and ran—for thirty years—a program in occupational
therapy and patient aid for immigrants detained at Ellis and
Angel Islands.

By the time the Daughters had begun to work with immigrants, the organization was just over thirty years old. The first
three decades had been good ones for the Daughters. It is true
that they had taken some criticism for their membership requirements. Like dozens of other patriotic associations that
formed in the late 1800's, the DAR limited its membership to
people with a certain lineage, as it does today. Also, press coverage in those early days often tended to concentrate on what the
president general was wearing and on the social aspects of the
organization. Some Americans got the impression that the
Daughters were more interested in petits fours than in patriotism. But despite such disparagements, the Daughters entered the decade of the 1920's with a fine public image. Their
programs had won applause. While not universally accepted,
their platforms were respectable and respected. Their links to
official Washington and their assistance to the government had
given them what one writer has called a "semi-official status."
The DAR that stood on the threshold of the postwar era was an
organization that many or most Americans esteemed and took
seriously.

The Daughters have not since that time been able to bask in so
kindly a light. Their image became and has remained the DAR's
most serious problem.

The turning point came in the mid-twenties. Subversion had
become a national concern during World War I, reaching a
point of near hysteria by 1919 under the shrill provocation of
Attorney General A. Mitchell Palmer. Many patriotic societies

rallied to the witch-hunt. Although the DAR alerted its members to possible dangers through a "Vigilante" column in *DAR Magazine* it did not enter the fray. Within a few years many Americans had concluded that they had overreacted to the threat of subversives in their midst. At that point many other Americans, the Daughters included, began to worry in earnest.

In the belief that calmer citizens were being duped, a number of "Red-baiting" organizations formed to get the message to conservatives that agents operating on orders from Moscow were infiltrating American society at every conceivable level. While this message was being passed along, a clash was brewing between Americans who favored a strong peacetime military establishment and those who opposed it. Patriotic societies stood against the pacifists. (This was not surprising because patriotic organizations and groups which formed to support a large standing army often had officers in common.) As the sides squared off, the loyalty of the pacifists was impugned. Some thought the pacifists might be the infiltrators. While at first not formally involved in these matters, the DAR strongly expressed itself against subversion. In 1925, House speaker Nicholas Longworth addressed the delegates to the DAR Continental Congress. He told the Daughters that in his opinion America had more to fear from the enemies within than from enemies without. The DAR responded by setting up a committee on national defense to combat "Red internationalists."

Led on by president general Grace Lincoln Brosseau and national defense chairman Mrs. William Sherman Walker, the Daughters stepped zealously into their combat role—zealously but not very judiciously. For a while they apparently satisfied themselves with radio broadcasts and rallies for members of like-minded organizations, but in 1927 an article in a liberal periodical, *The Woman Citizen*, gave Americans some shocking news. The Daughters of the American Revolution, said author Carrie Chapman Catt, were actively engaged in a smear campaign against loyal American citizens. Mrs. Catt accused the DAR of distributing lists and papers drawn up by parties unknown which slandered "thousands of Americans who never saw a Bolshevik in their lives."

The DAR stoutly denied that it had prepared any lists. This did not satisfy Massachusetts Daughter Helen Tufts Bailie. Mrs. Bailie investigated on her own and discovered that the DAR was in fact distributing lists of speakers who, by virtue of their alleged communist or socialist leanings, were not considered fit for DAR audiences. Unfortunately for the Daughters, the lists contained the names of some very prominent Americans, including some well known crusaders against communism and socialism and also including a few prominent men who happened to be married to Daughters of the American Revolution. Mrs. Bailie demanded an explanation from the DAR power structure and got nowhere. So, at a meeting of the Boston Ethical Society, she stood up and announced her findings. The DAR was being used by professional patrioteers as a cat's paw "in a tremendous conspiracy to crush free thought, free speech, and even liberty itself," Mrs. Bailie said. After the meeting she released the lists to the press.

Dubbed by *The Nation* magazine "an honor roll of American life," the blacklists, as they came to be called, brought ridicule down upon the Daughters' heads. *The Nation* threw a party for everyone whose name was included and invited Mrs. Bailie to attend as guest of honor. Listees who couldn't get to the party sent letters of regret full of scathing witticisms which the magazine published. *The New York Times* noted pointedly that the Daughters' ancestors had not been afraid to have issues thrashed out in public and added, "Fancy Sam Adams of Boston proscribed because his utterances might be radical." The Daughters responded to the furor by announcing that "blacklist" was not their vocabulary and by drumming Helen Tufts Bailie out of the DAR.

Things were not the same for the DAR after the blacklists. The incident eroded the Daughters' credibility and tarnished their heretofore gleaming image. Then in 1932 Franklin Roosevelt took office, inaugurating a period of liberalism which thrived almost unabated for decades. It was not an era that coddled conservatism, and the DAR was and is determinedly conservative. In that political environment the Daughters' pronouncements were almost bound to be unpopular.

But their pronouncements have been more than merely unpopular. Over the years the annual resolutions have actually helped to escort the DAR out of intellectual respectability in America. Although they are the aspect of the DAR about which outsiders know most and the Daughters themselves know least, the resolutions even in recent times have contributed to the notion held by some citizens that the DAR is harmful to America. In 1956, when President Eisenhower and Attorney General Herbert Brownell were attempting to liberalize the

McCarran-Walter Immigration Act, the DAR came out four-square behind restricted immigration, saying that our national security depended on it. In 1957, three years after the Supreme Court ruled in favor of school desegregation, two years after Rosa Parks precipitated the Alabama bus boycotts by refusing to move to the back of a public bus, the DAR demanded that the U.S. Congress "reject all pending civil-rights legislation and recognize the rights of states to protect all citizens as provided in the Bill of Rights." In 1958 the DAR urged the United States to get out of the United Nations, a position it reiterated as recently as 1973. Also, in 1958 the Daughters opposed fluoridation as part of a larger communist plot to take over the American government. In the last decade or so the DAR has opposed the Peace Corps, has opposed (of all things) UNICEF Christmas cards, and has come out against the Equal Rights Amendment.

To many Americans these positions are downright ludicrous. They seem predicated on a distorted view of America totally out of keeping with the nation envisioned by the Founding Fathers. They also happen to be pet positions of the John Birch Society, which is even more unpopular than the DAR. Many or most Daughters would not be pleased to be associated with the Birch Society in the public mind, but Americans who read the resolutions knowing the Birch stands have doubtless made the connection and drawn their own conclusions. As DAR public-relations consultant Paul Wagner puts it, "The DAR is up against the right-wing kook image. They have a fringe of superpatriots, and superpatriots don't do very well in the press."

These factors have all hurt the DAR in the public eye. But there is no question, even in the Daughters' own minds, that the biggest single reason for their unpopularity is the Marian Anderson incident.

In 1939 the DAR refused to let Miss Anderson give a concert in Constitution Hall because she was black. There is much more to the story, but it boils down to that simple fact. To Americans concerned about civil liberties, the DAR's decision was appalling. This incident became a cause célèbre. Eleanor Roosevelt resigned from the organization, and Marian Anderson gave her concert from the steps of the Lincoln Memorial before 75,000 people. The event dramatized as nothing had until that time what black Americans were up against in their own country. It also convinced many Americans that the DAR was a racist organization.

The Daughters did not attempt to answer this charge at the

time. This may be one reason they are still being asked to answer
it. Although more than three decades have passed, the incident
haunts the DAR. It comes up constantly. "DAR!" exclaimed a
woman in line at the Interior Department cafeteria who fell into
casual conversation with a Daughter visiting Washington.
"Aren't you the organization that refused to let Marian Anderson sing in Constitution Hall?" "DAR!" said a middle-aged white
taxi driver in Washington to a woman who directed him to the
Daughters' administration building. "There's one thing I hold
against them, and that is that they kept Marian Anderson out of
Constitution Hall." "DAR!" says prospective member after
prospective member. "I wouldn't join that organization. You
wouldn't let Marian Anderson sing in Constitution Hall." "Now
what about Marian Anderson?" reporters almost inevitably ask
Daughters they are interviewing. When the Kennedy Center
opened in Washington, DAR president general Eleanor Spicer
noted with dismay but no surprise that "*Time* and *U.S. News and
World Report* and any number of newspapers came out with
'Marian sat there, and she must have thought back to the time
when she was denied. . . ,' and so on, 'but now she sits as an
honored guest in the President's box.' " Miss Anderson is now in
her seventies. In the backs of their minds, some Daughters are
quietly bracing themselves for her death. They are afraid the
DAR is going to be "crucified" all over again. For years the DAR
and Marian Anderson have seldom been apart in the public
consciousness. One is almost inevitably a reminder of the other:
to think of the DAR is to remember Marian Anderson.

The Daughters can't understand why Americans don't forget
about 1939. They don't see why the DAR should still be held
accountable in the 1970's for something that happened in the
1930's, when any number of white Americans were guilty of
failing to accord blacks and other minorities their rightful place
in American society. The Daughters' question is legitimate. One
of the answers is that DAR members often raise the matter
themselves. They are extremely defensive about 1939. Talk to a
Daughter long enough and she is sure to mention that she wishes
everyone would just forget about Marian Anderson. Then she is
likely to attempt to justify the DAR's decision, arguing that it was
the only one possible.

If this is not the only reason people remember the DAR's
decision, it undoubtedly helps explain why they haven't forgotten it. The incident remains the one thing almost everyone
knows about the DAR.

As a result of the Marian Anderson incident, the DAR has become almost obscured in myth. Who joins it? Why? What do they do? Are they now or were they ever simply John Birch Americans, Lester Maddox whites, repressed women with schoolmarmish tendencies? Few outsiders could begin to answer these questions. Many Americans have drawn their conclusions on the basis of what happened in 1939 and absorb more recent information only if it substantiates what they already believe.

Painfully aware of how outsiders view them, the Daughters have sought ways to improve their image and in the process have developed quite a few myths about themselves. The Daughters badly want to believe that the women involved in the decision to refuse Marian Anderson were only law-abiding citizens trapped by the temper of the times and the strictures involved in being headquartered in a Southern city, and that the organization has been thus wrongly accused of prejudice. The facts do not support this view, nor do they support other, similar excuses.

There are also myths about the present floating about the DAR. Perhaps to compensate for the low regard in which they realize they are generally held, some of the Daughters have bolstered themselves by believing that the DAR is the largest women's organization in the world, that it runs the only Revolutionary War museum in the country, that a third of its members are under thirty-five, and so on.

Not all Daughters believe these myths. Some know and readily say that they are untrue. Somehow, though, the myths came to be thought of as true by some Daughters. One reason is that leaders have been less than diligent about setting the record straight. New administrations come in every three years bent on making a splash, and there's nothing very splashy about ferreting out dubious notions. Another reason is that many DAR members really don't know very much about their organization. They are susceptible to myths because they don't have the facts.

"We have a constant problem of educating our members," says Jeannette Osborn ("J. O.") Baylies, regent (head) of the DAR in New York State. "Many times when I speak at different chapters, women come up afterwards and say, 'I didn't know we did all that!' "

Daughters who know may be reluctant to say. "In my little talk I'm giving locally to chapters, I ask the question, 'How many times have you been at a cocktail party and been willing to admit you're a DAR?' " says Susan Barr, one of the organization's younger members. "And you should see the faces. They all know it's happened to them—where the DAR has come up or something's been said and they didn't volunteer information at all. They don't want to be the fall guy. What we need is ninety-nine-percent saleswomen in that group. But they hide in a corner."

Daughters have tended to blame the press, especially what they call the liberal press, for the distorted image outsiders have of them. Journalists have kept the Marian Anderson incident alive, they say, and ignored the DAR's projects. However, it's not hard to find DAR leaders who feel some of the responsibility for the image belongs to the organization itself. "We have never shown any great genius in our press relations," says Sally Jones, chairman of the DAR's national defense committee. "We could have been inept in the way things have been handled, too. We haven't presented our case as adequately as we might have—there's always that possibility." Curator general Sarah King is more blunt. "I think we've been a little arrogant and haughty about ourselves," she says. "We knew we were doing good things and didn't care whether we told anyone or not." It can fairly be said that the Daughters themselves have contributed to the general ignorance of their organization.

Ignorance of the DAR is not a condition that preys on outsiders' minds. Many Americans couldn't care less whether their heads contain fact, fantasy, or nothing at all about the Daughters of the American Revolution. But the DAR cannot be dismissed nearly so readily as many of its critics believe. For one thing, aside from the service auxiliaries and the General Federation of Women's Clubs, which is actually a loose association of independent groups, the National Society Daughters of the American Revolution is the largest women's organization in America. It is larger than the League of Women Voters, larger than the American Association of University Women, and vastly larger than any of the other hereditary patriotic organizations. (It is also bigger than all the men's clubs in that category.)

Furthermore, the DAR is growing. Its membership is at an all-time high. In the past five years, women have been joining the organization at the rate of eight or nine thousand a year. Many of them are young. As some Daughters see it, these young women are filled with dismay about certain trends in America and are persuaded that the DAR might be able to get America back on the right track before their toddlers become sophomores or soldiers or parents. Whatever the reason, well over a quarter of the women who have joined the DAR since 1960 have been between the ages of eighteen and thirty-five. Since 1890 some 600,000 American women have decided that the DAR is worth joining. They have laid out untold amounts of money and time and energy for the privilege of participating in and supporting the projects of one of the most reviled groups on the American scene. Women who for the most part consider themselves conservative and have led rather traditional lives as wives and mothers have apparently found challenge and pleasure and satisfaction in operating on their own. Some women, of course, are members in name only. They are on DAR rolls for no other reason than that their mothers or grandmothers are paying their dues. But many women take their membership very seriously. For them the DAR is clearly filling some sort of need.

The DAR is not a fly-by-night organization. It is almost half as old as the nation which fostered it. Withstanding all the criticism that has been leveled against it over the years, the DAR has found a place for itself in America, and that has implications for America. In a country founded as a republic, the DAR discovered fertile territory for an organization based on descent. In a nation which eschews monarchical trappings, the DAR has struck responsive chords with ceremony and insignia. In a nation which accused it of being retrogressive or silly or even dangerous, the DAR has survived and grown, binding certain Americans together into an organization that has almost continually attracted new members, if not on the strength of its ideas about America then in spite of them. Physically and ideologically and traditionally the Daughters of the American Revolution are part of America.

For a long time the Daughters have been viewed by many as irrelevant. But the tide could be coming in to float them off that sandbar. The DAR may soon be enjoying a position of respectability such as it has not known for many years, restored to America's good graces by the temper of these times. Severely chastened by the Watergate scandal, Americans have rediscovered the U.S. Constitution and taken a renewed interest in the American system as it was originally intended to operate. The resulting climate could turn out to be consonant with what the Daughters have been pushing all along.

The DAR has long been criticized for being behind the times, but the times may now be falling in step with the DAR. "The preoccupation of this country with the Vietnam War, the dissent and radicalism that have grown up, are at odds with this organization," said conservative California Congressman Bob Wilson in March of 1973. "Because of this unhappiness with Vietnam, 'flag' and 'patriotism' have become code words attracting opposition from the radical element. The Daughters have an opportunity now . . . to ride in on a rekindling of this spirit. The hippies are now sort of out of fashion. It's time for a rebirth of patriotic spirit. The DAR is in a good position to push it, especially with the Bicentennial coming up. That's right at the heart of what they're talking about."

If Americans are in a mood to celebrate the Bicentennial, they are likely to find the Daughters at the head of the parade. The DAR has dozens of Bicentennial projects in the works all over the country. "Patriotic organizations are at a low ebb," says former Congresswoman Clare Boothe Luce, "but comes this celebration to which no one is paying any attention, and we'll all find that the DAR has been working all along, and I say God bless 'em for it."

Clare Luce is a DAR member and a conservative. It is to be expected that she would have kind words for the Daughters of the American Revolution. But kind words about the DAR do not issue solely from conservatives and Daughters. It is possible to hear them from Americans who are neither—if they have seen the Daughters at close range and observed them without malice. In 1969 NBC project producer Pat Trese took a crew to Washington to film the DAR's annual Continental Congress for the program "First Tuesday." He was surprised by the experience. Trese said the ladies looked "a little Helen Hokinson-ish" with their brocade and banners, but he didn't care about that. (Miss Hokinson drew cartoons for *The New Yorker* for many years and was particularly devastating to clubwomen.) "The music was good, the pageantry was interesting, they were quite hospitable," Trese said later. "Not brainwashing, but very pleasant. I was raised a Roman Catholic, so ritual doesn't bother me! One evening some of the ladies invited us up for a drink. We sat there and had a couple of scotch and waters. I said, 'If it ever got out that I was sitting here in this room drinking with the DAR and having a good time, my reputation in the business would be ruined!' "

The DAR Pat Trese discovered in Washington is a DAR many people have never seen. Some refuse to believe it exists. It is a DAR that has relinquished the past to the extent of computerizing its operations. It is a DAR that could elect as its leader a woman who is not afraid to say she was moved by a rock musical on the crucifixion of Christ. It is an unknown DAR that has spent most of its money and most of its energies for most of its life on activities that the rest of us have never heard of and projects that have nothing whatever to do with banning UNICEF Christmas cards or subverting the Peace Corps.

All stereotypes contain some truth, of course, and there are certainly Daughters who resemble the DAR members in the traditional image—the tight-lipped, crotchety, unfulfilled women who dismiss every modification of the present with a single sniff and whose favorite sport is issuing reprimands to the rest of us. But the DAR in the image is not the true DAR. The true DAR has been shrouded in the dismal clouds of the Marian Anderson incident. As a result of that incident, it has been difficult for just about everyone, insiders as well as outsiders, to appraise the organization honestly. The DAR deserves an honest appraisal. Beneath all the myths is an organization that has commanded the loyalty and the efforts, the resources and the affection of tens of thousands of women over many decades. Its members are not outlandish proponents of extremist philosophies; they are teachers and secretaries and housewives who live down the street, stretch meals with Hamburger Helper, chauffeur their children, spoil their grandchildren, and share racial and political beliefs with many Americans who are not Daughters. The DAR has not been obliterated by the laughter and criticism leveled against it over the years. It is very much alive. It clearly serves a purpose in America. If 1939 was a mistake, it was also a long time ago. It's time to take a serious look at the DAR.

CHAPTER II

Who Are The Daughters?

Sarah King lives in a small mansion in Tennessee. At her dinner parties black servants move softly through elegant rooms pouring boiled custard and bourbon for guests out of cut-glass decanters. Mrs. King has entertained Tricia Nixon Cox's inlaws. She can get the local newspaper to cover the visit to her home of someone who would otherwise never make the society columns. She is different in all respects but one from the woman in Maine who had to pick and sell blueberries in order to buy herself a membership pin: Both belong to the DAR.

The Daughters at a glance seem surprisingly varied. Look at Libby Naisby. With her gray hair and largeish girth, Mrs. Naisby looks like an outsider's idea of a quintessential DAR member, but then without warning Libby Naisby opens her purse and pulls out her pink Playboy Club playmate card. She is obviously tickled to pieces to show it off. Or look at Janet Shay. Janet does not consider herself a typical DAR member, but she is acceptable enough to other members for her to be once honored as the outstanding young Daughter in Pennsylvania. She arrived at that high estate despite her deep involvement in astrology. Janet would probably argue that she was honored *because* of the signs. She takes the stars at least as seriously as she takes the Stars and Stripes.

Jean Scott Carroll belongs to the DAR. Mrs. Carroll was a Marine sergeant during World War II. More recently she has won blue ribbons in cooking, needlepoint, and rug-making at the Colorado State Fair, and she serves as chairman of volunteers for Pueblo Planned Parenthood. Jerry Roberts belongs to the DAR, flies her own plane in the Powder Puff Derby, and volunteers her services to a kind of airborne pony express which transports medicines bound for developing countries. Georgia Daughter Martha Cooper is sometimes too busy to wait for her Senator to get away for lunch with her. Mamie Eisenhower is a Daughter. So is Genevieve Morse, a Virginian Daughter who has published a volume of poetry and a history of her sorority. There is Jean Walter, a New Jersey Daughter who worries about her sons learning existentialism in college, who works as a secretary, who wrote for local grade schools a history of the community that begins with a delightful story of two children and an injured bird. There is Eunice Haden, now retired, a Phi Beta Kappa graduate of Oberlin, a school she is not very proud of these days because the dormitories are open all night; Eunice Haden who in her twenties went to work for the government because it had the best retirement program, who now paints and exhibits miniatures.

Susan Barr is a DAR member. Susan Barr has broken her wrist thirteen times ice-skating and calls herself an "apple-pie American," but she met her husband on a beach. "Put that in your book," says Susan Barr, " 'DAR Member Is Beach Pick-Up!' " At a party not long ago, Mrs. Barr had an argument with a member of her family. The relative said, "Your son would be lucky to marry someone like Diahann Carroll." Susan Barr replied, "Black, white, yellow, blue or pink, he won't be lucky to get her—some bitch will be lucky to get him!"

Stacia Peaster is a Daughter who lives on a plantation in Mississippi, but she refuses to belong to the United Daughters of the Confederacy because she thinks the members are still fighting the Civil War. The regent of the Wyoming DAR is Victoria Ewan, a registered medical technologist whose mother went to Wyoming from Montana by covered wagon in 1884. In Connecticut lives one of the National Society's top officers, Marietta Morriss, historian general, who appears at late-night DAR buzz sessions in bare feet, a knee-length robe, and false eyelashes half an inch long. In Chicago when she is not visiting Africa is Daughter Priscilla Mullen. Priscilla Mullen is seventy, carries a shopping bag, wears purple clothes and hats that are considered "the wildest" by the young Illinois Daughters who love her.

Delineating the DAR by describing characteristics of individual members is more fun than poring over charts and graphs, but it isn't very scientific. What do these characteristics say about the membership as a whole? Is Priscilla Mullen a typical member of the DAR? Is Libby Naisby? Is Eunice Haden?

It's impossible to say.

Surprisingly little statistical information is available on the women who make up the DAR. The Daughters have never felt the need to study themselves in any systematic way. They don't really know who their members are, and no one else does, either. They came closest to finding out in 1967, when a survey was conducted under the administration of the redheaded, popular Adele Erb Sullivan. The survey covered 126,675 Daughters, or 68.7 percent of the total membership at that time. (A questionnaire was sent to every chapter, but about a third of the chapters—978 out of 2,883—did not respond.) Leaders felt the results would surely refute the idea "that the DAR is a 'pink tea' organization, a group of society women without much to do with their time." The survey showed that of the Daughters reporting,

29,551 were professional women or held full-time jobs: 11,142 as teachers, 2,355 as business executives, 1,935 as nurses, 1,482 as artists, 1,192 as librarians, 835 as authors, 665 as newspaper-women, 263 as dental hygienists, 236 as doctors, 125 as scientists. In addition, 176 Daughters held various kinds of jobs in radio and television, and 8,889 Daughters held full-time jobs that fell into none of these categories. In all, these figures showed, twenty-three percent of all Daughters worked full time.

The survey also yielded some information on the Daughters' community activities. Of those reporting, 5,008 women said they served on church boards, 1,819 said they served on PTA boards, 1,014 were on hospital boards, 663 were on corporation boards, 453 were on school boards, 246 were on bank boards, and 10,807 were on the boards of other civic organizations. Four hundred and four Daughters reporting were city council members. One hundred and eighty-six served in state legislatures. (The tally doesn't show how many women checked more than one of these activities.)

Enlightening as it was as far as it went, the survey really didn't go very far. True, it sought more information than it got. Daughters were asked why they joined the DAR, what their favorite DAR committee was, and what their friends thought of the DAR. So few answered the first question, however, that an analysis of the replies would have been meaningless, and confusing instructions on the other two made analysis impossible.

Leaders did find out that the members of most chapters approved of the DAR because of its efforts in historical preservation. They learned that only about a quarter of the members subscribed to *DAR Magazine.* They discovered that on an average, 37.9 percent of the membership of any given chapter turned out for meetings. They also found out that 82.6 percent of DAR members were 50 or older and that 41.7 percent were over 60.

What the survey did not find out is everything else. Who in the world belongs to the DAR? What kind of woman joins, and why? Is she married? A mother? How old are her children? Does she belong to a church? Is she active in other organizations? Is she a Democrat, a Republican? Does she live in a shack, a condominium, an old people's home? Is she unhappy with anything the DAR does or stands for? Is she proud of everything America does or stands for? What does she want out of life, and what does she get out of the DAR?

These questions about DAR membership may go forever unanswered. The logistics involved in polling 197,000 people are overwhelming. More important, there is a feeling within the DAR that members might not appreciate a detailed poll about themselves. A president general who sponsored such a study might open herself up for criticism, Eleanor Spicer believes —"But ask Eunice Haden what she thinks." Eunice Haden ran Mrs. Spicer's campaign. She lives in Washington and serves as national chairman of the DAR lineage research committee. On the issue of a poll, Miss Haden upholds the president general.

"Most of us dislike questionnaires instinctively," she declares. "A question about income would be considered in very poor taste. Members with little wealth give valuable personal service on the committees. Many who have been very active in the past are now living on very small annuities. They should never be made to feel that this matters at all. Religious and political affiliations have absolutely nothing to do with DAR membership, and questions about them are taboo. Every member would resent those questions." Eunice Haden does not see that anything would be gained by querying members about other organizations they belong to. "Some people are 'joiners' and some are not," she points out. "So what?"

In the absence of hard data, few generalizations can be made with any certainty about the Daughters of the American Revolution. They join for all kinds of reasons. Sometimes the reasons seem to have little to do with wanting to belong to the DAR. One woman became a member because she was getting married and leaving the state and was worried about what her mother would do in her absence. She joined the DAR in order to get her mother to join, which her mother did. Some women join the DAR because their membership can help prove them eligible for Social Security. A Daughter in Virginia joined the DAR to forget about a broken love affair. Evelyn Waite joined because her husband wanted her to even though she was "not remotely interested." Florence Briggs, who says she "grew up" on ancestors, joined because she had no choice. Her mother had been a very active Daughter. Mrs. Briggs described her mother's activities at length and then said, "I tell you this so that you can see how I got into the DAR. I would not have dared say no."

There are lots of married Daughters, lots of single ones, lots of widows. Many Daughters are active in PTA, PEO—the meaning of the initials is known only to members—Eastern Star, other hereditary patriotic organizations, local historical societies, and church, and play bridge to boot. Other Daughters belong to nothing but DAR. Some belong to the American Association of University Women or the League of Women Voters, organizations considered too liberal by other Daughters. Some belong to the Junior League.

DAR members would probably agree on only three generalizations about themselves. The women who belong to the DAR are patriotic and feel the nation should be supported by its citizens. The women who belong to the DAR tend to be conservative and Protestant. Aside from those common characteristics, the women who belong to the DAR come in all shapes, sizes, vintages, and varieties.

The most persistent myth held by outsiders about DAR members is that they are primarily wealthy, upper-class women, a sort of American aristocracy. At one time such women apparently did dominate the organization. This is not true any longer and has not been true for some time. Most of the women who belong to the DAR today live in ordinary social and economic circumstances.

There are exceptions, of course. Some Daughters are former debutantes and travel in elite circles. Some are very well-to-do indeed. Women who rise to the top levels of the DAR are almost always women of considerable means. However, they are not necessarily members of America's upper crust. Eleanor Spicer's first job was as a file clerk. Her predecessor had been executive secretary to the Governor of Delaware. Of the Daughters' relationship to "high society," Ruth Seltzer, who has covered the Philadelphia social scene for many years, first for the *Bulletin* and currently for the *Inquirer,* notes, "There are a number of women in what you would call the 'upper elite' who belong to the DAR, but the DAR doesn't particularly represent that segment. There are many in the Social Register who belong to the DAR, but as a rule, you would find the majority of members not socially registered. By and large the DAR isn't a 'social' society—using the word in a Social Register sense—or an elite."

The Social Register, perhaps because it is a profit-making enterprise, grows thicker every year. Even so, very few DAR leaders are listed. Eleanor Spicer is not in it. No member of her executive committee is. None of the eight living honorary (past) presidents general is listed. Only two state regents in office in 1972/73 appear in the Social Register—"J. O." Baylies of New

York and Mary Houser of Massachusetts.

In short, the average member of the DAR has no more connection to high society than she has to the Vietnam Veterans Against the War. The average member leads a middle-class existence which very likely requires her to do her own cooking, her own cleaning, and her own laundry. Pennsylvania state regent Mildred Russell has estimated that the average family income of the Daughters in her state ran between $10,000 and $20,000 a year. The Maine Daughter who sold blueberries to buy herself a membership pin may be a particularly colorful exception to the myth, but in the real DAR she is not altogether rare. Actually she is a more accurate representative of the average Daughter than is Sarah King with her servants and her small mansion. Many of the older Daughters live on Social Security and little more. Nearly all the chapters quietly take care of the dues of at least one or two members who can no longer bear the cost themselves. The New York Society paid dues for 174 women (one and one half percent of its members) one recent year out of a Friendly Fund set up for that purpose. In any high-level DAR gathering there are women in designer clothes that obviously did not cost $49.95, but there are also women wearing clothes they have made themselves.

Daughters say they are unhappy to be thought of as society matrons, the implication being that they are superficial and not much interested in real work. They take pride in the diversity of DAR membership. "We're just like the citizens of the United States," said honorary (past) president general Adele Sullivan over lunch at New York's Harvard Club one winter Saturday. "Each one has different interests, and some of them are more interested in one field than another, and some of them just come for sociability. They come for many reasons. Everyone in the DAR is not alike."

Of course the Daughters don't exhibit nearly the diversity of U.S. citizens. But they aren't carbon copies of each other, either.

Mary Louise "Chick" Bell Anderson is fifty pounds heavier than she was when she married David Anderson in 1942, but her appearance is striking. Her hair is startlingly black. A roguish quality figures in her brown eyes that makes friends of strangers in very short order, and Chick bears an unmistakable resemblance to Jacqueline Kennedy Onassis. Chick's mien imparts a sense of fun that makes people feel good. She is a warm soul and a spirited one, wholly convincing when she says, "I'm rarely tired, and I'm never depressed." Chick enjoys life enormously.

She is in it up to her widow's peak. According to the crests dangling from the links of her gold charm bracelet, Chick belongs to ten hereditary patriotic organizations, but she would need half a dozen charm bracelets to fully represent her activities in the town of Huntsville, Alabama. The Huntsville Hospitality Club, the Huntsville Community Chorus (Chick majored in music and studied under two Metropolitan Opera stars), the Madison County Democratic Women, the Huntsville Council for International Visitors, the Alabama Historical Orchestra Guild—as Chick herself says, "Everything that's in town, I'm active."

Chick does not take her memberships lightly. She joins only those organizations she intends to support actively, and she feels very keenly the responsibility to complete a job she starts. To those who stand in awe of all she does, Chick says simply, "I'm organized. My word is good. If I say I'll do something, I'll do it to the very best of my ability. Some people like club work, and they love to be busy, whereas someone else wants to sit home and knit. They may have the background, but they're just not interested. I can do anything. I mean really, I feel that. There's nothing I can't do. Now somebody else may do it better than I can do it, but I'm going to do my best on whatever I do."

This is not mere theory. Chick knows from experience that she can do anything. She designed the two-story, ten-room, two-kitchen house that she and her husband and her mother share. She manages to thrive on a life crammed with meetings and parties in spite of being allergic to flowers, perfume, alcohol, and cigarette smoke. Although she says she nearly got run out of town for doing so, Chick once directed a Negro choir in San Antonio. She even sang at two Negro churches in Texas. Obstacles others might see as thick stone walls, Chick passes through as though they were tissue paper. Only a person with no limitations could find time in a schedule like hers to read historical novels, teach Sunday school, antique furniture, work on the family genealogy, help with elections, and write a cookbook. Chick does all that and more. She hates for a day to end. She often drags it out until two in the morning, sipping black coffee and laboring away at the desk in her cluttered little office off the breakfast room. A few hours' sleep and she is up again by six, rested and cheerful, ready to banter with her husband about his forthcoming day at the Southern regional office of the Department of

Defense or to chat with her mother about the society news in the morning paper.

On the paneled den walls of the Anderson-Bell household is a collection of photographs, portraits, certificates and coats of arms that testify to family roots deep in the royal houses of England and in aristocratic America. "Benjamin Harrison was a cousin of ours," Chick says, nodding toward the Harrison crest on the wall. But she says ancestors interest her mainly for themselves, not for anything she gets out of having them. Chick is proud of her accomplishments because she feels they are entirely her own.

Had she stayed in Texas where she was born, she believes that things might have turned out differently. Her father was a judge, as was his father. Her mother's great-uncle Dick, Hardin Richard Runnels, defeated Sam Houston in the Governor's race of 1857. His uncle, in turn, was Governor of Mississippi from 1833 to 1835. The Bells' home, ministered to by "colored" servants, had a living room big enough to accommodate seventeen tables of bridge, and the family was active enough in Texas politics to be invited to Lyndon Johnson's inauguration in 1965. Chick feels that all these elements would have combined to give her an unusual status. When she makes the society pages in Huntsville, as she frequently does, she knows she has won that honor for herself.

Chick is often asked to lead the singing of the *Star-Spangled Banner* at meetings of patriotic societies she belongs to, and at such times she pours her heart into the national anthem. She fervently loves the United States of America and describes her feelings of patriotism in lavish terms.

"It's appreciation. It's appreciation for freedom, for what we have. It's just gratefulness. And people who don't have it, they don't know what they miss, do they? They miss so much. They really do. It's love. It's a real deep love, it's just like lovin' a human being. I can look at my mother and I love her to death, but I see her faults, and she has lots of 'em, just like I do, but that doesn't keep me from loving her. And it's the same with America."

Such are the feelings that brought Chick into the DAR—these feelings and the belief that America is threatened from within by communism.

"What did Karl Marx say?" Chick demands. "And what did Khrushchev say? They said first that they're going to break us. If they can take our young people, and goodness knows, look at what some of them are doing, even burning the American flag. So yes, they take them from within. It's eat, eat, eat, eat. From within. I'm a fanatic on communism."

Politically, Chick Anderson is a Democrat with a high regard for the governor of her state. She would have supported George Wallace for President had he run. "I feel Wallace is dedicated to the American people *first*, not just for big money; states' rights against federal government control, military preparedness as a deterrent to war and communist nibbling and a possible devourment of our government and other democratic governments. He stands for law and order and uncorrupted government." Chick feels Wallace's stand on segregation a decade or so ago resulted from a pledge he made to the people of Alabama when he was running for Governor. She herself believes in all aspects of equal rights but one. "I do not believe in the mixing of races through marriage and birth," she says. "These are my own opinions and have nothing to do with DAR."

While Chick is a faithful Daughter, the DAR is not her life. Both she and her mother have trouble understanding why anyone would narrow his or her activities to one club. But Chick's memberships in patriotic societies do have profound meaning to her. They have such profound meaning that she has been able to accept what she sees as the rather frightening implications of belonging to them. In Chick's view, if the Communists achieve their goals, Mary Louise "Chick" Bell Anderson is a sitting duck.

"You know what I told Dr. Hobson's wife the other day, he's our minister? We had this discussion in Sunday-school class, and I said, 'You know, with all the things that we're members of, and as Christians, and with the background that we have, we'll be the first ones that are killed.' And you know, we've had a lot of Americans to die for their country and die for their religion, and really, I can't think of a greater way to die. You've got to die sometime. And really, I'm willing to. If it ever comes to that, to communism or any kind of insurrection, I'll be the first one out there with a gun if I'm needed. I just don't have any use for these yella people who won't fight for their country."

Chick won't be intimidated by the possibility that she might be risking death for her activities. If that is the price she must pay for what she considers to be her duty as an American, then so be it. Chick is going to keep right on doing that duty.

"A lot of people think 'It's my children's or my grandchildren's heritage,' " Chick says. "I don't have any children. I do it for love.

I'm trying to do my part on earth for other people's children."

Not all members of America's younger generation would appreciate Chick Anderson's efforts on their behalf. Elizabeth Duff and many of her friends, for example, have spent a great deal of time and energy opposing just the kind of patriotism Chick so fervently espouses. Elizabeth Duff is twenty-three. She is considered by her fellow reporters to be one of the most attractive women at *The Philadelphia Inquirer*. With skin like a spring day and long, shiny, dark brown hair, Elizabeth got some intent looks when she arrived in the city room to start her career in journalism. She is not only pretty but smart, articulate, and alert to what goes on in the world, and she has impressive credentials as an activist.

Elizabeth was at Northwestern during the final throes of the student protest movement in the early 1970's. She marched the streets of Evanston in peace demonstrations and helped take over the university administration center in an effort "to get more student input into high levels of administration." As soon as she arrived in Philadelphia, she became an active worker in the women's liberation movement. She boycotts non-union lettuce, wears jeans to the office, drives an air-conditioned Buick, belongs to a swim club, and lives alone in a small apartment in the center of the city where she does not devote her energies to such traditionally feminine pursuits as cooking. "When I go shopping I get cereal and milk and eggs and bacon and yogurt and bread and ham, maybe," Elizabeth says, adding with a smile, "And wieners!" Her apartment is decorated with communist posters brought from Moscow by friends.

Although few of her colleagues can really believe it, Elizabeth Duff belongs to the DAR. She has never been to a meeting, because she belongs to a chapter in Watseka, Illinois, where she grew up and where her parents still live, and she does not pay her own dues. Her mother takes care of that detail. But Elizabeth became a member of the DAR voluntarily. She transferred in from the Children of the American Revolution, a club sponsored by the DAR for the offspring of its own members or other children up to twenty-two years of age with similar genealogical credentials, soon after her twenty-first birthday.

Her reasons would not necessarily please the DAR. The Daughters ordinarily talk about how they can be useful to the organization, not the other way around. To begin with,

Elizabeth explains, "Someday I really might want to know all that nonsense is on file somewhere. I might really want to know where I came from, who my relatives were, where they lived, what life was like back then. It doesn't hurt anything, and since someone else is paying the bill, why not? If it was the Ku Klux Klan or the John Birch Society or the Republican Party or the Nazi Party, that would be one thing. But it's the DAR. Its primary purpose is historical. And it did put all that stuff in Independence Hall and Betsy Ross's home."

Elizabeth also believes that her DAR membership might prove useful if the FBI ever decided to look into her background. "I have been a member of and active in lots of very left-wing groups," she explains. "I've had my picture taken at a lot of demonstrations with a clenched fist, I have been up there with a bullhorn, I've been on a barricade with a Vietcong flag and all the other stuff that gets you in trouble. I have been involved with groups that burned American flags. I was marching with a group that did become involved in some violence. I didn't, but the group did. Oh, God, I've had my picture taken so many times! So I figured it might not be a bad idea to be a member of a group like that, because if the FBI is ever going to go down the list of memberships of groups, to have a couple of things like Panhellenic and the DAR and God forbid the Junior League, they'll think I'm a nut or a crank. Like I said, that was not the deciding factor."

Daughters who would be appalled at these comments might be comforted to learn that the person who made them was interested enough in her hometown to write a paper on it in college. Elizabeth speaks with relish about a rather traditional upbringing that featured, among other things, receipt of what she calls a "coveted" eighth-grade history award given by the Daughters of the American Revolution. One reason she belongs to the DAR is that she wants to keep her ties to her hometown. Elizabeth expresses this rather offhandedly, but she insists it's a serious wish.

"To a large extent it's a matter of retaining an identity with Watseka, with what I've come from," she says. "If I ever want to go back in a senile decline or whatever, that root is always there. That's where I came from. I don't want to deny it at all."

Elizabeth's older sister resigned from the DAR recently because she felt her membership impinged on her credentials as a radical. Elizabeth has no intention of following suit. "If I was going to make my life a clean-sweep political statement, then obviously the DAR would have no part in it, and part of my life would be dedicated to fighting organizations such as the DAR," she says. "But my life isn't geared like that. There *are* things I want to retain. This is symbolic of some of those things. And since they don't offer a belligerent confrontation with my conscience, there's no overriding reason to make a clean sweep of it."

As far as Elizabeth is concerned, the question of conscience is irrelevant because the DAR is politically impotent.

"If it was a very active racist, sexist, right-wing organization, then of course it would be bothersome," she says. "If it became serious like the Birch Society or the Minutemen, I would quit. I'd have no alternative. But as a political force, they are not to my mind to be taken seriously. If they became the leadership of this land, they could be dangerous. But they don't have the political consciousness. They don't have the political experience. I think their stands on the war, race, whatever, are impotent stands. They can't do anything to back them up, and I'm sure not all of the members agree with these stands. It's like the American Medical Association taking a stand on the school strike. It's completely irrelevant to their main purpose. Now while they might think this way, while most of them will feel this way, while some of them may act politically this way, as a body they will not be significant in that respect. As soon as they espouse a point of view they will disagree with others who are more experienced and more active and more powerful than they are, and they're going to come through it like pâté!"

As for the politics of Elizabeth Duff, some Daughters would find them very difficult to understand, even downright reprehensible. But Elizabeth considers herself a patriotic American. As she looks at it, she participated in demonstrations out of faith in the American system and its ability to correct its own faults, not out of a desire to overthrow the system. She hoped to help change the attitudes that created the war. She believes that blowing the whistle on wrongdoing is one of the responsibilities of a good American.

"If I had to do it again, I'd do everything exactly as I did it. It was such an experience to be part of the mass demonstrations in the Sixties. Thousands and thousands of people motivated beyond studying in the dorm, beyond Friday night, to *do* something. It was as if something might actually come out of it.

Nothing could have, really, due to the nature of the system we have. I didn't know that then, and I'm glad I didn't. I was too young to be a cynic."

Despite views that some Daughters would consider cynical, Elizabeth Duff thinks America has a place for groups like the DAR which try to preserve the furnishings and ideals of the American heritage. "I think that to give our own nation a sense of perspective and a sense of identity we should know something about, have some pride in, a very radical revolution, in 1776," she says, "and to have people go around getting artifacts, the desk that Benjamin Franklin sat in—it's fine with me."

If Elizabeth Duff were living in Maine and not Pennsylvania, Ada Helmbreck would undoubtedly make an effort to get her active in the DAR in Maine. Mrs. Helmbreck is not horrified by people whose views she does not share. She would not have been happy to see Elizabeth Duff up on a barricade next to a Vietcong flag, but as a person who goes out of her way to speak only for herself, Ada Helmbreck will rarely attempt to judge others, And she is adamant in her belief that the DAR should actively court and willingly utilize young women. An indefatigable evangelist for the DAR in Maine, Ada Helmbreck would probably go to some lengths to ascertain whether Elizabeth Duff had any interest in becoming an active Daughter, and, if she did, to help her become one.

Elizabeth would probably like her recruiter. A widow and retired teacher, Ada Helmbreck is direct, down-to-earth, and unconstrained by shibboleths. In entertaining friends for afternoon tea, she is likely to dress in a pantsuit and to serve wine along with the homemade cakes. The blue insignia ribbon she wears to DAR functions is laden with pins, but let a Daughter comment on the length of the string, and Ada Helmbreck jumps.

"My dear, but I have only one ancestral bar on there," she protests to the offender. "Those all represent offices that I have held and the work that I have done. And I get quite provoked when I go to Continental Congress and I see people with just one service or one office bar, and yet all those strings of ancestral bars. They're not the working ones."

Ada Helmbreck is a working one. In forty-odd years of DAR membership she has done "just about everything" on the chapter and state level, and when she was past sixty she became state regent of the DAR in Maine. For Ada Helmbreck the DAR is a full-time job. She is constantly on the go, visiting Maine chapters, speaking at DAR conferences in other states, attending board meetings in Washington. Daughters who admire her dedication but have never been to her home don't fully appreciate just how dedicated Ada Helmbreck really is. Her house is not elegant —six or seven comfortable rooms enclosed in a squat, modern exterior—but it stands on what must surely be one of the most desirable pieces of real estate in America: a cliff overlooking the Atlantic just a stone's throw from the landmark Nubble Lighthouse in the southern Maine resort town of York Beach. From her windows Ada Helmbreck can watch the ocean rile itself up in a storm or go very tame on a soft morning. She can hear gulls squawking over the sharp breezes that chase around the cliff all day long. A Marylander born and raised, she has become so enamored of her special spot of earth that she even writes about it in her DAR newsletters, wishing she could share it with all the Daughters in Maine. It is a spot that anyone would leave with reluctance, but Ada Helmbreck is able to spend very little time there. In just one year of her regency, she put 34,000 DAR miles on her car.

An abbreviated home life is by no means the only price Ada Helmbreck pays to serve the DAR. She also pays cash money in rather healthy amounts. The jobs in the DAR power structure are all unsalaried. (The president general and the chairmen of the DAR schools and national defense committees receive travel stipends.) Nonetheless, the women who agree to take them are expected to meet the minimum demands of the office. A state regent is expected to visit every chapter in her own state at least once during her administration, to participate in the board meetings held four times a year in Washington, and to attend Continental Congress in April. The state Society usually gives the regent money toward her expenses, but even the largest stipends of one or two thousand dollars doesn't begin to cover the actual costs involved. Maine is one of the poorest states in the union. Daughters there can't give nearly that amount.

"The Maine DAR gives three hundred sixty dollars a year, two hundred sixty for Washington and one hundred dollars for traveling in the state of Maine," Ada Helmbreck explains. "Now I can spend one hundred dollars in some months of the year traveling in Maine. I couldn't possibly do a Continental Congress for under six or seven hundred dollars."

Ada Helmbreck is somewhat concerned that women with the talent and the time to serve at the higher levels of the DAR can't always afford to do so. State regents can spend five, ten, fifteen, twenty thousand dollars of their own money during their two- or three-year terms of office. Mrs. Helmbreck wishes that the organization could make some provision for dedicated women who can't afford this kind of money.

But a problem that concerns her more seriously is the reluctance of some Daughters to make way for the younger women. She considers it "vitally important" to get young women interested in working in the organization. Unfortunately, she says pointedly, not all chapters are willing to give them jobs, and the problem goes beyond the chapters.

"I wish I could say that all states are willing, but I can't. That was one of the subjects that I talked on in Rhode Island last week. I spread it just as thick as I knew how. I told them that we must listen to these young girls, and though they may not do things exactly in the way we have been doing them and the way that we'd like to see them done, we have to at least let them try themselves. And we can be a sounding board for them."

While she concedes that the DAR has its weaknessess, Ada Helmbreck is very proud of the things she feels the DAR has accomplished. Being a member means a great deal to her. She was the first woman in her family to belong to the DAR, inspired to join when, as a very little girl, she watched a young friend of her mother's pack all her white dresses for Continental Congress. She joined in her twenties, after she had married, had a baby, and started teaching. "I think I can say that all my life I aspired to that," Ada Helmbreck says now.

In York Beach the Daughters of the American Revolution have a relatively unimportant status, according to Mrs. Helmbreck, but in Elkton, Maryland, where she grew up, the opposite was true. "The DAR in Elkton, Maryland, was a very important part of town life, and to be a member of the DAR gave one a certain status that I liked very much," Mrs. Helmbreck recalls. Status was not her only reason for joining. She had heard about some of the Daughters' activities and supported their goals. "As a young woman I felt they were having a part in making a better America. I liked the objectives. Those were the objectives that were very important to me because of the teachings of my father all of my life."

Ada Helmbreck describes the DAR as her first love, but it

has never been her only love. She has taught primary school and English and social science in high school and didn't retire from teaching until 1970. She was commander of the Navy Mothers' club when her son was in the Navy and now belongs to the National Education Association, the Episcopal women's organization, and the women's club in York Beach. Until recently she was also active in the American Association of University Women. She dropped out for philosophical as well as practical reasons.

"I was the president of the AAUW and had served a year of my presidency, but when I became state regent I knew I couldn't do both. And I preferred to do DAR because DAR is a conservative organization. And AAUW is a very liberal organization. And I knew that I couldn't possibly serve two masters."

Ada Helmbreck places herself on the side of conservatism without plying a party line. On issues that would inspire others to pontificate, she speaks out of her own experiences and according to her own conscience.

On race, for example: "I was born south of the Mason-Dixon line, and I feel that we have come a great distance in the last few years. I don't think that any of us have been terribly hurt by this integration. I don't think that the whites were hurt as much as they thought they were going to be, do you? But I think integration should have started earlier. I think it should have started immediately after the Civil War. I think we were about a hundred years too late.

"I believe in equality, but race is not something I discuss with too many people, because a great many people may not understand my feeling. I have lived both north and south of the Mason-Dixon line. I was brought up with colored people who were servants. My father's people were slaveholders. And yet I've come here to New England and I accept them in the town, taught them in the schools, and I have no personal feeling against them having all of the equal rights of the white people. I don't approve of intermarriage. I don't think that I would accept them as my social friends because I don't think that we would have the same cultural interests. If they had the same cultural interests that I had, I might.

"I am very fond of colored people. 'Course to me they're colored people. It's hard for me to say blacks. But they were always in our home. And I like them, I enjoy them, and I have taught colored children since I came to Maine. There were no black teachers, but I could teach with a black person. And I have no objection at all to teaching colored children."

On the peace movement, which she doesn't like but doesn't condemn: "I feel that if we had known as much in World War I and World War II and the Korean War as we know now through the medium of television, we would have had just as much revolution then as we are having now. But we didn't know about it. I think that the television has had a large part to play in the young people being of a revolutionary nature right now. Because they know, where we didn't know."

On President Nixon's visits to Russia and China, which she approved of: "I think just the idea of communication is a step."

On the Vietnam War: "I don't believe in peace at any price. I think peace with honor, and I think that would be making secure those things which we hold dear here and those things which the South Vietnamese hold dear there."

Ada Helmbreck is held in high esteem in the DAR, partly for the importance she attaches to getting young women active in the organization. She is a favorite of president general Eleanor Spicer and greatly admired by former president general Doris Pike White, a Maine Daughter herself. As a national committee chairman puts it, "Ada Helmbreck wags quite a tail." The DAR in Maine is comparatively small, fewer than two thousand souls. In the DAR as in national politics, people who aspire to high office have a better chance of being selected to run if they have plenty of votes behind them. Thirty-three states surpass Maine in DAR membership. But when slates were being assembled for the 1974 elections, Ada Helmbreck was asked to run for one of the twelve top offices in the DAR.

She accepted. National offices are very demanding, particularly for a woman nearing seventy, but Ada Helmbreck has no intention of sitting home for the rest of her life, seagulls and sea breezes notwithstanding.

In the amount of time and energy she dedicates to the Daughters of the American Revolution, Carol Glennon falls somewhere between Elizabeth Duff, who never goes to meetings, and Ada Helmbreck, who rarely misses one. Certainly in that respect she comes closer to being an average member of the DAR than either of the other two women. Like Ada Helmbreck, Carol was the first member of her family to join the DAR. The idea was suggested to her by her grandfather, who fought in the

Spanish-American War and whom Carol proudly describes as "pro-American all the way." Carol would undoubtedly be pleased to hear herself described that way. She saw the DAR as a way to do her part for her country and her town, Haddonfield, New Jersey, and joined in late 1960's.

Now second vice regent of her chapter and chairman of three committees, Carol spends at least an hour a week on DAR business exclusive of chapter meetings. These meetings are held on the third Thursday of the month, and Carol works full-time as a private secretary. She takes time off to attend. She is docked for the time, but she feels the meetings are worth it.

By outward appearances, Carol Glennon seems to have led a life blessed with advantages. She went to private schools, Quaker schools (Westtown in Pennsylvania, Moorestown in New Jersey), and then went on to Katherine Gibbs, one of the best secretarial schools in the country. In 1962 she spent two and a half months traveling in parts of the world that most tourists never see. Lebanon. India. Burma. In due course she married antique dealer Christopher Glennon and in the next few years bore two children, a girl, Jeannette, and a boy, Rogers. The Glennons live in the old section of Haddonfield in a two-hundred-year-old house that is partially furnished with antiques.

With nursery schools available and her mother nearby willing to baby-sit, Carol has held an outside job for most of her married life. She also manages to cook, sew, knit, do crewel and embroidery, raise plants (orchids, violets, tulips, cactus, mint, geraniums) in her own greenhouse and pursue some outside interests. Besides the DAR, Carol belongs to three clubs—the United Daughters of the Confederacy, the American Legion Auxiliary and the Haddonfield Newcomers Club. She did belong to the Junior Fortnightly, a woman's club in Haddonfield, but she thought the women were too interested in social climbing. "I wasn't interested in their pettiness," she says. "I tried to overlook it, but . . ." She shrugs. Carol does not miss the Junior Fortnightly. She believes that people who belong to too many organizations don't do a good job in any of them. Carol wants to do a good job, and she also wants to make sure she attends choir rehearsals every Thursday evening at the Presbyterian Church.

Despite all these earmarks of a full and happy life, Carol Glennon has had her worries. She and her husband separated recently, and for Carol the separation is only the most serious of several concerns. There is also the numbness in her leg, the aftermath of back surgery in 1972.

Along with physical problems, Carol Glennon has been disturbed by the awful things she sees happening in and to America. Just about everything, it seems to her, is going wrong. Parents aren't raising their children properly. Children who have had a proper unbringing are falling under the influence of those who haven't. College deans with no courage are giving students far too much say in matters they know nothing about. There are too many people, and there are too many bad apples among them, and the bad apples are getting far too much encouragement from lenient judges, the welfare program, and the Quakers.

Under it all runs the strong and relentless tide of what Carol calls the "anti-American faction." The anti-American faction, she feels, was behind the Marian Anderson incident. The anti-American faction was also behind the peace demonstrations. It uses the press, uses the kids, discredits patriots, threatens to undermine our whole way of life. Carol talks about it with alarm.

"I'm not going to brand it communism, because that's what everybody does. But everybody who's against America is going to go through the press. And not only DAR but any patriotic organization—the Auxiliary, the American Legion—they're kind of picked at, I think. The press is being used very successfully by the anti-American faction. And quite frankly, I think that these peace demonstrators are communistically motivated. It's so well organized all across the country that I think they've been put up to it."

Part of the reason the anti-American faction succeeds in this country, Carol believes, is that some Americans are all too willing to give aid and succor to the enemy. The mere mention of the Quakers makes her fume in anger.

"Don't get me started on the Friends. Boy, I wouldn't send anybody to Moorestown. I went there for three years. Westtown, I had a touch of existentialism at Westtown. They tore the Bible apart, and for about five years it messed me up. I have no use for the Friends. If you're an American you don't help the enemy, I'm sorry. There are children and women over there in North Vietnam who are suffering, that's war, war is hell, I'm sorry. If you're an American you don't help the enemy. You stand behind your country. The president of my class at Westtown was on the *Phoenix.* I would have shot that son of a b as soon as he came back in this country. For treason."

Carol adamantly opposes amnesty for men who chose to go to Canada rather than Vietnam, and she cannot understand why some of America's problems have been permitted to fester for so long. To her, the solutions are obvious.

"I think they ought to bring back the electric chair. And I think if anybody steals something, they should be thrown right in jail. And I don't think you need a jury. You need one man saying, 'Did you do wrong? Yes? Then you're guilty.'

"Who was it, Ruby, who shot Lee Oswald? I give him a lot of credit. Oswald would have been put away, and they'd go through this, 'Oh, he was put up to it and he was out of his head' and the whole bit. He was shot right there on the spot, and that's the best thing that could have happened. I don't go along with somebody taking the law into his own hands. I realize they have to find out why, and where he got his ideas, but then there shouldn't have been any waiting around.

"It's just they're too lenient on people. Of course there's going to be crime. Over in Arabia, for heaven's sakes, they cut off your hand for taking a loaf of bread, although I understand now they put you under anesthesia, right? It's terrible, I agree, but they've got to do something with the people who are sitting on death row. And the courts are so jammed up now.

"Of course it has to start in the home. And that's what the DAR is doing. Home and Country, that's the DAR motto. If you don't behave yourself, bam! And that's the way mine get it!

"But they're getting more lenient all the time. And then they worry about their cells and how comfortable they are. Heck, they should be dungeons or something. Anybody can make a mistake once. But two or three times. . . . And these women that are walking over there having babies like rabbits? And we're paying for their welfare? They should be fixed!"

Carol Glennon's views would sit very well with some members of the DAR. One Daughter who heard her express them agreed with almost everything she said. But two others were taken aback. Carol would probably be equally taken aback at hearing these women say that in comparison to her they are "liberal." She might feel that they have let themselves be swayed—perhaps by college-age children—into compromises. One thing is certain: Carol Glennon knows where *she* stands. Although she is only thirty years old, Carol has conquered life's ambiguities with a resoluteness usually attributed to much older people. And she's willing to do more for her convictions than just talk about them. That is why she belongs to the DAR.

"I'm pretty proud of it all," Carol says with feeling. "I feel I'm really doing something for the country and for the town. Our Indian schools, our DAR schools—we're helping people there. And we're promoting patriotism too. We have a national-defense program, and we're trying to eliminate these day-care centers that make everything so uniform. You go and plunk your children into them and leave them all day in this routine—it's like communism. The ones that begin at seven in the morning and go till seven at night. I'm breaking up the routine enough with my daughter. She's in school part of the time and with my mother in the afternoon. She's not under one influence all day. She's getting many different thoughts.

"And what we do for the town, well, we met at the library this week, and of course we gave them a book, a kind of tracing book for genealogy. And we also gave them a history book of our chapters. We're taking the fifth graders on a trip to Washington Crossing. We keep a historic site here de-weeded."

Carol laughs. "I'm in charge of that," she says cheerfully. "The one with the bad back!"

At a small post-cocktail party gathering late one evening in a room in the Mayflower Hotel, one of the older Daughters who had come to Washington for a DAR board meeting walked up to a much younger woman sitting on the bed and took her face in her hands. "And you're still a junior!" the older woman said. Although the two had never met, she spoke her single sentence almost lovingly. For a moment she stood looking down with great warmth into the face she held. "The work that we have been doing will soon be in your hands," she seemed to be saying. "We are glad you feel it is worth continuing. You will be us someday, and we were once you. We are glad you are here to remind us. And to be in our company. And to let us be in yours."

When Carol Glennon joined the DAR in 1968, twenty-eight percent of the new Daughters that year were juniors, women between eighteen and thirty-five. From 1965 through 1968 the DAR welcomed 31,208 new members, of whom 9,167, or twenty-nine percent, were juniors. In 1971, twenty-eight percent of the new members were juniors; in 1972, twenty-nine percent.

Many of these women are not active in the DAR and never will be. Many, like Sarah Casey, who received her DAR membership as a college graduation present from her aunt, had nothing to do with becoming members themselves. But many juniors are active and are assuming leadership roles. At last count 3,000 of them held offices or chairmanships on chapter, state, or national level. They are the society's pride and joy.

The special feeling older Daughters seem to have for juniors is rarely expressed as it was that evening in the Mayflower, but it frequently makes its way into casual conversation in the form of compliments about the "wonderful young women" who are working to forward the objectives of the DAR. When the Daughters are talking about the pages, the compliments become effusive.

Pages are juniors who volunteer to perform tasks of all kinds at a state conference or at Continental Congress. So that they may be quickly identified, the pages wear white—white dresses, white shoes, white gloves, white hats. They may be assigned to a given task such as handing out programs at the door, getting information for reporters, carrying a flag in a procession, or they may be assigned as personal pages to DAR officers. The Daughter who rates a personal page is escorted everywhere. The page renders every service the leader asks of her. She conveys messages. She settles a mink jacket on the back of the proper chair on the platform. She puts a stubborn zipper in working order. She lends a sympathetic ear. Paging is hard work. Pages have to be on their feet all day, constantly alert to what they can do to make the meeting run more smoothly and the officers feel more comfortable. Occasionally the efforts of these young women are expended on pure ceremony. When the president general is on the platform, her personal pages are expected to stand whenever she stands and for as long as she stands. Even if she rises just briefly to shift her skirt under her, they are expected to get to their feet, and they stand throughout her remarks to the assembly.

The Daughters say they could never hold their conferences and Congresses without the pages. Their very youth makes them practical. Unlike some of the officers they serve, the pages are surefooted and supple of limb; they can stand long hours without great discomfort, and they can get from one side of Constitution Hall to the other with a speed that would have impressed Paul Revere.

It's difficult to imagine that many young women outside the DAR would find the role of page to their liking. The pages, after all, are grown women between eighteen and thirty-five years of age, with husbands and children and careers. The work they do as pages, and the deference they show their leaders, would undoubtedly appall some of their counterparts outside the DAR, especially their liberated counterparts. Picture Gloria Steinem or Mary Tyler Moore running to fetch a fur at the behest of some vice president general, and then standing still long enough to be fussed over in gratitude.

But paging is considered an honor in the DAR. The pages love it. They would almost have to, because they pay virtually all their own expenses. They particularly love paging at Continental Congress. As they watch the proceedings and meet the women who run the organization, the women who page feel they're getting into the DAR on the ground floor. A woman running for high DAR office who has paged a number of times is considered to have a definite advantage over a candidate who never has.

"Paging is a magical experience," says Susan Gonchar, a veteran of ten years of paging who in real life is a young Virginia housewife with two teen-age daughters. "It's a fine way to begin learning about the National Society. And all the pomp and ceremony! So many people from different parts of the country!"

There are other appeals to paging, Mrs. Gonchar explains. "The speakers are good. I've met Al Capp, Fulton Lewis, Jr., Norman Vincent Peale. And I enjoyed serving the ladies. If you like meeting people and making new friends, paging is *good*." Mrs. Gonchar beams. "And the idea of getting dressed up! I felt almost like Cinderella! I hadn't put on an evening gown in ten years!

"It's quite a sacrifice to page. It's expensive, and it's hard to get a babysitter. But paging is an honor, because you're representing your chapter and your state. Your performance reflects on them. And to be personal page to the president general is the biggest honor of all."

Susan Gonchar does not recall any unhappy incidents in all her years of paging. Yes, pages have occasionally cried, usually because the women they were paging for were under a great deal of stress themselves. But that is rare. In almost all cases, Mrs. Gonchar says, the leaders are very nice with the pages. Most pages would be delighted to hear that they meant as much to the Daughters they serve as Ada Helmbreck says her pages mean to the Daughters in Maine.

"The older ladies *love* the assistance that these young girls give them. There isn't anything they like any more, particularly, I would say, guests and officers who have to step up to a platform for our state meetings. They love those girls being there to give them a little assistance out there. They love the girls helping them find something. They seem to be very grateful and appreciative of that."

The DAR is not a sorority of octogenarians, but the membership is not as young as many Daughters think it is. Many claim that a third of their members are thirty-five or under. This notion is widespread in the DAR and is becoming widespread outside the organization, with the help of reporters who don't ask enough questions. Eleanor Spicer used the one-third figure when she testified before a House committee on Capitol Hill in August, 1972. A Maine DAR leader gave the one-third figure to *The New York County Coast Star* in November, 1972. The state regent of Florida gave the same figure to *The Tampa Tribune* in March, 1973. The figure is a source of pride to Daughters. They like to confound outsiders with it. They have reason to believe their claim is authoritative because someone somewhere along the line authorized its use.

But the truth is that nobody really knows how many junior members the DAR has. For years nobody even tried to keep track. Then the national junior chairmen began to try by asking each state chairman to request a precise count of juniors from all the chapter chairmen in her state. As some chapter chairmen never responded, the count has never been completed. In 1963, at the behest of president general Marion Duncan, clerks at DAR headquarters began to mark the records of each new junior member with a small "j." This system enabled the DAR to find out how many juniors were joining.

But the number of juniors already in the Society remains a mystery that has never been solved. Only one statement can be made with authority on the number of young women in the DAR: Since 1963, when the organization began keeping track, 81,671 women have become members, of whom 22,239 were juniors—slightly more than one-fourth. (This tally does not include 1969 figures, as complete junior statistics are not available for that year.)

Not all Daughters are under the impression that a third of the DAR's entire membership is comprised of juniors. Jean Jacobs, executive secretary to Mrs. Spicer and to four presidents general before that, knows perfectly well that all juniors have not been counted. She readily gives the information when asked. But

DAR MEMBERSHIP BY STATE AS OF FEBRUARY 1, 1974

Alabama	4198	Nebraska	2185
Alaska	120	Nevada	305
Arizona	905	New Hampshire	1595
Arkansas	2158	New Jersey	4690
California	8782	New Mexico	1057
Colorado	2073	New York	12,090
Connecticut	3957	North Carolina	5667
Delaware	653	North Dakota	232
District of		Ohio	9069
Columbia	3130	Oklahoma	3074
Florida	7704	Oregon	1607
Georgia	7286	Pennsylvania	11,678
Hawaii	138	Rhode Island	831
Idaho	495	South Carolina	4082
Illinois	10,695	South Dakota	387
Indiana	8409	Tennessee	6036
Iowa	3781	Texas	12,264
Kansas	3655	Utah	258
Kentucky	5153	Vermont	928
Louisiana	4109	Virginia	7892
Maine	1726	Washington	1931
Maryland	2990	West Virginia	3331
Massachusetts	4233	Wisconsin	2159
Michigan	3772	Wyoming	423
Minnesota	1396	England	20
Mississippi	4488	France	110
Missouri	5808	Mexico	45
Montana	717		

Except for this chart, figures given in text are as of February 1, 1973. Statistics available as of February 1, 1974, showed a slight drop in total membership, probably reflecting the substantial dues increase approved at the 1973 Continental Congress. However, the number of chapters increased to 2,979 during 1973, and Texas replaced New York as the largest DAR state.

Daughters who don't ask may not find out. Too many, including leaders, have accepted the myth on faith, passing it along as fact. While the claim is not made in printed DAR brochures or fact sheets, it does occasionally crop up in a press release issued from Washington headquarters.

The DAR may not keep close or careful track of who its members are or how old they are, but it maintains very good records of where they are. In the ground-floor office of the organizing secretary general in DAR headquarters is a large U.S. map stuck with tiny white flags on red-and-white-headed pins. There is one pin for each of the DAR's 2,968 chapters. The pins are thickest in the East and South, nearly crowding each other out on the Boston coastline. To the left of a line slanting south-westerly from Minnesota to western Texas, the pins begin to thin out sharply. There are only six chapters in Nevada, four in Utah, seven in North Dakota, eight in Wyoming, and nine in Arizona. California, however, is studded with pins. Only sixth in DAR membership, the Golden State has more chapters—150—than any other state except New York with 175.

Fully six percent of all Daughters—12,332—live in New York, the biggest DAR state in the union. The second biggest state is Texas with 12,044 Daughters. Pennsylvania is third with 11,809. Illinois has 10,741 Daughters. Ohio and California have nearly 9,000 each. The smallest DAR state in the union is Alaska, with 124 members. There are 140 Daughters in Hawaii, 213 in Utah, 243 in North Dakota, 314 in Nevada, 399 in South Dakota, and 429 in Wyoming. In all, 13 states claim fewer than a thousand DAR souls each. In addition, 156 women belong to chapters in England, Mexico and France.

To some extent the geographical distribution of the Daughters of the American Revolution reflects the geographical distribution of Americans in general. California is the most populous state in the union, according to the 1970 census; New York is second, followed by Pennsylvania, Texas, Illinois and Ohio. These are also the six biggest DAR states.

But Daughters offer other explanations, too, for why they are where they are. America's independence was won by Easterners and Southerners. Many of their descendants have stayed on the side of the continent their forebears settled and defended. In that part of America, the Revolution is much more than a few pages in a history book. Parents take children to Revolutionary War landmarks—Lexington, Concord, Valley Forge, Independence Hall—on summer vacations. Families may own Revolutionary War relics. The Revolution is remembered on the oldest side of America. Many Americans who live there are eligible for any number of patriotic lineage societies, whether based on colonial or Revolutionary War service.

The DAR ensconced itself fastest in the northeast, though it is now growing by nearly 1,000 members a year in the southeast corner of the country. (Growth is especially swift in Florida, apparently because so many Americans are going there to retire.) Sentiment makes the East fertile territory, but there is a practical consideration. Proof of lineage is not as easy for Westerners to come by. They live far from the records of their roots in America. Easterners, on the other hand, have access to all kinds of institutions dedicated to preserving early American records: libraries, archives, historical societies, courthouses, cemeteries. Such records abound in the East. It is altogether natural that Daughters do too.

Though well-established east of the Mississippi, the DAR is growing at a rapid rate in the younger south-central region —Arkansas, Kansas, Louisiana, Missouri, Oklahoma and Texas. In 1971 New England and New York together suffered a net loss of 125 members, but the south-central states made a net gain of 868. Texas is the fastest-growing DAR state in America. For four years the Texas Society has brought more new members into the DAR than has any other state in the union.

A state regent is extremely happy if she can get five new chapters a year going during her administration. Julia Hubbard started nineteen during her term as Texas state regent, an all-time DAR record. The DAR's largest chapter in the country is the Jane Douglas chapter in Dallas with 785 members.

Julia Hubbard feels the DAR is popular in her state because her administration made special efforts to attract members. The Texas Daughters bought and restored a historic house in Jefferson and urged juniors to serve as docents. When the house was dedicated in 1972, the Daughters arranged to have a large hot-air balloon, piloted by the world champion pilot, take guests for rides. Publicity was so good that the Texas DAR had inquiries from all parts of the state from people who wanted to know how to join. The Texas Daughters also got good publicity when they succeeded in securing from its Dallas owner the "Lost Declaration of Independence," one of the sixteen original copies, for loan to exhibit in the DAR Museum in Washington.

Finally, Mrs. Hubbard explains, "We think there is a great surge in this part of the country back to patriotism. People are beginning more and more to ask about DAR."

Ada Helmbreck of Maine offers another explanation for the growth of the DAR west of the Mississippi. "I think you will find in the South and West the DAR is looked on as an organization of tremendous status, far more than we look upon it here in New England," she says. "Because here in New England the people have had it for so long. They have had the status, where those people who moved westward haven't had it. They haven't been there long enough, and when they can identify themselves with something so permanent as this is, I think they feel it's good for them.

"Here in York Beach it's not viewed quite that way anymore. We sometimes begin to be careless with what we have, and we take a lot for granted. Right here in York Beach, we have daughters and granddaughters and great-granddaughters of a lady who was at one time regent of Old York Chapter, and I can't get them in for love or money. We have in this town daughters and granddaughters of a lady from Massachusetts who married a lawyer here in town and raised her family here in town. They're not interested. Their children weren't interested in the CAR. But when people move into a community from someplace else, they are the ones that are coming in now."

However, Mrs. Hubbard doesn't feel that this necessarily holds true in Texas. "It appears to me that native Texans and those who have lived here over a long period of time comprise most of the membership," she says. "In our chapter we have many third-generation Texans as members."

Like those of any organization, the DAR's membership patterns over the years reflect national events such as wars and depressions and internal events such as an increase in dues and the election of a popular leader. The DAR was founded in 1890 by four women. Within two years the membership had reached 1,306. By the late 1890's women were joining at the rate of three, four and five thousand a year, and by 1931 the Daughters were 173,525 strong.

Then the Depression began to have its effects. The increase in DAR membership between 1930 and 1931 was the smallest increase in the history of the Society—566 members, as compared with 2,001 in 1930, 3,029 in 1929 and 4,910 in 1928. In 1932, membership showed a net loss of more than 4,000 women.

It kept dropping. By 1937 the DAR had lost more than 30,000 members and was no bigger than it had been in 1924.

Membership did not begin to climb steadily again until 1944. Through the war years, there were ups and downs, usually of only a few hundred members either way. Not until 1953 did the DAR get back up to its 1931 high of 173,000 members.

In each of the next seven years membership broke all previous records. Then the national dues went up a dollar. (They had gone up once or twice before, but only by fifty cents.) Besides being a financial hardship on a few members, the increase gave an excuse to women who weren't particularly interested in belonging to the DAR. The next year, 1961, membership dropped by 1,253 Daughters. It continued to go down until it fell slightly below the 1956 level of 183,447. Although the trend had slowed considerably by 1965, it was not brought to a halt until 1966.

In that year DAR membership went down by exactly two members. The next year it went up by more than 1,500, and in 1968 it went up by more than 2,000. Most Daughters would probably attribute the gains directly to Adele Sullivan, a very popular president general. The celebration of the DAR's seventy-fifth anniversary in 1965 undoubtedly contributed. To mark the event, the administration of Marion Duncan, Adele Sullivan's predecessor and also a popular leader, put out a slim book of pictures and text called *In Washington, The DAR Story.* The book is beautifully illustrated with lots of color reproductions, and the narrative is longer on fact than on propaganda, concentrating on the DAR's programs, history, and the fascinating articles to be found in the Museum at headquarters. *In Washington* came out the month Marion Duncan left office. Both Adele Sullivan and Eleanor Spicer feel it brought in members because it improved the DAR's image.

The upward trend didn't stop with Mrs. Sullivan. In fact, it didn't stop at all. For the year ending April, 1972, the month all DAR reports are made at Continental Congress, it showed the biggest net increase—2,377 members—since 1956. The following year the Society made a net gain of 2,317 women, bringing 1973 membership to its all-time high of 196,681 Daughters.

To record a net increase in size, the DAR must overcome annual losses which routinely total at least three percent of the membership. More than four thousand Daughters die every year. Another two thousand or more resign. Some resign on principle. For example, when the Daughters came out against fluoride, they lost a member whose father was a pioneer in

public health. A West Virginian says she resigned "because of
what they did to Marian Anderson" and also because "their
pronouncements have become so conservative that they're just
ridiculous—those women don't have enough education to know
what they're talking about." Others resign because they are too
old to participate, or too busy with activities they prefer. When a
family moves, the woman sometimes develops entirely new interests in her adopted environment, or she may simply not want
to bother starting all over again in a new chapter. Some women
resign because they can't afford to pay dues. Some are dropped
because they don't pay their dues on time. These Daughters are
reinstated when their money comes in, but sometimes it doesn't
come in.

A woman may decide to drop out of the DAR if her chapter
ceases to exist, although she could transfer. No one is happy
when a chapter has to disband. The conscientious state and
chapter regents will do everything they can to keep it from
happening. For thirty years or more the overall number of DAR
chapters has steadily increased, but every year she worked at
1776 D Street, N.W.—until 1973—Sue Large transferred about
a dozen folders out of the active chapter file into the disbanded
chapter file.

"Chapters die out for two reasons," Mrs. Large explains. "An
area will lose its income potential, and people will leave. This has
happened in Pennsylvania with the coal industry, and in Missouri. Small farmers can scarcely get by. West Virginia. Anytime
you have a depressed area.

"Or a chapter won't have any young members. The younger
ones leave the area, and there's no one to hold the offices. The
age of the chapter has nothing to do with disbandment. We
recently had one disband that started in 1966, and the five
original DAR chapters—Chicago, Atlanta, New York City, Nova
Caesarea in Newark, New Jersey, and Wyoming Valley in Wilkes
Barre, Pennsylvania—are still going strong."

In 1973, bowing to higher prices and to the decreased
revenues from Constitution Hall resulting from the opening of
the Kennedy Center, the Daughters of the American Revolution
voted to raise their national dues. The increase, from $3 to $7 a
year, was the largest in the history of the Society. The DAR is
bound to lose members when the increase takes effect in 1974.
Still, the Daughters hope to have 200,000 members by America's
two-hundredth birthday, and they very likely will. The woods
are full of prospective members. Some are Daughters' daughters

and granddaughters who haven't yet reached eighteen. Some are women who haven't kept track of their background and have no idea they could join the DAR.

To some extent an organization is defined by who is not in it as well as by who is. The woods are also full of women who know they're eligible for the DAR but have never joined. One of the most eligible, if eligibility has degrees, is Katharine M. Brooks. Miss Brooks' Aunt Carrie was none other than Caroline Scott Harrison, who served as the first president general of the DAR while her husband, Benjamin, was running the United States. Now in her eighties, living alone in an apartment in Washington, D.C., Katharine Brooks looks back with delight on the more than fifty years she wrote society news for *The Washington Star*. In that time she covered many DAR Congresses and what she calls the "pink teas," but like her mother, also a newspaperwoman, she never got around to joining. "Isn't that awful?" Katharine Brooks says, looking anything but stricken. "Frankly, I never had the time or the money." But those are only the second and third reasons why Mrs. Harrison's niece steered clear of the DAR. She doesn't at all mind telling her first. "I wouldn't go in because the women fought!" she says. "Oh, the fights were outrageous! One woman pulled the hair of another onstage!"

Jeannette Jenkins of Arlington Heights, Illinois, could belong to the DAR if she wanted to. Mrs. Jenkins enjoys getting out to sorority alumnae meetings because she learns something every time she goes, but she has no interest in joining the DAR. A neighbor of hers was never interested, either. She did keep her mother's DAR papers in a safe in case she ever decided to become a member, and now that her youngest daughter is in high school, this woman has been giving some thought to joining. But a DAR friend advised against it for now. "Wait till we get rid of all the old ladies in tennis shoes," the Daughter said.

Andrea Creed Razak, twenty-six, is not a member of the DAR. Mrs. Razak grew up in Baltimore, a member of a family descended from Pilgrims in a city which prides itself on old families. Andrea says her family is not well-to-do, but it owns land and big houses, and Andrea went to private schools. She also spent summers on her grandfather's estate in Connecticut. Her great-grandmother belonged to the DAR. Her mother, whom Andrea describes as "very family-history oriented," also belongs. She is not active, but she keeps her certificate of membership "framed, like a law degree, down in our basement." All in all, Andrea seemed almost destined to be a member.

But in the first place, she is not what one might describe as a joiner. Andrea Razak belongs to no organization. In the second place, Andrea has heard that black women are not permitted to join the DAR even if they prove their lineage. In the third place, it is Andrea's impression that the DAR is very conservative. She herself is liberal.

She is not, however, radical. At Wheaton College in Massachusetts, she boycotted classes and refused to take exams during the moratorium on the Vietnam War, and actively participated in peace demonstrations. But now Andrea has a job in Washington, D.C., with Action, the government agency combining Peace Corps, Vista and other volunteer programs. She looks back on the demonstrations as useless. Andrea feels she has changed a lot since she graduated.

"You mellow when you no longer live on your parents," Andrea says grinning. "I'm still liberal, but I'm less sympathetic with radicals. I've never been radical to the extent of the Weathermen. But I guess I'm still Establishment or whatever you call it. Maybe it's a philosophy of the moneyed class—you don't tear down buildings. You become protective."

While Andrea Razak does not tell a lot of her friends that she is eligible for the DAR, she is not at all ashamed to say she is a patriot.

"I love my country. It's very difficult for people in my generation to say, 'I'll die for my country' when they've never been through anything that would arouse patriotism. I've never lived through a world war. Vietnam turns people off. I don't know if I could die for my country or kill for my country. I've never lived overseas, but if I went overseas, I would probably defend my country. Not in all things. But I do like this country. It's certainly not a democratic system, but if you've lived abroad or done any reading, it's one of the best systems to live under. My husband was in the Peace Corps in Iran. There the Shah's word is all-meaningful.

"But here, if you want to march in the counter-Inaugural parade, you are allowed to. If you work for it, you probably could get power back to the Congress and out of the Executive Branch. You'd have to say it's one of the best systems in the world."

For an outsider, Andrea Razak can sound rather like a Daughter.

CHAPTER III

Living with Ancestors

Any woman eighteen or over is eligible for membership in the Daughters of the American Revolution if she can prove that she descends from a man or woman who fought for American independence or who rendered aid to someone who fought. (Adopted children are not eligible through their adoptive parents, but an illegitimate child may be acceptable. One family hired a lawyer to support the application for membership of a woman whose mother and father were not married to each other. The lawyer said the father had acknowledged the woman, and she was recognized by the state in which she lived as her father's issue. The woman's application was accepted.) A woman must also be "personally acceptable" to the chapter she joins, but most outsiders know only that certain Americans are kept out of the DAR because they were not born into the right families.

If the DAR were a garden club, dedicated to producing better amaryllis blossoms, few people would care how it chooses its members. But the DAR is dedicated, among other things, to producing better Americans. Many Americans find this ironic. In a nation which rejected the rule of a hereditary aristocracy and went to war to support the principles of a democracy within a republic, an organization which has appointed itself guardian of those principles is itself based on hereditary. In a nation whose founders pointedly noted that all men are created equal, Daughters seem to think that people with certain ancestors are better than people with certain others. Individual accomplishments alone won't get you into the DAR, nor will patriotic fervor alone. The Daughters want ancestors. Therefore, some people feel, they are ancestor worshippers. And as ancestor worshippers, they are out of place in America.

These charges are not reserved exclusively for the DAR. Either directly or by implication, they have been leveled at every similar organization that has ever taken root in America. As the largest and most conspicuous of these, the DAR bears the brunt of the criticism today. But even the DAR, however much its members think it has been vilified, cannot claim the all-time record for vocal opposition. That record belongs to the very first patriotic organization in America with a membership based on heredity, the Society of the Cincinnati.

Named for Cincinnatus of ancient Rome, who left his plow to defend his country and afterward returned to his farm, the Cincinnati was founded in 1783, more than a hundred years before the DAR was born. Its members were Revolutionary War

officers. Its first president was George Washington. Its purposes, said the founders, were not merely social but charitable
—to provide for needy officers "some lowly shelter for the
unfortunates against the storms and tempests of poverty," for
example. Having given this rather innocuous description of
itself, the Cincinnati dropped what turned out to be a grenade.
Its membership would be hereditary, and it would pass only to
the eldest male descendant of each original officer.

Citizens couldn't believe their ears. American jaws dropped to
American chests and then began articulating in angry protest. A
hereditary society in America? More likely it was an effort to
develop an American aristocracy. Americans were suspicious
and downright hostile. Benjamin Franklin took one look at the
decorations and declared that the Society's founders had been
"too much struck with the ribands and crosses they have seen
hanging to the buttonholes of foreign officers." Washington,
uncomfortable about both the insignia and lineage requirements, went to one meeting and never went to another. By 1800
the Cincinnati had little more force than a club dedicated to
perfecting amaryllis blossoms. It was weakened by the hostility it
encountered, by westward migration, and by the members' own
indifference.

Whatever its own misfortunes, however, the Cincinnati had
established a precedent in America. Hereditary as a basis for
association, while attacked, was not wholly repudiated. In the
latter part of the nineteenth century, hereditary patriotic
societies began sprouting up on the American scene like dande-
lions in spring. By 1890 there were some thirty-five such
societies. In the next ten years the number doubled. The craze
was no respecter of sex. Seized by the desire to prove themselves
eligible for one organization or another, men and women alike
pored over records they didn't know they had and rummaged
through trunks that hadn't been opened for years, hoping to
find themselves related to the right people. Ancestors had come
into their own.

The women got organized a little later than their male counterparts. In 1875 a group of men met in San Francisco and
formed the nucleus of what became, on April 30, 1890, the Sons
of the American Revolution. Colonial Dames of America was
founded in New York that May, the nation's first hereditary
patriotic society for women. The second, which began to take

shape in July, was the DAR.

The Daughters would have preferred to join the men. That option was not open to them. The SAR decided right off that no women would be admitted. The one concession it made to the distaff side was to permit a woman to file with the SAR's registrar a record of her ancestor's service and of her line. At a meeting of the Sons in Washington in July, 1890, Senator John Sherman unwittingly rubbed the women's noses in the Sons' decision.

"They might not have done any fighting," he said of the females of the Revolution, "but they kept the farm going, raised the crops that fed the army, spun the yarn and wove the cloth that clothed the soldiers, looked after the homes and the children, kept the country alive, and it is most fitting that women should be present here tonight to help in commemorating the names of the Sires of the Revolution."

When Mary Lockwood read Sherman's statement in the *Washington Post*, she was not pleased. Mrs. Lockwood was a writer. She sat down and wrote a letter to *the Post*. "If there were true patriotic women, why is not the patriotism of the country broad and just enough to commemorate the names of women also?" Mrs. Lockwood demanded. She invoked the name of Hannah Arnett. One evening in December, 1776, a group of town leaders had met in the Arnett home in Elizabethtown, New Jersey, for an agonizing discussion of Britain's offer of amnesty. When it seemed as if the men had begun to lean toward acceptance of the offer, Mrs. Arnett not only gave them a successful pep talk, implying that they were traitors, but threatened to leave her husband if he should ever forsake the cause. In her letter to the *Post*. Mrs. Lockwood urged American women to produce the names of heroines for an honor roll.

The letter appeared on Sunday, July 13, 1890. On Tuesday Mrs. Lockwood's mail contained a letter from Miss Mary Desha offering to help organize a society of Daughters of the American Revolution. The two women met that week. On July 21 a letter appeared in the *Post* supporting a women's patriotic society. The writer was William O. McDowell of Newark, New Jersey, a great-grandson of Hannah Arnett and an *eminence gris* behind several other hereditary organizations that formed in the 1890's. McDowell offered to assist in the formation of a Daughters of the American Revolution. Six women in Washington responded to his letter—Miss Mary Desha, Miss Eugenia Washington, Mrs. Hannah McLaren Wolff, Mrs. Louise Knowlton Brown, Mrs.

Mary Morris Hallowell, and Mrs. Roger A. Pryor. Miss Desha wanted advice from McDowell. He suggested that a meeting be called, and the two of them scheduled one, inviting the women they thought should attend.

The meeting was held on July 29 at the home of Mrs. Louise Knowlton Brown. Because many people were away from the city on vacation, only five women attended. Mrs. Lockwood was absent and was to miss other meetings that summer. (She was on the Board of Lady Managers planning the 1893 Chicago World's Fair.) Those five women who had come to Mrs. Brown's decided to defer action till fall. Miss Desha so informed McDowell.

"Washington is the deadest place in the United States in the summer," she wrote him.

Torrential rains, illness, and absence from the city kept all but three women from the next meeting on August 9 at the Langham Hotel: Mrs. Ellen Hardin Walworth, who lived at the hotel, Miss Desha, and Miss Washington. The three made plans anyway. They decided to make the Society national in scope and to ask Mrs. Caroline Scott Harrison, the wife of the U.S. President, to become its first president general.

On August 17 a notice appeared in the *Post* proposing the new Society of the Daughters of the American Revolution and urging those eligible to write Miss Washington. On October 8 Mrs. Flora Adams Darling, another Washingtonian who had been corresponding with McDowell about a women's hereditary patriotic association, issued a call for an organizing meeting to be held on October 11. Among those in attendance were the three planners present at the August meeting. By the time the October 11 session was over, the Society had eighteen members, a constitution, three objectives (the same three it has today— historical, patriotic, and educational endeavor), and thirty-three dollars in the treasury. Mrs. Lockwood announced that Mrs. Harrison had accepted the post of president general. Mary Lockwood, Eugenia Washington, Mary Desha, and Ellen Hardin Walworth took their places in history as the founders of the Daughters of the American Revolution. The Society was incorporated in 1895 and received its charter from the U.S. Congress on May 5, 1896.

The popularity in the 1890's of societies that were both hereditary and patriotic had nothing to do with coincidence. To begin with, associations of all kinds were becoming popular. While a lull followed the formation of large veterans' organizations after the Civil War, the century drew to a close in a burst of organizing. Along with the Sons and Daughters and Dames of this and that, other groups—among them the Elks, the Masons, the early women's clubs—formed and flourished. Americans who found themselves living closer together in a city than they ever had in the country also discovered that joining was fun. While the city provided the place, increased leisure provided —to middle-class Americans, at least—the time.

Along with their new-found discovery of each other, Americans were rediscovering their past. The reason for this development is not altogether clear. The celebration of America's centennial doubtless had something to do with it. The increasing social and economic tensions brought on by the Industrial Revolution may have made it more comfortable for Americans to look back instead of forward. Family trees became the rage. Patriotic feeling ran so high that magazine articles sometimes described the phenomenon as "a renaissance of patriotism."

The good feelings Americans had about themselves did not extend to foreigners. The descendants of colonists viewed with alarm the "New Immigration" of the 1880's, which brought in waves of people from eastern and southern Europe. Unlike the people who had come from northern and western Europe, the Slavs and the Latins and the Jews were not blond or fair of skin, and they spoke in strange tongues. Native Americans considered the newcomers radicals, anarchists, opportunists who wanted to make money and take it back home. And if they stayed? How could Italians and Bohemians and Poles understand American ideals and institutions? And how could American ideals and institutions be preserved if so many of this country's inhabitants were Italians and Bohemians and Poles?

When all these forces converged, the development of hereditary patriotic organizations was almost inevitable. With industrialization changing the old order and immigration introducing new elements, bonds no longer seemed common to Americans. Many turned to patriotism, according to historian Wallace Davies, "as a sort of secular religion to unite the American Republic." The descendants of the older stock took for granted that they were best qualified to indoctrinate the newcomers. As an early DAR leader put it, "Our founders realized that with the steady immigration of foreigners to our country something must be done to foster patriotism and love of country and our flag and to make Americans of them, or there was danger of our being absorbed by the different nationalities among us."

Many Americans viewed the proliferation of hereditary patriotic organizations with approval. Proponents felt the societies could be useful in fostering patriotism and respect for America's past. Because they stressed nationalism over sectionalism, the societies were considered by some a potentially useful tool in helping to erase the bitterness left from the War Between the States.

Approval was not unanimous, however. By 1890 no American viewed lineage societies as a threat to the republic, but plenty of Americans felt that the members of these organizations had pretensions which simply did not belong in a democracy.

The societies seemed to go out of their way to prove their critics correct. They deliberately sought members with social standing in addition to genealogical credentials. Membership in some groups was not automatic but by express invitation, and the invitation was extended to very few. While DAR leaders envisioned an organization of much greater size and scope than the other societies, the Daughters, too, began by seeking recruits in the upper echelons. As one early leader expressed it, "The society is to become large, of course, and no invidious lines should be drawn or aristocratic distinctions established, but in the beginning, you must have what our coloured brethren, with their natural and distinctive discrimination, call 'quality folks' if the organization is ever to become attractive to that element which secures social success everywhere." Therefore, she suggested, the Daughters should entrench themselves "within the charmed barriers of Revolutionary descent *and* of social consequence."

The societies were quite successful in their efforts to thus entrench themselves. Many people who joined were professionals and well-to-do businessmen, and the smaller organizations were made up almost exclusively of listees in the Social Register. Since people of social consequence tended to be people with money in their pockets, they tended to dress beautifully. Skeptics wondered just whose glory was actually being celebrated. Writing in a small-town Pennsylvania newspaper, one critic scolded, "All honor to the men who achieved American independence, but this is a practical age, and men of today are taken for what they are, not for what their forefathers did, and to bank on the ever-glorious reputation of a past age is not wise, save it be to emulate their example."

Such comments inevitably put Society members on the defensive. "No, it is not for the aristocracy," Mary Lockwood said of the DAR, "but to honor the men who carried the muskets and the boys who beat the drums and fifed 'Yankee Doodle' for liberty. It is for the honor of the women who served their country, in their homes and in the field, while the men were away fighting the battles for freedom; so that their names, too, should be rescued from the musty annals of the Revolution and for the first time inscribed on the pages of history as factors in making the nation." Nevertheless, all the while the hereditary patriotic societies were forming, their members were charged with being undemocratic, snobbish, and overly concerned with ancestors and social position.

In all the years since, the members of these associations have never succeeded in convincing their critics that these charges are false. "I don't know why *they're* so puffed up," says New Jersey housewife Olive Roeder, a septuagenarian who lives in a community where the DAR is active. "They haven't done anything *themselves.*"

Of course, Olive Roeder is precisely the kind of person from whom the Daughters expect such criticism. To put it bluntly, she is not eligible for the DAR. Although Mrs. Roeder claims to be perfectly happy with her activities in church organizations, some Daughters feel that people who criticize them do so because they wish they had the bloodlines to join the DAR. This phenomenon is described by Pennsylvania Daughter Georgie Anderson as the "jealousy factor" or the "little greeen monster."

"There is a problem with a majority of·people today," Mrs. Anderson informed two younger Daughters one evening in her no-nonsense voice. "You tell them that they can't do something, that's what they want to do. Now we have certain requirements for entrance into this organization, and when they can't meet those requirements, it is then easy for them to say, 'Oh, they're a bunch of old women.' "

Though Daughters feel that mere envy is behind some of the attacks against them, they can't shrug them off. They become incensed when they hear criticism such as Olive Roeder's. It implies that the only thing they do or know how to do is swell with pride in their antecedents.

That, the Daughters say, is ridiculous. While they respect or even revere their ancestors, they definitely do not worship them. They certainly do not believe that having special ancestors makes *them* special.

"We are what we have made of ourselves," Maine regent Ada Helmbreck says flatly. "Our own ambitions and desires and interests make us what we are. I think our ancestors have given us an opportunity. I'm just grateful that I had them, because they have made it possible for me to serve in an organization that does such wonderful things."

Daughters say the DAR's lineage requirements are designed not to humble women who don't qualify but to attract those who do. "What we do as a Society has very little to do, actually, with our lineage," Eleanor Spicer says. "We are envisioned as ancestor-worshippers, and we are only in a very broad sense —that we appreciate our ancestors and feel that our objectives are to perpetuate their traditions and ideals. Lineage is our common bond. You have many organizations founded on something they have in common. For us, having that bond emphasizes the responsibility of our heritage as well as the privilege."

In Eleanor Spicer's mind there is no contradiction between the hereditary DAR and the democratic U.S.A. Mrs. Spicer even argues that the DAR is right in line with American principles. For one thing, the Daughters' Continental Congresses are modeled after the original, with voters being elected representatives of the body at large. For another, the soldiers and patriots from whom the Daughters descend came from all walks of life. The Daughters do, too. Of all the hereditary patriotic organizations in the country, the DAR is the easiest to get into. If a woman wants to join the Order of the Crown, she has to prove that she descends from a royal line. If she wants to join Daughters of Colonial Clergy, she has to find documents that will link her to one of fewer than ten thousand colonial clergymen. The man who wants to join the Order of the Founders and Patriots of America, generally considered the most difficult hereditary society to get into, must descend from someone who was in America before 1657, and that someone must have had a descendant who fought in the Revolutionary War and must bear the surname of the mother or father of the man who wants to join. No wonder only about 3,500 men have joined the Order since its founding in 1896. Only about 1,450 founding ancestors have been identified. The Daughters of the American Revolution, on the other hand, have identified 106,200 men, women, and children who helped win the Revolutionary War. More such patriots are being discovered every year. All of their descendants are eligible for

DAR membership. When Eleanor Spicer hears people criticize the DAR for being exclusionist, she becomes a little indignant.

"The DAR is wide open," she protests. "And to vilify us— and they do—because we don't take everybody in without restrictions, throw it wide open, is just unreasonable and illogical. Everything about the organization would have to change if we did that, from the charter on down. It would lose its idea. I don't think that even with double the number of members we'd be as effective without that particular incentive, that sense of shared responsibility the lineage gives us. Look at B'nai B'rith. I can't belong to that. Does that make them subject to criticism? Not everybody can be a Black Panther, either!"

Lineage does provide the Daughters with a common bond, but it clearly has importance beyond that in the DAR. Some Daughters obviously feel that the quality or quantity of their lines has a definite relationship to their own quality. "I have seven Revolutionary War ancestors," one Daughter boasted to a total stranger. Since she thought it unnecessary to say who the ancestors were or what they did, the woman was apparently trying to give some clue not to them but to herself. An older Daughter, a grandmother with high rank in the DAR, announced that her given name had been borne by a woman in every generation of her family for seven centuries. She evidently felt this detail indicated something about her own standing. A Daughter in her thirties looks to her family's coat of arms as proof that she is solidly respectable even though she smokes marijuana, drinks rather heavily, and dreams of living one day on the Left Bank. "Since the coat of arms was kept up, they were serious family people," she explains of her ancestors. "Any family that kept track of its coat of arms weren't just drifters. I'm bohemian and so forth, but I think I have some substance. Anybody interested in genealogy or biography has substance. You want to be respectable according to the law and to morals."

Lineage also figures in DAR politics. This is not to say that Daughters who descend from officers have a better chance of getting into the DAR power structure than Daughters whose ancestors were foot soldiers. Although it happens that Eleanor Washington Sullivan Spicer and former president general Marion Moncure Duncan both descend from the Washington family (Mrs. Duncan descends from Colonel John Washington's line), many women have risen to the top ranks of the DAR without benefit of such illustrious antecedents. But a candidate for office in the DAR will use her background to whatever advantage she can, much as a candidate for national office will. When Eleanor Spicer was campaigning, she always brushed up on her ancestors before a trip and mentioned them in her speeches.

"I went to Vermont, and I knew I had five Green Mountain Boys, and of course it was a nice thing to be able to say to the Vermont Daughters," she says. "In New York I could talk about the Sullivans and the Van Guyslings, and in New Jersey I had some Quakers who were patriots."

Mrs. Spicer's opponent, Elizabeth Barnes, pointed out in her campaign that she slept in the bed she was born in, and her mother before her, and a grandparent before that. "I must say this is something I respect and admire," Mrs. Spicer says. "I mean this is great if you can have that tradition and keep the same house. It's wonderful. I know there are people with homes like that, established homes. But it didn't happen in my lifetime. I was a nomad." Candidate Barnes wore two ribbons bearing, among other things, fourteen ancestor bars. Candidate Spicer had never bothered to prove more than one line. At her campaign manager's urging, Mrs. Spicer permitted Eunice Haden to complete papers on eighteen more ancestors. The additional bars came to what Mrs. Spicer describes as "a whole string of stuff," and she says she wore it feeling "like something out of a circus." But Eleanor Spicer won the election. If her ancestors didn't hand her that victory, they certainly didn't obstruct it.

Daughters who feel that ancestors do more for them than get them into the DAR and inspire them to work for a better America are unlikely to say so. Outsiders might laugh. The Daughters know as well as anyone else that status ought to be earned.

But sometimes it's tempting to take the easier route. Eleanor Spicer acknowledges that in a story she tells on herself. In trying to close a gap in her father's line, she sought the help of a genealogist, a woman, who discovered that one of the missing ancestors was a smith. Mrs. Spicer was not overjoyed at the news.

"I said, 'A blacksmith! Forget it!' She said, 'My dear, you don't know what you're talking about.' I said, 'That doesn't sound very aristocratic.' But she told me that the smiths of those days were wagon constructors, people who were very well established. They owned fleets of wagons which they rented out.

"Now that, I'll have to admit, was snobbish. If I had any sense I'd be proud of him. But we're all two or three different people, and it was the snob in me that answered."

While most Daughters probably stand a little taller because of their connections to the early patriots than they would without those connections, most DAR members do not seem preoccupied with ancestors. An occasional state or chapter regent will make a game of asking everybody at a meeting to stand up and describe her ancestor in ninety seconds. But ancestors are rarely mentioned at a DAR gathering otherwise, and Daughters say they just never sit around and chat about them. They also say it wouldn't occur to them to make a fuss over a woman known to have an unusually high number of patriots in her past.

"If some vice president general has ancestor bars on a ribbon down to her belly button, I notice," says Pennsylvanian Janet Shay, laughing, "but I don't talk to her about it!"

What Daughters do talk about is lines. Establishing a line for the DAR is more involved than worshipping an ancestor. A woman who wants to join must find written evidence that every person linking her to an American of two hundred years ago was born, was legally married, and died. Whether she starts with herself and traces back, hoping to find a suitable ancestor, or starts with an ancestor she already knows about and traces forward, proof can be extremely elusive (just for a start, how many people would know where to look for their grandmothers' birth certificates?), and, as Eleanor Spicer points out, "We go in on the *easy* lines." Family Bibles, cemetery records, county histories, tax lists, wills, deeds, church and census records, historical societies, libraries and courthouses are all possible sources; but a genealogy buff may research the logical places for months and come up with nothing more telling than a few ancestral footprints which disappear at the foot of a tree.

All kinds of obstacles impede the search. Names have more than one spelling. Records are handwritten and sometimes illegible, and certain letters look alike in many of the older scripts. Marriages were performed by circuit riders who cantered off into the sunset carrying their records with them and years later died in another county. Families gave babies the same name again and again until one of the babies lived. The Quaker calendar begins in March, making May the Quakers' third month. Records of any kind may be incomplete, listing one brother and ignoring another. County lines change. Courthouses were burned during the Civil War. Old people who know the facts may not be able to remember them.

"You can't just say, 'What was his name?' to some older people," Eunice Haden says. "They go blank."

"Doing genealogical research is like stumbling around in a swamp," genealogist Thomas Wilgus says without smiling, sitting on his desk at the Library of Congress. "It's murky." Many daughters find the swamp an absorbing place, full of tests and surprises. To these women, the mysteries shrouding the search for almost any ancestor can be fascinating subjects for discussion.

The case of Estelle Irwin illustrates how murky the genealogical swamp can be. While most women have trouble coming up with documents written a century or two ago, Estelle Irwin, who had been orphaned at an early age, was stumped by the very information most people start out with—the date of her parents' marriage. Her problem was knotty enough to require the attention of two genealogists, both members of the DAR.

Elizabeth Estelle Benton was born in Adairville, Kentucky, in 1902. Not long thereafter the family moved to Trenton, Missouri, where her father, John Bryant Benton, served as a Baptist minister. When Estelle was only seven, her mother, Myrtle Cooke Benton, died.

The young father sent his three children to live with relatives. John, the youngest boy, stayed in Trenton, Kentucky, with an uncle. Estelle, the oldest child, was put on a train with her brother, Will Cooke, then five. They got off in Smiths Grove, Kentucky, where their maternal grandfather lived with his wife, their step-grandmother. The children had no other grandparents. Their father's parents were dead. Within a year after they moved in with their grandfather, he, too, died.

In the summer of 1910, Benton came after Estelle and took her by train to Owensboro, Kentucky, where he proposed to his childhood sweetheart, Tina Owen. The young woman's mother had once opposed her daughter's marriage to a struggling young minister, but this time she did not prevail. Benton and Miss Owen were married at Christmastime, 1911. They took Estelle and Will Cooke to live with them in St. Louis. Six months later, as the family was beginning to knit itself together, Estelle's father died of emphysema.

Will Cooke was sent back to his step-grandmother's. Estelle went to live with a sister of her mother's, Aunt Mattie Porter, and Aunt Mattie's husband, Bennie, on their big farm in Bowling Green, Kentucky. Estelle was not happy there. The Porters had no children. They would not permit their niece to go anywhere. She was frightened by Uncle Bennie, who would hold her over the sty and threatened to feed her to the hogs. Looking for a way out, Estelle hit upon the idea of finishing her last two years of high school in one year. Her plan worked. After she graduated, she attended Tennessee College for a year and then went to Ohio. Her stepmother was in charge of the office at the Conservatory of Music in Cincinnati. Estelle enrolled at the University of Cincinnati and majored in chemistry and French. After graduation she married chemist Clarence Irwin and bore him two children.

As the children grew up, Estelle continued to study voice. She was often invited to sing for groups of clubwomen. One of the organizations that kept asking her back to sing was the United Daughters of the Confederacy. They invited her to join. Estelle considered it futile to try. She had been uprooted so many times. She was sure she could never trace her family.

Then one Christmas the Irwins received a card from Mary Bryant Benton Brooks, a cousin in Owensboro, Kentucky. Estelle didn't know this cousin. Her brother, Will Cooke, had visited Mary Brooks and given her his sister's address. Estelle added Mary Brooks to her own Christmas card list. Though the two never really corresponded, they exchanged greetings for several years. On one card Estelle asked her cousin whether she might be eligible for UDC. "And because I was writing," Mrs. Irwin says, "I included the DAR."

Mary Brooks replied that Estelle was eligible for both. Estelle decided to join if she could trace her lines. She wrote back to her cousin asking for proof if any was available. Like many people who have never set foot in the swamp, Mary Brooks proved to be something less than an avid unearther of documents. Although Estelle wrote many letters asking her cousin for photostats that would help prove the line, offering to pay the copying cost, no photostats appeared. Estelle Irwin took matters into her own hands. She began hunting for Bentons in the Historical Society of Cincinnati. She found a Joseph Benton. He was listed in the first Maryland census.

About this time Mary Bryant wrote to her cousin suggesting that she contact a certain genealogist in Calhoun, Kentucky, Mrs. W. Leachman, to whom the Bentons were distantly related. Estelle Irwin and her husband got in their car and drove to Kentucky.

Mrs. Leachman was a member of the DAR. At her suggestion Estelle Irwin wrote to DAR headquarters in Washington and learned that the DAR had records establishing Joseph Benton of Maryland as a patriot by virtue of his having signed the patriot's oath of allegiance to the Colony of Maryland. Joseph Benton was born in 1730 and died in 1807. One of his descendants, Mrs. Irwin was informed, was Eunice Haden, who happens to be a genealogy buff.

Mrs. Leachman wrote to Miss Haden. Had the Joseph Benton who died in Montgomery County, Maryland, in 1807, had a son named Joseph? Eunice Haden sent Mrs. Leachman a copy of the will of Joseph Benton, Sr. He had been married twice, the document showed, first to Elizabeth and then to Rachel. In the will, Benton had named his son Joseph first among the eleven children of his first wife. Joseph, Jr., had been the executor of the will. In addition, Miss Haden told Mrs. Leachman where the will of Joseph, Jr., was recorded and referred her to some unpublished Maryland Revolutionary records listing Joseph, Jr., as a soldier in Maryland troops.

From the Hall of Records in Annapolis, Maryland, Mrs. Irwin received a copy of Joseph, Jr.'s, will, dated April 3, 1815. That will established Benjamin Benton as Joseph's son. (Joseph left Benjamin all his wearing apparel.) A book called *History of No Creek* yielded a little more information on Benjamin, and the existence of Benjamin's son, Erasmus, was ascertained in a book called *Spider Webs, A Steamer-Trunk and Slavery.* A third book, *Ohio County, Kentucky, In the Olden Days*, recorded Erasmus' marriage. It also noted that Erasmus' family took up residence in Daviess County, Kentucky. In Daviess County census records Mrs. Irwin found Erasmus' son, William, listed. Daviess, Ohio and Muhlenburg counties merged to form McLean County in 1854. The McLean courthouse had a record of William's marriage.

When she found William Benton, Estelle Irwin had found her grandfather. She had never even known his first name.

When she found a book on Baptist preachers in Kentucky linking William to John, her father, Estelle Irwin had reached a point that for most people tracing lines marks the end of the hard work. All she had left to do was to connect her parents with each other and establish herself as their issue. But the most frustrating part of the search still lay ahead.

Knowing that the DAR would accept cemetery records giving

birth and death dates, the Irwins drove to Smiths Grove hoping to find the graves of Estelle's parents. They found no Benton graves. The woman in the cemetery office couldn't find any records of the Benton burials.

However, while they were in Smiths Grove, the Irwins had learned that a cousin on Estelle's mother's side lived there. When Estelle returned home, she wrote her cousins asking if she knew where the Bentons were buried. The cousin wrote back and said they were buried in the very cemetery the Irwins had visited. The Irwins finally got an official copy of the cemetery records. Apparently they had simply been overlooked by the cemetery employee.

Estelle then had to get a copy of her own birth certificate. The courthouse in Adairville, Kentucky, her birthplace, had burned down. The doctor who delivered Estelle was dead, and so was the attending nurse. Estelle had once obtained a birth certificate from Bowling Green, with the help of her high-school records, but when the time came for the Irwins to apply for Social Security in 1965, Clarence Irwin sent his wife's birth certificate to Chicago. The Irwins wrote to Chicago and heard nothing. They wrote to Bowling Green and heard nothing. They drove to Kentucky. After a whole day traipsing from bureau to bureau, they finally got a copy of the birth certificate from the Department of Health.

Back in Ohio, Estelle received news that Eunice Haden had discovered a record of Joseph Benton, Jrs.'s service in a Maryland battalion. Until then Estelle had not known that Joseph, Jr., had taken part in the War. She knew only that his father had taken an oath of allegiance. Miss Haden's find established Joseph, Jr., as an acceptable DAR ancestor, meaning that other women could possibly become members on his line. From the Maryland Historical Society Mrs. Irwin obtained a copy of the page of an old muster roll listing Joseph's name.

Armed with all this material, Estelle Irwin applied for DAR membership. Back came a letter from the genealogist who examined the application. The letter informed Mrs. Irwin that she would have to submit the exact date of her parents' marriage.

Estelle was almost ready to give up. Early in her search she had written to the city clerk in Bowling Green requesting information on the marriage of John Bryant Benton to Myrtle Cooke. The clerk wrote back saying the county had no record of the marriage. When she got the bad news from the DAR genealogist, Estelle thought, "This is the end. There's absolutely nobody who would know. I do not know one person whom I might ask."

Out of what she calls sheer desperation, Estelle Irwin got out a map and sat staring at it. Suddenly she realized that the counties on the map weren't clearly delineated. In fact, it was almost impossible to determine with any certainty which county Smiths Grove was really in. And the Butler county seat was actually closer to Smiths Grove than was Bowling Green, the county seat of Warren County.

Estelle Irwin wrote one more letter to the Butler county seat. The reply came from Bowling Green. Estelle looked at the envelope and knew she must have been mistaken. Smiths Grove was in Warren County after all. Butler County officials had sent her letter on, and now Bowling Green was writing again to tell her there was no record of her parents' marriage in the courthouse there.

Estelle was half right. Smiths Grove is in Warren County, and the Butler County people had sent her letter on. But the envelope did not contain bad news. It contained, for one thing, a letter handwritten by an apparently elderly woman, the relative of an employee at the Bowling Green courthouse. The woman apologized. The county officials had neither the time nor the personnel to do research, she explained. She herself had done some and had come up with the document she thought would help.

The other piece of paper in the envelope was a copy of a marriage bond. It stated quite simply that John Bryant Benton had posted one hundred dollars as proof of his intent to marry Myrtle Cooke. At the bottom of the page was a copy of the marriage certificate.

In October 1970, after two years of work on her line, Estelle Irwin became a member of the DAR.

Some women would never have joined the DAR if they had had to work as hard as Estelle Irwin did to trace their lineage. To many Daughters, slogging through the genealogical swamp is about as tempting a prospect as going to tea with Jane Fonda. Working on a line is no guarantee of becoming addicted to tracing. Even if it were, many Daughters would never become addicted because they have never worked in the swamp. For any number of women, joining the DAR involves the time it takes to copy someone else's papers, usually Mother's. The prospective member only has to prove that she is her mother's daughter. Only the addicts keep on proving supplemental lines after they've joined the DAR, and there are no more than a few addicts in each chapter. Most Daughters prove one line and stop.

Other Daughters find that the fringe benefits derived from tracing an ancestor prove almost as valuable as the DAR membership itself. After spending eighteen months on a search that involved figuring out how her great-great-grandfather could possibly have died at the age of one year (the author of the book was in error), Florida Daughter Jesslyn Downer could say enthusiastically, "I have learned a great deal of the history of my county, some geography, a little civics, such as the structure of county governments. I learned of the migrations of the citizens, why they migrated, and some of the routes they took. In searching the census we began to notice that the same families were always neighbors and after migrations the group settled in the new location with hardly a family missing. I have enjoyed all of this search for unknown ancestors. There were frustrations and disappointments, but when things went well the excitement and pleasure made it all worth the trouble. There was anticipation with every mail delivery. One never knew where the next letter would come from and what information it would contain."

Tracing a line shows the searcher a little of what America used to be like, not in the offices of government but in the homes of individuals. It produces friendships with other stumblers in the swamp. It opens eyes: Karen Kiser dreamed only of Danish modern before she joined the DAR, but now, to her mother's complete astonishment, she is mad about antiques and crazy about quilting. (Karen is in her early thirties.)

And it puts kin in touch with each other. A woman in her seventies, recently widowed and living alone in Oregon, gets a letter every so often these days from a distant cousin in Illinois she never knew she had until Linda Lee, a young mother, joined the DAR and discovered her.

Americans who think that interest in ancestors is proof of eccentricity may soon find themselves surrounded by eccentrics. Addiction to genealogy is a communicable passion that is presently spreading all over the United States. In the past decade, several hundred genealogical societies have sprung up in this democratic land, and the number of books and magazines devoted to genealogy has doubled or tripled. Daughters—of the American Revolution or anything else—no longer have a corner on the ancestor market. Americans of all kinds are poking into their past.

One explanation of this revival comes from Kenn Stryker-Rodda, president of the National Genealogical Society. Noting that most of the new societies are in the Midwest or Southwest (Texas alone has more than fifty, which may have something to do with the DAR boom in Texas), Stryker-Rodda says, "The reason for so much interest beyond the Appalachians is probably a desire for roots. We are also finding an increasing number of descendants from late-nineteenth-century immigrants doing research on their own, or hiring researchers." Perhaps, too, a parallel can be drawn between the stresses of the 1960's, when any American who was awake saw his nation threatened by divisions, and the stresses of the 1890's, when a nation in the throes of an identity crisis seemed to take comfort in the past.

Library of Congress genealogist Thomas Wilgus does not suggest any explanations for the trend. He says he hasn't really questioned people who come into the Library as to why they're there. But if Wilgus can't explain why genealogy is popular today, he does have an idea why people in any period of history try to trace their lineage.

"A lot of people may not have anything," Wilgus says, "but they all have ancestors."

Without apparently intending to, Wilgus made perhaps the strongest argument that can be made for the perpetuation of a hereditary society in twentieth-century America. His statement, of course, does not describe all members of the DAR, or even most of them. Some of the Daughters have not only families but friends, money, education, social position, professional standing, intelligence, personality, and ability. They don't need the DAR nearly as much as it needs them.

But most Daughters don't have all these attributes, and some undoubtedly have none. Yet the work of an organization makes different kinds of demands on its members. Even women in the Junior League sometimes have to tote cartons, letter name tags and make phone calls. If she can qualify genealogically, and can convince a chapter that she is sincere, a woman with nothing but ancestors can do some work, earn some pins for her ribbon, and make some friends. She can, in other words, find herself a niche in the DAR.

It is this aspect of the Daughters of the American Revolution that causes sociologist Dr. Albert I. Gollin almost to sputter in indignation at the idea that a hereditary society is an anachronism in America.

"That's silly! Is B'nai B'rith an anachronism? Are the critics saying that our society is so well integrated, with rewards so evenly distributed, that people have no need for groupings to defend their positions or to seek greater personal satisfaction? Are they saying that all the social identification you need is to be a New Yorker?"

Gollin, who has studied social movements while working for the Bureau of Social Science Research in Washington, D.C., believes that a misunderstanding of the concept "hereditary" lies behind such criticism of the DAR and similar organizations.

"When the word 'hereditary' is used, people generally now take it to mean race," he points out. "That's saying, 'You're permitted in these groups because of your genes.' But, 'hereditary' as applied to the DAR does not mean biological transmission of traits or capacities through genes. It's kinship—a social status transmitted through kinship from generation to generation.

"Membership in B'nai B'rith is based on identity with the status of Jew. B'nai B'rith is exclusivistic and has goals which are not those of nonmembers. But so are and so do thousands of other organizations. How is the DAR different from Knights of Columbus, which consists mainly of Italian Catholics, or from the Friendly Sons of St. Patrick? These are based on an ethnic identity. The DAR is based on a temporal identity: Members trace their ancestry to people who were in the U.S. at a certain stage."

Not only does Gollin refuse to view the DAR as inconsistent with democracy; he argues that its very existence is a hallmark of democracy.

"If belonging to the DAR automatically conferred a greater measure of society's goods on its members, or greater access to these goods, then it would resemble a hereditary class or caste system, and it would threaten democratic institutions," he says. "But the DAR is an association of people where membership has a hereditary base with no particular economic or even social consequences except what the members themselves think. Their satisfactions are mainly social or emotional, not political or economic.

"Pernicious? It's quite the contrary. This tendency to form groups based on common interest or shared identity is commonplace in the American experience. It is characteristic of autocracies or dictatorships that they don't permit such organizing because it threatens the rule of the state. But democracy is *preserved* by the formation and maintenance of precisely these kinds of societies and interest groups.

"The DAR provides satisfactions for its members without exacting any price on the larger society. To say that groups that you don't think serve any particularly useful purpose should not be available to those for whom they do is the ultimate bigoted perspective."

Gollin's views are upheld, surprisingly enough, by activist Daughter Elizabeth Duff. "Most qualifications for any group are kind of absurd," Ms. Duff says. "Professional societies of journalists sit around and huff and puff about journalism. Is that any less absurd than people who had relatives fight in the American Revolution sitting around? The DAR is excluding no one whose destiny is significantly affected by the DAR, or who wants to get in that badly."

The subject of Daughters and ancestors is primarily but not exclusively controversial. One statement can be made that most Americans in and out of the DAR would readily agree with, and that is that the Daughters of the American Revolution give more thought to ancestors than does almost anyone else in America. They would have to even if they didn't want to. The DAR is the only organization in the United States charged by the U.S. Congress to locate and mark graves of Revolutionary War soldiers. As they locate and mark those graves—two or three hundred a year—the Daughters inevitably give some thought to whose old bones are in them. As they try to perpetuate the memory and spirit of the men and women who achieved American Independence, the Daughters inevitably think about what those men and women were like and in what spirit they decided to risk their lives, their fortunes and their sacred honor.

The ancestors the Daughters think about are a very motley crew. Some of the men who fought and some of the patriots who rendered service were criminals. There were vagabonds among them, and scalawags, and some were rogues, and not a few were what archivist Phoebe Jacobsen of the Maryland State Archives describes as "bums." A recent book describing the Continental Army almost tells the story in the title: *Rag, Tag and Bobtail*. In the book author Lynn Montross calls the American soldiers a "mixed bag" that included, along with men who were plucky, audacious, brave, and individualistic, men of "uncouth beginnings" who were illiterate, poor shots, untrained, undisciplined, cowardly, and given to swearing, drinking, pillaging, smuggling, entertaining women of dubious reputation, and wandering away from the ranks never to return. In *The Spirit of 'Seventy-Six* the editors note that when Washington took command, "The Army was not an army in any accepted sense of the word, but a haphazard collection of volunteers, skillful enough in the use of musket or rifle, but almost wholly without experience or training, disrespectful of officers, fiercely resentful of discipline, ignorant of the rules of hygiene, wasteful and disorderly." As Eleanor Spicer says, "Some of those men who fought in the Revolution came out of debtors' prison or were in the prison for real crimes and pardoned if they'd get out of the country. They came to America. They used to deport prisoners to America to get rid of them. America was a catch-all, to some degree. Certainly not all of them were second sons of noble families who couldn't inherit and so came to America to find their fortunes."

Some were, of course. "To say that the Continental Army was composed of jailbirds, ignorant backwoodsmen, troublemakers, and general riffraff fails to take account of George Washington, Benjamin Franklin, John Adams, Nathanael Green, Thomas Jefferson and their kind," writes Albert Britt in his book on the Revolution called *The Hungry War*. But not everyone can descend from such stars. Some Daughters undoubtedly descend from rogues. Many descend from people who contributed relatively little to the cause. Americans who fought are not the only Americans who qualify as patriots for the DAR's purposes.

For example, New Jersey Daughters Doris Ballengee and Carol Sutton were talking one evening about Aunt Betty Frazee of Westfield, New Jersey. As the story goes, Aunt Betty was baking bread when Lord Cornwallis and his troops rode by. Apparently he smelled the bread and inquired if she would give him some. She replied, "I give this bread in fear, sir, not in love." Those words, said Doris Ballengee, "made Aunt Betty a patriot!" (To finish the story, Cornwallis is said to have responded with a deep, courtly bow. "Then neither I nor one of my men shall touch a bite of it, madam," he is supposed to have said. Off went Cornwallis, presumably to find a less discriminating baker.)

In general the Daughters don't kid themselves about their ancestors. They know that some of them were not paragons.

They also know that in a revolution, every little bit helps. No matter what their ancestors' weaknesses, no matter how small the services they rendered, the Daughters are loyal. Many of them accept the foibles of some of the Revolutionaries with astonishing equanimity. At a recent New Jersey state conference, Libby Naisby rushed up to a visitor and said with considerable amusement that she was "dying" to find out about an ancestor of hers who was a key figure in a scandal involving a married woman and an illegitimate child. Eunice Haden laughs when she says she has found no document to prove that two of her antecedents were married to each other and not just living in sin. Eunice Haden also says, "Of course Benjamin Franklin was a woman-chaser, and I can't think of *anyone* who wouldn't be delighted to be his descendant!"

When the musical *1776* was made into a movie, Eleanor Spicer received an indignant letter from a certain American male. The gentleman objected to the "lewd conduct" he thought the movie implied about Thomas Jefferson and his young wife. He was asking the president general of the DAR to protest the movie.

Eleanor Spicer had seen the play. She felt the characters were rightly portrayed as non-saints. "I suppose they played up the same incident they did in the play—the young Jeffersons in the house by themselves in the middle of the afternoon, and Franklin and Adams and who was the other one outside cavorting and making a few off-side remarks," Mrs. Spicer says. "And this man thought that that was blasphemy. And I. . . ." The president general laughs. ". . . I answered, and I said that I thought the musical really told a great deal about the men who founded our country. That while there were some episodes that were perhaps not in the best of taste, while we knew and revered our Founding Fathers for their patriotism and courage, we certainly didn't revere them as saints. That they were ordinary human beings, and they had the pleasures and failings of ordinary human beings."

Mrs. Spicer did not protest *1776*.

CHAPTER IV

Waving the Flag

The American's Creed

"I believe in the United States of America as a government of the people, by the people, for the people; whose just powers are derived from the consent of the governed; a democracy in a republic; a sovereign Nation of many sovereign states; a Perfect Union, one and inseparable; established upon those principles of freedom, equality, justice and humanity for which American patriots sacrificed their lives and fortunes.

"I therefore believe it is my duty to my country to love it; to support its Constitution; to obey its laws; to respect its flag; and to defend it against all enemies."

—William Tyler Page
Clerk, U.S. House of Representatives
1917

The American's Creed is virtually unknown outside the DAR, but to the Daughters it is gospel. They repeat it at just about every DAR gathering. It is a succinct expression of their intense faith in America and of their sense of responsibility as American citizens.

DAR members believe that America is the light of the world. Its representative form of government assures the best for the most; its free-enterprise system assures that every person who really tries can get ahead. The Daughters have little patience with Americans who believe otherwise. They have even less patience with Americans who, while claiming to be acting in the best interests of their country, make an issue of its faults. To the Daughters such behavior is the very antithesis of patriotism. Men who burned their draft cards are in this category. So are men who went to Canada instead of Vietnam, and men who went from Vietnam to Sweden, and Americans who marched in peace demonstrations, and clergymen who led them. Former Attorney General Ramsey Clark is in that category because he criticized the war effort. Joan Baez is in it because she withheld her income taxes as a war protest. (The Daughters showed how they felt about that by refusing to let Miss Baez give a concert in Constitution Hall in 1965.)

At the top of the DAR's bad-American list is Jane Fonda.

There are Daughters who have vowed to themselves that they will never go to see a Jane Fonda film because Jane Fonda went to North Vietnam and criticized America. While a Daughter here and there will concede a remote possibility that Fonda and the peaceniks and the draft dodgers were acting out of what they conceived to be patriotism, most would probably say with New Jersey Daughter Joanna Friedrich that the lot of them are traitors.

To the DAR, good Americans are those who obey the law, uphold the government, support the police, and respect the military. When good Americans are unhappy with a law, they work to change it. When they disagree with their elected officials, they vote for others. When they have complaints against the police, they seek a hearing. When they oppose what the Pentagon is doing, they write to their congressmen. Good Americans do not go around criticizing their country. America may not be perfect, but it's the best nation there is.

Standing up for America has gotten the Daughters of the American Revolution into more trouble than almost anything else they have done. Nobody ever criticizes the DAR's historical or educational programs. But when the Daughters wave the flag, they raise hackles. They appear to be trying to rally the support of all citizens for a version of America that many Americans vehemently oppose.

The Daughters' version of what America should be like is set forth in a series of resolutions issued each year at Continental Congress. The resolutions are the policy of the Society, which translates to mean that they are policies to which the Society subscribes. Technically that is all they are. The DAR is registered with the Internal Revenue Service as an educational institution. It is proscribed from supporting issues in a way that could be construed as lobbying. But the Daughters make no secret of their hope that Americans will pay attention to their policy. The resolutions do not merely represent what the resolutions committee deems best for the DAR. They also represent what the committee deems best for America.

Americans have failed to appreciate the committee's efforts. Year after year the Daughters have issued their list of ways to keep America pure and strong; year after year the resolutions have been pounced on by newspaper writers, public officials, and ordinary Americans who denounce them as old-fashioned, silly, reactionary, ridiculous, un-American, and even anti-

American. Sometimes the resolutions are at odds with national policy. They have frequently seemed pinched and negative, the product of a constricted view of the world, the admonishments of a scolding spinster aunt glaring down her nose through her pince-nez. Though the DAR has moderated its stands of late, some resolutions still strike Americans as wholly removed from the spirit of a time the Daughters of the American Revolution purport to revere.

The rather curious fact is that the resolutions are more important outside the DAR than they are inside. In the life of the average Daughter they take up less time than the annual trip to the dentist. The average Daughter couldn't list all of last year's resolutions if she were threatened with expulsion from the Society. She has only a foggy idea of what purpose the Society's policy is supposed to serve and what relationship it is supposed to have to the individual member. The DAR has no programs relating to the resolutions. The membership does not study them in any organized fashion. Members don't even get copies unless they send fifteen cents to DAR headquarters in Washington. When asked to name the accomplishments of the DAR, the average Daughter never mentions the resolutions.

This raises interesting questions. If the resolutions reflect the views of the average Daughter, why would they affect her so slightly? How can the resolutions affect her so slightly and still be issued as Society policy? Given the impact of the resolutions, and their consequences for the DAR, the matter of who formulates Society policy and how is of utmost importance.

Briefly, the national resolutions committee drafts the annual resolutions during the week before Continental Congress, relying heavily on state resolutions which have been passed during the year. On the first day of formal sessions the resolutions are read from the platform to Congress delegates. The next morning the delegates discuss them one by one, make changes, and vote. The resolutions are not ratified either by state Societies or by individual chapters. They become DAR policy as soon as the vote is taken in Washington. It is expected that the resolutions will be read aloud in the fall in chapter meetings throughout the country. It is hoped, according to silver-haired Virginian Genevieve Morse, resolutions chairman under Eleanor Spicer, "that the individual member will work toward these things, will be in agreement with them, and will support them."

Anyone who masters this sketch comprehends only the bare

bones of the resolutions process. The real shape of the animal can be grasped only by those who understand the workings of the DAR's national-defense committee, the stated purpose of which is to keep the membership informed about national issues. The purpose of the resolutions committee is to draft resolutions. On an organizational chart the two are totally distinct from one another, but in real life they are intimates. The resolutions cannot be understood apart from national defense. The women who are interested in one are to a large extent the women who are interested in the other. They are known in the Society as the "national-defense-minded" members, or "national defenders" (unless they are conspicuously shrill, in which case they are referred to as "national-defense nuts"). Because of this overlap, and for less innocent reasons, the resolutions almost always represent the concerns of the national-defense committee.

Americans who don't belong to the DAR generally understand the term "national defense" to refer to the men and machines of war. Inside the DAR the expression is said to have broader connotations. As explained by Sally (Sara Roddis) Jones, who has served as national-defense chairman under three administrations, "We've always conceived of national defense as something more than just national defense, I mean in terms of guns and ammunition. I've sometimes said that national defense is a thing of the spirit as well as of guns and planes and so on. It really covers a wide spectrum of material. It emphasizes the significance of the Constitution. Our youth program. The committee is concerned with trying to keep alive and well the ideals of our country." The committee has been trying to do that since 1926, when the intensifying pacifist movement and fear of subversives in America led the Daughters to scrap their old Patriotic Education Committee and divide its work three ways, establishing national defense as a separate committee.

Each month the committee publishes a pamphlet called the *National Defender* which sells for ten cents a copy. Along with one, two, or three reprints of articles or speeches which in the opinion of the national-defense chairman bear on the national interest, the *National Defender* is mailed to chapters free and to interested individuals in and out of the DAR for the subscription price of $2.50 a year. A recent packet contained the text of a speech by Illinois Congressman Philip M. Crane, "Can Business Survive Government by Crisis?" and a reprint of an article by Captain Paul R. Coloney, USN (Ret.) called, "Is American Defense

Adequate?" The eight-page *National Defender* for the same month contained eight articles, including "Reds Detain Rivals as 'Socially Insane' " by Michael Padev, reprinted from *The Indianapolis Star*, and "Family, Not Government, Should Rear Children," reprinted from *The State* of Columbia, S.C.

The committee also issues a four-page price list from which Daughters or outsiders can order pamphlets on subjects which interest them. Ranging from three to fifty cents a copy, the materials fall into eleven categories: Constitution and Constitutional Rights (twenty-one pamphlets), Communism and Socialism (nineteen), World Government (four), Immigration (three), Education (eleven), Fluoridation (five), Mental Health (two), Religion (six), Disarmament (nine), United Nations and United Nations Specialized Agencies (twenty), and Miscellaneous (thirty-nine pamphlets). Sample materials from the list include "The Role of Money in Soviet Espionage Operations" by J. Edgar Hoover, "The Pied Pipers of Sex" by Fr. Robert E. Burns, C.S.P., "What Price the Dollar" by Sara Roddis Jones, "Law and Order" by Ezra Taft Benson, and "Operation Peace Corps—A Pig in a Poke" by Elizabeth C. Barnes.

The literature of the national-defense committee is notably lacking in balance. That does not happen through oversight. In Sally Jones' opinion, "many things that go on in Congress and in our day and age are really not discussed very fully" in newspapers, and one side of an issue is often given more coverage than another. To the extent that the press is liberal, the position that gets slighted, she feels, is often that of the conservatives. Sally Jones's objective as national-defense chairman has been to supply the Daughters with the missing side of the American story.

"We don't insist that we're always right," Mrs. Jones explains, "but we do try to make information available which may not necessarily have been given wide coverage in the press." The motto of the *National Defender*, printed under the logo of each issue, is a quote from Abraham Lincoln: "Let the people know the facts and the Country will be saved."

Daughters who fail to order literature from the national-defense committee do not go uneducated. National-defense articles appear in *DAR Magazine* each month. Every DAR chapter is supposed to allocate five to ten minutes of every meeting to national-defense reports, usually a reading from the Washington materials. A chapter wishing honor-roll status must devote one whole program to national defense, perhaps inviting a speaker from the community.

Congress delegates may attend the national-defense luncheon at the Mayflower Hotel on Monday and the Tuesday evening program in Constitution Hall. No other committee has an evening all its own at Congress, or, for that matter, two events. National-defense night visitors often include Congressmen and Senators who can be expected to applaud the views of such speakers as conservative Congressman Philip M. Crane, General William Westmoreland, and former FBI agent Dan Smoot, some of whose writings can be purchased from the John Birch Society. The national-defense luncheon is one of the best-attended extracurricular functions at Congress. Like the schools luncheon, it always sells out. Recent speakers have included Dan Smoot; former Notre Dame law school dean Clarence Manion, a member of the national council of the John Birch Society; and Daughter Phyllis Schlafly, a leading opponent of the Equal Rights Amendment.

In its efforts to complement the so-called liberal press, the national-defense committee has consistently utilized the resources and representatives of extreme right-wing conservatism. Most Daughters seem truly unsympathetic to the Birch Society and other forces considered reactionary by many Americans, but the national defenders offer the membership a steady diet of Birch-like views. This is not to say they get materials from the Birch Society itself. Nothing on the DAR publications list is identical to anything on the Birch publications list. Still, materials used by the DAR treat certain subjects almost exactly as Birch materials treat them. (The DAR sells "UNICEF—Trick or Treat?" by Elizabeth C. Barnes; the Birch Society sells "UNICEF—Trick or Treachery?" by William E. Dunham.) It is scarcely surprising, therefore, that the DAR resolutions dealing with concerns shared by most conservatives—the dangers of communism and world government, the importance of national sovereignty and American military might—frequently express the paranoia of the extreme right.

DAR policy-makers have seen threats to their America in places other Americans would never think to look. In 1970 the DAR worried that agents of the Marxist-Socialist-Communists were seeking to win the hearts and minds of American youth through, among other things, rock festivals. In the Daughters' opinion, these events were characterized by "music of hypnotic rhythm and subtle lyrics tending to break down moral restraints and to expose the young to the dangers of communal living and illicit sex."

In 1962 the DAR went on record against UNICEF Christmas cards with this explanation: "This plan to associate the UN with Christmas and have it replace the religious aspect of Christmas is believed to be part of the broader Communist plan to destroy all religious beliefs and customs so that one day we shall awaken to find that December 25 is being celebrated as a one-world peace festival instead of the birthday of Christ."

In 1961 the DAR asked the Post Office Department to stop issuing stamps depicting foreign people and places. The same year the Daughters opposed the fledgling Peace Corps, arguing that volunteers would be working with communists, would risk dying or being injured abroad, would suffer separation "from the moral and disciplinary influences of their homeland," and would burden the taxpayers.

In 1958 the Daughters came out against the United Nations. They had given their "hearty cooperation and support" to the UN in 1946, but events had caused them to change their minds. They felt the UN was anti-Christian. It had proven itself unable to deal effectively with strife in Korea, Hungary, and the Middle East. Although the U.S. was paying a third of the UN's bill, it was being outvoted in the General Assembly by tiny nations in a bloc. Having the power to form agreements and treaties, the UN had the means to supersede national sovereignty. Daughters also felt that American money was being used by the UN in behalf of a socialized, one-world state.

Such stands as these account for a polarity within the DAR. Members are either national defenders or they aren't. There is no question that the resolutions and national defense have a committed following among the Daughters. Some women care intensely about the issues involved. Others feel the resolutions prove to the world that DAR members are capable of more than just drinking tea. Some, like New York resolutions chairman Betsy Wiedle, who is 35, joined the DAR because of the resolutions. Mrs. Wiedle is proud to belong to an organization which is not afraid to speak out, even if speaking out stirs controversy. A Southern state regent says she has gotten "a great deal" out of national defense.

"I've been forewarned of things," she explains. "In years past I would go to some of these national-defense meetings and would come home in tears to tell my husband some of the things I'd heard that day. At first he began to laugh at me. Then he realized. He began to see things in the next few years develop that I had told him before—with the churches, for example. Many of them are so terribly liberal. They've gotten away from what a church stands for, really." Lots of other Daughters would agree with Janet Shay, who says she feels she is better informed because she pays attention to the resolutions than she would be if she didn't.

But there are also some Daughters who barely tolerate the resolutions. They almost belong to the DAR in spite of them. A Daughter of Quaker background, the first vice regent of a good-sized chapter, says she doesn't understand why the DAR gets involved in certain issues. "I'm interested in work with children," she says. "I'm not an isolationist. I think we've all got to get along in this world. If there are any steps we can take to make sure we do, that's fine with me. Isolationism should be a thing of the past."

This woman says she is not clear what relationship the resolutions have to either the work of the chapters or the DAR's three goals. "I must say, sometimes they're farther afield than they should be," she says. "Really far removed. They sometimes get into things that for the life of me I can't figure out who's behind it. The resolutions seem to go on aside from the life of the chapter. The grass roots, the women in our chapter, are very enthusiastic about the projects we're working on. I know *our* women don't get involved in all that stuff. I wonder about other chapters."

All Daughters no doubt believe in national defense as it is described in the DAR's broadest definition, stressing the education of young people in honorable values and sound principles. It may be true that most Daughters are sincerely concerned about weaponry and treaties and national sovereignty and potential communist take-overs, but quite a few women feel that the DAR's national-defense program emphasizes those issues too much. Some don't think the DAR should get involved in them at all. These women may not register their dissatisfaction publicly, but they don't treat it as a state secret, either. According to one Society leader, there is support, though muted, for giving the national-defense committee back its old name of patriotic education. A number of Daughters believe that one of the two national-defense committee functions at Congress should be dropped. Of members' receptivity to national-defense speeches, Sally Jones herself says, "In some places they don't even want to see you come down the road." One state regent was heard to complain to friends about an outing she had taken with some national defenders. "We heard 'national defense' from morning till night until I was really tired of it," the regent said. "I was glad I was driving a Volkswagen. It's noisy, and it drowned out everything!"

However disjointed it may be, there is opposition within the DAR to the role of the national defenders. "A lot of the members have been bullied into thinking national defense is the most important," says a state vice regent. "I've heard members complain about it. They think it's a small clique."

No one knows how many national defenders there are in the DAR. Interest in the national-defense functions is strong among Daughters who attend Congress, but some Daughters feel that the members who attend Congress tend to be those interested in the resolutions. The sale of national-defense literature tells another side of the story. In 1972 the committee sold $10,408.60 worth of materials. Assuming all of it went to members, which it did not, that would mean purchase of just over a nickel for each Daughter—one pamphlet. The $10,408.60 could also represent the sale of complete sets of committee materials to 1,480 Daughters—fewer than one percent of the members.

Daughters commonly assume that there are a few national defenders in each chapter. Eleanor Spicer thinks the national defenders comprise perhaps ten percent of the Society. That would mean an average of six or seven women per chapter. Not even the strong national defenders claim that they constitute a majority in the DAR.*

Yet they are defining policy for the majority.

The resolutions system is set up to give every Daughter a say in forming organizational policy. Ideally, say DAR leaders, if Phoebe Garland in Illinois gets an idea for a resolution, she introduces it to her chapter, and if the chapter votes favorably, the resolution goes to the Illinois resolutions chairman for consideration as a state resolution. If delegates to the state confer-

---

*Opinions vary as to whether being "national-defense-minded" helps a candidate for high DAR office. Some Daughters say a national defender has never been elected PG. Others say that candidates for PG known to be interested in national defense have a good chance to win.

ence approve the resolution, and if it has national scope, it goes to the chairman of the national committee. If it is proposed, and if the Congress delegates vote favorably, Phoebe Garland's resolution becomes part of DAR policy.

But the system rarely operates as intended.

The DAR Handbook states that the national committee "welcomes resolutions from members, chapters, and state Societies." In practice the committee gets them only from state Societies. Many members don't know that they can send their suggestions direct to the top. Few ever send any. Some chapter regents don't realize that resolutions are supposed to originate at the grassroots level. "I've never known it to happen in our chapter or any other," said the regent of a large metropolitan chapter. "I just personally don't know of any in this area. To the best of my knowledge that's done by a committee on the national or state level."

The states have no better luck than the national committee getting resolutions from the chapters. For the nine years that Adelaide Rice chaired the Pennsylvania resolutions committee, only one or two resolutions a year came in from chapters. Committee members wrote the rest. Smaller chapters may not even have a resolutions chairman.

Resolutions which *are* submitted by chapters to state Societies, as well as those submitted by state Societies to national, are often the work of only one person. "Sometimes a particular woman will influence the others and get the chapter to pass about ten," says Anne Musgrave, bylaws chairman under Eleanor Spicer. "Very often in state resolutions committee, one woman writes most of the resolutions. It could occur." It occurred in New York in 1973. Because she did not receive a single suggestion from any of New York's 12,000 members or 175 chapters, state resolutions chairman Betsy Wiedle wrote all six New York resolutions herself.

Anne Musgrave intended her statements as a description of the resolutions system, not a criticism of it. But as a description they carry considerable authority. Mrs. Musgrave worked on the national resolutions committee on and off for forty years. She knows how resolutions work. Their evolution as she describes it, and as others confirm, is not the result of grass-roots procedures.

The truth is that the resolutions system as it works almost precludes a Society policy that fully represents the views of the

Society's members. The women on the national resolutions committee are appointed each year by the president general, often in consultation with the committee chairman. The PG tries to select Daughters she feels might have a special interest in or talent for the job. "Some women are definitely interested and fitted to work on resolutions," says national resolutions chairman Genevieve Morse. "They have a certain type of mind. They are interested in current events and well-informed." Those who accept the appointment are not necessarily national defenders, of course, but they are interested enough in resolutions to be willing to travel to Washington a week before Continental Congress and put in six or seven days of hard work while paying hotel bills and buying their own meals. Some women serve on the committee for years. Furthermore, when the committee convenes, it works with a liaison to the executive committee, and often the liaison has been the national defense chairman.

State resolutions committees are chosen for the same attributes prized in members of the national committee. In fact, the state resolutions chairman and the state's representative on the national committee are often one in the same woman. A chapter regent can't always find someone who is interested in resolutions, but a conscientious chapter chairman, like a dedicated woman on the state or national resolutions committee, will apprise herself of current issues and read national defense committee materials bearing on recent resolutions. Fifty-two of the 139 pamphlets available through that committee are the work of just three Daughters—Sally Jones, Elizabeth Barnes, and Enid Griswold.

These women are well-known in the DAR for their deep interest in national defense. All three have served in the Society as national defense chairman, making speeches and selecting speakers and choosing articles for *National Defender* and gathering reprints that have helped inform the Daughters of the American Revolution on national-defense issues for a total of fifteen years. It is impossible to estimate the impact of these three women on the thousands of other women who belong to the DAR. But their positions and those of the Society have generally coincided. While the thinking of national defenders may not control the entire resolutions apparatus, it is difficult to imagine that Phoebe Garland or any other Daughter could get very far with a resolution that contradicted it.

"You'd be surprised at the similarity of thinking," says

Genevieve Morse of the resolutions that come in from state societies.

According to Wisconsin state regent Barbara Janikowsky, the Daughters who are both interested in the issues and able to articulate them are so vocal that they seem more numerous than is actually the case. "There are really a very few," Mrs. Janikowsky says. "This is where it does its job. Those who are writing resolutions are influencing those who otherwise wouldn't be informed."

The Daughters emphasize that they establish their policy by democratic procedures. While every member does not necessarily submit a resolution, every member may vote for the delegates who will represent her at state conferences and at Continental Congress. In New Jersey and perhaps elsewhere, resolutions are written early and discussed in chapters before the state conference. But this is an exception. Insofar as the national resolutions are concerned, a Daughter actually has less control over her delegate than an American citizen has over his Senator or Congressman. The delegates can't be instructed in advance by their chapters. They don't learn what the resolutions are until they arrive on the scene. They don't have time before the vote is taken to even sound out, much less poll, their constituency back home. They are entirely on their own.

Theoretically, of course, state resolutions submitted to national have been discussed and refined at state conferences. New Jersey historian Jean Walter says that when she disagreed with a resolution she was asked to state her reasons and rewrite the resolution to suit her. However, Mrs. Walter's experience is unusual. Adelaide Rice says in her dozen or more years on the Pennsylvania resolutions committee she doesn't recall a single Daughter ever criticising a resolution. "They're very proud of what we do," she says of the delegates. At the 1973 New York DAR conference Daughters passed six resolutions without a single comment. Apparently the regent expected none. Although she asked for discussion after each resolution was proposed, she only once looked up to see if any was forthcoming. It was lucky none was. The printed conference schedule allowed virtually no time for discussion on the resolutions.

Even if a delegate knew her chapter's views and wanted to convey them, she would have little opportunity to do so, especially in Washington. Discussion there is strictly limited. According to Congress rules, "No member shall speak more than once to the same question on the same day, or longer than two minutes at one time, without leave of the Assembly, granted by a two-thirds vote without debate." Once in a while a delegate seeking clarification or additional information has been made to feel by the presiding officer that she is questioning not the resolution but the women on the resolutions committee. Finally, Constitution Hall is an enormous place. Full of delegates, it is a powerful incentive to a shy Daughter to stay out of the discussion and vote with the masses.

Some Daughters are unhappy with these procedures. They believe that the chapters ought to learn about the resolutions before they become policy, not afterward. Although there seems to be no movement afoot, any number of Daughters share the sentiments of the Pennsylvania grandmother who says, "I've always felt the resolutions were thrown at people when they got to Congress. I think they should be discussed at chapter level first, and the chapter should advise delegates how to vote. It's very hard for anybody to stand up there in that hall and say anything at the time, so they just pass them without talking about them too much. Of course I'm just a little Indian, not a chief."

Among the chiefs, the belief predominates that the present system is the best and perhaps the only one possible. National resolutions chairman Genevieve Morse points out that if the resolutions were drafted early enough to be discussed in chapters prior to Congress, they might not be as timely as the committee would like. States which hold conferences shortly before Congress wouldn't have a chance to submit their resolutions for national consideration.

Expense would be a problem. Committee members who are going to Continental Congress anyway, as most do, spend the same amount for travel whether they arrive in Washington on April 12 or April 19. But if the committee were to prepare resolutions for advance consideration by chapters, committee members would have to make an extra trip to Washington. Cost, says a Daughter who has served on the committee, is why the system is unlikely to change.

The system wouldn't necessarily change even if that problem could be solved. Leaders express concern over how the resolutions would fare in chapter meetings. "In the average chapter you wouldn't have the background and wouldn't be able to vote as intelligently as members of the committee," says Genevieve Morse. "Maybe I shouldn't say that. It's easier for the resolutions committee to present the resolutions."

Anne Musgrave upholds Mrs. Morse's view. "The average chapter would not have the information necessary to make a really wise or discerning determination about it," she says. "I think it adds nothing whatever to send out a resolution which may never be brought in [to Society policy] in any way. I would not work to send them out in advance, after fifty women who are supposed to know something about them have done their work. When you send resolutions out into the hinterlands with no discussion, it's just too bad. Chapters aren't that discerning."

Genevieve Morse and Anne Musgrave are experienced women. They know first-hand the work that the national resolutions involve. But if chapters aren't discerning enough to make policy, are they truly meant to carry it out?

Or, to put it another way, can the policy of the Society be entrusted to the members? And if it can't, then why is it the policy of the Society?

The explanation seems clear. The resolutions are drawn up for the few by the few. The few have convinced the many that resolutions are not for the masses. The masses, agreeing, have abdicated.

If this were not true, the masses might be raising these and other pertinent questions about the resolutions procedures. According to the DAR Handbook, resolutions must always conform to the historical, educational, or patriotic objectives of the Society. So into which category does the 1973 resolution against aid to North Vietnam fit? Like most other resolutions, it is neither historical nor educational. But what does it have to do with patriotism? Similarly, is the DAR's stand against the Equal Rights Amendment to be construed as an aspect of historical, educational, or patriotic endeavor?

None of the above, Genevieve Morse concedes. Still, Mrs. Morse defends the ERA resolution. "We're women," she argues. "It affects every one of us." A Daughter who has served many times on the national resolutions committee sees the matter differently. "The one on the ERA had no business getting in there," she says flatly. "It doesn't fit in with the three objectives and could be political. And we're not supposed to be political."

It is possible for an outsider going around making inquiries to learn that quite a few Daughters oppose the DAR's opposition to the United Nations. These women object to certain things that have happened in the UN, most recently the ejection of Taiwan and the ensuing gleeful celebration, but feel that the original idea had merit. They believe that as long as the UN exists, America should stay in and try to get it back on the right track. These Daughters make no secret of their feelings. A few even dare to speak to the issue at Congress. They may truly be in the minority, but no one knows for certain. If a stranger can find these dissenters with ease, surely most DAR members have run into them. Why does the DAR continue to oppose the UN when so many members of the DAR apparently support it, however joylessly?

Beyond a doubt, the DAR resolutions represent the best efforts of the women on the national resolutions committee to put forth thoughtful and timely positions in the national interest. They do not represent the unanimous views of the Daughters of the American Revolution, or even the primary concerns of more than a small percentage of the membership. No leader pretends that they do. What the leaders do say is that the resolutions represent the will of the majority.

But it seems more likely that the will of the majority is to let the women who are interested in resolutions set the policy for everybody.

The reason is not difficult to understand. In the mind of a citizen trying to plan what she will teach her literature students next year, or how she can care for an aging, ailing parent this month, or what to feed her family besides beef, the right of Americans to buy, sell, and make contracts in gold is not a burning issue. Women's liberation may have helped convince women that they ought to be looking into such matters, but it hasn't changed the fact that most people, women and men, worry about things closer to home. Making contracts in gold is at best peripherally relevant to most Daughters, and so, naturally, are resolutions about making contracts in gold. Most Daughters probably wouldn't care to help in the work of formulating such a resolution if Genevieve Morse sent a coach and four to pick them up.

Once formulated by the people who are willing to do the work, the resolutions go out to the chapters with no instructions on how they should be implemented. The chapter regent is supposed to apprise the members of the contents of the resolutions but doesn't always do so. The average Daughter has no clear idea how she is supposed to support her organization's policy. Daughters may write Capitol Hill, of course, but they can't write as DAR members, and the Society must be very careful about encouraging them to write as individuals so as not to appear to be lobbying. Furthermore, members are asked not to speak for the DAR on resolutions. To avoid misunderstandings about Society policy, only the president general is authorized to speak for it.

The DAR is supposedly devoted to democratic tradition, but the resolutions process as it operates is the very opposite of democratic procedure. In a real sense the Society's policy does not belong to the membership at all. The average Daughter has no say whatever about who serves on either the state or the national resolutions committees. Technically anyone can submit a resolution, but a great many Daughters don't have the nerve. They believe that the women who write resolutions are vastly more intelligent and informed than average Daughters, and the women who write resolutions have done little to discourage this notion. The average Daughter can become a delegate, but unless she is more forceful than average, she won't get her two cents in. At state conference she may face a regent who not only fails to encourage discussion on the resolutions but doesn't even look for it. At Continental Congress she is faced with Constitution Hall. Practically speaking most Daughters have no say in formulating policy of their organization. They have shown themselves willing to let that policy be set by women appointed, not elected, to their posts, women who exercise virtual control over policy-making procedure.

The national defenders are not trying to perpetrate a coup. They are serving the Society in the way they feel most qualified to serve. Letting people work at what they enjoy most is sound management practice. It is also a convenience for everybody else. Obviously the resolutions process as it operates is the resolutions process most Daughters prefer, or they would have changed it.

But the Daughters who aren't much interested in either national defense or resolutions have put themselves in a very ticklish position. They have let themselves be represented to the public by a group of women who may not truly represent them. They have all had to take the consequences.

And what results have the resolutions produced?

Consider the record. The DAR's viewpoint seems to have prevailed in a few cases, though it would surely have prevailed even if it had not been the DAR's viewpoint. The U.S. government has not signed the Genocide Convention. Americans have been granted the right to buy and sell gold. There is rising concern in many quarters about immigration, though because the size of the population has begun to threaten the quality of that life, not because foreigners are thought to pose a threat to the American way.

But the Daughters' failures have been legion. In spite of DAR efforts, the Bricker amendment was killed. The 1962 resolution notwithstanding, Americans are still buying UNICEF Christmas cards. Despite DAR warnings, rock music has not been banned from the airwaves. Over DAR opposition, the U.S. has announced its willingness to drop "in perpetuity" from the treaty with Panama and intends to eventually cede the administration of the Canal to the Panamanians. Notwithstanding the DAR's expressed concern that such matters belonged in the hands of the states, the federal government enacted civil-rights legislation. Heedless of DAR policy, Americans are still joining the Peace Corps. No matter what the DAR has said, America is giving aid to North Vietnam.

Daughters believe that events have proven virtually all their positions right. "The Society has been vindicated," they often say. Adele Sullivan wrote recently, "If the public were to look back at the record of the DAR, it would find that we did predict many of today's problems, which would have been avoided if the Society's words of wisdom had been heeded." As Exhibit A, the Daughters usually cite their stand on the United Nations. When the DAR came out against the UN, the women were ridiculed. Now, Daughters say, most Americans oppose the UN. Eleanor Spicer singles out the UN stand when she notes her belief that the resolutions have sometimes posed a challenge to the U.S. Congress.

"I think because we were not afraid to speak out on such things as the United Nations when everybody else was saying how wonderful it was and we said we didn't like it, why, there was a challenge there, too," Mrs. Spicer says. "And a lot of people tried to convince us that we were wrong. Now they agree with us. The very things we're saying. But we've often been as much as ten to fifteen years ahead of time, ahead of popular thinking."

One could argue, of course, that even if Americans now feel widespread disaffection with the UN, the DAR was not necessarily justified in opposing it in 1958. An outsider looking at a ten-year-old marriage can say it will never work, and if the couple later gets divorced, the outsider can say he was right all along. But flaws in a ten-year-old marriage may still be worked out, and the couple doesn't necessarily split. A prediction of trouble is not proof of farsightedness. For the DAR to be vindicated on its UN stand, most Americans would have to want out of the UN, and conservative columnist William F. Buckley, for one, does not believe they do.

"I think that most Americans feel that so long as we don't understand the UN to be a policy-making body that guides the U.S., it is, to quote a phrase of my own, 'a useful forum within which to exchange bribes, threats, insults, and intimidations,' " Buckley told a visitor to his New York office in 1973.

Buckley may be wrong, and the DAR may be right. No one knows whether most Americans now oppose American participation in the UN. But America is still participating in it. Daughters have been passing resolutions against U.S. participation for fifteen years, and Americans haven't cared to heed them. Perhaps they haven't even heard them. "I can't imagine that anybody reads the DAR's resolutions," William Buckley says softly.

There are strong indications that this is true. The Daughters believe that the resolutions are read on Capitol Hill, but this is open to question. There was a time when the DAR sent copies routinely to every Senator and Representative in Congress. Then a dozen or so years ago a Daughter writing in *National Defender* urged DAR members to write to their Congressmen and object to a pending bill on the nuclear test-ban treaty. This struck a district Internal Revenue Service agent as an attempt to lobby. The national office of IRS did not share his concern and threw the case out, but the Daughters, intent upon keeping their tax-exempt status, were chastened by the experience. They have been meticulously careful ever since about staying within prescribed limits. Contrary to what many Daughters believe, the DAR no longer sends the resolutions to Congress unless Congressmen ask for them. Not many do. According to one DAR employee, only about fifteen or twenty requests a year come in from Capitol Hill.

The resolutions don't seem to penetrate other levels of government, either. As the State Department, for example, the DAR's opposition to dropping "in perpetuity" from the U.S. treaty with Panama draws only amusement.

"There are members of Congress, Danny Flood and others, who are very much against the revision of the U.S. position, who pull more weight than the DAR," says Latin American public-affairs officer Kate Marshall with a giggle. The Department's special adviser to the Office of Interoceanic Canal Negotiations says that while the U.S. will defend the Canal with or without Panamanian approval as long as America has treaty rights there, the DAR's resolution to this effect had no bearing whatsoever on the State Department's stance. "It's like whistling to keep alligators away," John Sheffey suggests waggishly. "You whistle, the alligators don't come, so you assume it was your whistling that kept them away."

There may be several explanations for the irreverence with which outsiders respond to DAR resolutions. The Daughters themselves feel that the liberal turn the country has taken since Franklin Roosevelt's day has provided rocky soil for conservative philosophies. In the old days, they insist, the United States Congress used to wait to hear what the DAR would say. Now, in Eleanor Spicer's view, "There are men in Congress who would have been openly labeled traitors forty years ago."

DAR public-relations consultant Paul Wagner feels that the Daughters' gender is a factor in how their stands are received.

"They have some resolutions that are not credible for a women's organization, with the image that they have," Wagner says. "Frankly, no one understands paper gold in this world, and they had a resolution on paper gold in 1971. When I was talking with them about this the other day, Sally Jones said, 'I understand it,' and she went and got a fairly good paper on it. So I told them the story about the President going off the gold standard. He held briefings with Arthur Burns and John Connally. Nixon said, 'Don't ask me or Connally what it means because we don't understand it, and Burns does, but he can't explain it.' Almost no one understands paper gold, and frankly, that's not credible for a bunch of women."

A similar opinion is expressed more flatly by "right-wing watcher" Wesley McCune of Group Research, Inc., a one-man, one-secretary Washington firm which keeps tabs on conservative organizations for subscribers. "The last time I read some of the DAR's resolutions they were so way-out I couldn't believe it," McCune says. "These gals go way out of their field of competence."

William Buckley believes the problem may lie in the way the Daughters express themselves. "They've always been, as you know, an object of fun," he says with a certain gentleness. "A lot

of people find it terribly easy to proceed with the Helen Hokinson simplistic DAR mother idea. And this is to be expected,
because they tend to be people like my own mother who are not
primarily verbalists and who aren't primarily ideologically
oriented, but who feel a sense of tradition and a sense of attachment to ideas that they view as constantly threatened, which, I
might add, they are. But the Daughters tend to be sloganistic and
predictable."

The resolutions open the DAR to criticism for reasons that
have nothing to do with their content. They are often exceedingly long, prefaced by three, four, or even six "Whereases."
Daughters believe that many of the DAR's positions have been
misunderstood by the public because they are not fully reported
in the newspapers, but most newspapers couldn't devote the
space to printing even one resolution in its entirety. Whenever
material is deleted, of course, there is always the risk that meaning will change.

In addition to being burdened by length, some resolutions
lack concision and may sound quite negative. "The women on
the resolutions committee are supposed to be women with
judgment and ability," says a woman on the resolutions committee, "but sometimes they put too many things together and get a
dog's breakfast. Frequently there's more preamble than resolution, and the preamble is full of brickbats. A resolution should
never have a brickbat in it, and you shouldn't preach a sermon in
every resolution. They should be constructive and nothing else."
Though the Daughters have made an effort in recent years to
phrase the resolutions in positive terms, their reputation for
being negative is still well entrenched.

The bibliographies attached to some resolutions almost invite
ridicule. The Daughters like to point out that the facts supporting the resolutions are fully documented, but the documentation relies heavily on a single source or group of similar sources
apparently selected because they uphold the committee's biases.
For example, the 1972 resolution on sea power was buttressed
with an official publication of the U.S. Navy League called "Sea
Power," and with nothing else. An outsider can only conclude
that the Daughters either sought documentation that would
prove their point or swallowed the line of a party that could
hardly be called disinterested.

Some bibliographies have been downright unscholarly. The
1973 resolution on "Communist Encroachment in the Carib-

bean" was backed up with two dated but unnamed articles from the Society's own *National Defender*, two DAR national-defense committee publications dealing with the Panama Canal, and five dated but not named articles from the Congressional Record, *The Chicago Tribune*, and *The Pittsburgh Press*. A reader must either go to the trouble of looking up the seven untitled items or to take on faith the word of the resolutions committee that the articles cited bear on communists in the Caribbean with some authority. Delegates may follow the latter course. Reporters are unlikely to do either. Even if the articles were titled, the bibliography would not inspire confidence. Newspapers are not primary sources of information, of course, and the Congressional Record contains material from a variety of sources, all of which may not be unimpeachable.

When they get down to hashing out the fine points of the resolutions as proposed, the Daughters all too often lead with their chins. So esoteric are some of the issues involved that ordinary Americans are highly unlikely to be informed about them, and some delegates lack sophistication as well as knowledge. The "conspiracy" as an explanation of events, probably discounted by most Daughters, finds its way into the deliberations with fair frequency, and emotional or sentimental considerations often take precedence over the practical. One example: When the Daughters were discussing a UN resolution in 1972, several delegates said in essence that the U.S. should not hang around with non-Christian nations, or, as one woman put it, "The ladies are going to have to decide whether they are going to go along with the nude, pagan god Zeus in the Soviet United Nations or are they going to accept Christ and the Bible."

The more knowledgeable and articulate Daughters don't necessarily prevail in these discussions. In 1971 three delegates spoke on a resolution opposing the legalization of marijuana. The second, a member from Arizona, urged the Daughters to insert a phrase asking that the penalty for mere possession be reduced from a felony to a misdemeanor. "I am a volunteer probation officer," the Daughter said to the assembly, "and I have worked with the Juvenile Courts. Many young people have come in and been given a felony offense because they have been caught with marijuana. This goes on their record for the rest of their lives. They are not marijuana addicts. They are just beginning, and I think it is a crime to saddle our young with a felony offense before they become felons."

The president general thanked the Daughter from Arizona and recognized the first vice president general, who spoke to an earlier question. The PG then asked for further discussion on the resolution, got none, and took the vote. The "ayes" had it. An Illinois Daughter stepped to a microphone on the floor.

"Madam President General, we had a very interesting comment by the probation officer . . . from Arizona on changing or adding in the 'Resolved' to recommend that the law on marijuana be made a misdemeanor rather than a felony," she said. "Perhaps some of us are not aware of parliamentary procedure. She didn't make it in the form of an amendment or a motion. I think we are missing what she was trying to add, wherever she is, and I think if she wanted to make an amendment she should come forward and have another chance."

The president general replied, "I am sorry. The only way that amendment could be added would be for those voting on the prevailing side to decide that that is the thing to do. The motion has been completed."

The Illinois Daughter said, "Can't you help the speakers and direct them and ask them if they want to make a motion to that effect when they come to speak at the microphone?"

The president general replied, "I am sorry, the motion was given and the comments were received, but the motion has now been completed."

The resolutions have undeniably kept many Daughters abreast of world affairs over the years. They have engaged the interest of some members who might never have thought about some of these issues otherwise. They have undoubtedly given many women the feeling that they can and should be concerned about matters beyond their own little bailiwicks—a sense of citizenship and even, perhaps, a sense of worth. These are not trivial accomplishments.

But the resolutions have had little apparent effect on America. While they may have served as ballast for conservatism over the years, they have failed again and again to achieve specific goals. They have not transformed the nation into the DAR's America, and they have hurt the Daughters themselves. Cast against the DAR's racist reputation, the resolutions have made the Daughters seem WASPish in the extreme, fervently dedicated to preserving a pure breed of American wholly isolated from the richness of new influences of any kind. While jet travel makes friends of strangers and even enemies, the DAR seems to prefer its own backyard. While the world is talking cooperation, the

Daughters are talking American superiority. In an age marked by revulsion for war, the DAR preaches guns and ammunition. These stands have turned people against the DAR. Perhaps they have even turned people against causes the DAR champions. The resolutions have almost certainly cost the DAR what remained of its credibility after 1939.

"The good things that we do never make headlines," Sally Jones lamented one day. "Our controversial stands are the things that subject us to criticism and controversy. So a lot of people don't know anything about the DAR except the controversial positions that we take."

Mrs. Jones was bemoaning what she saw as the tendency of the press to concentrate on more startling aspects of the DAR agenda, but her point deserves consideration for other reasons. A member of the Washington press corps looks at it this way: "I've always felt that the good the DAR does is submerged by the resolutions."

There are hints that some Daughters share this view. In New Jersey a state officer who does not oppose the resolutions on principle expresses serious reservations about their actual effect. "It gets very sticky," she says. "Even if we're right, the point is that we go on record for these things, which opens us up to a lot of controversy. The point is it brings in the press." This Daughter says she knows two or three CAR members who refuse to join DAR because of a 1970 resolution on ecology. Sally Jones says some women join the DAR because of the stands it takes, which is doubtless true. But one state regent, a candidate for national office, says, "If we dropped the resolutions we'd probably lose ten members and take in twenty."

A move to eliminate the resolutions would undoubtedly meet strong opposition within the Society, just as there has been opposition to moderating them. Although the resolutions are less strident than they used to be, public-relations consultants have tried to get the Daughters to tone them down even more. The Daughters have thought it over and refused. They would rather risk their popularity than appear to be pussyfooting. It is a source of pride with the Daughters that they have not been afraid of controversy.

But they might ask themselves whether that controversy has served either their America or the DAR.

If the resolutions were ever dropped, the major part of the

DAR's patriotic endeavor would remain intact.

The Daughters make Braille flags for blind people. They badger public officials to proclaim February as American History Month permanently and throughout the land. Texas Daughters have given an American flag to a mother whose son was killed in Vietnam; California and Nevada Daughters have commended a girl who rescued a burning American flag from anti-war demonstrators. West Virginia Daughters run an American Heritage camp for sophomore girls each summer. Chapters across the nation give receptions for new citizens. The National Society sponsors an annual American history essay contest in which fifth-through-eighth graders compete for four $100 savings bonds, and although these are modest prizes in these inflationary times, the DAR's contest engaged the interest of nearly 54,000 students in 1972.

These represent the day-to-day, week-to-week, year-to-year efforts of the Daughters of the American Revolution to put their brand of patriotism into individual communities. Whether national, state, or chapter projects, all share a single goal: to firmly lodge the meaning of America in the hearts and minds of its citizens. Some of these activities have been going on for decades. New and old, they require incalculable expenditures of time and energy and cost the Society thousands of dollars a year.

The oldest of these efforts, and by far the DAR's largest youth program, is the Junior American Citizens clubs. Organized in 1906, the JAC program is open to youngsters of all races, creeds, and religions, from kindergarten through high school. It now reaches three or four hundred thousand children in more than ten thousand clubs in forty-one states. The purpose of the clubs is to train children in citizenship so they do not grow up to be like Jane Fonda or Ramsey Clark. The Daughters would like the children to observe American rituals, learn something about their American heritage, and practice being what they consider to be useful citizens.

Many Daughters think of JAC as fully organized clubs conducted according to *Robert's Rules of Order*. Actually a club can be any group of children using the DAR materials regularly. The program has found its way into schools, settlement houses, detention homes, homes for dependent children, Campfire Girls and Scout troops, children's hospitals, neighborhood organizations, 4-H clubs, and Head Start programs. Membership costs the child nothing. The DAR provides handbooks, pins, certificates, suggestions, a few dollars, and, if a club has no leader of its own, leadership. It also sponsors annual contests, giving the children a chance to compete for cash prizes by submitting essays, posters, poems, plays, programs, songs, scrapbooks, and descriptions of special projects, all relating to an American theme.

The character and activities of the JAC clubs vary greatly. Children from many clubs volunteer their services at veterans' hospitals. Some club members are confined to institutions themselves—a Texas Daughter who had polio of the throat started clubs in schools for handicapped children. A Missouri JAC club raises $1,200 a year for a children's hospital. Members of a Florida club had a Christmas bazaar to raise funds for a trophy case for their school. Club members in Mississippi helped teach English to Spanish-speaking children. A high school group in Missouri raised $8,000 to pay the hospital bills of a JAC member who had suffered a cerebral hemorrhage.

Not all clubs are so active. A JAC meeting may require nothing more of the children than their passivity. Such a meeting took place in a Southern state one late November afternoon, with a DAR member presiding and another as guest speaker. About a dozen girls in fifth, sixth, and seventh grades gathered in a living room and sat down quietly on chairs arranged in an oval. When the guest speaker came, the girls stood. They were told that their visitor, an older woman who had driven over from a nearby town, was the state DAR flag chairman. The girls greeted her politely.

Sitting with the girls, the flag chairman read to them from a red paper notebook:

" 'You and I are living in the era of the U.S. Bicentennial'—that's a big word, isn't it, Bicentennial?. . . . 'Now our country is not really very old because people have been fighting and dying for freedom for thousands of years. . . . Of course you've heard of the War of the Revolution back in 1776. . . . America grew from vast wilderness . . . one of the truly free nations in the whole world. . . .' "

As the flag chairman read, the children sat quietly, looking at her or at their folded hands, apparently listening.

" 'We never hurt what we love. . . . Americanism and patriotism should be dear to our hearts. . . . When we raise our flag on a flag pole we raise it quickly and with joy. . . .' In closing may I say God bless each of you fine young American citizens."

The flag chairman put her notebook down. "Now you've been such attentive young ladies," she said, "that I have a little remembrance for you." She picked up a box and took off the lid. The girls, who had been solemn, gasped. The box contained some tiny silk flags on little poles and some bronze-colored plastic holders. At a word from the flag chairman, the girls got in line, and as they filed past their guest, she presented each with a flag in a holder. A few of the girls smiled. They remained quiet but were obviously pleased. The meeting ended a moment or two later when the JAC president, a blonde, leggy child, stood to announce shyly to the flag chairman, "We are very happy with the flags, and thank you for your speech."

In spreading the American gospel to American children, the Daughters sometimes meet with resistance. Most of the JAC programs are in public, private, or parochial schools. Since the Daughters can't get into the schools without permission, they are heavily dependent on cooperation from school administrators and faculty members. Many school officials have proven enormously helpful. Others have not. School administrators are increasingly wary of outside groups seeking access to the children under their care. Administrators sympathetic to the DAR might keep the Daughters out rather than set a precedent that other groups could use as leverage. Some aren't sympathetic.

Even the Daughter who gains entry is not necessarily successful. Linda Lee started a JAC club in Naperville, Illinois, that got national DAR recognition its first year of operation and then nearly perished because it lost its school sponsors. If anyone could get a successful JAC program going it would probably be Linda Lee. The mother of two teen-agers, Linda is young, direct, friendly, and respectful of children. She is careful to separate truth from nonsense, and she does not lack courage. She and her husband have taken two large groups of children to Washington, and Linda tries to take DAR programs into schools even though she feels self-conscious about never having gone to college.

"It takes guts to go into a classroom when you've had no training and see these kids that know more than you do, you know!" Linda says.

Linda Lee's assets as chapter JAC chairman included an excellent relationship with the superintendent of schools and considerable credit with the system, which she had served for years as, among other things, Home and School president. While chapter flag chairman, she had encouraged some schoolchildren to produce a flag assembly. They came up with a program called "My Country 'Tis of Thee" which they carried off beautifully.

Linda got some of those children together as the nucleus of a JAC club. The club members put together a program which they performed for their own school, and then for other schools, and then for boys at the DuPage County Boys' Home, and then for a DAR chapter. It went over so well with the Daughters that the children were invited to perform at the state DAR conference.

"They've never forgotten it," Linda says. "Those kids still talk about that. They got standing ovations. The program got a first place for Patriotic Programs both at state conference and DAR Congress. Two of our girls wrote a play and presented it to the younger grades. They got students from the younger grades, gave them the parts, rehearsed it. It got a first place from the state DAR and an honorable mention at Continental Congress. And they did it all on their own."

When the summer was over the club members returned to school to discover that one of their three faculty advisers had become principal of another school, and the second had had a schedule change.

Like that the club began to disintegrate. Linda Lee found herself begging for teachers to put it back together.

"I won't give up," she says. "Last year in the lower grades I sent a note to the teachers saying, 'Please ask the students if they'd like to write anything about the flag and read it at our flag program to the other students.' And you know how many I got? Thirty-five. And it's just a little school, like a hundred and some students. Thirty-five of those students stood up before a microphone and read what the flag meant to them. They're not ashamed of it. It does your heart so much good. There's no limit to any of these youth things, really. To me it isn't just waving the flag. It's 'Do you care about someone else, will you do something for someone else?' The kids are so willing if people will just give them the opportunity."

Although the school superintendent supports the JAC program, Linda feels that the DAR can't relax its efforts. "You've got to keep plugging all the time," Linda says. "You've got to watch your Ps and Qs. You cannot step on anybody's feet. You have to be very careful. You have to tread very lightly."

If it seems ironic to members of the DAR that they have to tread lightly while trying to encourage American children to love America, they don't say so. They do sometimes refer with looks of confusion or indignation or hurt in their eyes, to the occasional youngsters who turn down awards which the DAR has tried to confer upon them. Usually the Daughters can forestall embarrassing situations by asking the school principal or guidance counselor to make sure in advance that the girl or boy who qualifies for the honor will agree to accept it, but an occasional Marlon Brando turns up who doesn't refuse the award till after he has received it. Accompanied by explanatory letters, the rejected awards once in a while make their way to the president general's office.

It is Mrs. Spicer's view that the kids simply lack an understanding of the DAR. "They get into one of these groups, and they become imbued with the idea that we're racist, or that we believe in war, or that we support the police—which of course we do —and they send us back their medals with all these childish declamations," she says, sounding slightly miffed. "This happens, oh, maybe a couple of times a year. It's not common, but it does happen."

The Daughters find it easier to forgive children who return awards than school administrators who won't let awards be given out. The children, after all, are impressionable. They may have swallowed a line. In time, it is hoped, they will learn the truth. But school administrators should have learned by now that the Daughters only want to instill patriotism, which is what, as the Daughters see it, the administrators themselves should be doing.

School administrators see the matter differently.

"Our decision not to let any groups into the schools to make awards rested on the difficulty of making a decision as to which groups and which awards," says superintendent John F. Fanning of the Lower Merion School District outside Philadelphia. "There are literally thousands of groups that for various and sundry reasons—some admirable and some questionable— want access to schools to exhibit their interest in young people. To avoid a court battle, we decided that they can give an award to a child on their own time. We won't set up a special assembly or bring them in to give fifteen-minute ceremonies."

Noting that this policy has been practiced in Washington, D.C., for a decade and is spreading to other parts of the country, Fanning points out, "In the past, schools were never questioned. If they decided to let DAR in and not John Birch, nobody questioned it. But now the community does ask. I would have to defend the John Birch Society, the Sons of Italy, Pennsylvania Polish-American Society, Boy Scouts, Girl Scouts. There are just an awful lot of groups, and some I've never heard of. And some awards are very specific in nature—$100 to a caucasian male seventeen to nineteen who is the grandson of a Polish immigrant. That gets pretty touchy."

The Daughters tend to look upon such explanations as excuses. But in spite of occasional antipathy or lack of cooperation from students or school administrators, the DAR manages to confer quite a number of awards each year. The awards are of several varieties, but they all go to students who qualify as good Americans as DAR members mean the term. In 1972 Good Citizenship honors—lapel pins and bronze medals—went to 4,800 elementary, junior or senior high school students exhibiting qualities of honor, service, courage, leadership and patriotism. The same year 1,500 ROTC cadets received bronze or gold medals for outstanding dependability, character, adherence to military discipline, leadership ability, and "a fundamental and patriotic understanding of the importance of ROTC training." Also in 1972 Good Citizen awards went to students in nearly a third of the secondary schools in America.

Good Citizens is the DAR's biggest award program and also —because it carries a monetary prize above the local level—the Daughters' favorite. Instituted in 1934 to recognize girls when "there were all kinds of scholarships and things done for boys in schools by men's organizations," as Eleanor Spicer puts it, the Good Citizens program honors senior girls, one per school, who have shown outstanding qualities of leadership, dependability, service, and patriotism. Local winners receive a pin and a certificate; state winners receive a pin and a $100 bond; the national winner receives a $1,000 scholarship to the college of her choice. She is also brought to Washington during Continental Congress so the Daughters can applaud her as she accepts congratulations and a sterling silver bowl from the president general.

The 1973 Good Citizen winner was Helen Louise Hatlelid of Ponca City, Oklahoma. Miss Hatlelid was a straight-A student, first in her class of 525, winner of a National Merit commendation and president of the National Honor Society in her school. She received school honors in Latin, French, biology, and orchestra. Besides being an accomplished swimmer and flutist, Helen was a longtime member of the Presbyterian church choir. She wants to major in education in college and be a foreign-language teacher.

Any chapter would have been happy to sponsor Helen Ha-tlelid. Her qualifications and achievements are just the kind that the DAR values highly. Not all Americans would view them in the same light. A veteran Illinois teacher describes the Good Citizens program as one which recognizes "our lovely and in-stitutionally oriented" girls.

"No one," says English instructor Kenneth Schaller, "ever questions the worth of either the award or the recipient."

But the Good Citizen award can be a source of great pride to the girl who wins it. Pennsylvanian Karen Fad, now a medical secretary in Delaware, took the trouble to write a letter to a local newspaper reporter describing the day she received local Good Citizen honors as one of the most memorable days of her life.

"I was so impressed by the patriotism, enthusiasm and love for our great country that was displayed by all of the members of the DAR present at the luncheon," Karen wrote. "I felt very proud to be an American, and especially grateful to be the recipient of an award given by this dedicated National Society. At the close of the luncheon, everyone joined together and sang 'God Bless America.' As I looked around at the happy faces, I noticed tears in the eyes of many. That same emotion took hold of me. I just can't understand how any American citizen could overlook the cause of such a great organization."

Americans have found it increasingly easy to overlook if not the causes espoused by the DAR, the DAR itself. Many years have passed since the Daughters were headed by a prominent American woman. United States Presidents do not routinely address Continental Congresses as they once did. President Nixon spoke at Constitution Hall, but both Lyndon Johnson and John Kennedy passed up the opportunity. Vice-President Spiro Agnew sent his regrets the year he was asked to deliver the Congress keynote. Even Senators who are friendly to the DAR are difficult to snare these days. The Daughters must settle for such lesser lights as a member of the House of Representatives from Mount Prospect, Illinois. It seems to be the feeling in most quarters that the DAR as an organization wields little power in today's America.

One who disputes this view is South Carolina's U.S. Senator Strom Thurmond. Thurmond calls the DAR "an organization of prestige and influence" and says that the Society's positions are not ignored on Capitol Hill. "Many members of Congress would prefer that they and the DAR would be together on as many points as possible," Thurmond says.

Few politicians would wish to incur the wrath of an organization of 197,000 voters, of course, and as Thurmond points out himself, he is not completely neutral. His wife and sisters are members of the DAR, as was his mother; he himself belongs to the Sons of the American Revolution and once served on the DAR advisory council. Another Congressman who, like Thurmond, is fond of the DAR says he never sees Daughters on Capitol Hill and admits with some embarrassment that he is not conscious of "any great area of accomplishment" as far as the organization is concerned. William Buckley doubts very much that the DAR is "a force." Even right-wing watcher Wesley McCune doesn't consider the DAR a part of the right-wing he needs to watch.

"Until their annual meeting, I forget about them," McCune says. "They disappear, like the American Legion. I clip the resolutions, not because it's the DAR but because the story usually has something on their speakers. They always have at least one outstanding clinker from the right wing, a flannelmouth who'll tell 'em exactly what they want to hear. Phil Crane is the most conservative member of Congress. Thurmond and J. Edgar Hoover have been their favorites."

The Daughters themselves don't dispute their diminished influence on the American scene. Though they console themselves that the "pendulum is swinging back" in their favor, many share with Eleanor Spicer the opinion that the DAR was most influential in the 1920's. That is the view of DAR member and political conservative Clare Boothe Luce, who feels that the DAR ceased to be the "in" thing "when the influx of immigrants and ethnic groups were beginning to find themselves." Speaking out of what she described as vast ignorance, Mrs. Luce told a reporter in 1973, "It is my impression that the DAR has never really tried to exert political power, has none, and was always attacked because outsiders thought it had it, or was supposed to." Then speaking out of personal knowledge, and wryly, Mrs. Luce noted that when she ran for Congress, "It was more important that the labor unions be for me than that the DAR be for me."

These are opinions, of course, not evidence. It would be difficult to prove that the DAR as an organization wields no power in America. Even if such a thing could be demonstrated beyond a doubt, it would not fully measure the DAR's impact. The DAR is not just the president general or the executive committee or the national board of management. It is Ramona Bradley in Arlington, California, and Sylvia Hansen in Jackson, Wyoming, and Edna Burns in North Manchester, Indiana, and Marian Rehler in Portsmouth, New Hampshire. If DAR membership doesn't make these women any more powerful than the average American citizen, it certainly doesn't make them any less powerful. When a Daughter acts as an individual, she may expect to accomplish things that any individual in America can accomplish.

In the early 1960's, using a DAR textbook study but working as individuals, Daughters in Texas joined forces with concerned members of other organizations in an effort to make sure Texas schoolchildren were taught the "right" version of American history. The effort was successful. The crusaders prevented Texas schools from adopting certain history textbooks. They had certain passages in other textbooks rewritten or expunged.

In 1973 the Maine state legislature refused to ratify the Equal Rights Amendment. Maine residents who happened to belong to the DAR felt they had had a large part to play in that action. "We did nothing as an organization," Ada Helmbreck wrote later, "but we worked in a quiet way, individually contacting our Senators and those who had influence." (The Maine legislature did ratify the ERA in 1974, however.) Seeing the rather unusual opportunity for specific action related to DAR policy, women in several states left their DAR ribbons at home and went out to work against the ERA. According to Nebraska state regent Esther Hunter, Nebraska Daughters felt they had had "a significant part" in rescinding their state's ratification.

Such grass-roots influence is precisely the kind some Americans worry about. The DAR as an organization is unlikely to spearhead a textbook censorship project, but a few Daughters with fair organizational skills and a sense of mission managed to rally enough support to change the history books in one state and modify the teaching of history in several others, causing Gene Roberts, Philadelphia *Inquirer* executive editor and coauthor with Jack Nelson of a 1963 book called *The Censors and the Schools*,* to refer to the DAR as "the most formidable adversary

---

*Boston: Little, Brown, and Co., 1963.

of free speech" in the textbooks-censorship era.

By Roberts and those who share his philosophies, the DAR has sometimes been viewed as harmful to America. Just as the DAR feels that peace demonstrators twisted the rights of freedom as America's Founders meant those rights, many outsiders feel the DAR, too, has twisted the original version of America out of shape.

"I don't know if they're harmful now, but in the past they've done harm," Wesley McCune says of the Daughters. "They have given a measure of respect to stands that are not respectable. The UN. Immigration laws. When these gals can say the same things the John Birch Society says, they're taken seriously by a lot of gals around the sewing circle. Things that wouldn't get much comment or ink otherwise. Their roots are very deep in the community. They're not laughed at out there."

McCune, of course, does not consider himself a friend of the DAR. Strom Thurmond, who is, believes that the principles espoused by the DAR are precisely the principles that made America great. "I don't know anything they stand for against the best interests of this country," Thurmond says. "They've held out for the Constitution. That's what's gotten them into trouble. Their strength and forte has been to stand for the Constitution of the United States. As a whole, the DAR has stood for America, the decent things in our public life. I know of no harm they've done this country."

CHAPTER V

Race—The Past

In 1973 the following statement was drawn up for distribution by DAR headquarters:

"Many times since 1939 the National Society Daughters of the American Revolution has been referred to as 'a racist organization.' Usually the 'Marian Anderson' incident is cited as an example. This allegation is untrue.

"In fact, Constitution Hall, a few years after its dedication in 1929, was the scene of a concert by Roland Hayes, a great Negro tenor. The date was January 31, 1931. A few months later, on March 21, a black choir from the Hampton Institute, Virginia, sang in the Hall to an integrated audience. As far as can be determined, this was the first instance of its kind in the nation's capital since Reconstruction days.

"The DAR thus took a pioneer step in the historic movement to end segregation.

"Miss Marian Anderson sang in Constitution Hall on at least eight occasions. Her farewell concert, upon her retirement, was given in the DAR Hall. Over the years, many eminent black singers and actors have appeared there, and others will appear in the future.

"The incident referred to occurred in 1939, when an agent of Miss Anderson's requested use of Constitution Hall on the same day it was scheduled for the National Symphony of Washington, D.C. Because of a series of unfortunate misunderstandings afterward, a controversy developed, and Miss Anderson sang on the steps of the Lincoln Memorial in Washington. International publicity which followed was extremely detrimental to the DAR, and dramatically but incorrectly made a segment of the public regard the DAR as racist. It has been said that the incident was the first successful Civil Rights activist event.

"In 1939, Washington was, as it had always been, a segregated city. This was still the situation in 1945, when Eleanor Roosevelt wrote in her column, 'My Day': 'I do not think one can hold the DAR alone responsible.' Other concert halls, theaters, churches, restaurants, hotels, schools, golf courses, and even government cafeterias were segregated in Washington as they were over much of the country.

"Segregation was an ugly part of America's history and most of our institutions shared the blame."

This statement was put out by president general Eleanor Spicer. It is the latest in a series of statements issued by the DAR in an attempt to set the record straight about what actually happened in 1939. Revised by succeeding administrations, the statements are sent to every Daughter and every outsider who writes to the National Society asking about or mentioning the Marian Anderson incident.

Mrs. Spicer's version is far more conciliatory than anything the DAR has said about the incident since it occurred. The statement it replaced was querulous in the extreme. "One of the greatest hoaxes perpetrated upon the American public is the charge, repeated for more than a quarter of a century by the news media, that the DAR denied Constitution Hall to Marian Anderson," the 1970 statement began. "Nothing could be further from the truth. Whether the statement is true or false makes little difference to the biased reporting. . . . The press always takes license with the truth, under the guise of a free press."

This statement was issued by Eleanor Spicer's predecessor, but it went out in Eleanor Spicer's name for more than two years after she took office. Although the tone and the content of the statements change from administration to administration, their message has remained essentially the same: The DAR did not deny Constitution Hall to Marion Anderson in 1939 because of her race; the DAR is not prejudiced against blacks; the press and the public have chosen, then and now, to overlook the truth. The message implies that if Americans possessed the whole truth, they would cease to condemn the DAR.

The whole truth is not to be found in the statements issued from headquarters. Though Eleanor Spicer's is more nearly true than earlier versions, it is not wholly accurate. Past DAR statements have been misleading or downright false. They have consistently conveyed the message that the DAR was merely acting in accordance with prevailing policy and custom in Washington when it said no to Marian Anderson. Many Daughters argue that the DAR would have violated a District of Columbia law or ordinance if it had permitted her to sing. There was no such law or ordinance on the books in 1939. There apparently never has been one. The statements from headquarters have consistently informed the Daughters that all District theaters and auditoriums at that time barred black artists and performers. This is not true. Other Daughters point out, and the statements stress, that the April 9 date requested by Miss Anderson's agent had been booked for months. That is true. A schedule printed in *DAR Magazine* the previous October shows that the National Symphony had reserved Constitution Hall for April 9. But in a full explanation of the Marian Anderson incident, the booking conflict is equivalent to "Once upon a time," as DAR leaders have known or should have known.

The whole truth about 1939 cannot be found in any one pamphlet or file or building or city. Some of the pieces may be lost irretrievably. Decades have passed since Marian Anderson sang from the steps of the Lincoln Memorial that Easter Sunday. Memories have faded. Most of the principals have died. Some of the pertinent materials have been removed over the years from DAR files, leaders claim. Furthermore, the incident cannot be considered apart from the policies governing Constitution Hall before and after 1939, and those policies are very puzzling indeed.

Still, much of the background of 1939 and the details of the incident itself can be pieced together. The story sheds light on why DAR leaders acted as they did. It also suggests that other people involved may have acted out of motives that were less than totally pure. But the facts of the story do not exonerate the DAR. Instead, they make the Daughters' efforts to defend 1939 seem badly misguided. In light of the extremes to which the Daughters have sometimes taken those efforts, such as making the preposterous statement that Miss Anderson has assured them that she does not believe the DAR discriminated against her, it seems more than likely that the DAR has done greater damage to its reputation by trying to justify 1939 than by barring Marian Anderson in the first place.

In 1935 Marian Anderson came back to the United States after a two-year concert tour in Europe. She returned under the management of Sol Hurok, who had immigrated to the U.S. from Russia as a young man and become one of this nation's leading impresarios. "You won't be able to give her away," someone told Hurok when he signed the black contralto. The forecaster was proven wrong almost immediately. On December 30, Miss Anderson gave a homecoming concert in New York's Town Hall. While some reviews were reserved, *New York Times* critic Howard Taubman gave the young singer superlative praise, using such terms as "stunning" and "transcending." Taubman called Miss Anderson's performance "music-making that probed too deep for words." So much excitement did the concert generate that Hurok quickly arranged for Miss Anderson to sing at Carnegie Hall on January 30, 1936. That concert was also successful. He booked her again into Carnegie Hall on March 9. That concert, too, was sold out, and Marian Anderson was again heartily acclaimed by critics.

Later that year, apparently acting for Sol Hurok, V. D. Johnston, treasurer of Washington's black Howard University, requested the use of Constitution Hall for a concert by Miss Anderson. (His request was made through the Howard concert bureau.) Fred E. Hand, a DAR employee, was the manager of the Hall at the time. As the Daughters had inserted a "white artists only" clause in all Constitution Hall contracts beginning March 23, 1932, Hand advised Johnston to apply to the DAR's National Board of Management.* Johnston evidently did not follow up the suggestion. (Hand is now deceased. The part he played in the Marian Anderson incident is described in a statement he wrote entitled "Facts Concerning the Management of Constitution Hall Dating From 1929 to 1940.")

Three years later Hurok decided that the time had come for Marian Anderson to sing in Constitution Hall. She had previously sung in churches and schools and smaller theaters in Washington, but her reputation as a singer had grown, and, as Hurok puts it, "Constitution Hall was the only concert hall in Washington." By 1939 no one was thinking of Marian Anderson as anything but a concert artist. As Hurok still insists, "There was nowhere else for her to go."

So in mid-January of 1939, Charles C. Cohen, chairman of the Howard University Concert Series, went in person to see Fred Hand. He asked Hand for the use of Constitution Hall for a concert by Miss Anderson on April 9. According to Hand's account, "It was explained to them that the Hall would not be available to them on that date because of a contractual obligation with the National Symphony Orchestra. They then proposed to make an effort to change the date, at which time I advised them that it would be impossible for me to book Miss Anderson in the Hall because of the restriction placed upon me by the Executive ruling of March 23, 1932, and I suggested to them that if they sought a waiver of this ruling that they address a letter to the National Board of Management which would meet early in February."

Two days after the meeting between Cohen and Hand took place, an open letter from Howard University treasurer V. D.

*National officers and all state regents.

Johnston appeared in *The Washington Times-Herald* and, on January 17, in *The Washington Star*. The letter criticized the DAR for its stand. It said, in part, "The question arises . . . whether there are not a sufficient number of persons in Washington and vicinity interested in hearing Miss Anderson and what she represents to impress upon the DAR that this restriction may not represent public opinion in Washington." The *Times-Herald* editorialized on the matter on January 15, concluding, "Prejudice rules to make the capital of the nation ridiculous in the eyes of all cultured people and to comfort Fuehrer Hitler and the members of our Nazibund."

On January 23, Hurok wrote Hand saying, "Without attempting to discuss the justification of such a policy, we are asking whether you would waive that restriction in the case of Miss Anderson. It need not be pointed out to you, we hope, that Marian Anderson is one of the greatest living singers and the application of such a restriction would be to deny a great musical experience to the people of your city, since it is impossible to present her in any other hall in Washington. Would you, or a possible board of managers whom you might represent, take up this request as soon as possible and advise us of your decision." (This letter and other pertinent documents in Hurok's possession were quoted in an article by Carleton Smith in the July, 1939, issue of *Esquire* magazine.)

Hand claimed he acknowledged receipt of Hurok's letter. "I replied to Mr. Hurok's letter on January 25th," Hand wrote in his "Facts," "telling him, as I had told the original applicants, that the Hall was not available on April 9th and suggested that if he wished to request a waiver of policy that he address a communication to Mrs. Robert, our President General." Hurok told *Esquire* that he did write to Mrs. Robert on January 27, saying, "The cultured people of America would be gravely offended by your decision to exercise the restriction above-mentioned."

On January 30, 1939, Interior Secretary Harold L. Ickes wrote to Sarah Corbin Robert. "My dear Mrs. Robert," the letter began, "The President of Howard University, Dr. Mordecai W. Johnson, advises me that in his effort to secure Constitution Hall on Easter Sunday for a recital by Miss Marian Anderson, internationally known Negro contralto, he was informed that the regulations prohibited the use of the hall for Negro artists. This is such an astounding discrimination against equal rights that I am loath to believe that the Daughters of the American

Revolution should invoke such a rule. I am writing you to inquire whether Doctor Johnson was correctly informed."

Also on January 30, Metropolitan opera stars Kirsten Flagstad and Lawrence Tibbett wired the National Association for the Advancement of Colored People protesting the DAR's decision. It is uncertain just what prompted them to express their dismay on that date to that organization. Hurok readily acknowledged that at some point during the negotiations—he could not recall just when—he decided to exert pressure on the DAR. As he explained his efforts shortly before his death in March 1974, strong traces of Russia still in his voice, "I took over the Washington Hotel, a whole floor upstairs, and I brought in my press agent and all to start to bombard the whole country, you know—artists, actors and so on and so on. A big campaign, we made. It was to protest that the DAR are not allowing Marian Anderson to perform there. The whole thing was just a question of mass protest. I raised the sentiment all over the country and all over the world, as a matter of fact. The world protested."

Whether the world protest was inaugurated by Tibbett and Flagstad on January 30 is not clear. Hurok claimed he did not remember on what date he began the campaign. His memoir, *Impresario*,* doesn't mention it. His account and others indicate that the protest did not begin in earnest until the end of February. The Washington Hotel destroys its records after five years, and a hotel spokesman says it is impossible to ascertain on what date Hurok rented the floor or checked out. Hurok believes he had the space for several weeks. How many other letters or telegrams the DAR received before its National Board of Management met on February 1 for its regularly scheduled meeting is not a matter of public record. The Philadelphia Orchestra protested on February 28, but whether that dates Hurok's campaign is unclear.

The president general was to imply later that the issue had raised considerable public comment before the board met. She maintained that "with no request yet in writing, letters began to appear in the press." This statement seems rather disingenuous. Newspaper comment before February 1 was limited to one editorial, one news story, and two brief letters to the editor. *The New York Times* did not carry a story on the affair until February 23. Neither *Time* nor *Newsweek* mentioned it until March 6.

Impresario, by Sol Hurok (New York: Random House), 1946

At any rate, the Daughters who met on February 1 were not swayed by whatever protest had been registered. By a vote of 39 to 1 the Board elected to maintain its "white artists only" rule. On February 3 DAR president general Sally Robert wrote two letters. One went to Interior Secretary Ickes. "My dear Mr. Secretary," the letter said, "In reply to your letter of January 30, Constitution Hall had already been engaged for Easter Sunday for use by another musical organization. Dr. Johnson was informed of the existence of a policy of several years' standing, limiting the use of Constitution Hall to white artists. The artistic and musical standing of Miss Marian Anderson is not involved in any way. In view of the existence of provisions in prevailing agreements with other organizations and concert bureaus, and the policy which has been adopted in the past, an exception cannot be made in this instance."

The president general's second letter went to Hurok. "At the time that the Chairman of the Howard University Concert Series approached the Manager of Constitution Hall," Mrs. Robert said in part, "the Hall had already been engaged for Sunday, April 9th, by another musical organization." The DAR maintained—and maintains—that Hurok did not request an alternate date in his January 27 letter.

Hurok said in his book that Mrs. Robert's letter contained "no mention of the discriminatory clause." In his view, the letter ignored the issue. "Now it was our move to ask for another date," Hurok wrote. "Mark Levine, my good friend, of National Concert and Artists Corporation, wrote to Mr. Hand at this time asking for available dates for a concert by Ignaz Paderewski in Constitution Hall. Hand replied with a list of dates which did not include the ninth, but did mention the eighth and tenth as open. I wired the University's concert manager that the eighth and tenth were open and he promptly applied to Hand for either date."

Hand wrote, "On February 9th, I received a Registered letter signed by Mr. Charles C. Cohen, requesting the use of the Hall on April 8th or 10th for Miss Anderson's concert and in reply on February 10th I advised him that the Hall would not be available on either date. Before any of these letters had been received by me, numerous open letters in the press had appeared."

On February 13, the DAR president general issued a press release saying, among other things, "The rules governing the use of Constitution Hall are in accordance with the policy of theaters, auditoriums, hotels and public schools of the District of Columbia." On the same day, following a Society tradition that continues to the present, Mrs. Robert boarded a train for the spring tour of state DAR conferences. She was to be gone nearly seven weeks.

On February 15, Charles Cohen announced receipt of a letter from Fred Hand which said, "The Hall is not available for a concert by Miss Anderson."

On the same day Cohen made application to the Board of Education of the District of Columbia for the use of the Central High School auditorium for a recital by Miss Anderson. On February 19 Dr. F. W. Ballou, Superintendent of Schools, said no. The District of Columbia was operating, by law, under a dual school system at that time. Central High School was white. Although school board members pointed out that District educational facilities could not be used for commercially sponsored events, board minutes make clear that the deciding factor in the board's decision was Miss Anderson's color.

On February 20 the Marian Anderson Citizens Committee, composed of representatives of twenty-four local and national organizations, convened a mass meeting, attended by 1,500 people, and picketed the Board of Education. Thousands of people signed a petition protesting the Board's decision. "We regard such action," the petition read, "as contrary to the spirit of democracy, and as a backward step in the development of interracial goodwill in the District of Columbia."

On February 24 Hurok announced that Marian Anderson would give her Washington concert out of doors. According to his book, Hurok made this announcement and then contacted Secretary Ickes about having the concert at the Lincoln Memorial. Again according to the book, the arrangements were made by Hurok's press agent, Gerry Goode, and by NAACP president Walter White, who met in Washington and approached Ickes together. (Asked how Walter White became involved, Hurok replies that White was interested in the "colored movement.") In recounting the story recently, Hurok said he, too, went to Ickes. Perhaps both he and Goode spoke with the Secretary.

As Hurok recalled the conversation with the Secretary, "I asked him what's to be done. I said I want to have the Lincoln Memorial for a concert, a big concert. So, well, he says, 'I want to talk to the President.' Ickes liked the idea right away. He took it up immediately. So he came back to me and said, 'Go right ahead, but we don't pay; you'll have to pay all expenses. Government institution, we're not allowed to spend money this way. You go ahead."

On February 26 Eleanor Roosevelt, wife of the President of the United States, resigned from the DAR. She had belonged only since 1933, the year after Franklin took office, when DAR president general Edith Scott Magna, a moderate and a woman who understood public relations, had prevailed upon her to become a life member of the Society. Leaders wanted the First Lady on their rolls. They had not only paid her initiation fee but given her, at the traditional White House reception, an embossed certificate inscribed with the names of her six Revolutionary ancestors. Obviously Mrs. Roosevelt was free to reject these attentions if she had wished to. Despite the furor over the blacklist incident in the late 1920's, the DAR apparently had enough good works to its credit that DAR membership in the early 1930's was not a blot upon the record of the lady in the White House.

But 1939 confronted Mrs. Roosevelt with a very stark option. She could either retain her membership and thus appear to confer White House sanction upon the DAR's decision, or she could get out.

Still, she debated with herself. Would it be better to stay in the DAR and try to change its policy? She had followed this course before when she found herself in disagreement with an organization she belonged to. "I have often found that the thing in which I was interested was done some years later," Mrs. Roosevelt wrote in her column on February 28. "But in this case I belong to an organization in which I can do no active work. They have taken action which has been widely talked of in the press. To remain as a member implies approval of that action, and therefore I am resigning."

Her decision seized America's attention. "This released the gutters of publicity," wrote Carleton Smith in the 1939 *Esquire* article. "Club women wrote letters, columnists wisecracked, newspapers editorialized, Congressmen and Senators jumped on the bandwagon. L'affaire Anderson rivalled Hitler's coups as a front-page item."

On March 3, under considerable pressure, the D.C. Board of Education reversed itself by a vote of 6 to 2 and agreed to allow Miss Anderson to give a concert in the Central High School auditorium. The Board said it had made this decision "as proof of goodwill to Marian Anderson and the Colored people of the District." But there was a catch. The concert would be permitted only if sponsors gave "positive and definite assurance and agreement that the Board of Education will not in the future again be asked to depart from the principle of a dual system of schools and school facilities." The sponsors accepted the use of the auditorium but rejected the conditions attached. The Superintendent of Schools promptly withdrew the offer.

On March 18 the results of a Gallup Poll were released showing that sixty-seven percent of the people in America approved of Mrs. Roosevelt's resignation. Only the South disapproved, and by a narrow margin. "Southerners dissented by an average vote of fifty-seven percent but even some of the dissenters declared they had no objection to Marian Anderson's singing as a paid performer," noted the statement issued by poll officials. "It was Mrs. Roosevelt's 'making a fuss about it' that they disliked."

On March 30 Secretary Ickes announced that permission had been granted for Marian Anderson to sing on the steps of Lincoln Memorial on Easter Sunday. "It seems to me to be a good use of the public facilities," Ickes noted. Interior Department permits were issued on that date.

On the afternoon of April 9 Marian Anderson gave her concert. Nearly 75,000 people gathered to hear her sing. Among the people on the platform behind her were Ickes, Treasury Secretary Henry Morgenthau, Supreme Court Justice Hugo Black, six U.S. Senators, and a number of members of the House of Representatives. Miss Anderson began her concert with "My Country 'Tis of Thee" and "Nobody Knows the Trouble I've Seen" and went on to sing "America the Beautiful," the aria "O mio Fernando," Schubert's "Ave Maria." Then she sang three more spirituals—"Gospel Train," "Trampin'," and "My Soul Is Anchored in the Lord." After she had finished, it seemed to Miss Anderson that "the tumult of the crowd's shouting would not die down."

These are the basic elements of the Marian Anderson story. They make it patently clear, contrary to the DAR's 1970 statement, that the DAR did deny Miss Anderson the use of Constitution Hall. It did not deny the Hall to her because the hall was booked or because Hurok failed to follow the proper procedures. While maintaining that Hurok had never posed the proper question properly, the board nonetheless gave an answer. The answer was to refuse the use of the Hall to Marian Anderson. The reason was that Miss Anderson was black, and that a performance by a black in Constitution Hall was against the policy of the DAR.

These are harsh facts, and Daughters who concede their accuracy tend to wince at the baldness with which they are sometimes stated. When Joseph P. Lash published his book *Eleanor and Franklin** in 1971, Eleanor Spicer received a number of letters from DAR members who were upset at the author's treatment of the incident, which he tersely characterized as "a local episode of bigotry" turned into an international cause célèbre by Mrs. Roosevelt's resignation. The president general herself was upset.

"That we denied Marian Anderson the use of Constitution Hall because she was black is basically and essentially an unfortunate truth. But they didn't go into why we had to, and what we could have done about it if they'd given us a chance to do it, which wasn't given us. All of this furor of the press came down upon our heads before we had ever been asked if there was any way we could make an exception, anything we could do about it. The first date they had asked for was April ninth, and there was a concert in the Hall that day. And her manager never came back and made the request until after the press had blown us off the map as far as they were concerned."

The question can legitimately be asked why Hurok did not address a letter to Mrs. Robert requesting other dates, as it appears he did not. Hand claimed he told Howard University's Charles Cohen when Cohen first approached him on January 9 that Hurok would have to apply to the DAR Board of Management. Instead, on January 23, Hurok wrote to Hand. According to the part of that letter that appeared in *Esquire*, Miss Anderson's agent was requesting a waiver but not another date. Hand's January 25 answer—again as supplied to *Esquire* by Hurok—noted again that Hurok would have to write to Mrs. Robert. Nothing in Hurok's book or in the *Esquire* article indicates that Hurok did ask for another date when he wrote Mrs. Robert on January 27. He apparently asked only for a waiver. In his book he states that only after Mrs. Robert's February 3 reply did he consider it time to ask for another date. But if Hurok could ascertain *after* February 3 which dates were open, which he

*New York: W. W. Norton, 1971.

did by applying for a Paderewski concert, he could just as easily have found out *before* February 3. When he did find out, he empowered Cohen to request the date for Marian Anderson. Cohen wrote not to Mrs. Robert but to Fred Hand.

However, the question can just as legitimately be asked why the DAR didn't offer another date. In Hurok's January 23 letter to Hand he specifically asked that Hand "or a board of managers whom you [Hand] might represent" reconsider a Constitution Hall concert for Marian Anderson. If the DAR had been willing to have her sing in its auditorium, it seems unlikely that technicalities, such as whose name was on the envelope or which date was at issue, would have mattered a whit.

That the DAR was operating under considerable pressure during those weeks of 1939 is undeniable. No matter how one regarded the "white artists only" clause, as defensible or indefensible, it was the DAR's established policy at the time. The policy had become a public target. While there is nothing in the Washington press to substantiate the DAR's argument that public criticism had become full-blown before the board met, the fact that Tibbett and Flagstad had wired the NAACP on January 30 and the fact that there were any letters at all in the papers before February 1 proves that at least some feeling had been aroused. How many expressings of protest had arrived at DAR headquarters only the DAR knows. Whether the feeling had been aroused by Hurok's campaign is immaterial. Accurately or inaccurately, some Daughters felt that the DAR was under pressure. Rightly or wrongly, some Daughters felt that the Society was being used in a test case for civil rights. The essential task facing the board members who convened on February 1 was not merely to decide whether they wanted to change the policy at all, but whether they wanted to change it while it was being publicly attacked by outsiders. That they failed to change the policy even when the attacks ceased proves that outside pressure had nothing to do with the Daughters' basic position. In fact they reaffirmed the ruling in 1945. But at least as board members viewed the situation those first few days of February, 1939, the justness of the white artists clause was not the primary issue. The primary issue was this: Would the DAR permit its policy to be dictated from without? The board decided that it would not.

At Continental Congress, which convened only eight days after Miss Anderson's historic concert, president general Sally Robert described to the delegates the dilemma in which the board members had felt themselves when they met eleven weeks earlier.

"Information and letters received during this period clearly indicated that the question was not one regarding a single artist, but involved far-reaching changing social forces," Mrs. Robert said in her address. "By the time the National Board met on February first, the real question had been so involved with entanglements that it could not be considered alone. . . .

"The membership should distinctly understand that to have made an exception would not only have been in violation of signed agreements of the Society, and customs for all similar properties in Washington, but would have meant that the Society retreated under fire of widely scattered groups and organizations, many of whom knew nothing of the facts, and whose interest had nothing to do with the real question. To have changed a rule while it was entangled with so many factors having nothing to do with the rule would have been to surrender the Society to influences inimical to its purposes and efforts. When independence of action is threatened, and when fog beclouds real issues, there can be no surrender."

Mrs. Robert also made clear in her address that outside pressure was not the only factor bearing on the board's decision to sustain the white artists only policy. "An important consideration was that to make an exception would be in direct contradiction to existing agreements with concert bureaus who have regularly used the Hall for some years and whose agreements cover a period of years," she informed the delegates. "The Society would therefore have opened itself to legal responsibility for violation of its own agreements. This was an important factor affecting the action of the board." Apparently Mrs. Robert felt that local concert bureaus would actually take the owners of the biggest hall in Washington to court. She also was apparently unaware that the DAR had few if any long-standing agreements for future use of Constitution Hall. Her implication was that the Society had already signed contracts for events scheduled over "a period of years," but most DAR contracts at that period provided for events that would take place within a few months.

Another factor said to affect the DAR's decision was the feeling within the Society itself. This information comes from Anne Musgrave, who was Sally Robert's dearest friend right up until Mrs. Robert died in 1972. In 1939 Mrs. Musgrave was not only DAR program chairman but was also revising the bylaws. Like

Sally Robert, she lived in Maryland. Unlike many of the DAR's
top officers then as now, she was close enough to Washington to
be able to spend three days a week in a little office next to that of
the president general. Although she claims to have had no role
in the Marian Anderson incident, Mrs. Musgrave was in a position to know what was happening.

"Many of the members had become very indignant—they
weren't Southerners, either—about the pressure," Mrs. Musgrave recalls. Asked if the members objected to what they saw as
pressure on the Society to change its policy, Mrs. Musgrave
replied, "Apparently. It was a question of doing things the right
way. I think many of the members would have been upset if we'd
let her come." In an earlier interview, Mrs. Musgrave had noted,
"Now I must say that in the Society women from Massachusetts
and Ohio and Illinois were much more vehement as being not
favorable to concessions than the women from the deep South.
Surprising."

The board's decision was not universally supported in the
DAR. Two hundred Daughters in Texas joined forces and requested a large block of seats for the concert that finally did take
place. Others were angry enough to resign. Some women quit
even before Eleanor Roosevelt did. How many left for that
reason is impossible to say, however. DAR membership did drop
slightly in 1940, showing a net loss of 256 Daughters. At that
point membership had been increasing for two years, and it
continued to increase in 1941 (by 316 members) and again in
1942 (by 146). The loss in 1940 was definitely if minutely out of
line with a trend. Since it is possible to run across women today
who are proud to say they quit the DAR over Marian Anderson,
there is no question that the board's decision encountered some
opposition within the Society.

Once that decision had been made, the DAR was obliged to
live with it. No matter how much it displeased outsiders or even
insiders, there could be no changes. The reason, Mrs. Robert
reminded her listeners at Congress, lay in the voluntary character of the organization.

"The members of your National Board of Management serve
entirely without compensation," Mrs. Robert said. "They pay
their own expenses, both for traveling and for hotels. They
cannot, therefore, be called together for special meetings as
need arises, because the Society has no right to put that added
strain upon purely voluntary service, however willing the mem-

bers themselves may be." In other words, the board could not be reconvened in Washington to reconsider its decision. No one else, including the president general, had the authority to alter that decision. In the DAR, what the National Board of Management devises, only the National Board of Management may put asunder.

Throughout the difficult period ending with Miss Anderson's concert, the DAR made no attempt to reply to its critics. On the surface, such a strategy seems puzzling. If the Daughters believed that their decision was defensible, why wouldn't they defend it? Mrs. Musgrave points out that there was really no one around to reply. The DAR had no public-relations director in 1939. Mrs. Robert had left Washington for her seven-week tour immediately after news of the DAR's decision had been announced. The torrent of publicity that would be triggered by Mrs. Roosevelt's resignation was still two weeks off. Today a crisis could be handled at least temporarily by the Daughter serving the Society as first vice president general, but in 1939 that office didn't exist. While the DAR did have ordinary vice presidents general, the duty of the highest-ranking was limited to presiding over a meeting in the president general's absence. A vice president general was not authorized to make decisions. Mrs. Robert apparently felt that continuing her carefully scheduled tour was more important than returning to Washington. Since her board had already determined the DAR's course, there was little she could do in the capital anyway. Once she was reached and informed of what was happening, she was unwilling to comment from a distance. Anne Musgrave ascribes the latter decision to Mrs. Robert's code of ethics in dealing with matters relating to the President of the United States.

"I think if Mrs. Robert had been less ethical, she would have jumped in," says Anne Musgrave. "But she said, 'The Society has never permitted any word to be said in criticism of the President of the United States or his family, and we simply cannot raise our voices. We must say no word.' "

It could be that Sally Robert simply didn't know what to say. She was new at the job of PG. Elected only ten months earlier, she had yet to preside over her first Continental Congress. Her decision could have been a smokescreen. But there is a fair possibility that she was truly reluctant to appear to be squaring off against the President's wife. For one thing, Sally Robert was trustee and parliamentarian for *Robert's Rules of Order Revised.*

Her father-in-law was the originator of the book, and Mrs. Robert took it over when her husband died in August of 1937. She had undoubtedly given a lot of thought to propriety. (She later taught parliamentary law and procedure and served as a consultant for organizations adopting *Robert's Rules*.)

Furthermore, respect for men and women in top echelons of government runs deep among Daughters of the American Revolution. A reluctance to express any sentiment that might possibly be construed as criticism persists, particularly among DAR leaders, to the present day. When two angry Daughters made known their unhappiness with Mrs. Roosevelt during a session of Continental Congress that ill-fated year, Sally Robert squelched them instantly. In the same vein, when the 1971 resolutions committee wanted to oppose President Nixon's visit to China, committee members were reminded by a DAR leader that Richard Nixon would be addressing Continental Congress that week, and that good hostesses did not criticize their guest, particularly when their guest was the President of the United States. The resolutions committee saw the point.

Whatever the reason for the decision to maintain silence until after Miss Anderson's concert was over, the statements Mrs. Robert finally did make at Congress won the Daughters a compliment from *The Washington Post*.

"Because of the furor over the Marian Anderson concert," the *Post* editorialized on Sunday, April 23, "the forty-eighth annual congress of the DAR, which adjourned on Friday night, attracted more than customary attention in Washington. There was widespread community interest as to the way in which the Society would face, or evade, the issue.

"Now that the Congress is over it must be said that a delicate situation was handled by the Society with admirable restraint and common sense. In her report last Tuesday Mrs. Henry M. Robert, Jr., the president general, did not sidestep. She emphasized, but did not exaggerate, the fact that Constitution Hall was engaged for April 9—by Washington's own National Symphony Orchestra—months before the sponsors of the Anderson concert requested it for the same date.

"Mrs. Robert also noted, but did not stress, that misleading statements about the Society's position would have made a change of attitude very difficult even if no other factors had been involved. And she further pointed out what none can successfully refute, that the underlying issue is one for the community itself to solve. When that is accomplished, the DAR 'will be willing, at all times, to adopt its policies' in conformity with community standards."

The real mystery about what happened in 1939 is not why the Daughters of the American Revolution barred Marian Anderson but why they had bound themselves to a policy that barred all black artists.

Constitution Hall was dedicated on April 19, 1929. The Daughters had built it exclusively for their annual Congresses, but because it was the only hall of its kind in the nation's capital, the DAR made it available for community use. When the top DAR officers met in October of 1929, they passed the following ruling: "That a special request of any lessee of Constitution Hall to set aside a small group of seats for Negroes be granted." In passing this rule, the Daughters of the American Revolution afforded the blacks of Washington their first chance to hear world-renowned artists.

The very first concert to be given in Constitution Hall took place on November 2, 1929, under the management of a Mrs. Wilson-Greene. The next summer, according to Hand's notes, the DAR entered into a blanket contract with Mrs. Wilson-Greene which provided for a series of concerts. The artists who were to appear in the series were not named at the time the contract was signed. Under the terms of the contract, Mrs. Wilson-Greene presented black tenor Roland Hayes in concert in Constitution Hall on January 31, 1931. The question that remains unanswered is this: Did the DAR sign the contract knowing that Mrs. Wilson-Greene might schedule a black artists—or not knowing?

Whatever the answer, the DAR soon had an opportunity to decide in advance whether to let a black performer appear at the Hall. Early in December of 1930, just a few months after Mrs. Wilson-Greene got her contract, the Metropolitan Musical Bureau of New York applied for use of Constitution Hall for a concert by Negro baritone Paul Robeson. "On December 10, 1930," Fred Hand wrote, "the Executive Committee refused this request."

Early in 1931, however, the DAR contracted with the T. Arthur Smith Concert Bureau for use of Constitution Hall for a concert by the black Hampton Institute Choir. The concert, a benefit, was scheduled for March 21, 1931. Hand's notes say that the proceeds were to be used to erect a Negro War Memorial in Washington, but the concert program shows that the proceeds would go toward a National Memorial Building "in honor of the Negro's contribution to America and his achievement along all lines." By the terms of the contract, Hand wrote, "sale of seats to Negroes was restricted to two hundred in Sections H and O of the tiers"—and the lessee agreed to refund the money of any Negro who arrived for the concert holding a ticket for any other part of the auditorium.

There are two very different versions of what happened at the Hall the night of March 21. According to Hand's notes, "So much pressure was brought to bear upon the committee sponsoring this concert that the Daughters of the American Revolution waived its contractual rights in the matter and permitted the sale of tickets to Negroes in any part of the auditorium." The Daughters have since stated that the choir sang to an integrated audience, claiming that to their knowledge this was the first time blacks and whites had sat together in a Washington auditorium since Reconstruction days.

However, an editorial in *The Washington Daily News* after the concert contradicts this version of the incident.

"The DAR showed a double face in the matter of Saturday night's concert by the Hampton Institute Choir at Constitution Hall," the *News* stated. "The DAR, whose fine auditorium is the best place to hear music in town, was willing to rent its Hall to a colored organization but succeeded, through an odd ruling, in keeping many colored people away from the event—even though the concert was given by the finest colored singers in the world, and was for the benefit of the National Memorial Association, which is seeking to build a memorial here to the achievements of the colored race.

"The DAR management ruled that only two blocks of seats, those on the corners of the surrounding tiers, might be sold to colored people. After these were disposed of, hundreds of colored people were turned away with the information that the seats were sold out.

"It being a Saturday night concert, the turn-out of Washington's regular concertgoers was small, although the boxes were filled, consequently the Hall was two-thirds empty. The seats assigned to colored people were packed; beside them were empty blocks. Here and there through the hall, a few other colored people sat, doubtless in seats sold personally by members of the memorial association.

"The choir that has sung in the music centers of Europe, that sang by invitation in Westminster Abbey, that was entertained at a formal tea in Berlin by Ambassador Frederick Sackett, a Kentuckian; that choir sang to empty seats because only two hundred of its own people were permitted to come into the DAR's Hall and hear it."

The matter did not end there. A few days later an open letter appeared in *The New York Herald Tribune* which was signed by Walter White, Secretary of the National Association for the Advancement of Colored People. Based on the *Daily News* editorial, White's letter criticized the DAR for not cooperating with the Negroes. Hand notes, "All the facts contained in this letter were untrue and based on the terms of the original contract rather than on the actual happening." Hand does not say in what respects White's facts were untrue. Pointing out that the letter was signed by an NAACP official, Hand continued, "As a result of this criticism and the unwillingness of the original sponsors of the concert to restrict the sale of tickets as per their contract, an application made in April, 1931, for the use of the Hall by the Columbian Educational Association (colored) for a convention to be held in July, 1931, was refused by our Executive Committee on April 11, 1931."

The following year the Daughters began to insert the "white artists only" clause in Constitution Hall contracts.

It has been the contention of many DAR leaders that the clause was added at the specific request of white theater owners in Washington. Or, as this is often phrased, the DAR "was forced" to insert this clause. The "Statement re: Constitution Hall" put out by the DAR in 1966 includes the following passage: "Negro artists and performers were barred from the stages of all schools, theaters and auditoriums, except those exclusively for Negroes. This segregation policy was followed until the early 1950's. In order to bring Constitution Hall into line with public policy and customs, and to comply with public opinion and usage, the DAR, in 1932, was forced to put the 'white artists only' clause into its rental contracts."

This is pure fantasy. Blacks performed on "white" Washington stages all through the 1930's and before. Sometime prior to 1927 black actor Charles Gilpin starred in *The Emperor Jones* at the Belasco. On May 1, 1927, also at the Belasco, the Armstrong High School players, all black, presented *On the Slopes of Calvary*. In 1929 Lew Leslie's "Blackbirds" played at the National Theater. In 1931 Ethel Waters played the lead in *Rhapsody in Black* at the Shubert-Belasco, and the same month Marian Anderson sang at that theater. In 1933 Marc Connolly's play about black heaven, *Green Pastures*, was produced at the National. In 1936 black actor and singer Todd Duncan starred in *Porgy and Bess*, also at the National. *Porgy and Bess* was followed by Ethel Waters in *As Thousands Cheered*. In 1937 Abigail Mitchell played in *Mulatto* at the Belasco. Bill "Bojangles" Robinson and other blacks performed in vaudeville at the Capitol Theater all through the Thirties, according to Washingtonian Ray Bell, who was at the Capitol from 1933 to 1940, ending up as director. Marian Anderson sang at the Rialto in 1938. This is not necessarily a complete list, but it proves that black artists were not barred from Washington stages.

In addition, people in a position to know something about Washington theater say they never heard of a "white artists only" clause in the District except at Constitution Hall. Ray Bell says that. Richard Coe, who has been theater critic at The Washington *Post* since 1938, says he never heard of another theater that used the clause. Scott Kirkpatrick, who began working as an usher at the National Theater in 1932 and is now its manager, agrees. So does impresario Patrick Hayes, who wasn't in Washington in 1932 but was there from 1941 on and would certainly know if black artists were barred at that time. So did Sol Hurok, who said he never ran into a white artists clause anywhere else in Washington. So does black actor Frederick O'Neal, immediate past president of Actors' Equity. So does Edward Love, who once worked at Constitution Hall and left to found Theatrical Services Incorporated in Washington, which supplied ushers to Constitution Hall beginning in 1952. So does Reverend Gilbert V. Hartke, O.D., chairman of Catholic University's speech and drama department, who has been a highly respected fixture on the Washington theater scene since the late 1930's. One searches in vain to find any mention of the "white artists only" clause in books about theater or segregation. For example, a recent book by Loften Mitchell called *Black Drama** has an entire chapter about the Thirties which says nothing about a white artists clause anywhere. In *An American Dilemma,*** Gunnar Myrdal's classic study of blacks in America, the author states in a footnote that "Negroes cannot get on the

*New York: Hawthorn, 1970.
**New York: Harper and Row, 1962.

opera stage, and they are occasionally restricted on the concert stage," but the sole example he gives for the latter is the Marian Anderson incident.

In fact, what confounds Washington theater buffs about the DAR's policy is its very uniqueness. Many writers have pointed this out, perhaps none with more relish than Paul Cooke in the 1959 U.S. Commission on Civil Rights study, "Civil Rights in the Nation's Capital." Then a professor of English at D.C. Teacher's College and Director of Howard University's Workshop on Intergroup relations, Cooke wrote, "For those who love the paradoxes and contradictions of racism, no better examples than the National Theater-Constitution Hall situation ever existed. In the theater the Negro artist could perform but could not be watched by his Negro brother. On the other hand, at Constitution Hall the Negro was seated indiscriminately but not to watch any Negro." (Cooke went on to mention Marian Anderson.)

Since their white artists clause was unique in Washington, the DAR's explanations for why it was invoked don't wash. Obviously white theater owners would not ask the Daughters to bar black artists when they weren't doing so themselves. Daughters have sometimes argued that the DAR inserted the clause because the Society didn't want to compete with local theater owners, but even if every theater in town had had a white artists clause, it is difficult to understand why a charitable organization that sometimes leased its Hall for commercial enterprises would have cared what commercial theater owners wanted. Though the women might have wanted to treat their colleagues respectfully, as they maintain today, it seems unlikely that the DAR would conform to anyone else's policies without strong reasons of its own for doing so.

Sally Robert's defense of the white artists clause in her speech to the 1939 Congress hints that the decision to insert the clause had everything to do with the situation precipitated by the Hampton contract. However, the statement is oblique in the extreme and sheds no light on the decision. Fred Hand's statements also indicate that the Hampton incident was the motivating factor. "From that time forward," he wrote, referring to the events of the first few months of 1931, "we had several applications for the use of the Hall by colored groups and for the presentation of colored artists so that on March 23, 1932, the

Executive Committee by ruling instructed the Manager of Constitution Hall to insert the words 'White Artists Only' in all contracts for the use of Constitution Hall."

Hand's comment clearly implies a causal relationship between applications for use of the Hall by blacks and the addition of the clause barring them. In other words, the DAR inserted the clause when it became apparent that black groups were going to continue to ask to use the Hall.

It seems quite possible that the clause was intended not to keep black artists out but to keep too many blacks from buying tickets. After all, by contracting for the Hampton concert the DAR had shown itself willing, at least initially, to let blacks perform in Constitution Hall. Someone close to the Daughters says he has been told that some of the members protested use of the Hall by blacks at the time of the Hampton concert. Eleanor Spicer says she has heard that some Washington subscribers protested Roland Hayes's concert. But if the issue was black artists, why would the Daughters have contracted with Hampton after protests over Hayes?

A major difference between the Hayes and Hampton concerts was the audience. Mrs. Wilson-Greene apparently did not request a block of seats for blacks for Hayes's performance. (If she did, no mention of it is made in the contract.) Therefore, as the DAR has claimed, the first time blacks ever sat in the Hall was at the Hampton concert. Since the 1929 ruling was not invoked until March 21, 1931, it might have escaped the Daughters' notice. Then their attention was called to it by a newspaper editorial protesting restricted seating. Perhaps the Daughters foresaw that black artists would again draw more blacks than sections H and O could accommodate—more, in other words, than the Daughters were willing to seat. This is the view of National Theater manager Scott Kirkpatrick.

"I think they felt if they had black artists there would be large numbers of them in the audience," Kirkpatrick surmises. He points out that the same prediction was made by the man who was booking for the National in 1948, when Actors' Equity boycotted the theater because it would not permit blacks in the audience. As a result of that boycott, the National was closed until 1952. "It was so unrealistic from an economic standpoint," Kirkpatrick says of the National's refusal to yield. "Negroes at that period were economically deprived. It was said they would just flood the place. Of course it didn't happen."

If seating was the real issue in 1932, the Daughters must have been in a predicament about how to control it. They couldn't just tell outside sponsors that the DAR had not really decided to permit blacks in the audience because Hampton had shown otherwise. They could have rescinded the executive committee ruling of 1929, but that might have appeared as a rebuke to the previous administration, and such a rebuke would be considered very bad form in the DAR. The discriminatory clause may have seemed the only solution. The Daughters could circumvent seating problems by allowing only white artists in Constitution Hall.

Their decision to bar black artists was not necessarily a result of protests within the DAR. It is quite possible that most of the protests came not from DAR members but from concert subscribers living in or near the District. If this is true, the Daughters' decision to insert the white artists only clause was very likely made for commercial reasons. The DAR could retain subscribers by offering assurance that they would not have to sit next to a Negro in Constitution Hall.

The Daughters have generally claimed that the blacks who came to the Hall sat wherever they wanted from the first. They can't prove this. Given that the 1929 ruling specifically mentioned a "group" of seats, and that the Hampton contract specified which seats blacks could sit in, it seems likely that the Daughters originally intended to segregate. Mrs. Dorothy Porter, a black Washingtonian prominent in library circles for her work with the Moorland Collection at Howard University, says that she used to purchase Constitution Hall tickets through a friend or by mail because she refused to sit in the section reserved for blacks. On one occasion in 1930 or 1931, Mrs. Porter recalls, she was asked to leave the Hall. (She did not do so.) Perhaps the Daughters changed their minds as a result of the Hampton incident.

At any rate—for those who love paradoxes and contradictions—it is apparently true, as the Daughters claim, that Constitution Hall was integrated before any commercially operated theater or auditorium in Washington. That is the recollection of National Theater manager Scott Kirkpatrick and of *Post* critic Richard Coe, among others, who say that there was no segregation in the Hall from the 1930's onward. Their recollections are supported by odd clippings here and there. According to a "Segregation Survey" in *The Washington Post* on May 8, 1949,

Constitution Hall "follows a unique custom [of excluding black artists]. . . . Since its establishment, a policy of integrated audiences has been observed without racial discrimination, despite segregation practices elsewhere. . . ."

The facts, as they can be assembled, support this claim. The National Theater closed for more than four years rather than seat blacks anywhere in the theater. It reopened integrated, but not until 1952. The Gayety restricted blacks to a gallery until 1949, when it ceased operation as a burlesque house. It was not integrated until it opened as a playhouse in 1950. The same year the Arena Stage opened on a fully integrated basis. The Belasco, which turned Negroes away in 1937, was bought by the government in 1940. The Rialto was torn down in 1940. According to one reliable but secondhand report, the Rialto audience was integrated when Marian Anderson sang there in 1938, but nothing in the extensive press clippings on theaters at the D.C. public library suggests that the Rialto operated on a policy of integration. The Lisner Auditorium at George Washington University kept blacks out until 1947.

In 1948, the Dupont Theater opened under an integrated policy, but most of the other white movie theaters refused admittance to blacks until 1953. When Dwight Eisenhower took office in 1952, *Collier's* Magazine noted, forty of Washington's sixty-two movie houses barred Negroes entirely, four art theaters "permitted all comers," and eighteen theaters in Negro neighborhoods "were attended almost entirely by Negroes, though whites were not barred." The DAR's closest contender for first-to-integrate honors is Catholic University, in whose theater blacks were welcome to sit where they chose from the time the theater opened in 1937. Of course C.U. was not operating a commercial hall.

Whatever the full explanation for the DAR's decision to insert the white artists clause, it is undoubtedly explained in part by the fact that in 1932 the Daughters of the American Revolution were rank amateurs in the theater business. Daughters who ran for office expecting to head a women's organization discovered that their job involved running the biggest hall in Washington. The issue of seating blacks was one that even the professionals in the District did not resolve until 1953. In discussing the white artists clause recently, Scott Kirkpatrick, a native of Arkansas, said, "I don't think you would ever find anybody who was a professional in the arts who would deny the expression of an artist. The National was run by professionals in the arts. Constitution Hall was run by a group of ladies who were leaders in their local communities but who did not have training in the arts." Eleanor Spicer wasn't there at the time, but she is probably close to the truth when she says, "We were just blundering along."

Many Daughters insist today that if 1939 had been properly handled by the outsiders involved, the DAR would definitely have given its permission for Miss Anderson to sing in Constitution Hall. "There's no question that if her backers, if *anybody* had asked, if Mrs. Roosevelt had asked once, they could have gotten permission from the board," Anne Musgrave declares. "But after six weeks' vilification campaign, then they came in and asked for Easter Sunday. Of course they knew they couldn't get that date. They didn't want that date. Then they said, 'Oh, any date.' The members of the executive committee felt that because of what had happened it was not prudent to go ahead. It would be much better to wait and then at a quiet time invite her."

Actually, the record offers little reason to suppose that the DAR's decision would have favored Miss Anderson even if her agent had followed prescribed procedure to the letter. After the Hampton concert in 1931, no black artists appeared on the Constitution Hall stage for more than a decade. Then, on September 28, 1942, Fred Hand wrote to Sol Hurok and invited Marian Anderson to sing in the Hall. The concert, a benefit, would be undertaken as part of the DAR's program of war activities. Hurok replied on October 3. He accepted the offer but stipulated two conditions. First, he wanted "a specific agreement that no segregation in the seating arrangements be exercised." Second, he wanted the DAR to understand that Miss Anderson would construe her performance "as a precedent that hereafter Constitution Hall will be open to her in the normal course of her tour."

Hand wrote back ignoring the first condition, perhaps because segregation had not been practiced in the Hall for some time, and saying, "I am instructed to advise you that the invitation sent to you under date of September 28, 1942, was the same as that thus far extended to other artists for War Benefit Concert. It is regretted that Miss Anderson, through you, her manager, has not accepted the invitation as extended. No appearance of any artist, attraction or event can ever be considered as a precedent insofar as future engagements in Constitution Hall are concerned."

Hurok replied saying that Miss Anderson did not want to

deprive the Army Emergency Relief Fund of the income which would result from her concert. Therefore she would sing without insisting on the precedent. But Hurok was taking no chances on seating. "Since the Executive Committee has not referred in its letter to the matter of segregation in the seating arrangements," he wrote, "Miss Anderson understands that this is no barrier." It wasn't. On January 7, 1943, Marian Anderson sang in Constitution Hall to an integrated audience.

But in September of 1945 DAR leaders refused a request for black soprano Hazel Scott to sing in the Hall. A number of DAR chapters passed resolutions strongly opposing the decision. Connecticut Congresswoman Clare Boothe Luce threatened to resign from the organization. The board did not relent.

Five months after saying no to Hazel Scott the DAR turned down a request for Eddie Condon to bring his jazz band to Constitution Hall. Fred Hand explained that the DAR didn't permit jazz in its auditorium "because of the type of audience which attends and which in some cases may be very destructive." The band, which had played in Carnegie Hall five times with no destruction, was mixed. Condon himself was white.

Upon hearing of the Condon decision Clare Boothe Luce took to the airwaves. She made a nationwide appeal for all Daughters to join in an effort to eliminate the "white artists only" clause. With nine other Daughters, she formed the DAR Committee Against Racial Discrimination in Constitution Hall. The Committee contacted Daughters who had opposed the ban, urging them to retain their membership and rally as much support as they could before Continental Congress.

Then Mrs. Luce learned that the DAR had refused a request for the choir from black Tuskegee Institute to sing in Constitution Hall on June 1. She wired the president general, who wired back saying that Mrs. Luce's committee was hurting, not helping, the choir's case. A few days later, out of the blue, the president general announced that the Tuskegee Choir would sing rent-free in the Hall on June 3. The DAR would donate the services of its employees. The concert would benefit the United Negro College Fund.

Viewing this decision as a maneuver around the real issue, protest committee member Mrs. Denny Vann of New Jersey submitted a resolution to the National Society opposing the white artists clause. Almost as soon as the 1946 Congress opened, the fate of the resolution was clear. For a time it looked as if Mrs. Vann would not even be permitted to read it from the platform. Finally she did read it, and then, before it could be voted down, she withdrew it. The protest committee had had the last word, but it did not prevail. Mrs. Luce resigned from the DAR. She was joined by Republican Congresswoman Frances Bolton.

In 1947 Hand refused to permit the black Armstrong High School choir to give a benefit concert in Constitution Hall. Also in the late Forties, according to National manager Scott Kirkpatrick, the DAR refused to let a choir from Cardozo High School sing on its stage. Kirkpatrick worked for the National Symphony at the time. As he tells the story, the choir had won top honors in a District competition, and concert sponsors had arranged for the winning group to perform with the National Symphony, which used Constitution Hall for its concerts. When the DAR discovered that a black choir had won, the arrangements were modified. The choir could sing, the Daughters said, but not from the stage. Contest sponsors pleaded to no avail. The Cardozo singers performed from seats in the audience.

In 1952 black soprano Dorothy Maynor appeared in a program with the National Symphony in Constitution Hall. According to *The New York Times* of February 18, 1952, she was the first commercially sponsored black artist to appear on the DAR's stage since before 1939. She was apparently the first since Roland Hayes sang there in 1931—and the second in Constitution Hall history. Miss Maynor appeared as an exception to the white artists clause. Perhaps with the reopening of the National Theater on an integrated basis that year the Daughters realized that discrimination of any kind in public auditoriums was on its way out. There was also a practical explanation. Again according to the *Times*, DAR public-relations director Tom Wrigley said that the president general was "disposed to favor" the request of the Orchestra for Miss Maynor's appearance because the Orchestra "always has cooperated and has been a good customer."

The white artists only clause was not dropped until 1953. Until it was eliminated, the Daughters followed a pattern of clear discrimination which was interrupted only occasionally by benefits, school choirs, and Dorothy Maynor. That being true, it is unlikely that Marian Anderson would have sung in Constitution Hall in 1939 under any circumstances.

In choosing to deny Marian Anderson access to the Hall, the board members were saying in essence that they had agreed to do what they felt the majority of the members wanted. They had decided to take no financial risks. They had decided against changing an established policy which some outsiders believed to be wrong. Neither at the time nor since have the Daughters ever said they thought the policy was morally right. They have simply pointed out, as they pointed out at the time, that the DAR had no choice. The policy was merely an expedient. It was functional in the circumstances.

In other words, the DAR chose to be safe rather than to take the risks that seemed to be involved in securing for one black American one of the blessings of liberty.

The Daughters committed no crime. They had every legal right to make the decision they made. They even had human precedent on their side. Electing to be comfortable rather than courageous is a common human decision. In 1939, very few Americans or American institutions were going out of their way to assure blacks an equal chance at the pursuit of happiness, liberty, or even life.

"The decision was obviously wrong, pathetic, and badhearted," William F. Buckley said thirty-four years later. "On the other hand, that's the way most Americans were in the late Thirties. They just plain were that way. It was incredible. But I think the incident hurt the DAR more than anything they could possibly have done. Especially since it was done to a woman. And it was done to a great artist. And it had that horrible sort of feel to it of a lack of magnanimity."

Buckley raises an important point. If most Americans "were that way" in 1939, why did the DAR's decision provoke such intense protest in America?

Two explanations are suggested by liberal Jewish writer Robert Rice. "The Marian Anderson thing happened at a time when people were very conscious of race," he points out. "After all, it was after Munich. Hitler would invade Poland four months later. And Marian Anderson wasn't singing pop or soul. She was singing Verdi."

Most important, perhaps, the Marian Anderson incident brought into the open an American disease most Americans had successfully ignored. In *The Secret City: A History of Race Relations in the Nation's Capital*,* author Constance McLaughlin Green

*Princeton, N. J.: Princeton University Press, 1967.

writes, "The furor aroused in the city and throughout the country exceeded any outburst of indignation within the memory of Washington's oldest inhabitants. White people were jolted out of their assumption that Negroes with ambition and talent could make their way anywhere, for here was a woman of utmost distinction being treated as an obnoxious nonentity. Marian Anderson revealed to the nation the depths into which white ignorance and prejudice had forced all Negroes."

The Daughters who today acknowledge that Miss Anderson's race was the issue in 1939 seem compelled to try to put the decision in as favorable a light as possible. They have not allowed reality to stand in their way. The conviction that Marian Anderson does not feel the DAR discriminated against her is the prime example of the willingness of some Daughters to believe almost anything except the truth. Ed Sullivan once reported in his *Washington Star* newspaper column that a Daughter had told him "that Miss Anderson, a fine person as well as a great singer, will be the first to tell you she does not feel that DAR has discriminated against her." Although she would hardly need to, Miss Anderson herself denies the statement firmly.

"One year after I had sung in the Hall, the president general came back and said she hoped the incident was all over," Miss Anderson says. "I probably said to her that I did not make comments on the affair. But I never assured the DAR that I did not feel I was discriminated against."

Also in the far-fetched category is the notion some Daughters seem to have that Marian Anderson got a big professional boost by the concert at the Lincoln Memorial. In 1935 maestro Arturo Toscanini told her, "A voice like yours is heard once in a hundred years." In 1936 she sang at the White House. By 1939 Miss Anderson was already a world-renowned concert artist. She had sung in the great halls of Europe and the United States. In 1941, she was to be one of the highest-paid concert artists in America. In 1939, she was still sixteen years away from her debut at the Metropolitan Opera, but she had been decorated by the kings of Sweden and Denmark, and the government of France had bestowed official recognition on her. Of course Miss Anderson was not hurt by the publicity, but, as *Time* magazine pointed out in its review of the concert, she hardly needed it. She was booked for seventy-five concerts that season. Her customary fee was from $1,750 to $2,000 a concert. Yet in 1957 DAR public-relations director Mary Spargo expressed these views in an article that appeared in the Moline (Illinois) *Daily Dispatch*— which some Daughters still hold:

"What this matter boiled down to was that Miss Anderson had sung once here in Washington without receiving much attention. The promotion of a controversy involving the DAR was a means of hitting the front pages. It was effective, and Miss Anderson was made as a singer."

Many Daughters today advance the argument that the racial situation in Washington in 1939 foreclosed all options except the one the DAR took. "Washington was a Southern city, a segregated city," these Daughters say. To illustrate the racial climate in Washington at that time, Daughters—and some DAR literature—note that when Hurok was turned down by the DAR, he and Charles Cohen tried to book Miss Anderson into four different Washington theaters and were refused by all of them. Fred Hand, in his "Facts," makes this statement: "It is not known, however, and I am reliably informed that it is true, that applications were made to the Belasco Theater, the National Theater, the Rialto Theater and Loew's Capitol Theater in Washington for this concert and that each of these applications was refused." Hand did not cite his source, nor did he say why the applications were refused. The 1966 DAR "Statement" said that the applications were refused "because of the then existing racial barriers in the District of Columbia against all Negro artists performing in white auditoriums and theaters." Of course this is false.

In a presentation to the DAR National Board of Management several months after the concert had taken place, Washington Cathedral Dean Anson Phelps Stokes did say that the Rialto had been out of the question for the concert, but not because of Miss Anderson's race. It was closed under a receivership, Stokes reported, and the receiver was unwilling to make a binding contract for a single engagement. In the written application to the Board of Education for the use of the Central High School auditorium, Charles Cohen noted the Rialto receivership and went on to say, "Several auditoriums of government cannot be used for affairs at which admission is charged. The National and the Belasco are tentatively available. However, because of the policies of the United Booking House, from which their attractions are obtained, these corporations cannot enter into binding contracts more than two weeks in advance of concert dates. Obviously it is quite impossible to make adequate arrangements for such a major concert in so brief a period as two weeks." Since black artists had been appearing all along in the nation's capital, Miss Anderson's color could not have been a factor in negotiations for other theaters.

It is quite true that Washington in 1939 was anything but integrated. The school system maintained, by law, separate schools. The school playgrounds likewise were open to either black children or white, not both. There were separate public tennis courts and baseball diamonds for whites and for blacks. Harold Ickes himself, as Interior Secretary, administered segregated public golf courses. Hotels and restaurants, by social custom, were segregated. Miss Anderson did not go back to her hotel after the concert at the Lincoln Memorial. She did not have a hotel. The Washington Hotels which provided lodging suitable for a concert artist would provide it only to concert artists whose skin was white.

"Segregation in Washington seems an accepted fact," wrote Sterling A. Brown in a 1937 study of blacks in Washington undertaken as part of the Federal Writers' Project. "Public buildings and public conveyances are not segregated, although on every southbound train Negro passengers are 'jim-crowed.' Negroes are not served in restaurants, saloons, hotels, movie houses, and theaters, except those definitely set aside for them. Some stores will not accept their trade. Some governmental departments have separate accommodations, and some discriminate in the type of work offered to Negroes.... The Negro of Washington has no voice in government, is economically proscribed, and segregated nearly as rigidly as the Southern cities he contemns."

However, while it may not have been the most enlightened city in the nation in 1939, Washington was not the least enlightened. Blacks and whites alike had access to trolleys, buses, and taxicabs, which was not the custom in many Southern cities at that time. The waiting room and the dining room in the D.C. railroad station were open to blacks. So were the public libraries. So were all lectures, meetings and concerts in government buildings.

Both the Board of Education and the Board of Public Welfare had black representation, as did the Community Chest and many of its member agencies. Blacks could feel at home in Washington parks, as they could not in those of many cities of the South. There was a Negro judge on the Municipal Court. Black Episcopal ministers belonged with their white colleagues to The Clericus of the Episcopal Church, and blacks attended services and concerts at the Washington Cathedral along with whites. By prior arrangement, blacks and whites could meet together for business or civic lunches or dinners at such places as the Wardman Park Hotel, the Y.W.C.A., the Willard Hotel, and several restaurants.

So Washington was not quite as rigidly segregated as the Daughters often imply. Furthermore, for Daughters to say that Marian Anderson couldn't sing in Constitution Hall because Washington was a Southern city is to ignore both sentiment and practice relating to black performers and artists in some parts of the South. The editors of many Southern newspapers deplored the DAR's decision. For example, this editorial appeared in the *Montgomery Advertiser*, Montgomery, Alabama, on February 28, 1939:

" 'Blind Tom,' great pianist, and 'Black Patti,' great vocal soloist, appeared repeatedly in their day in the white music halls of the Deep South. More recently the famous Tuskegee choir has been in demand before white audiences throughout the Deep South, and the Dawson symphony is as warmly appreciated by Southern whites as by Negroes. Roland Hayes, great tenor soloist, who, like Marian Anderson, has appeared before the crowned heads of Europe, is as popular in Alabama as in Maine or Yugoslavia. Anderson and Hayes have sung repeatedly in Alabama. They have appeared at Tuskegee and Birmingham and in Montgomery, the first capital of the Confederacy. It is but a few months since that Hayes sang at the city auditorium in Montgomery. . . . Why there should be any objection to the appearance of Marian Anderson in Constitution Hall at Washington passes all human understanding."

The Democrat-Times, Greenville, Mississippi, had this to say on March 10, 1939:

". . . The DAR has evidenced more than its share of such unreason in its refusal to permit Marian Anderson, gifted Negro singer, to perform in Constitution Hall in Washington. We fail to see how the DAR achieved a single worthy purpose in denying the Hall to a Negro woman whose voice brings pleasure to men and women of every race. Here in Greenville, for instance, there is no uproar when a Dr. Carver speaks in the theater to a white and Negro audience; nor do Delta pleasure seekers think it unseemly for a nationally known Negro orchestra to appear on a white dance hall stage. It seems to us that the DAR, like lesser folk, should realize that it is possible to preserve racial taboos without erecting new barriers. And certainly the organization in Washington should realize that it is better to encourage artistry in any race than to discourage art because of the color of the man or woman who expresses it. . . ."

And in Staunton, Virginia, *The News Leader* had this to say on March 1, 1939:

"If the DAR's employee or its officers closed Constitution Hall on racial grounds, the membership should certainly be heard from. In view of the discredit already reflected upon the organization, we hope the ladies will insist on developing the facts, and in accepting the precedent of George Washington, who in Revolutionary days wrote to Phyllis Wheatley, a Negro poet: 'If you should ever come to Cambridge, Miss Phyllis, or near headquarters, I shall be happy to see a person so favored by the muses, and to whom Nature has been so beneficent in her dispensations. I am, with great respect, your humble servant, George Washington.' "

Without question there were Washingtonians who felt the DAR had been right to refuse Miss Anderson. One of them, Alvin R. Schwab, expressed his views in a letter which appeared in the March 20, 1939, issue of *Time* magazine. "Sirs," Schwab wrote, "In *Time*, March 6, there appeared an article dealing with the refusal of the DAR to permit the Negress Anderson to sing in Constitution Hall in Washington. In this article, Washington was referred to as 'provincial.' This was spiteful and entirely unjustified. Remarks of that nature show that all small people do not live in small towns. . . .

"You mention a mass meeting of 1,500 (probably all Northerners) who protested the DAR's action, but no mention is made of the four hundred-odd thousand of white citizens of Washington who do not want the theaters they patronize contaminated by colored entertainers. . . .

"I am not sympathetic toward the DAR in most matters, but I feel that in this case they have acted in the only decent manner possible. After all, it is better to pique Mrs. Roosevelt than to insult the entire white population of a big city. P.S. As a matter of fact, there is a colored theater, the Howard, which could have been used without arousing any protest as it is a fit place for Negroes to sing."

Citing sentiments such as these, Daughters today argue in effect that the DAR in 1939 was steering a treacherous course between Scylla and Charybdis and that any decision was bound to incur criticism from one side or the other. Since black artists were welcome on other white stages, this seems unlikely. Scott Kirkpatrick believes that a majority of people in Washington probably sided with the DAR, but whether they would have protested aloud, and whether that criticism would have reached the major proportions of the protest that did take place is quite another question. Would the Daughters have been subjected to pressure, as they sometimes argue, if the board had made a different decision in 1939? Not in the opinion of Joseph Rauh, a Washington civil-liberties lawyer who attended the concert at the Lincoln Memorial.

"If there were to have been any pressure on the DAR, there would have been ten times as much when she sang in a public place," Rauh says. "Why didn't people rise up when she went to a public place?" News accounts of the event mention no protest groups around the Lincoln Memorial. It is axiomatic to people in public life that critics are more likely to write letters than supporters, but between March 1 and March 15, 1939, the D.C. Board of Education received 104 letters from individuals and organizations favoring a concert by Marian Anderson in a public school and only thirty-one opposing such a concert.

There is a feeling among many Daughters that the DAR in 1939 was at the mercy of people who were interested at least as much in publicity for themselves as in the rights of black Americans. This theory was given credence even at the time by several leading publications. Calling for pressure on the U.S. Congress—which served as the District's government—to set more equitable community standards, The Washington Post editorial of April 23, 1939, concluded with these rather pointed remarks:

"Some pressure might also be constructively exerted on Secretary Ickes, who was active in promoting the Anderson concert at the Lincoln Memorial but who should not be content to stop with that handsome gesture. The real solution for the problem, of course, is found in the municipal auditorium to which the National Capital is so thoroughly entitled. No single individual is in a better position than Mr. Ickes, through his power as head of the PWA, to push this overdue project. His activities on Easter Sunday were spectacular, but transient in effect. Active advocacy by Secretary Ickes of the much-needed local auditorium would be an appropriate follow-up and proof that publicity for himself was one of the least of his concerns two weeks ago today."

Mrs. Roosevelt herself, some people suggested at the time, may have had more than one reason for resigning from the DAR. Americans would go to the polls in 1940, and Franklin Roosevelt wanted to be reelected. He was actively courting the Negro vote. Noted *Time* on April 10, 1939, "In Alabama the Presidential special pulled up while Franklin Roosevelt devoted his attention to Southern Negroes, who usually can't vote but who have enfranchised Northern brothers who could play hob next year by swinging back to the Republican Party. At famed Tuskegee Institute (for Negroes) he locked arms with its distinguished, white-wooled Agricultural Chemist George Washington Carver, called the students 'my boy and girl friends.'

"To the appeasement of Negro voters, Mrs. Franklin Roosevelt also contributed last week. Having resigned from the DAR after they barred colored contralto Marian Anderson from Constitution Hall in Washington, she promised to appear this summer on a program with Miss Anderson in Richmond, Virginia."

It is perfectly true that Mrs. Roosevelt's decision sparked much more publicity than the DAR's decision had sparked on its own. The Marian Anderson incident did not become a cause célèbre until Eleanor Roosevelt resigned from the DAR. Miss Anderson herself acknowledges that, saying, "Of course people became aroused when Mrs. Roosevelt resigned. She was a powerful person. People lived according to her example." It may even be true, as some Daughters say, that the whole issue would have died down and faded away if the President's wife had stayed in and said nothing. Mrs. Roosevelt cannot have failed to realize in advance that her decision would cause a stir. To what extent publicity was actually a factor in the decision will always be open to surmise.

Nevertheless, Mrs. Roosevelt's resignation was neither her first nor her last stand on behalf of civil rights. She championed the black cause long before 1939, and she continued to champion it long after black votes had anything to do with Franklin's career. Black leaders recognized her as a firm ally. Furthermore, Harold Ickes was viewed as the person in Roosevelt's Cabinet most willing to walk an extra mile for black Americans. He blistered people who turned blacks away from the Interior restaurant, and in 1940 he would take steps to wipe out segregated recreation areas in Washington that were under Interior Department control. So neither Eleanor Roosevelt nor Harold

Ickes was acting out of character in 1939. Moreover, it can be argued that if they saw something to gain from the stand they took, many Americans must have felt the cause was just.

In any event, Mrs. Roosevelt's resignation and its effects have nothing to do with the basic issue. Whatever their motives, Eleanor Roosevelt and Harold Ickes did not become involved in the affair until it *was* an affair. What Mrs. Roosevelt did, what Ickes did, whether for cynical or honorable reasons, neither explains nor mitigates nor erases the DAR's decision to say no to Marian Anderson. The DAR alone is responsible for that decision.

Of all the people who were involved in 1939, the person the Daughters are least likely ever to forgive is Sol Hurok. Some Daughters say today that neither Eleanor Roosevelt nor Marian Anderson herself really understood what she was doing, and that what the two women were doing was letting themselves be manipulated. This could be considered highly insulting to Miss Anderson and Mrs. Roosevelt, but the Daughters don't really mean it that way. They simply feel that Hurok was too smart for everyone else's good. He wanted publicity. By putting on a show at the DAR's expense, using everybody he could trick into his service, Sol Hurok could get his name in lights all over the land, exposure which would yield quite palpable returns.

Perhaps Hurok was sensitive to this charge, because in his book he made a point of saying that publicity was not his motive. Having described some of the difficulties involved in managing a black artist in the 1930's, he writes:

"Once it was given to us to be part of a great, a dramatic demonstration of protest. After the constantly recurring offenses, from unwilling cab drivers up to segregated concert halls, it was almost a relief when the Daughters of the American Revolution presented Marian's friends with an issue big enough to bring out into the open." After describing the event, Hurok wrote, "We gave our services, we paid the incidental expenses, but this is one event I do not claim as a publicity stunt. Anyone who has read the record knows it was as nearly spontaneous an arising of men and women of goodwill in Washington as there can be in our times. Well managed, of course. No untoward events. No jarring notes."

That the response to Miss Anderson's concert was a spontaneous rising is undeniable. That Sol Hurok was masterfully astute in matters of publicity is known by virtually everyone in the entertainment world. There is no doubt that Hurok stood to profit from the 1939 incident, or that he exploited it to the full. "Being in that world myself," says Catholic University's Father Gilbert V. Hartke, "I suspect it [the Lincoln Memorial concert] as a dramatic gesture, and I think it was a very good one."

But, as in the case of Miss Anderson herself, Hurok did not need publicity to get ahead. He had inagurated his career as an impresario in 1912 by presenting Efrem Zimbalist, by that time a prominent violinist. A few years later he started a series of extremely well-received Sunday afternoon concerts at the Hippodrome in New York. In the words of Philadelphia music critic Daniel Webster, "Hurok started at the top and stayed there." Hurok did not have to wait for the Marian Anderson incident to get himself in the spotlight. He was there already.

Furthermore, while Hurok exploited events as they developed in 1939, he cannot be accused of contriving the whole affair. Approaching the DAR for the use of Constitution Hall was more than merely justifiable. It was the only logical step for Hurok to take. He had been Marian Anderson's agent for four years. It was his job to arrange her concerts. Since she was a concert artist, naturally he would arrange for her to sing in concert halls. Hurok is absolutely right when he says there was no other concert hall in Washington except the one belonging to the DAR. There were legitimate theater stages, and there were vaudeville and movie stages, but there was only one concert stage, and that was the stage owned by the Daughters of the American Revolution.

Finally, many Daughters today insist that the DAR was made the scapegoat in what was essentially a test case for civil rights. Hand wrote in his "Facts," "I would also like to call to your attention that at 1215 U Street, N.W., Washington, the Lincoln Theater, catering to colored trade, has a seating capacity of 1,800, which is approximately the same as our high-school auditoriums or any of the theaters mentioned except the Capitol which is larger, hence, I am inclined to believe that this application for a concert in a white theater or auditorium was based more on the desire to hold it in such a theater rather than through the necessity for a larger seating capacity."

This theory may have originated with the DAR, but it was given some consideration outside the organization as well. In the July, 1939, *Esquire*, Carleton Smith wrote, "There is certainly more in l'affaire Anderson than appears on the surface. It was not merely a matter of finding a hall for Miss Anderson in Washington. Nor were the DAR alone to blame. The Lincoln Theater, belonging to the Negroes, has a capacity of 1,800—equal to that of the white high-school auditorium. It could have been used, but the sponsors wanted the concert elsewhere. They saw a good opportunity to force the issue of racial equality. Washington groundhogs heard in the distance the firm voice of Walter White, secretary of the National Association for the Advancement of Colored People."

If a test case was in the making, the request for Constitution Hall for a concert by Marian Anderson is the weakest possible evidence for it. Less than three weeks before she was to sing in Washington, Miss Anderson gave a concert in the City Auditorium of Houston, Texas. All 4,300 seats were taken. Extra chairs were brought in. People paid to stand in the aisles. Perhaps some members of the audience had come just to see the woman on whose behalf the First Lady resigned from the DAR. But Eleanor Roosevelt did not fill the Pittsburgh Mosque for Marian Anderson when she sang there to an audience of 4,000 about the time the DAR board was deciding not to let her sing in Constitution Hall. Miss Anderson had sold out Carnegie Hall —2,500 seats—when she came back from Europe in 1935. White or black, the Lincoln Theater was simply too small for Marian Anderson.

In a 1973 interview Hurok skirted the question of whether he was trying to force the issue of racial equality. "Every case that you lose is a test case," he said with a shrug. "I didn't think of this as a test case. It's simply the question that a great artist like Marian Anderson should be deprived not to sing in the Constitution Hall in the capital of Washington, the capital of the United States. But she sang in all the capitals of the world, you know, kings and queens and everything else. I felt it's a great insult, not only to the black but to the white as well."

Still, Hurok admitted that Walter White was "a great friend" of his and of Miss Anderson's. He admitted that White was of the opinion "that we should do it." The NAACP was involved in at least part of the incident. On March 13 its board passed a resolution urging Howard University to refuse the use of the high-school auditorium as proposed by the D.C. school officials, saying it would be better "for Miss Anderson to sing out-of-doors, for example, at the Lincoln Memorial" or "not to sing in Washington at all till democracy can surmount the color line in the nation's capital." In his book *Fight for Freedom*,* author Langston Hughes notes that "NAACP intervention helped to secure the open-air platform of the Lincoln Memorial for her [Miss Anderson's] concert."

The personal correspondence of Walter White, on file at the Library of Congress, includes nothing about the incident for December, 1938, or January or February, 1939. It does include two letters to Miss Anderson in March, 1939. The first, dated March 7 and mailed to her in Los Angeles, begins, "A very large part of our thought, time and energy these last few days has been devoted to l'affaire Marian Anderson—and never have we worked with greater enthusiasm." Most of the rest of the letter deals with a forthcoming benefit concert at Carnegie Hall, but White does mention that Mrs. Roosevelt had asked his opinion on inviting Miss Anderson to the White House when the King and Queen of England would be there on June 8. He also mentions enclosing a clipping from *The New York Evening Post*—"one of the several thousand on you and Washington." On March 24 White wrote to Miss Anderson again, who was by then in Texas. The letter was almost entirely devoted to discussion of the April 9 concert and reads in part:

"Hurok's office telephoned me this morning about the proposal of Howard University to stage the April 9 concert at the Belasco Theater. When my opinion was asked I told them that I thought it would be most unfortunate and unfair to you to ask you to sing there. The Belasco was once a famous theater but that was thirty years ago. It is now a run-down, second-rate place which is dark a good part of the time and when it is open it is used for the showing of films, some of which are on the risqué side.

"I suggested to Hurok that if an open-air concert is given it be held at the Lincoln Memorial because of the peculiar appropriateness of that place under the present circumstances. Our Board of Directors last Monday also passed a resolution, copy of which is enclosed. . . .

"I shall be in Washington next Wednesday and I am going to make inquiries about the glass booth from which the President broadcast when he was inaugurated. This will protect you from any inclemency in the weather and will be less of a strain upon you.

"I discussed with Mr. Goode of Hurok's office today a sugges-

*New York: W. W. Norton, 1962.

tion we made of organizing a very distinguished sponsoring committee for your concert at the Lincoln Memorial, if one is held there. I am sure that I could get Mrs. Roosevelt without any difficulty to head the committee. I have in mind asking the President also, Vice-President Garner, Justices Frankfurter and Black of the Supreme Court," and so on. "Mr. Goode asked about the NAACP taking charge of this. I told him that nothing would make us happier, not only to do the work but to bear the expenses, because of the principle involved. I suggested, however, that since the NAACP is known as a propaganda organization, it would be far better to have the sponsorship under such a committee, which would keep it on the highest plane of art and justice."

Nothing in Hurok's book, in Interior records, in Ickes' diary on file at the Interior Department, or his papers on file at the National Archives, in NAACP board minutes or White's papers on file at the Library of Congress indicates when or how the NAACP became involved. Nothing in any of those sources indicates that the NAACP was involved from the beginning. The Marian Anderson incident is not given a separate folder among the NAACP papers in the Library of Congress, as are many of the special cases the organization worked on. Metropolitan Opera singers Kirsten Flagstad and Lawrence Tibbett and perhaps others made protests to the NAACP, and Walter White did sit on the platform that day at the Lincoln Memorial. But there is simply no evidence that would even suggest that the Marian Anderson concert was something White and Hurok cooked up in advance.

But suppose they did. Suppose Hurok was in league with the NAACP from the beginning. Suppose he did not tell the truth in his book. Suppose he really was primarily interested in publicity for himself. Suppose he was trying to force an issue, not merely to put on a concert. Many auditoriums all over the country, including the South, were open to black artists. The largest hall in the nation's capital was not among them. The Daughters undoubtedly had their reasons in 1932 for deciding to permit white artists only to appear on their stage, but even in the 1930's segregation was beginning to relax its hold on America, albeit slightly. In 1935, when she returned from Europe, Miss Anderson had been admitted to a Los Angeles hotel only on the condition that she use the freight elevator. By 1939 she had been a guest in hotels in a number of major cities. No one enjoys being sacrificed for a greater good, even if he agrees that the greater good should be served, and the DAR is understandably dismayed to emerge as the villain in the piece. As Eleanor Spicer points out, "Ironically, you know, it was in a sense a sort of beginning of the civil-rights movement. People woke up to what was happening. But we were the goats." Still, an organization dedicated to aid in securing for mankind all the blessings of liberty should not have thought it inappropriate in 1939, and should not still be arguing that it was, for Hurok to say, as he said to Marian Anderson then, "We have to do it. It's time."

Marian Anderson now lives in Danbury, Connecticut. Her husband has not been well. Because of his health, because of the snow, or because of her calendar, she finds it difficult to schedule an interview to talk about 1939. She resists, in a gracious way, for eight months. Miss Anderson says she has never really talked about the incident. She makes clear, always graciously, that she sees nothing to be accomplished by talking about it now. In 1939 she did something she felt she had to do. It was difficult for her. Hurok wrote in his book that Miss Anderson called him at midnight the night before the concert, "in actual fright," to ask, "Must we really go through with this?" Miss Anderson describes herself in her autobiography as a noncombatant. The book is powerfully persuasive on that point. She did not want to embarrass anyone by commenting at the time; now, she says, "It's not necessary that I should try to discuss it."

But she does say a little about that Easter Sunday. She speaks softly but without hesitation; she has surely thought about the events of that day many times. As is her custom, she resorts very little to first-person singular.

"Certainly we wanted to be a part of whatever we thought was right," Miss Anderson says. "Some things are inherently wrong or inherently right. This was one. Though one would not get out and use one's fists or use one's mouth to say bad, inhuman things, things can be done in different ways."

Did she expect such a huge response?

"We had no notion that people would turn out in such numbers. We went over in the afternoon to rehearse, and people were already milling around. It was hours before the performance.

"I think there were people waiting and working diligently, trying to bring something of this sort about. Some things lend themselves to something like this. When a thing of this sort comes to pass, it means that enough people were interested enough to bring it to pass."

Do people still ask her about it?

"Occasionally people bring it up, but there would be nothing gained if people knew every aspect. I am sufficiently in love with this country to want to add to anything that is for its good or its edification. Unfortunately, we are oriented to what is spectacular. There are people in this country who do things none of us is very happy about, and these are spread on the front pages. Many people do things that are good but don't do them willingly. The attitude of the person waiting on someone can affect the person being waited on.

"I would hope that concert would not be the most important thing people know about me. It's something like a person with a child on drugs. The parents are sorry for it. The child doesn't care. But the paper says, 'John Smith, son of Henry Smith,' linking the two. Some people will not let what you do be mentioned without bringing in in some way that particular incident. While it was an important thing, it was not the most important thing for us. We had a contest that we won to appear at the Lewisohn Stadium in New York. That was more important, but there was less coverage."

And the most important thing?

Miss Anderson says, "We dreamed in high school of appearing at the Metropolitan with the Met company. When that happened, it was a dream come true."

On April 15, 1939, six days after Marian Anderson sang at the Lincoln Memorial, an athletic meet took place at the University of Missouri. The meet did not go off as scheduled. It was to have been a triangular event. Athletes from the University of Wisconsin and from Notre Dame would compete against each other and against University of Missouri athletes. But the University of Wisconsin bowed out. Ed Smith, Wisconsin's star hurdler, was black. The host school had stipulated that Negro athletes would not be permitted to compete.

America has changed since 1939. Black Americans are not so estranged from the rights and privileges of citizenship as they were then. Many more white Americans are determined that blacks should have those rights and privileges. The struggle is nowhere near its end. But some achievements have been made.

The third largest city in the nation has a black mayor.

By almost any measure, 1939 was a long time ago. Babies born in that year are now watching their own children proceed into high school. Thousands of Daughters who supported the 1939 decision at the time it was made are no longer living. Only one person who had a leadership role in the DAR in 1939 is active at the national level today. Marian Anderson was a young woman of thirty-seven when she sang at the Lincoln Memorial; she is now past seventy. Sol Hurok celebrated his fifty-first birthday on that historic Easter Sunday; now he is dead at 85. Sally Robert is dead. Fred Hand is dead. Harold Ickes is dead. Eleanor Roosevelt is dead. Constitution Hall and every other hall in the country have long since integrated—Marian Anderson gave half a dozen concerts on the Daughters' stage before she started her farewell tour there in 1964. Yet the Daughters of the American Revolution are still being held accountable for the events of 1939.

Eleanor Spicer does not think there is anything the DAR can do to lay the matter to rest. Public-relations consultant Paul Wagner has suggested that the Daughters sponsor a Marian Anderson scholarship, but Mrs. Spicer thinks that would solve nothing. Wagner also urged the DAR to say to the world, as he puts it, "It was a very unfortunate thing, it's too bad the country and the city were segregated, it's in the past, we're all guilty for being a part of it." Eleanor Spicer won't hear of that, either. Like most Daughters, she feels that the DAR has been persecuted for simply abiding by the custom of the times. While she can face the fact that the Marian Anderson decision turned on race, she will not say anything that might look as if the DAR were pleading guilty to racism.

"There have been some things suggested," she says slowly, "which I think would in effect say, 'Oh, we were guilty.' Beating of breasts and mea culpa, sackcloth and ashes, that kind of thing. We don't feel that we were, and why admit to something you didn't do?"

Along with other Daughters, Mrs. Spicer believes that the DAR will eventually receive and accept some applications from black women. But it is doubtless true, as the president general points out, that blacks would never constitute a high enough percentage to have much impact on the public. The one possible way she sees for the Daughters to offset 1939 in the minds of their critics has been foreclosed in precisely the place it might, in her opinion, be most effective.

"The one thing I would *love* to see that I think might help a lot right here in the District especially, where we are the hardest hit always, I would love to see a black child win our great big $8,000 history scholarship. I would be *happier than I can tell you.* But the District of Columbia school board will not allow any of our programs in the public schools. The District of Columbia Daughters, I think it was, passed some sort of resolution about bussing, or discussed a resolution about forced bussing. And on the basis of that we were declared to be racist by the school board.

"I had two very nice colored gentlemen come to my office when I was historian general, because part of my job was the American History Month contest. They were heads of the parent-teachers association here in the District. They asked for information to refute this charge of racism, because they wanted our programs kept in the schools. But the teachers were adamant. And these men were so very nice, and so very earnest. They saw the picture clearly. They knew that the people being hurt were the children. *Their* children."

Eight thousand dollars is a healthy scholarship. Almost anyone would be thrilled to win it. If District policy changed and the money were to go to a black child there, the DAR might very well get a little good publicity.

But it would likely not be much publicity, and it would be unlikely to move the public very much. Institutions and organizations of all kinds have been going out of their way to give scholarships to black children for a decade or more. The DAR itself was giving scholarships to blacks as early as 1953. The public has apparently not noticed.

Out of her conviction that nothing the DAR can say or do will put an end to talk about 1939, Eleanor Spicer did nothing about issuing a new Marian Anderson statement for nearly two years after she took office. Even when several of her staff members began badgering her to work on a new statement, Mrs. Spicer resisted.

Then early in 1973 Mrs. Spicer received what she describes as a new bit of information that she thought worthy of notice. The information came from one of Eleanor Roosevelt's "My Day" columns. This particular article appeared in 1945, but a Daughter visiting in Ohio had just seen a clipping of it in a scrapbook. She had alerted the president general. The president general thought the members should have "this much extra ammunition to use *if* it's needed," even though she does not really believe that one more attempt to set the record straight will make any difference. The ammunition, Mrs. Spicer said, was Mrs. Roosevelt's statement that "the DAR was not by any means alone to blame, that there was a social situation in Washington at the time over which they had no control." So in June, 1973, Eleanor Spicer put out the latest in the DAR series of statements on 1939.

The 1973 statement is a vast improvement over its predecessors. It doesn't tell the whole truth, but with the exception of the claim that Constitution Hall was integrated when the Hampton choir sang there, it is truthful as far as it goes.

What the statement will accomplish, however, is something else again.

The cold truth is that Americans are never going to listen to the DAR's protestations, no matter how they are phrased. By offering explanations of any kind whatever, the Daughters put themselves in the position of appearing to defend something that outsiders long ago decided, or prefer to believe, was indefensible. Far from convincing an outsider that the DAR was not prejudiced in 1939, this strategy is more likely to convince him that the DAR is prejudiced now.

It may be true that the Daughters can do nothing to obliterate the Marian Anderson incident from people's minds. If they were to repudiate the decision now, they would repudiate not only their leaders but all the members still living who supported the decision in 1939. A public apology to Marian Anderson would be painfully awkward for all concerned and is far too late anyway. An extraordinary leader might bring it off, but the odds against her would be extremely high.

Some members feel the DAR should simply refuse to discuss 1939. The statute of limitations has expired, they believe. Journalists and prospective members and ordinary citizens ought to be asking newer questions. Americans who "still have Marian Anderson stuck in their craw," as one Daughter so vividly put it, are just as guilty of prejudice as they say the DAR is. These points are well taken. But silence on the part of the Daughters will not eradicate the memory or the knowledge of others. Washington impresario Patrick Hayes says, "There has to be an element of forgiveness here," but Americans will remember 1939 even if they come to forgive the DAR. The incident has become part of

American folklore.

Yet the DAR is not necessarily stuck with its racist image. It is conceivable that the DAR could take steps that would show the Daughters today to be indisputably on the side of equal rights for black Americans. Such a move would certainly not be easy. As Eleanor Spicer has said, almost anything the DAR did might be construed as artificial, a contrivance it didn't really mean. But if the Daughters were willing to bear those accusations, there is nothing else to stop them from affirming in some concrete way their belief that the blessings of liberty should accrue to blacks as well as whites—if, that is, they truly believe this, and if they truly want it established.

So far the Daughters have done much less than they have said. They have asserted their innocence, and they have argued with their critics, and they have issued statements. They have tried to prove they are not prejudiced by boasting about two concerts by black artists in Constitution Hall more than forty years ago. "We have black children in the Junior American Citizens clubs," they say. "We give awards to blacks." But black JAC members and black award winners do not signify nearly as much as a racist reputation of thirty-five years' standing. Children and medals will not destroy that reputation, nor will concerts which took place in 1931, nor will one $8,000 scholarship.

The DAR's reputation rests fundamentally in the hands of the Daughters. They have been willing to let it shift for itself, but it still belongs to them. While they might not be able to change their racist image completely, they could conceivably change it a lot. The possibilities for doing so remain almost totally unexplored.

The starting point is obvious. The Daughters need to face the whole truth about 1939. Until they do face it, they will continue to defend their decision. As long as they defend it, they will be held responsible for it.

There are worse crimes than belonging to an organization in the 1970's that discriminated against blacks in the 1930's. One of them is denying that it did.

CHAPTER VI

Race: The Present

A critic willing to yield 1939 to the past and observe today's Daughters without bias will see racial attitudes manifested in ways both pleasing and displeasing.

Although a few Jewish, Oriental and American Indian women belong to the DAR, the organization has never knowingly had a black member. According to sociologist Albert Gollin, the DAR has almost certainly had black members without knowing it. A government genealogist substantiates this view.

"I have heard rumors in years past that there were black members in the New York Society," he says. "They were people who were masquerading. There have to be some present members who, if their lineage were correctly traced, would have had to be traced back to a black person." So many blacks passed successfully for whites in the past, Dr. Gollin points out, that their descendants might never even have realized they were not one hundred percent white themselves. If they realized it, they have not had to mention it to the DAR. The Daughters' application form asks no questions about race.

Daughters are quick to inform outsiders that blacks are not barred from membership. The reason there are no black members, they say, is that blacks can't produce the proof of ancestry that the DAR requires. Noting that she, a genealogist, has been unable to find the baptismal record of one of her great-grandmothers, lineage chairman Eunice Haden goes on to point out, "If it is hard to prove one of my lines, it will be doubly hard for a black person to prove her lineage. In addition to loss of records, it was a fact that during the Revolutionary period many blacks did not use a surname; and then and later most of them mated without benefit of clergy. . . . I know researchers who believe that it would be a rare Negress who could prove her lineage with legal documentation." The DAR will not accept anyone, white or black, without proper documentation.

Miss Haden's comments reflect conventional wisdom held by genealogists for years. Today, somewhat sheepishly, many experts are beginning to come around to a different point of view.

"We have found that we have more black records that I would have assumed a few years ago," says Gust Skordas, assistant archivist at the Maryland State Archives. "We're trying now to index what we do have. Marriage licenses issued beginning 1777 often indicate race. A freed black was often given a certificate of freedom registered with the Clerk of Circuit Court or the Registrar of Wills. Even in the Colonial period there were free Negroes. They were freed by will and by regular deeds of manumission, which would be recorded like any other transfer of property.

"The main obstacle is that records don't always show that a black is a black, and in the colonial period, most blacks had only a given name, not a surname. It would be difficult for a black to trace back to the Revolution, but I think it's perfectly possible to do it, and with documentation. The reason this tracing is uncommon or still rare was the assumption on the part of people that it was not possible, that blacks couldn't do it."

James Walker, genealogical and local history specialist at the National Archives, upholds Skordas' view. Walker admits there are problems in obtaining documents, but says more information is available in some states than in others. "Tracing is no more difficult for blacks than for whites," he maintains. "That is also the impression of Nancy Chudacoff, Historical Society reference librarian in Rhode Island, the state whose First and Second Regiments comprised a higher percentage of blacks than any other regiments in the Revolutionary War.

Still, finding a black who has done the tracing and can produce the proof that the DAR would accept is not an easy matter. A cursory search, utilizing leads offered by several genealogists, proved fruitless. The fact is that until recently, not many blacks have even tried to trace their ancestry. Some weren't interested. Some believed, along with many genealogists, that the task was impossible. At least one was actively discouraged from looking up his past. Phoebe Jacobsen, a colleague of Gust Skordas' at the Maryland State Archives, recalls that when she was working in a Pennsylvania library, "the librarian had an inquiry there from a black man who wanted to join the SAR. She was highly indignant, and she refused to give him any information." That, Mrs. Jacobsen said in 1973, happened only fifteen years before.

Blacks who have become interested in tracing their ancestry are unlikely to be seeking documentation that might be acceptable to the DAR. "I don't know of any blacks who have tried to join," Phoebe Jacobsen says, "and I don't know a black who would *want* to belong either to the SAR or the DAR." Some black women might once have aspired to DAR membership, but since blacks are less and less eager to identify themselves with white groups, it seems highly unlikely that there are more than a few black women in America who would make an effort to become Daughters. The issue of black DAR membership is all but academic.

Daughters say that black women who would like to join and who can come up with the necessary documentation would be welcome in the Society. Some members would be delighted to see a black woman in the DAR and would bend over backward to make such a woman feel welcome. Others definitely would not. The DAR as an organization has never gone looking for black members, perhaps because many Daughters can't imagine having anything in common with a black woman. While individual Daughters have made individual efforts in behalf of black membership—junior Cheryl Haddock spent an entire afternoon with a black woman she met in a library helping her trace her ancestry because the woman said she wanted to join the DAR—many would oppose an "outreach" campaign of the mildest sort. A national committee chairman says she knows a state regent who receives periodic phone calls from a black woman asking how she might join. The woman claims she can prove her ancestry. She is told that she cannot join without two sponsors. Period. The way such a phone call would usually be handled in the DAR is that the caller would be given the name of a Daughter or a chapter in her vicinity, or the chapter would be told that there was a potential member in the neighborhood. Many chapters are delighted to have new members. Chapter officers see to it that Daughters get to know the prospective member well enough to testify to her "personal acceptability" and to sponsor her.

The National Society is clearly not ready to bend far to see to it that black women join. Consider the DAR's reaction to this letter, written to headquarters in 1973 by a member of an Illinois chapter:

"I would like to bring a matter of some delicacy to your attention. I have a friend living in Rhode Island who has a Negro friend interested in joining the DAR. Her friend says positively she can trace her lineage back to a Negro who served in the First Rhode Island Regiment during the American Revolution.

"I've personally checked the Regiment and have found that Negroes apparently did serve in it.

"Now my friend and I don't share the same views on these things, but we do agree on this: Above all, discretion. Neither she nor I wish to see her friend's feelings hurt, nor do we wish to see any confrontation. And I, particularly, wish to avoid anything which might hurt my friend, which is why I'm writing you.

"If there is any standard (as there was in my old sorority) restricting Negro members my friend has agreed to 'ward off' a showdown. She simply won't sponsor the girl and will let the matter drop.

"But if there is no such rule they will go ahead and frankly, I fear the result. In the best interests of everyone's feelings I am asking you if any standard exists which will stop her and her friends.

"I am looking forward to your reply."

This letter, written to test the waters, was addressed to lineage chairman Eunice Haden. Miss Haden replied:

"The rules of membership of our Society are set forth on pages 29 and 121 of the DAR Handbook (1972 edition). Applicants must be endorsed in writing by two members of the Chapter who are in good standing and to whom the applicant is personally known; and then she must be approved by a majority vote of the Chapter, taken by written ballot.

"In my own Chapter and many others, it is required that a prospective applicant be brought to visit the Chapter one or more times before she is voted upon. When the vote is favorable, she may be given the application forms to fill out.

"This process is a precaution so that all new Chapter members will be personally acceptable to the other members. If they are not, the stability of the Chapter could be threatened. No member should do anything which would cause the weakening or disbandment of her Chapter.

"In the instance you describe, I would think it wise for your friend to ascertain ahead of time the personal reaction of all the other members of her Chapter. Unless *all* are in agreement, your fears could be realized.

"The well-being of the Chapter should take precedence over the desires of one person.

"Finding such a service record is not surprising. It is known that there were Negroes in the Revolutionary Army. In the attempt to prove descent from one of them, the difficulty will be to find acceptable *documentary* evidence to connect the generations and to prove the dates and places of birth, marriage and death for each person in each succeeding generation.

"In replying to your letter, I have, of course, told you the way I understand the rules and see the problem."

Eunice Haden apparently went to some pains to deal with this specific situation as carefully as she could. That aside, the reference to how things are handled in her chapter indicates that the Society has no policy that would encourage or even appear to encourage black membership.

This position was clarified in New York a few months later when, during the New York DAR's annual conference, a black woman from Queens came up to the registration table one afternoon and announced that she was a member.

Eleanor Spicer and honorary president general Adele Sullivan convinced her that she was wrong. The two leaders talked with the woman for nearly an hour. (The conference was not in session at the time.) Apparently she had written to headquarters requesting information about how to join. She had received a packet of materials. She took that to mean that her membership was confirmed. She wanted to register for the New York conference. The Daughters wanted to find out whether she was a plant.

"It was a very pleasant conversation," Eleanor Spicer told a reporter the next day. "We took the tack, and I think it worked very well, that she was convinced by her own sincere assumption that the packet constituted membership. We simply explained that there was a misunderstanding. We told her what the requirements were. She was from the West Indies and had been told that her family descended from Spanish conquistadors who went through the West Indies in the 1500's. We explained that we require Revolutionary ancestry. We told her how to go to the Archives and how to get a census. We said if she found she had a line she could trace she should get in touch with us.

"I talked to her as I talk to anyone. She can't say to anybody that she didn't get the most courteous treatment. She was smiling when I told her some of the little stories about troubles I had finding ancestors. She was either a superb actress or a perfectly sincere, misled person. I think the latter. It could have been unpleasant if she had been unpleasant, but she was a perfect lady. I was determined there would be no hard feelings. We were just as charming as we knew how to be."

Then Mrs. Spicer said, "We got a very nice letter not long ago from a black woman who said she was president of the black Republican women's club. We sent stuff off saying that she must prove every step of her ancestry in order to join, and we never heard any more. Someday I honestly believe it will happen. I think it's coming. We are not making any effort to integrate the Society, but we are certainly not going to resist."

The president general elaborated on her statement. The "we" she referred to is the National Society. The National Society determines only whether an applicant's genealogical credentials are in order. The applicant's personal credentials are strictly the business of individual chapters. "The National Society doesn't solicit members, though we do try to make it attractive to people," Mrs. Spicer said in New York. "Soliciting members is the job of the chapters."

Requiring women to be personally acceptable to the members of their chapter before they may join is explained by Daughters as a way to keep troublemakers and insincere persons out of the Society. Some women, members say, want to join only to get their lineage documented. They have no intention of becoming active or, in some cases, even paying dues. Others are disruptive; they start right in criticizing the organization even when they are attending meetings as guests. One Daughter describes the personal acceptability requirement as "our escape clause so that we do not have to take everybody if we don't want them." One time this clause was useful in her chapter, the Daughter said, was when it permitted the members to escape from a prospective member who turned out to be under indictment for federal income-tax fraud. Of course a chapter could easily invoke the escape clause against blacks if members were so inclined.

Sooner or later the DAR is going to be put to the test. Black genealogy has begun to catch on. A great deal of interest was generated by an article appearing in *The New York Times Magazine* in 1972 called "My Farthest-Back Person—The African," then published as a book, *Roots*, by Doubleday. In the article, writer Alex Haley described his search for his origins. Genealogists intensified their efforts to learn what information might be available to blacks. Haley himself set up the Kinte Foundation in Washington where documents relating to black lineage are available to researchers. Furthermore, there are Daughters around who would be happy to get black women into their chapters. There are undoubtedly chapters which would welcome them. One of these days a black woman who wants to join the DAR will come up with both the proof and determined sponsorship. As long as her documents are sound and a chapter wants her, the National Society cannot turn her down without violating or changing its bylaws. Very likely it would accept her. Whether it does or not, its decision will provide a fair basis for judging the DAR's racial attitudes.

The DAR as an organization has no programs specifically

aimed at blacks. It carries on a number of activities from which blacks as well as whites may profit both directly—scholarships, Junior American Citizens clubs, DAR Good Citizens and other award programs, the work in veterans' hospitals, the donation of flags and citizenship manuals, the DAR Museum—and indirectly, as, for example, conservation. At their 1972 Congress the Daughters presented their annual Army Nurse of the Year award to a black woman, Lt. Col. Hazel W. Johnson of Malvern, Pennsylvania. The award is presented in memory of the Daughter who founded the Army Nurse Corps. Nominated for the award by the Corps chief, Lt. Col. Johnson saw no irony in the DAR's recognizing a black.

"I feel it's a great honor," she said. "It's a great honor to be the first member of my race to receive it. Everything has a beginning, a step forward. This is a good vehicle. I think they have been looking for a vehicle that wasn't too obvious. I have been to presentations of this award before and have been treated very cordially. I can't think race will enter into it anymore, or let's put it this way: I hope it won't."

As individuals the Daughters express the range of racial attitudes that might be found in almost any large group of conservative Americans. There are few, if any, women active in both the DAR and what is left of the civil-rights movement. For many Daughters, racial exchange has been limited to conversations with servants. Their idea of treating blacks as human beings is loving their maids and giving them their old clothes. Like other white Americans who have not had nor sought the opportunity to become acquainted with black Americans on an equal basis, some Daughters seem anxious or hostile about blacks. Occasionally a Daughter may express these feelings openly.

"I taught in the public schools of Washington until 1945," said an elderly woman in a DAR receiving line to someone coming through. She spoke tightly, as if 1945 were still bothering her. "We had *good* students. I didn't teach when the schools were integrated. I suppose I shouldn't say that." A Florida Daughter was moved to snap to some DAR friends over cocktails that "nigras" were behind almost whatever trouble broke out in America. "Well, I don't know about that," one Daughter said. The rest maintained an embarrassed silence.

Most Daughters would not make such comments, certainly in front of strangers. They may, however, seek safety from new attitudes in old notions or stereotypes. There is a Daughter in Alabama who feels the Communists are at the bottom of the trouble between blacks and whites, and that blacks who don't protest about their lot in life are patriotic. There is a young

Daughter in Virginia who is proud of the fact that her forefathers held slaves because they took care of them, and who feels blacks should go slow. "For me and my friends, and for most, I would say for most of the Southerners, they feel for the colored," she says. "And why build it all out of proportion and make for another civil war? I think we're making more harm now with all these programs than we are good."

There is a Daughter in New Jersey who told some DAR friends that she had gotten in a taxi in Washington only to discover that the driver was black. She delivered that information as if it were a punch line. Then she went on to say that the driver had pointed out some prostitutes on the street. Boy, did she get out of that taxi in a hurry! The Daughters listening to the story didn't get the point. Their friend thought they were very naive. To her it seemed clear that the cab driver was trying to set her up for the evening.

But the DAR has any number of members who view blacks much differently. One of them is Clare Booth Luce, who rejoined the organization many years after she resigned over race and who does not now find the DAR's views inimical to her own. One is Daisy Daniels, an Illinois Daughter in her eighties. "I have this feeling that DAR has lacked in not doing anything for the Negro," says Mrs. Daniels, a local historian. "Now I'm very proud of DAR, but that's one thing I feel a little bad about. That would be a criticism with me." One is California junior Karen Landers, who recently transferred into DAR from CAR, who has lived most of her life on military bases, holds medals for shooting, wasn't afraid to wear a Girl Scout uniform to high school, and says she would marry a black man if she loved him. One is the friend of a black secretary in Washington. "My friend and I agree the DAR members have a long way to go," says the secretary, "but they're getting younger and less conservative."

One is Lucille Fryxell. Lucille Fryxell worked for many years as the registrar for Augustana College, a small Lutheran liberal-arts school in Illinois. In 1961, when race problems were making national headlines, a number of students and community residents gathered one evening to hear a panel discuss civil rights. It was the first such program many of the people present had attended. As they began to reevaluate themselves in light of what they were hearing, emotions began to rise. They showed up rather starkly in comments directed at the panel. The discussion was becoming ragged and edgy when the white-haired registrar rose and asked permission to speak.

Few people on campus really knew Lucille Fryxell. She was a private person, older than most of the faculty members. She had a voice that was very soft and very dignified. All her years in the North had not erased her Southern accent. Lucille Fryxell said to that room full of people that while she believed in civil rights in theory, it was difficult for her, with her upbringing in the South, to think of black people as true equals. She was trying to accomplish that, she said, but she didn't know whether she could ever really do it, if she was honest with herself. And then Lucille Fryxell said something that some of the people who heard her have never forgotten.

"I don't know if I can ever truly feel the way I would like to feel," Mrs. Fryxell said quietly, "But I know one thing: I have made up my mind that no matter what, I will never knowingly be unkind to anybody."

There is Pat Thompson, of Wytheville, Virginia, a Daughter in her forties. "I grew up in a protected world," Mrs. Thompson writes. ". . . The first time I came up short with white racism was when I was twelve. My mother had bought me a new white dress with cherries embroidered on the pockets. I had white stockings, white shoes, and a big white bow in my hair. Standing in line to get my books a black child wrote all over my dress and punched a hole in the back of it so I jumped, and she got in the line ahead of me. I was hurt and mad and cried. All the way home all I could think of was what did I do to her? My mother tried to tell me the girl liked my dress but my father told me what all her other feelings must have been.

"A short time after that my father (a Methodist minister) and I were walking, and we met up with his friend, the African Methodist preacher. The black man recounted a story which I do not recall, but at the end of the story tears flowed from both men's eyes. My father said at that time, 'I have carried on the fight, but this child will take up the banner when the time comes.' These words seared my brain, and I have never forgotten them. At about that age I was asked to join the CAR. I had no reasons for refusing that I can remember, but I'm sure I had questions, and I did not join.

"I was at West Virginia Wesleyan College the first year black students were allowed to go to classes there. The maid in our dorm was the first black student in my class. One day as she was cleaning my room she asked me if I did not see the difference in the way I talked to her and the way the rest of the girls did. I replied no. She replied in my room she had dignity. In my class she was an equal. She should have been—her grades were far better than mine, her wisdom in understanding poetry more realistic. We were not equals. She had something to give to me.

". . . I got married, I moved to Charlottesville. My mother-in-law was DAR, Daughters of 1812, Daughters of the Barons of Runnymede, the Order of Washington, UDC, and on and on. My job was to join everything possible or have virtual war. I helped entertain at tea parties, luncheons, breakfasts, and country-club affairs. One year later we moved to Wytheville, Virginia."

In Wytheville Pat Thompson joined the DAR and soon headed the chapter. "My stipulation for being regent was that national-defense reports be limited to two minutes," she says. "I ran a well-ordered social club, and the ladies loved me."

In 1968 Pat Thompson's life changed. "A black man came to wash my windows, and he sang all day," she recalls. "Lots of young people came to my house that day, and at lunch I asked him to sit down and eat. He did so. But when he prayed, he did so with tears. We talked for three hours. He told me the story of his life. . . . He invited me to his church, and I went and I went again and again and again. Without my realizing it I became a white doll. 'Mrs. Thomas, will you sing us a song? Mrs. Thomas, will you read us a poem? Mrs. Thomas, will you, will you—oh, you are so elegant.' One day my brother came to see me, and as I went out the door, he said, 'Good-bye, Mrs. Bountiful.'

"I could not enjoy church. I squirmed, I turned, I agonized. I immediately went to my friend and told him my plight. He laughed and laughed and laughed. He said, 'I wondered how long it was going to take you! Why don't you start on yourself —do some soul-searching, talk to your own people. We need you, but as a friend. Your white friends need you more.'

"I curtailed my activities until I came up with what I thought was an answer. I invited six of my black friends with my family, and we sat down and talked honestly and openly for the first time. One of them said, 'What can we do?' We decided to form an organization. Our first meeting was stiff, but for a year and a half we have struggled on. My relationships have changed. As for the blacks, I have gained a modicum of trust. Sometimes they tell me, 'Don't push too hard.' They call me the woman with the black heart. . . . The greatest comment that was ever made was in our last meeting—one of our men said, 'Our people are dying to break up this group. They'll do anything to destroy it. We've got to stick together because for the first time in our lives Mrs. Thompson has shown us the way.' My greatest success was when our school teacher of the group called me Pat.

"As for my white community, they asked my parents questions like, 'Aren't you afraid to let her go into such dangerous places? The work Pat is doing is so charitable,' etc. But the Mayor, the president of the college, the councilmen all appeared at our home for the black beauty pageant. The state senator said it was the greatest party he had even been to. We have not had one turn-down from anyone we have invited to speak from the white community. *Today* I was invited to join a five-county DAR regents club. People stop me on the street to give me money for our projects.

"The South is paternalistic still. Much of the money we get for our projects comes from people who have had black people work for them. They still see them as children. But yet they contribute to the cause. Many DAR women have told us what great work we are doing. Our contributions have come from all types of local society. The first offer of actual work came this week from a leading wife of the community, a DAR member, who offered to help us paint a house.

"We have not won the battle, but I have learned not to be Lady Bountiful, or condescending, but a being who loves. It's catching on. I feel it."

And there is Betsy Campaigne.

For a woman in her early thirties, Betsy has already led a rather full life. She grew up in Washington and Maryland, graduated from American University, works as a systems analyst for IBM and has traveled widely. She has a peace symbol in her living room (unusual, to say the least, for a member of the DAR). She lives with her husband in an apartment building in Washington, D.C., that is almost entirely black. She cheerfully passes along the news that a prostitution ring was broken up there recently. Betsy used to spend most of her spare time with other whites in the CAR, which she joined at eleven, and the DAR, which she joined after college. In fact, in her senior year at American University she was national president of the CAR.

Betsy now spends a good part of her spare time with blacks. She had never really known any blacks until she had finished college, but Curt, her husband, is associate minister in

Washington's Foundry Church, one of the largest black Methodist churches on the East Coast. She is on the church health and welfare committee, has taught sewing to some of the women in the community, and with Curt has participated in a seminar where blacks and whites met and discussed racial feelings. She has joined the League of Women Voters and wants to do some projects in the neighborhood "helping people help themselves."

Betsy and Curt were married in Foundry Church by the pastor of Foundry, Frank Williams, in 1970, and the wedding plans involved more than they would have if the marriage had taken place somewhere else. Betsy had to decide who her friends were. "I didn't want a large wedding," she said, "and I knew among some guests there'd be bad feelings. It made it very easy in my mind that if they couldn't accept it, they weren't really friends, and we wouldn't invite them. I knew the only thing some people would remember about Betsy's wedding is that a black man performed the ceremony. I thought, 'It's not worth it.' You just sort of eliminate them from the invitation list."

Betsy was so active in the DAR as Betsy Bennett that Mrs. Bennett, also a member, used to identify herself as "Betsy Bennett's mother." Betsy is no longer active. She has less time than she used to, and more responsibility, but those are not the only reasons.

"The DAR doesn't have as strong a hold on me as it did at one time," Betsy says. "My thoughts and philosophies have changed since marriage. Let's say my horizons have widened and I see more of life than I've ever seen. This comes from being in a church situation, meeting people from all walks of life—this would be true also with a white congregation—living in a downtown, inner-city area and doing community service. I have come to have more understanding for and patience with people whose background and values are different than mine. I have to choose what is best for me and what I am most comfortable with, so I am not always in the 'DAR corner.'

"I feel that I have become more liberal and more open in my expression of feelings among friends and acquaintances. I do feel I can give some light in cases of prejudice. There needs to be more of an individual accepting another individual on what they are themselves, versus the race to which they belong."

Betsy feels that the DAR has a way to go before it reaches that point.

"At chapter, when I got engaged, they asked me where my husband was a minister. When I told them, one lady said, 'Why that's a black church!' This lady is seventy-five years old. She still calls them 'nigger babies.' I don't know if I can ever get through to her. Every once in a while when somebody talks about the riots or the Indians taking over the Bureau of Indian Affairs, I say, 'Have you ever thought about what the British thought about us putting tea in the harbor?' They say, 'That's different.' I say, 'No, it wasn't. It's a revolution.'

"Now, then, if a black woman asked me if she could come to a DAR meeting I would be happy to take her, but I don't feel my chapter members would be as cordial as they should be, and I think they would be very unhappy with me. I don't think the DAR is racist, but I don't think any of them live in integrated neighborhoods."

Betsy has two DAR friends in Washington who feel as she does—that black members would be good for the organization and should be encouraged to apply. Asked what effect the "personal acceptability" requirement could have, Betsy replied, "I would hope that would not be a block to blacks joining."

Despite her differences with the DAR, Betsy Campaigne has no plans to resign, though that possibility is not as remote as it once was. "I have a lot of friends in the DAR I've collected over the years," she says. "I get something from the programs. A unity. I like the work that they have done and what they are doing. But if it ever got to the point where DAR membership was going to hurt my husband's position, or be detrimental to us in any way, I would just resign."

One of the most interesting things about Betsy Campaigne is that the DAR is not hiding her. It is perhaps to be expected that Adele Sullivan speaks about her in superlatives, since Betsy worked in Mrs. Sullivan's administration. It is a bit more surprising that a Daughter at headquarters would steer a reporter directly to Betsy Campaigne's door, saying, as Grace Porter said rather proudly, "She's done some interesting things in the community on a one-to-one basis. She's in today's world, a modern world, and still has worked hard for this organization." In 1971, when the editors of *McCall's* were thinking of running an article on DAR juniors, headquarters got on the phone to Betsy Campaigne.

In 1973 the man who gave the keynote speech on opening night of the DAR's Continental Congress was, for the first time in the organization's history, a black. He was Air Force Major General Daniel "Chappie" James, public affairs officer for the

Pentagon. In the thirty years James had given his country as a combat pilot and commander, he had participated in 178 combat missions in the Korean and Vietnam wars. Most recently, as Eleanor Spicer pointed out from the podium, he had been seen on television standing at the foot of gangplanks, welcoming home the American prisoners of war.

Among liberal blacks in Washington, Chappie James is not a favorite. "He'll give you his 'I Am an American' speech," one liberal black warned a Congress guest in advance, pretending to gag. James did give that speech. He announced that it was the only speech he made, and then he proceeded to make it. He argued for military strength. He referred to President Nixon several times as "my President," or "my commander-in-chief." He described his visits to campuses during the peak of the anti-war period. When students had asked him, "Why don't you go back to Africa?" he told the Daughters, he had replied, " 'This is my home. I was born here. I am an American. I speak for the democratic dignity of the individual.' When the black militants hollered for separatism, I told them I was once under separate-but-equal, but I'm not going back under that blanket, no sir. When I came into this man's Air Force, I vowed I'd be a general. I am, as you see."

The Daughters seemed to like what they were hearing even though James didn't spare them. "While we build and unite to heal the wounds of a long, costly war, we must get involved," he said, pausing to let his words permeate the big hall. "You can't sit there in righteous indignation and say, 'I'm not part of it. I didn't throw the rocks. I didn't burn the flag. I didn't call him honky. I didn't call him nigger.' If you just stood there like you didn't hear it or see it, that may be what's wrong with you."

When James had finished, most of the Daughters gave him a rousing standing ovation. One state delegation did not stand. The others clapped and clapped and clapped. Eleanor Spicer had to wait for them to quiet down. Finally she was able to thank General James for his talk. After she had said a sentence or two, she stopped and half-turned toward him. So he could hear, and so the Daughters could, she said with emotion that most of the Daughters seemed to be feeling: "We are intensely grateful." Her voice was almost a whisper. When the colors had been retired, General Daniel "Chappie" James was surrounded on the stage by Daughters of the American Revolution who wanted to shake his hand.

CHAPTER VII

The DAR and the Press

Continental Congress always convenes the week of April in which the nineteenth falls, because that date marks the anniversary of the Battle of Lexington. There is no more perfect time to be in the nation's capital. Many of the Daughters still have winter back home, but they pack for Washington expecting spring, and Washington rarely fails them. The sun can be dazzling in D.C. in April. Lady Bird Johnson's red and yellow tulips open wide. The grass brightens to sharp green. The water in the Tidal Basin sparkles; the white monuments to Washington and Lincoln and Jefferson stand out against sky that is likely to be deep turquoise blue. And as Mayor Walter Washington has repeatedly told the Daughters on opening night, the famous cherry trees are in flower.

It is commonly said in the DAR that once a Daughter goes to Washington for Continental Congress she's hooked on the organization. This is not surprising. Congress week brims over with activities that bring pleasure to DAR hearts and tears of pride to DAR eyes. There is ceremony, marking death and acknowledging life. The accomplishments of a year are summed up and celebrated. Plans are discussed and projects voted on. Officers are elected, prizes given, VIP's honored, choirs and bands heard. Children from DAR schools give speeches of gratitude. There are banquets and teas and meetings, and there is a reception at the White House given by the First Lady of the land. Friends see each other again. First-timers explore the DAR's impressive buildings. Everybody has a chance to dress up in formals and long gloves and corsages. Everybody has a good time.

And everybody takes home and savors the unforgettable memory of the outstanding moment of the DAR year.

Congress always opens promptly at 8:30 on a Monday evening with a processional. The president general enters last. The instant she steps across the rear threshold of Constitution Hall, a Daughter standing in a rear balcony gives a signal, and a huge American flag—one of the biggest ever made in America —snaps open in the upper reaches of the Hall. It commands the Hall. For a few seconds, as every eye watches, the banner ripples and wafts in the delicate currents stirred by the breathing of four thousand people. Then, like an enormous kite guided by marionette strings. it is brought under control to hang high over the audience, nearly motionless from its own weight, a reminder to the Daughters of what the forthcoming proceedings are really

all about. The whole ceremony takes less than a minute, but it
sticks permanently in the mind of anyone who has ever seen it.
Even journalists, who don't get their jobs unless they can produce documentation that they descend from cynical and hard-
bitten stock, are not immune. When NBC's Pat Trese filmed
Continental Congress, he said he really felt the patriotic juices
flowing when the flag unfurled. "You'd have to be a vegetable
not to respond to that," Trese says without embarrassment.

Continental Congress turns half-hearted Daughters into zeal-
ous ones, but its significance is much broader than that. Congress gives outsiders most of their impressions of the DAR.
While small-town papers cover chapter activities fairly regularly,
metropolitan dailies ignore the Daughters most of the year. But
Congress gets attention. Reporters from both Washington papers invariably write about the resolutions and usually cover the
speakers as well. Their articles often go out over the wire to be
picked up by newspapers around the country, and even reporters from other cities may cover Congress. DAR news doesn't
exactly blitz the nation even then—Americans can certainly go
about their normal lives even when Continental Congress is in
session—but to the extent that outsiders have learned anything
at all about the DAR, they have probably learned it in April.

In some ways this is unfortunate, because the DAR in Congress assembled is not necessarily the DAR at its best. In fact, the
opposite may be true. "In Indianapolis and other places they're
wonderful," says retired Washington reporter Katharine
Brooks. "They keep things like patriotism before everyone's
minds, which is good. But here, the place is practically taken
over. You can't even get a seat in a restaurant because of the
DAR's dripping with orchids!" In Miss Brooks' opinion,
"Washington sees them at their worst."

Things have changed a little since Katharine Brooks wrote
society news for *The Washington Star*. The days of multiple corsages, which made most Daughters look, according to one, "like
the horse that came in first at Hialeah," are over. Still, the
Daughters who gather in Washington for Congress often help,
albeit unwittingly, to reinforce the image outsiders hold of them.
A reporter who goes to Congress looking for the DAR in the
traditional image can certainly find it. Washington is where the
myth begins.

To begin with, many delegates may closely resemble the traditional image. Getting to Washington and staying there is not

cheap, and Congress lasts nearly a week. Mothers with children at home often can't find a baby-sitter for five or six days. Working women may not want or get their vacations that week. In either case the cost of Congress may be prohibitive. The Daughters who have the money and the time to go to Congress tend to be older women in comfortable circumstances. They are retired; their children are grown. They don't have to worry over every penny. Even those Daughters who stay at the YWCA aren't paupers, and many can afford to stay at the Mayflower, the Madison or the Hay-Adams. Some of these women dress very well indeed, although it is possible to see some rather dowdy outfits at Congress, as at other large gatherings. Persons with a certain sense of humor can laugh at the idea of a white-haired woman in a brocade formal without ever having to see her. Strings of insignia and sashes denoting rank are ridiculous to some people, fine for Girl Scouts but silly for grown-ups. Even the common breeds of clubwomen have always been considered fair game, and when the Daughters assemble in full regalia, some look almost exotic. The Daughter who carried the American flag at one recent Congress wore feather earrings like wings. This is an extreme example but one that could put even a sympathetic photographer to the test.

Congress proceedings, too, have helped convince some Americans that the DAR is not to be taken seriously. In general the business sessions go exceptionally smoothly. There is a lot to be done in five days, and the Daughters try to ward off snags by adhering strictly to a detailed schedule and *Robert's Rules of Order* as well as by observing common courtesy. Pat Trese helped produce NBC's coverage of the 1968 political conventions, and he describes Continental Congress with a laugh as "much more orderly!" On the DAR meeting, Trese offers these thoughts: "One gets the feeling that you are watching something that's been pretty well decided in caucus ahead. It's more or less like, but less unruly than, stockholders' conventions. I did not see and did not expect a floor fight. It was all very ladylike and proper. Nobody interrupts anybody else. Nobody gets angry."

Anger felt may be anger unexpressed when TV cameras are watching, but it is true that Congress rarely if ever erupts in crisis. Although some order must be imposed on any meeting of several thousand delegates, the Daughters' docility proves to some outsiders that the DAR is a rubber-stamp outfit and that the Daughters are sheep. And of course at no time are the

Daughters more vulnerable than when the resolutions come up for discussion.

The Daughters have been extremely unhappy from time to time with what Americans have been told about them in April. They feel that representatives of the press arrive at Congress biased, with the flowered-hat image firmly implanted in their minds. Instead of writing about what actually takes place, reporters look for evidence to support the conclusions they have already drawn. They pick out the "sensational," Daughters feel. They always manage to quote some member who doesn't know what she's talking about and ignore those who do.

"We've been very badly maligned by reporters hearing what irrational women say," says Eleanor Spicer. "Some women preen themselves and come to town and don't know one cotton-pickin' thing they're talking about."

Reporters take statements out of context, Daughters believe. They blow up incidents into events. They slant their stories. The liberal press is particularly guilty of these sins, DAR members feel, but sometimes their friends have let them down, too. Even news photographers show bias. Whenever a photographer comes around, Daughters say, he seems to look for the oldest woman he can find with runs in her stockings and a rain hat on her head, then he pushes aside five juniors wearing Jerry Silverman fashions so he can get a good, clear shot of her. In general, DAR members feel that the press wants to perpetuate the image, not convey the facts or present a well-rounded picture.

Like other clubs, the DAR is usually covered in feature sections of today's newspapers. The reporters who write for those sections readily acknowledge that they don't necessarily describe an event or an organization in full. That, they say, is not their job.

"The Congressional Record will give a complete record of what happened [in U.S. Congress sessions]," says a Washington feature writer who asked not to be quoted by name. "We're not interested in recording a complete record of what happened, in detailing every side's argument for the record. The complaint that we use things out of context is perhaps legitimate in the sense that in covering anything, one seeks the unusual or salient or unorthodox view or act. The views reflected in the paper are sometimes the oddball things or passing remarks—views, statements, and so on which fall out of the majority view. If you look at journalism as a matter of record, in which reporters should strive above all to give an exact record and reflect the tenor of the assembly, that's a different approach than the one that we have."

The DAR and the press have not always been so far apart in their concept of how the DAR should be described. In the old days a club member could simply give a newspaper the latest information about meetings or other activities and the paper would print it. Reporters would cover annual club events almost automatically and write about them even if nothing earthshaking occurred. Some smaller newspapers still cover local organizations this way. But on the feature sections of large metropolitan dailies the policy has changed. "Straight" coverage is often less than fascinating to the reader who can press a button and get his information in living color. "Duty" coverage, in which an event is reported just because it happens, has largely given way to selective coverage. Writers on feature sections try to be accurate without necessarily being comprehensive. Stories that appear are written to interest the reader, not to please the dramatis personae.

Today most newspapers no longer view their mission as one of purveying "handouts" or other information provided by individuals and agencies seeking to put themselves in a good light. Even before Americans learned that high government officials were successfully managing the news, editors and reporters had begun to exercise a healthy if belated skepticism in their assessment of sources and their evaluation of events. This trend went beyond the newsroom into society and even food coverage. But the journalist's course was never so clear as it became with the revelations of the Pentagon Papers and Watergate. "Papers *were* a publicity agent," says Washington *Post* social editor Donnie Radcliffe. "We can't be any longer."

Given their differences, the press and the DAR were almost destined to clash, and in 1970 they did. The issue was the DAR's resolution on "Total Environment." The Daughters gathered in Constitution Hall resolved three things: that the DAR call upon policy makers to urge the federal government not to adopt "unnecessary and harmful control programs which the nation would later regret"; that the DAR "suggest personal responsibility of the individual citizen be emphasized as one of the most effective ways of decreasing pollution"; and that the DAR "recommend that the Council on Environmental Quality direct attention and emphasis to the dangers of pollution of the mind in its considerations and studies of the dangers and threats to our total environment." Delegates got to bickering about whether the so-called "real" problem of pollution was being "exaggerated" or "distorted". Of course the press heard them.

According to Eleanor Spicer, several of the comments were made by someone who wasn't even a member. "We don't even know how she got in there," the PG protests. Be that as it may, it happened that the Daughters were arguing about pollution at the precise point in history when pollution was on American minds as it had never been before.

The Washington Post made the connection in its lead. "While thousands across the country yesterday marked Earth Day, some of the Daughters of the American Revolution labeled the environment movement 'subversive' and 'distorted' and 'exaggerated,' " *The Post* observed on April 23.

Eleanor Spicer argues that the DAR was only saying, "Don't move too fast in anti-pollution because inexperienced people were getting programs in it," but on that first Earth Day, this warning was about as welcome as six beer cans in a trout stream. Americans howled in indignation and disbelief. So strenuous were the objections that president general Betty Newkirk Seimes went on nationwide television to say that the DAR was not opposed to anti-pollution efforts.

What the DAR distinctly was at that moment was incensed with the press. Urged on by DAR public-relations director Stanfield McClure, Mrs. Seimes bought a full-page ad in the *Star* and ran all the resolutions in full. She wanted the man in the street to be able to read the environmental resolution as it had been written by the DAR, she said, and not as it was interpreted by the Associated Press and *The Washington Post*. The next year, as one of her last acts in office, Betty Seimes barred reporters from the resolutions session of Congress for the first time in DAR history. Although she cited "biased reporting" by *The Washington Post* and the Associated Press as the reason for the ban, Mrs. Seimes made it clear that no reporters were to be admitted to Constitution Hall while the resolutions were discussed. Sally Jones, finishing her term as first vice president general, explained to reporters, "We felt that being a private organization, we were entitled to our family squabbles without having them aired on the front page."

Stanfield McClure was less circumspect. "We've survived the slings of outrageous fortune for eighty years, and we've always turned the other cheek," he stormed. "Not anymore." Claiming to be speaking unofficially, McClure took advantage of the occasion to get something else off his chest. "*The Washington Post* ignored all our nice-looking ladies and searched out the older, less attractive ones for pictures," he told a *Washington Daily News* reporter. "Now here's a picture of an attractive lady, but taken from an unattractive angle with shadows. All in all we really got a hosing last year, so why should we set ourselves up for it again?"

Washington reporters did not take kindly to the DAR's decision. Ruth Dean of *The Washington Star-News*, who the Daughters feel has been sympathetic to them, said later, "I was incensed that they forgot who their friends had been. It was ridiculous the way it was handled. One of the worst things you can do for a bad press is to keep them out or tell them how to do the story." *Washington Post* reporter Nancy Ross decided not to abide by the DAR's decision. Looking to begin with as if she could blend with ease into a very posh crowd, Ms. Ross put on a suit and a strand of pearls and went over to Constitution Hall to eavesdrop. A page recognized her and asked her politely to leave. Ms. Ross went into a room where she could hear the proceedings over a loudspeaker but could not take notes without being observed. She ended up under the stage with her ear against the ceiling but was discovered and ordered out. Finally a page caught her in a corridor looking over the shoulders of non-delegates who had copies of the resolutions. The page escorted Ms. Ross out of the Hall. Ms. Ross went back to *The Post* and wrote a piece explaining how she had been thrown out of Constitution Hall, mentioning that she had the blood to join the DAR, but not the guts.

At the end of the 1971 Congress Eleanor Spicer was installed as president general. Interviewed by *Post* columnist Dorothy McCardle, Mrs. Spicer said she believed in freedom of the press and had an open mind about opening the resolutions sessions to reporters. However, in 1972, she decided to sustain the ban, although she agreed to give reporters advance copies of the resolutions on the understanding that they not be printed until they had been passed. Ruth Dean wrote, "Mrs. Spicer put the onus on elements of the DAR membership 'who often raise questions that are not pertinent, which leads to confusion and distortion of the true meaning' as her reason for closing the resolutions session."

DAR public-relations committee chairman Mary Pierce told a reporter later, in private, that she thought Eleanor Spicer was more willing to open the sessions than were some other officers, and members of the press felt that the Daughters' position had become less rigid. "Eleanor Spicer was trying to pour oil on troubled waters," one reporter said later. "The press committee overdid it with kindness—you sort of felt like each was a personal bodyguard—but they meant well. They were trying to recoup some of the mistakes of the previous administration."

During the 1973 Congress advance copies of the resolutions were again issued to the press, but reporters were told that the ban on attending the discussion session was still in effect. It has not been rescinded.

This problem is not an easy one for the Daughters to solve. Many would feel powerfully inclined to agree with the Washington reporter who says, "If they claim to be a democratic organization, democracy at work should be publicized." Eleanor Spicer leans toward reopening the sessions, and there are Daughters in the upper echelons who would probably support such a move, who feel that the DAR can withstand scrutiny. But others would probably agree with Sally Jones that the DAR has a right to privacy. There are closed sessions on Capitol Hill, after all, where democracy is also supposed to be at work. While public pressure may eventually force open public meetings, organizations which fund themselves have no obligation to let outsiders in. From the DAR's point of view, if reporters can be expected to entertain readers at the expense of the Daughters, why should they be welcomed?

For all the paranoia they have developed about the press, the Daughters in some instances seem fully justified in their mistrust. When Daughters in Washington gathered to celebrate the DAR's birthday with a luncheon and fashion show, an eight-paragraph story appeared in a Washington newspaper under a fairly large three-column headline reading, "No Hats at the DAR." The first three paragraphs of the story discussed the dearth of hats. The next three told where the meeting was held (Shoreham ballroom), how it opened (drum roll), and who blew out the candles on the cake (Eleanor Spicer). The seventh conveyed Mamie Eisenhower's excuses for her absence. The story ended with a Daughter's comment on the fashion show: "I can't see most DAR's wearing any of these clothes," the Daughter was quoted as saying. "Maybe some of our Juniors could get into them."

The same dubious editorial instincts showed up in press coverage of a DAR meeting in a big Eastern city which Eleanor Spicer attended shortly after she took office. As the PG recalls, "The photographer was taking pictures of lovely young pages and young women, attractive people. Even I'm not too hard to take a picture of. And what did they have in the paper? The one odd-looking woman in the place. When she came in the night before, I said to whoever was sitting next to me, 'I'll bet you that's the only one who gets her picture in the newspaper.' Because she came in with a wig on that was all dalrymple curls, just a queer-looking creature, and the next day she was dressed in a tri-corn hat on top of those curls, and I tell you right now she was the most ridiculous thing you've ever seen. Yet she's one of their best workers."

A predictable press is not a creative press. If the Daughters know in advance how the press will portray them, the press is guilty at the very least of too little imagination. Permitting a group to be represented in a photo by one woman who is conspicuously dissimilar to other members nears the realm of distortion. Journalists have sometimes seemed willing to play for a laugh rather than probe the myths. While it is possible that a few reporters or editors might wish to deliberately hurt the organization, it seems more likely that sheer laziness accounts for much of the press coverage to which the DAR objects. Of course laziness has the same effect as outright antagonism. Both factors violate the principles of good journalism. Either way, the Daughters come out behind.

Still, a lazy press does not wholly explain the DAR's image problems. The Daughters themselves have worked against good coverage for the DAR. They have frequently used a rather heavy hand with members of the press, making clear that they expect reporters to follow DAR orders and abide by DAR conventions. Instead of fielding a question on a touchy issue with "No comment" or asking that the answer be off the record, a Daughter may say, "That has no business in the story." A reporter asking a leader to confirm information learned elsewhere may be told, "I don't want that in there." A Daughter might say to a reporter interviewing her, "Don't put that down." No matter what happens at any given event, reporters get the message that they are supposed to print the most charitable interpretation. But, says a reporter whose coverage of the famous ecology resolution the Daughters did not like, "When you're going to dictate on deadline, you're not going to tippy-tippy worry about stepping on somebody's toes. You try to give the hard news kernel."

Reporters are expected particularly to observe the strict and intricate taboos that obtain in DAR politics. The Daughters have a rule that candidates for national office must not discuss their candidacy until it is formally announced after the Congress just prior to election year. Obviously any Daughter can refuse to answer any questions a reporter might put to her. Yet one reporter was flatly told by an officer not even to ask a candidate for president general about the forthcoming campaign because she had not yet announced, even though it had been common knowledge for some time that she would be running. Another reporter made the mistake one year of printing the slate before the Daughters were ready. "I went to a DAR reception and got wind of who the candidates would probably be," this reporter says. "I thought since I had talked to several people and quoted no one, I didn't see why the story shouldn't be broken. A local DAR called me at home, got me out of the shower, and blessed me out for giving the names."

The reporter continued, "They want you to play by their rules. The papers used to keep those things confidential, but hell, it's news. Why should I keep these petty politics? If you can dig the story out, print it. You use judgment, of course—I'd protect someone's reputation—but you're not paid to flack for them."

In addition to treating reporters on occasion with a certain imperiousness, the Daughters sometimes make it rather difficult for members of the press to get information—even information they want them to have. In 1972 reporters couldn't get comments on the resolutions from national resolutions chairman Genevieve Morse, because Mrs. Morse was not permitted to speak on Society policy without a go-ahead from the president general, and the president general, presiding over Congress sessions, was not available to give it. In 1973, the president general agreed to let a reporter have an advance copy of the resolutions, but when the reporter arrived in a taxi to pick it up, the two people who knew that permission had been granted were not around. The resolutions chairman, who was, said she couldn't release the resolutions because she didn't have the authority to do so. The reporter got back in the taxi empty-handed and angry.

This modus operandi can be annoying. The reporter who has to leap hurdles to get information only to be ordered rather than asked not to use some of it is going to sit at the typewriter feeling less than kindly disposed toward the DAR. A reporter with integrity will not write a vindictive story. An editor with integrity wouldn't run one. But the same facts can be treated both warmly and coldly. A story won't reflect enthusiasm if the reporter doesn't feel any. While few members of the press want coddling, they would naturally like to have smooth paths, not bumpy ones. And sometimes the Daughters drop boulders in the road.

Some of the Daughters' problems with the press might be solved or at least eased if the DAR had a good, strong, professional public-relations operation. It doesn't. In the last seven administrations, eight different people have been hired to handle public relations. One of them, Stanfield McClure, was hired three separate times; one left after less than a year to get married; several were asked to resign; one returned from lunch one day to find her belongings in shopping bags. The public-relations staff today has the full-time services of just one person —Sharon Parsons, a secretary.

Until recently the public-relations office was administered by Aileen Jordan, a dedicated Daughter who never had any professional training for the job she held. She learned what she knew about public relations from her husband, who was a newspaperman, and from many years' experience on the DAR public-relations committee. The professional services of Paul Wagner were available to Mrs. Jordan only part-time. (Wagner, of course, works out of his own office and has many other clients.) Mrs. Jordan was also supposed to work in tandem with DAR public-relations committee chairman Mary Pierce, but Mrs. Pierce lives in Wisconsin.

Candor and an understanding of journalism and of how members of the press operate made Mrs. Jordan more valuable to the DAR than some Daughters realized, but she was fired in 1973, in part because of budget considerations and in part because she is not a writer. Even if she had had all the experience in the world, Mrs. Jordan was up against a task that would be difficult for any one person to do well. She had no time to be creative and little money to pay for the creative ideas Paul Wagner was retained to think up. Her budget for the 1972/73 DAR fiscal year was $25,000. Out of that and a few thousand left from the previous year came her salary, the salaries of a secretary and part-time writer-editor, Wagner's retainer, and all supplies, photographs and telephone bills. Twenty-five thousand would just about buy the services of one full-time professional publicist.

Adele Sullivan describes the DAR's public-relations history as "very poor, very poor," but the Daughters have never been much inclined to spend money promoting themselves. They feel it is far more important that their money go to their projects. A classic illustration of this philosophy occurred in 1939. In the aftermath of the Marian Anderson incident president general Sally Robert consulted a public-relations expert, as the DAR didn't have one of its own at the time. According to Anne Musgrave, "The public-relations man came to Mrs. Robert and said, 'We can make you the most popular organization in America by bringing out, publicizing, all of these wonderful things that you do, particularly for black people. But it'll cost money. It'll cost as much as twenty-five thousand dollars to really do it right.' Well, now, Tamassee DAR School for under-privileged children needed a high school. There had never been a high school in a hundred miles. What was the DAR to do, make themselves look popular, or take that twenty-five thousand dollars—which was what it took—and build a high school at Tamassee? Well, we built the high school."

The DAR is still operating under this philosophy. Certainly it is an admirable one, but it underestimates the importance of image. Unpopular organizations go unheeded. Many people won't join one. Allocating minimum resources to public relations might have been a more workable policy when the press was willing to stand in as publicist, but today the ball lies squarely in the DAR's court. "If there's a bad image, it's as much their responsibility to change it as it is ours to tell it like it is," says *Washington Post* social editor Donnie Radcliffe. "If there are areas in which they're not getting full credit, it's incumbent upon them to get those cleared up."

Some Daughters do believe in spending money to tell the DAR story. In 1972 state regent Hope Sasportas convinced the Con-necticut Daughters to spend $5,000 on a sixteen-page Sunday newspaper supplement on the DAR. The cost would be borne by individual Daughters, who for two dollars could have their names and their ancestors' names listed on the back pages. As Mrs. Sasportas explained in a speech to New Jersey Daughters before the supplement came out. "Connecticut has seven hundred fewer members than you have, but members don't mean too much. The elder stateswomen are carrying the load. As nice as all of us are, we're not going to last forever. *The Hartford Courant* has seven hundred thousand readers on Sunday. Their editor has been there thirty years and doesn't know what the DAR does. I promised our Daughters seven hundred members out of seven hundred thousand readers. Some of our members voted against the supplement. They wanted to put more money into our two houses. I said, 'Go paint 'em. It won't increase your membership. They've been there two hundred years and never got us one member.' "

After the supplement appeared, the Connecticut Daughters got more than a hundred letters from women seeking information on becoming members. They were still receiving letters four months later. A hundred members is six hundred fewer than Hope Sasportas promised, and fifty dollars per member could be considered high. But a hundred new members would be a hundred more than Connecticut would have had otherwise.

Furthermore, the supplement undoubtedly told the Connecticut residents who read it some things about the DAR that may have replaced old notions. One woman who wrote said that while she didn't know whether she was eligible, she was concerned about natural woodlands and had been impressed with a story in the supplement about a forest maintained by the DAR. Admonished by their regent to be nice to everyone who called whether eligible or not—"I don't care whether she's black or what," Hope Sasportas told a reporter at the New Jersey meeting. "If someone calls who isn't eligible, we'll at least make a friend"—the Connecticut Daughters may have given some outsiders an entirely new impression of the DAR. They consider their money well spent.

A bigger public-relations budget might help the National Society, but in the meantime the Daughters could probably improve their image without spending a cent. They could do it by knowing their organization. ("We used to have a saying," Aileen Jordan says: " 'The DAR's can't read, or they won't.' ") They could do it by being willing to admit that they don't know the answers to certain questions and then getting those answers, whether the person asking is a radio interviewer or a neighbor down the street. Since Continental Congress convenes every year, and since resolutions are put out every year, and since reporters almost always want comments on them, the president general should not wait to authorize the resolutions chairman to make those comments until after reporters have gone back to their papers angry.

Leaders need to make absolutely sure that no pamphlet or

release containing factual errors is ever distributed and that communications from headquarters are always dignified. A few years ago a president general, aggrieved over an article that had appeared in a high-school newspaper, wrote the student editor of the paper a three-page letter. Instead of simply setting the record straight, the letter bristled with such sarcastic comments as "After all, casting the DAR in the role of a villain makes good copy. Why kill a good story by telling the truth?" The article the president general objected to appeared under the headline, "DAR Wrong Organization to Honor Good Citizens." Any Daughter would want to defend her organization in such a situation, but blasting a teenager is not the way to go about it.

In dealing with the press, Daughters could do a lot worse than to follow the example of Maine Daughter Florence Norris. When Mrs. Norris became regent of her chapter. she was told she'd have a terrible time with publicity. She went straight into the newspaper office for a talk with the society editor. "I went in and told them I was as green as grass, which was the truth," says Mrs. Norris. "After all, I knew nothing about newspapers; I didn't know what their policy was." Florence Norris has never had a terrible time with the press.

"They have been wonderful," she says. "But I never told them how to run their business."

Oddly enough, the women's liberation movement, which many Daughters oppose, may help ease the DAR's image problems. It is becoming less and less possible to poke fun at women's clubs with impunity, particularly in public. Male members of the media, often at the prodding of the females in their midst, are increasingly careful to show that they are not chauvinist pigs. Eleanor Spicer thinks the DAR may very well profit from the change in attitude governing coverage.

"It's possible that it won't be as funny or as profitable, let's put it that way, for cartoonists to lampoon us," she says, "because in lampooning us they'll be lampooning other women's organizations that'll crack back at 'em."

On opening night of the first Continental Congress at which she presided, Eleanor Spicer welcomed the Daughters by saying, "We gather in our building to hear reports and renew friendships." She wasn't leaving out a great deal. Every three years in Washington the Daughters elect new national officers, and every three years they vote on a president general's project, and every year they elect seven of twenty-one vice presidents general, and every year they vote on budgetary matters and bylaws changes which are usually minor. But the real work of the DAR does not take place at Continental Congress during one week in April. Congress offers the merest glimpse of what the Daughters of the American Revolution is really about. It is not to the DAR what Atlantic City is to the Miss America contest—the purpose and culmination of a year's work. It is more like what the annual report is to General Motors—a summation. A fair evaluation of the organization cannot be made on Congress alone. The DAR should also be judged by its other incarnations its best-loved project, its chosen leader, and its grass-roots self.

CHAPTER VIII

The Daughters' Favorite Project

To judge by appearances, the children who board at Tamassee DAR School in the South Carolina mountains are healthy and whole. Their eyes are clear. Their faces are candid. Their bodies are alert, spirited, well nourished. Sitting together at tables in the dining hall drinking milk and eating fried chicken and sweet potato soufflé, the children of Tamassee look like a *Saturday Evening Post* cover painted by Norman Rockwell. Leaving their dormitories for school, they sound like campers on their way to the lake. They show an ease and warmth with strangers that hint at a background unusually blessed—how else does a child get that kind of confidence?—and except for their clothes, which are worn or inexpensive or both, they could be the treasures of the best families, preparing for lives that will continue to be charmed.

The facts are much different. Most of the children of Tamassee come from the worst of families. Their mothers and fathers, if they have mothers and fathers, are unable to take care of them, or don't want to take care of them, or are unfit to take care of them. Some of the Tamassee children have lived in unspeakable circumstances and seen unspeakable things. They have had very little to lean on, hurt by the very people who should have protected them.

Their stories are frightful. There are the Porter children, two of them, whose father got drunk and shot a man and was sentenced to twelve years in jail; whose mother remarried and couldn't keep the children because her new husband was also sent to the penitentiary. There are the Surrett children, three of them, whose mother and father separated, whose father started running around and was sent to jail when the girl he was seeing ended up at the bottom of a well.

There are the Wooten children, nine altogether, five at Tamassee. Their father murdered their mother with a poker the night he found her in bed with one of his bootlegging partners. There is Patricia Meece, who once saw her parents, both alcoholics, draw guns on each other. There are two youngsters, a brother and sister, whose mother has told them that she doesn't ever want to see them again. There are the two Crane children, whose stepfather used to beat them every night of their lives, slapping them away from the dinner table and almost starving them to death.

The older girls talk about Martha Ballew, a bright, popular student who left Tamassee in her senior year to live with her

foster mother. Martha Ballew's real mother had been confined
to a wheelchair which her father used to push up against the coal
stove to burn his wife's feet. Martha Ballew's mother died when
Martha was in second grade. After Martha went to Tamassee her
father used to show up drunk and demand to take his daughter
home, but Martha cried to stay, and she did stay.

In any given year there are about 150 children in the Tamassee boarding department. They range in age from six to eighteen and come from South Carolina, North Carolina, and Georgia. Ten percent of them have been referred to Tamassee by the
courts. Forty percent have been referred by social agencies.
Seventy percent of the children come from broken homes. A
third of their families receive public assistance. Some of the
children have lived in shacks and slept on pallets. Some have
emotional problems, and some do poor work in school, a direct
result, according to Oconee County guidance counselor Wilma
S. Murphree, "of the previous experiences of the children, ir-
regular school attendance, poverty, improper diets, and homes
broken by desertion, death, or jail sentences."

The DAR opened Tamassee in 1919 to educate mountain
children living nowhere near a school. That need no longer
exists. Public schools are now accessible to every child in the
state. More than half the children attending Tamassee Elementary School on the Tamassee campus are local students going to
the nearest public school. All are white; no blacks live in the
immediate community. Naturally the children from the community live at home. So the Tamassee boarding department has
gradually, almost radically changed. Once a convenience for
children who had homes but no access to a school, it has become
a refuge for children who have access to a school but no real
homes. (The boarders, too, are all white. Technically a black
child could be referred to Tamassee by the courts or by social
agencies, but Tamassee's business manager says no black child
has ever applied for admission to the boarding school.) The
children who have applied and been accepted suffer needs
which are far more complicated than the needs of the Tamassee
students of 1919, and far more difficult to meet. These children
need security almost desperately. They need attention. They
need consistency. They need food, clothing, shelter, medical
and dental care, but they also need love, and they also need
peace. The Daughters of the American Revolution, who mostly
do not believe in welfare but do believe that children are

America's most important natural resource, are trying to provide those things.

The child who goes to Tamassee enters another world. Off by itself in the foothills of the Blue Ridge Mountains, the campus is a thousand acres of oak, pine, and scrub timber that have been cleared in places for pasture. It is on a spot which Cherokee Indians once called "the place of the sunlight of God." The land is crossed by streams and the Little River. Scenic Highway 11 traverses the campus, but the road is quiet, unmarred by gas stations, billboards or other marks of civilization, and it can't be seen from the school proper.

The school proper looks almost like a miniature suburban town. Aside from a few large structures, Tamassee is predominantly brick and stone and frame houses surrounded by lawns. The houses are furnished like homes, which is what they are. The children live in them, one or two to a room, thirteen to thirty-four in a house, with houseparents. Many of the buildings and the walkways that connect them are shaded by elegant, tall old trees that spread the sunlight in dapples on the ground. At the base of the trees, two peacocks of lustrous blue and green wander at will. Overhead, crows and blackbirds scream and squawk. In the woods around the buildings, a child with sharp eyes may pick out at various times squirrels, quail, rabbits, raccoons, foxes, even a deer. A little way from the school is a farm which the students help work. There is also an apple orchard. Tamassee doesn't look like an institution for underprivileged children. It looks like a college for children of the well-to-do.

The first person a child meets at Tamassee is a man who signs himself W.L. Jones. In his sterner moments, Lincoln Jones could scare an adult. He is not tall, but he is big, with a big square face, and his eyes behind his glasses steel to size up whatever they see. Jones is paid by the DAR to run the boarding department and he and his wife, a DAR member, live on the campus and take their meals in the dining hall. Mrs. Jones serves Tamassee Elementary School as librarian. The two have been at Tamassee since 1960. Before that Jones was a high-school teacher and a superintendent of schools, but he looks more like a politician than an educator. Although he works in Appalachia, he wears a suit and tie to the office.

Lincoln Jones doesn't run the boarding department so much as he presides over it. He demands and almost always gets obedience. Jones goes by a strict moral code that some might consider too strict, but he has a strong sense of responsibility to the children in his care.

"Some people say it's bad for children to be out of the home at this age, but they haven't investigated the conditions as I have," he says. "When a mother runs off with another man, it's not only my duty but society's duty to do something for the children."

Jones will not accept just any child as a boarding student at Tamassee. He wants students of good character with a good record, or, as he puts it, "worthy" students. "If the child is not worthy, we don't take him." Jones says simply. "We would have the boarding department overflowing if we accepted every application or referral that we receive. But we want to keep our student body above reproach. In order, in other words. We don't want to turn it into a correctional institution.

"We go according to need and the child's record and behavior. We check on the financial statement and try to visit the home wherever possible. We try to get information on trouble in court. I check the court record. We sometimes check with a minister. We turned a boy down this week from a broken home. The school says he gave trouble to all his teachers, had a parent in a number of times, and there were bad reports of his behavior at home.

"We look at a girl's character or a boy's, but mostly a girl's. If a child has been cutting school, meeting boys, staying out at night, we don't take her, because we feel she would be a bad influence in the dormitory. If we feel there are good reasons—if the parents are solely to blame—and if we feel there's a good chance for the child, we give her a chance. We don't take unwed mothers here. There's no written policy, but we feel they'd be a bad influence."

The child who meets with Jones's approval walks out of his office into an exceedingly demanding life. Tamassee is a bastion of the work ethic. A visitor feels guilty on the first day for lying around in bed till 7:00 A.M., and by the second becomes distinctly uncomfortable about not wielding a bucket and scrub brush. The children get up at 6:30 and straighten their rooms. After breakfast they do assigned dormitory chores, such as sweeping the walk or carrying out the trash. Buses leave at 7:45 and 8:00 to transport the older children to Tamassee-Salem High School two and a half miles away, and buses bring them back again at 3:00 in the afternoon. The little children, who just walk across campus to Tamassee Elementary School, stay in class from 8:20 to 2:30 or 3:00 depending on what grade they are in. When school is over, the children may go to the canteen for thirty or forty-five minutes. Then they do their jobs. Every child on campus from the fourth grade up is expected to help run the campus by doing some kind of non-paying work—washing dishes, setting or clearing tables, cleaning, or working in the office, the canteen, the kitchen, or the elementary school library. The older girls like to be assigned as breakfast cooks, because by getting up at 5:00 A.M. they can get their work out of the way for the rest of the day. The littlest child has some kind of chore, even if it is only straightening chairs or dusting. Supper is served promptly at 6:00. When it is over the children are expected to go straight to their dormitories, where they may relax until 7:30 or 8:00. Then they go to the dormitory study hall and study for twenty minutes to an hour, depending on their age. After study, they may watch television until the time for devotions. The youngest children are normally in bed by 8:30, and lights out for the older children is 10:30 at the very latest.

On Saturday morning everybody works. Grounds are neatened; walls, floors, and furniture are scrubbed. Bright and very early, before other little boys across America have even begun to stir in their beds, before their mothers have placed a half pound of bacon in the skillet, Gerry White, eleven, with eyes like oversized black olives and more tummy than he needs, is lying flat on that tummy on the bottom shelf of the big cooking table in the kitchen at Tamassee, rubbing away the flour drifts and spaghetti stains with a huge, wet white rag, as part-time cook Linda Chastain, who doubles as his housemother, supervises.

Such activities represent the minimum work schedule at Tamassee. Some children do even more work than they are required to do, and for this they are paid, usually a dollar an hour. They may be assigned a job to do all year in addition to their regular duties—a girl may work as a dormitory aide, living in a house with the smaller children and helping the houseparent put them to bed at night; a boy may feed hogs or work as a painter or a plumber—or they may work as work becomes available. "The other day we put up five hundred bales of hay," Jones said one morning. "We didn't finish in the afternoon, and I asked at dinner for volunteers. Seven or eight went out and worked till nine o'clock." This kind of work is dispensed almost like a treat. Jones always says he "lets" the kids take on these extra burdens. "A housemother told me some kids staying over

Thanksgiving needed some toothpaste and so on," Jones said. "I let 'em rake leaves at a dollar an hour for four hours on Friday morning. Those that don't have any family money, we let 'em work. If it stops raining this week, we'll probably have a good many raking leaves. They like to get things at the canteen."

The schedule at Tamassee doesn't leave much time for mischief, but just in case, there are rules to obey. Discipline is stringent. It is predicated on the belief that even good children get into trouble if they have the opportunity. At Tamassee they don't have the opportunity. Their houseparents must know where they are at all times, and nothing could be easier since the children aren't allowed to step beyond the porch unless they have permission. They must be at the right place at the right time, period. In fact the students at All States, the residence for older girls, may not go to another floor without permission. During study hall in their dormitories the children must ask permission to go to the bathroom. They may not walk on campus without a very good reason, at night above all. "If you want exercise," says one older girl, "you have to walk around your bed." The girls in All States may smoke, but they're allowed to do so only in the first-floor bathroom, perching on the sink or wherever they can find a place to sit down.

Sixteen-year-olds may date, but until quite recently, dating at Tamassee meant just this: A boy went to All States Dormitory at one o'clock Sunday afternoon and met his lady friend in the parlor there, and the two of them were permitted to be together, in that lounge, for an hour and a half. If they wanted to neck, no one stopped them (though sometimes people watched), and at 2:30 the boy went back to his dormitory. Now the juniors and seniors who obey the rules the rest of the week may go off campus, boys and girls together, a couple or a group, on Friday evenings until 11:00 o'clock P.M. and on Sunday afternoons between 1:00 and 7:00 (or dark), but boys and girls are not permitted to pass time together on campus except at the canteen during canteen time. They are expected not to "go around loving it up," as Jones puts it.

Infractions are punishable. The child who walks into the dining hall when it's not mealtime or worktime may be assigned ten extra hours of work. The student who misses the school bus more than a few times gets ten hours of work. Some penalties are more severe. If a boy brings alcoholic beverages on campus or becomes intoxicated on campus, he immediately goes home. If a girl leaves a dorm at night to meet a boy or a man, she immediately goes home. If a student leaves the dorm just to run away, he may be suspended for a week. If a boy is caught at a girl's dorm or out with a girl without permission, he is automatically suspended and may be out for the rest of the year. These prospects apparently make their point. "We might have one or two cases a year," Jones says. "It's not often." In addition to all these restrictions, the children are required to go to all meals and to Sunday school and church every week at the nondenominational campus chapel.

Restrictions govern life at Tamassee, but they by no means constitute it. The children receive other kinds of care which they are meant to enjoy. To begin at the beginning, the food is anything but a chore to eat. Presided over by the attentive Mrs. Owen, Tamassee's kitchen turns out large, delicious, noninstitutional meals. For another thing, the kids from poor families get clothes when they come to Tamassee. The girls get uniforms sewn on the premises for school, and everybody is sent with a houseparent to "the rummage" above the post office to get something to wear after school and on weekends. If the rummage doesn't yield anything the right size, clothes and shoes are bought new. The clothes are far from elegant, but at least no child need feel shabby.

There is recreation at Tamassee, and there are parties. On Saturday and Sunday afternoons there are team sports outside—basketball, baseball, volleyball. The dormitories may plan suppers. The kids in each dormitory—there are seven—are organized into Junior American Citizen clubs, and the clubs have parties most weekends. There is something called a Junior-Senior, a dance held in the dining hall with a live band, to which Tamassee kids may invite boyfriends or girl friends from Tamassee-Salem High School. Tamassee children who attend Tamassee-Salem may get Mr. Jones's permission to attend any school event they wish. Sometimes whole busloads of children head off down Scenic Highway 11 to Tamassee-Salem basketball games. Tamassee is well represented both on the team and on the cheerleading squad, and also has a girls' basketball team.

A big event for the children and the community is the annual beauty contest at the high school. (A Tamassee girl was named Miss Senior in 1972.) The kids also look forward to commencement and awards day, to Thanksgiving dinner, to the music program put on by the Tamassee Elementary students at Christmastime.

There is a Christmas dinner and a box of presents for each child. In addition, families in the community sometimes invite Tamassee children home for a weekend. A teacher in the elementary school may take one of his students someplace special in the evening and keep the child at his own home overnight. A child doesn't have to feel he is freeloading on these occasions. Children who want spending money can get it. They don't usually get it just for the asking, but they can always get it in advance. If Jones announces after supper on Friday that there's a bus going to a basketball game, he will peel off six or seven dollar bills for children who want to buy whatever the vendors will be selling. The children appear in Jones's office the next morning for work assignments to pay what they owe.

For all the watchfulness of the Tamassee staff, the kids are free to have fun within the prescribed limits. One Friday night not long ago, Linda Chastain gave a party for her boys in Pouch Cottage. The boys had invited the girls their age—fourth-through-seventh graders—from other cottages, and the girls went to some trouble to make themselves look smashing for the occasion. The boys were waiting for them in the big basement of Pouch. They had moved all the furniture off to the sides of the room, so the dance floor was ready when the girls got there. Mrs. Chastain put herself in charge of the record player. She let the kids dance and goof around a little to wear off the shyness that some of them obviously felt. There was plenty of goofing. Tall boys teased girls; small boys teased each other.

Then Mrs. Chastain gave a whistle that would have done credit to a truck driver and announced a multiplication dance. There was a lot of suspense in the room while she chose the couples. The kids remained impassive when their names were called, but Linda confided later that she had deliberately chosen the children who were known to like each other. She had had a fistfight the year before, she said. A solemn little blonde named Cheri had told four different boys she would "go" with them. The boys, unfortunately, had bragged to each other.

Linda set out punch and cookies, and the children helped themselves. Some of the older ones disappeared out the basement door. Linda said they went out there to smoke. She did nothing to stop them. "I keep them sexually segregated, and that's about it," she said calmly. The kids danced on and on. After the fashion of the day, they danced with their arms around each other. Some weren't the least bit interested in dancing close, and some really couldn't. The girls were too tall. These girls bent almost double in an effort to dance cheek-to-cheek with the shorter boys. One girl was big enough to pick her partner up and carry him across the room, which she did with determination in spite of the fact that he was beating on her shoulders, close to tears, looking to Linda for help and getting none. She wasn't about to interfere. Between dances the kids laughed and joked and pushed at each other. Spilled punch was treated as a minor crisis, which was all it was. Except when she was announcing dances, Linda didn't raise her voice with the children the entire evening.

Not everyone had a marvelous time. Some of the smaller boys sat along the sidelines hoping they would not be asked to dance. "I'm afraid," one said softly to a forward female. The tallest girl, the young woman whose mother had told her she didn't want her, sat for a while with her hands over her face. But in general it was a good party. The kids let off steam (there was a tug of war with a mop at one point), enjoyed each other's company, and, when the time came to clean up, seemed to enter into the task in a happy frame of mind.

When the day is over, a child at Tamassee knows that someone will be there to pull the covers up and turn out the lights, literally or figuratively. Four widows, a widower, and two younger couples with children of their own serve as houseparents. They may have homes and kin and roots elsewhere, but they are anchors for the children of Tamassee. Like most parents, they are on the alert twenty-four hours a day. They serve snacks when the children come in from school. They repair hems when hems go. They get up with sick children in the middle of the night and hold their heads if they throw up and sponge their faces before putting them back to bed. Those who are able to do more do. Earl Chastain, a brickmason whose brother went to Tamassee, takes the Pouch boys fishing and acts as their cubmaster. As den mother and JAC sponsor, Linda Chastain has taken children all over the county—to the dairies, to the courthouse, to the offices of the Seneca *Journal*, to Tamassee Knob for a hike, to the state park for a picnic. The Chastains are young—their daughter is only six. Linda has a high-school education. A doctorate in child psychology never could have provided her with her gift for getting along with children or her regard for them.

"Boys show emotions in different ways," Linda says, contrasting her charges at Pouch to the girls they invited to their party.

"They're rough and mean with each other. They'll cause trouble in school or get into petty thieving for attention. I don't do anything about it till after Christmas. I just work with 'em. Then I have a stern talk with 'em and tell 'em it's time to settle down.

"We have more trouble with the parents than with the kids. One mother, an alcoholic, comes to the campus drinking. The children beg her not to drink because if she were caught they'd be taken away. She says, 'I will stop. I love you more than the bottle.' But when she comes back, she's been drinking again.

"And we have kids from good families that are having a rough time. A man's wife had a mental breakdown. He brought four children in here and put two more in a day-care center. He works two jobs. He's torn between his kids and his wife. He's got decent kids. They'll grow up to be something."

Lincoln Jones does not believe in coddling the children of Tamassee. He respects them, and sometimes he is angry with them or disappointed in them, but he will not show them that he pities them no matter what they have been through, and on the rare occasions when he gives them something they haven't earned, the gift is intended as a lesson that the child is expected to learn.

But Jones isn't running a boot camp. He has three grandchildren of his own in Ohio, and he is both father and grandfather to many of the children of Tamassee as well. Jones knows the importance of leaving space for occasional exceptions. In fact granting privileges seems to be one of the parts of his job he most enjoys.

When a child asks special consideration, it is not given without a brief interrogation. A teen-aged girl came into Jones's office one afternoon to request permission to go to a basketball game. "Do you know anybody on the team?" he asked with a half-smile. The girl fidgeted. He waited. Finally she said, "He's goin' back to Patsy."

Jones regarded her for a moment. "Can't you do your part to get him back?"

The girl twisted and hung her head, smiling herself but in embarrassment. Jones said, "You can go."

She stood up straight and happy. "Thank you, Mr. Jones," she said softly.

It is patently obvious that Jones cares about his charges. Sometimes he seems to interrogate the children purely for his own amusement, calling them over to pick on some detail of dress or behavior, just to pleasure himself. When they answer, he releases them with a laugh. "Go on!" he says. "You're a cute little thing, anyway!" Although Jones says it is not required, the children stand when he comes into a room. The younger ones are afraid of him. The older ones jump when he calls their name. No child would dream of cutting up while Jones was giving his announcements in the dining hall after meals. Yet, old and young, the children of Tamassee, like the staff of Tamassee, praise Lincoln Jones until they run out of words.

Support of education has been a major DAR effort for more than sixty years. Including individual contributions made directly, the Daughters have spent about ten million dollars on education in that time, according to schools chairman Amanda Thomas. Today, exclusive of student loans or grants-in-aid, they are able to raise between $200,000 and $250,000 a year for their schools program. This amount may not seem a staggering sum for an organization whose membership is approaching the two hundred thousand figure, but support of the schools is just one of the many DAR activities to which members contribute above and beyond their dues. The education of youth is far and away the Daughters' favorite endeavor. For that reason and because the schools help the DAR retain its tax status as an educational institution, this program is the biggest item in the DAR activity budget.

In the year ending April, 1973, the DAR spent $207,672.33 on the two schools it owns and the five it helps support. Ten thousand dollars of this money was appropriated by the National Society. About twenty-two thousand was raised by the junior members through jewelry and stationery sales. The rest came, as one Daughter puts it, "from the little old ladies having their teas and their card parties and their fashion shows."

The second largest program in the DAR activity budget is Indian scholarships and aid to Indian schools. Although this program is technically educational, it is handled as a matter of convenience by an American Indians committee whose endeavors and expenditures are totally separate from those of the DAR schools committee. Most of the money raised for Indians is divided between St. Mary's School for Indian Girls in South Dakota and Bacone Junior College in Oklahoma.

St. Mary's gets most of its funds from the Episcopal Church, but the DAR provides about $30,000 a year which is used for scholarships, general operating expenses, and special DAR projects such as furnishing the school's chapel-auditorium. Bacone is largely supported by American Baptist churches and by the nearby city of Muskogee, but the school receives about $25,000 a year from the DAR which it uses in a variety of ways. A special project at Bacone in the Spicer administration has been the endowment of a silversmithing chair on the Bacone faculty. Both schools receive used clothing from individual chapters as well as items to sell in the school thrift shops.

In addition to helping St. Mary's and Bacone, the DAR makes scholarships available to Indians around the country. For the year ending April, 1973, the scholarships given totaled $6,300. A publication put out by the federal Bureau of Indian Affairs lists forty-nine organizations which give scholarships to American Indians. Of the forty-nine, eleven do not restrict their awards as to tribe or course of study. The DAR is one of the eleven. BIA information specialist Mary Ellen Ayres believes scholarships represent a useful way to aid Indians. "It's realistic," Miss Ayres says. "They're not trying to tell the child what to do." Miss Ayres further says that the DAR, whose American Indians committee was set up in 1936, is "one of the major secular organizations with a continuing interest in Indians."

Because some DAR committees operate with appropriations and some with contributions, it is difficult to describe precisely how the organization's educational expenditures compare with its patriotic or historical expenditures. What can be said is that the largest of the DAR programs supported by appropriation is national defense, and that for the year ending April, 1973, the Society spent $60,596.32 on national defense, not even a third of what the Daughters gave to the schools. (Half of the national-defense appropriation went to staff salaries; another quarter went to printing; the rest went to postage, supplies, literature and subscriptions, other incidentals, and travel. The national-defense and schools chairmen are the only DAR committee heads who receive travel stipends.)

Sixteen percent of the DAR's school money for the year ending April, 1973, went into the five so-called "approved" schools. To qualify, an institution must serve underprivileged children or be involved in the "Americanization" of foreign-born students or students of foreign parentage. It must also satisfy the DAR schools chairman that it maintains high scholastic standards and teaches patriotic American principles. Then it must be approved by Continental Congress delegates. The DAR has contributed to a number of such schools over the years, but the five currently on the list, and the approximate amount of money the DAR gave each for the year ending April, 1973, are: Crossnore School, Inc., Crossnore, North Carolina, $18,300; Hillside School, Inc., Marlborough, Massachusetts, $9,150; Hindman Settlement School, Inc., Hindman, Kentucky, $2,900; Berry College and Berry Academy, Mount Berry, Georgia, $2,000; and Northland College, Ashland, Wisconsin, $1,660. The lion's share of what the DAR spends on education is always divided between Tamassee and Kate Duncan Smith DAR School in Grant, Alabama, which the DAR established.

In an article in *The Columbia Record* in 1966, a reporter described Tamassee as a place "where every stick and stone is accounted for." The subhead over the article read, "Every Bush, Every Building Bears a Plaque." It's true. Little brass plates are scattered throughout the campus like oblong freckles. You find them on furniture, on walls, even on rocks. The plaques cost from four to eighty-seven dollars apiece. They mark DAR contributions to Tamassee which over the years have come to several million dollars.

The DAR owns the land. The DAR owns the buildings, thirty of them. Five, including the building once used as a high school and now used for the elementary school, were projects of the National Society, the latest being the Adele Erb Sullivan Administration Building. Others were projects of individual states, among them the South Carolina Cottage which houses older elementary school girls, the Michigan laundry, the Pennsylvania health house, the Texas Friendship Cottage for guests, and the Illinois dormitory for older boys. Several states have collaborated on some of the buildings. Individual gifts have helped finance others. Lincoln Jones sees that the buildings are kept in good repair, but renovation is taken care of by special DAR fund-raising campaigns. "An Ohio member offered five thousand dollars, and I suggested the renovation of a room off the dining hall with a new roof," Jones says. "The Ohio Society seemed interested and asked what else I would suggest. I suggested a new fire escape and some other things, and it came to nineteen thousand dollars. Ohio is going to do all of it." Altogether the Tamassee buildings and grounds are now worth between four and five million dollars.

The DAR pays the boarding department staff: four full-time

and two part-time employees in the kitchen, a woman who operates the laundry, a day nurse, a night nurse, seven house-parents, two full-time employees for the rummage, four full-time men who handle farm maintenance, three office workers, and Lincoln Jones. (Jones receives his home on campus, meals in the dining hall, a car for school business, and $12,000 a year.) The woman who does the laundry also helps serve lunch in the dining hall. The husbands of the two married housemothers help with discipline, and they and their own children may eat in the dining hall whenever they wish.

The DAR fully supports at least forty percent of the children in the boarding department for nine months of the year. Housing, food, clothing, school fees, and medical and dental expenses run to about a thousand dollars per child. Families are requested to put a little money toward their children's care if they are able. When a child comes from a home where the father was killed or has died, Social Security may be available, and the family is asked to pay ten or twelve dollars a month. One family is paying $50 a month. The mother, who went to Tamassee, separated from her husband and then remarried. She had what Jones calls "a conflict in the family" and sent her two children to Tamassee because she felt they would be in good hands there. But this is an unusual situation; the other families don't pay nearly this much. (The boarding department sometimes runs on a deficit which is made up for, Jones says, by faith and bequests.)

DAR contributions to Tamassee come in different forms. The National Society appropriates five thousand dollars a year for the general fund. The juniors recently raised five thousand for dental care for the children. Every so often Jones issues a list of "needs" ("washing machines, $225; filing cabinets for office, $165; music scholarships, piano and voice, $50"). If he gets a check in the mail for fifteen or twenty-five dollars he puts it in the general operating fund, but, he says, "They like to have these projects." State Societies often raise money for specific purposes. West Virginia has given a herd of beef cattle, for example. California recently sent $1,500 for work scholarships enabling the children to earn pocket money. Michigan bought a commercial washer and dryer for $3,800. New York gave a pickup truck. Wisconsin sent two sewing machines. Individual Daughters send cash, trading stamps, and stuff for the rummage, which is open to the public and makes $18,000 a year.

Daughters also send presents or money for Christmas. In one

recent year the Iowa Daughters made cash contributions to Tamassee totaling $1,935, donated 1,253 pounds of clothing, and sent twenty boxes of Christmas gifts. Cartons come in at Christmastime from all over the United States. So many come in, in fact, that from Thanksgiving on, two or three Tamassee employees work until nine or ten o'clock almost every evening, opening boxes and sorting their contents into piles that house-mothers will then further sort into a package for each child. Most of the cartons contain used clothing, but some of it is new, and there are always odds and ends such as jewelry and stuffed animals, usually used, which the children at Tamassee especially like to receive.

Since the late 1960's the DAR has provided Tamassee with approximately $95,000 a year. Not all of it goes to the boarding department. Some goes to Tamassee Elementary School. Because the building is owned by the DAR, many Daughters are under the impression that the school is run by the DAR, which is not true. The principal and most of the teachers are hired by the county and paid by the county and the state. (Because the school serves a community population that is considered low-income according to federal standards, it receives federal assistance under Title I of the Elementary and Secondary School Act. In 1973 that aid came to $11,491. In addition, some of the children receive free lunches under the Department of Agriculture school lunch program. All day students, as well as all boarding students who attend Tamassee Elementary School, eat their lunch in the Tamassee dining hall.)

The teachers follow a basic public-school curriculum using textbooks approved by the county. However, Tamassee Elementary School is the only school in the county with full-time music instruction and with teachers for arts and crafts and home arts. The DAR empowered principal Willard Johnson to hire three teachers for those subjects and is paying their salaries as well as buying supplies. The arts and crafts teacher receives his salary from the DAR juniors, who recently established an arts and crafts center at the school which they also equip. The Daughters also buy books for the library—three-thousand dollars worth in one recent year. Besides enriching the curriculum, the DAR pays the water and heating bill if it goes over a thousand dollars. Responsibility for building maintenance lies in some vague realm between the county and the DAR, but the Daughters have renovated the rest rooms a time or two.

The Kate Duncan Smith story is in some ways very different

from the Tamassee story. To begin with, no children board at
KDS. It was opened by the DAR in 1924 to provide an education
for the children in the immediate vicinity, and it exists today for
the same reason. Children on Gunter Mountain go to KDS for
both elementary and high school. Like the Tamassee Elementary School, KDS is a physical plant owned by the DAR in which
the public school district operates a public school. The teachers
are hired by the county; except for enrichments, the curriculum
and textbooks are those utilized by the county. But the relationship between KDS and the community it serves is a special
relationship.

The school has apparently been a catalyst on Gunter Mountain. Expansive claims are made for what it has accomplished.
"This community is a success story to the DAR," says KDS
executive secretary John Tyson. "The DAR's health program
has revolutionized this mountain. True, it took industry in
Huntsville. But the preparation—that's the DAR's work."

Tyson is a DAR employee. People who aren't have said similar
things. A writer for *The Chattanooga Times* wrote in the 1950's
that the DAR was changing the face of the mountain by changing the minds of the people. When the school celebrated its
twenty-ninth anniversary in 1953, two lifelong mountain residents wrote the DAR, "We want to express our appreciation to
you for giving us the fine school, and all the other things you
have done for Gunter's Mountain and the surrounding communities. You can never realize just how much the school has
done for these people."

There have been no studies done to determine just what effect
KDS has had on Gunter Mountain. That the mountain has
changed is not a subject for debate. When John Tyson first went
there as principal of the school in 1945, there were two telephones on the entire mountain, an area of about a hundred
square miles. The town of Grant, the largest on the mountain
and now a bustling community of nearly four hundred souls,
had been incorporated for only a couple of years. One of its first
laws was that every house must have a sanitary pit toilet. There
was no paved road until after World War II. Before that, anyone
who drove on the mountain was likely to need to be pulled out of
a mudhole by a tractor. Fortunately there were a few tractors
around, because most people on the mountain made a living by
farming.

The mountain as John Tyson found it had advanced considerably beyond what it was when the DAR found it. In 1919 the Alabama DAR decided to build a DAR school in honor of state regent Kate Duncan Smith. The Daughters spent some time trying to choose a suitable site. They investigated twenty-seven communities, and finally chose Gunter Mountain for several good reasons.

First, it was isolated. Cheap land had drawn settlers to the mountain, but the land was cheap because it sloped steeply, and water was a serious problem, as it is to this day. To get to Guntersville, the county seat, a distance of thirteen miles, a resident of the mountain had to cross the Tennessee River by ferry and then spend a full day on a wagon. There was a school or two, but they were one-room affairs that operated only a few months of the year. There were residents with little regard for the law. There was no doctor on the mountain. Malnutrition, rickets, and TB were commonplace. There was a high infant-mortality rate. There was widespread ignorance and superstition about good health practices. No one had electricity and didn't until the late 1930's.

The Daughters were impressed with the people's interest in having a school. When DAR members came to investigate the site, they were met by a man on a horse carrying the American flag, by adults singing songs of welcome, and by children strewing flowers. The Daughters received promises of land and assistance. To make matters even better, the people on the mountain were almost all descendants of Revolutionary soldiers. (Today Marshall County is ninety-seven percent white. There are no blacks on Gunter Mountain.) Finally, the site was beautiful. At an elevation of 1,200 feet it looks out over a lovely range of green hills called Kennamer's Cove.

On February 6, 1924, KDS opened in a four-room building of rock that the residents of the mountain had built. It had two teachers and fewer than a hundred students. It replaced a one-room wooden school with a tin roof appropriately called Old Tintop. In 1938 the Daughters established a health center. The nurse they employed had responsibilities that were much more far-reaching than taking care of children in school. She served the people on the mountain as a sort of itinerant health expert and midwife, paying visits to homes, advising mothers how to best care for their babies, suggesting better ways to nourish their children, helping them develop proper health habits. She also had health clubs at her house. The nurse who works at KDS today still visits the families of poorer students.

Today Gunter Mountain looks like a rather prosperous little community. There are tumbledown houses, but there are also neat frame or brick veneer homes like those that can be found in any suburb. Roads are paved. A majority of houses have telephones, and all newer houses have inside plumbing. Women do their shopping in shopping centers where they can also pick up their copies of the weekly newspaper, the *Tri-County Shopper*. Most people on the mountain now earn their living in something other than agriculture. Many of the men commute from the mountain to nearby communities or even Huntsville. They hold jobs with such companies as Arrow Shirt, Goodyear, H. D. Lee Slacks, and Monsanto Chemical, or they may be employed at the Redstone Arsenal or by the Tennessee Valley Authority. While the man of the house is at the office, the women and children may be raising chickens. Unable to mechanize after the war because their farms were so small, farmers turned their buildings into broiler houses, so now many families have income from two sources. Stills have not become obsolete on Gunter Mountain, and the oldtime sins of drinking and bootlegging—white lightning or wildcat whiskey—have hung on, but unfortunately the mountain now has modern crimes, too. There are burglaries, for example. The KDS vault was blown one night, leaving the school a little poorer.

There is at long last a doctor. He graduated from KDS, went to medical school, and came back to Grant. The people were so happy to have him that they helped him build his house. They are not wealthy even now—KDS has the highest percentage of children on the federal school lunch program of any school in Marshall County—but they're lots better off than they were.

KDS itself has changed a great deal in fifty years. The campus has more than doubled in size and now spreads out over 240 acres. Even though the students live at home, KDS has even more buildings than Tamassee, thirty-four of them. Twenty are homes for KDS faculty. There is a log cabin that was the first library and is now used as DAR headquarters and Tyson's office. There is a water tower of native stone in which the Pennsylvania Daughters are installing a carillon. The newest structure is the low-slung modern-looking Seimes-Thomas Classroom Building. Of course KDS has a rummage, too, which nets the school about $15,000 a year.

Because about half of the graduates settle on the mountain

and do not go on to college, KDS emphasizes home economics and business and industrial training. Among the buildings there is a home-economics practice house where the students live for a few weeks at a time and a vocational shop that is one of the best-equipped in the state. The buildings, grounds, and equipment are valued today at three million dollars. KDS doesn't have Tamassee's trees, but eyes that gaze over the hills in Kennamer's Cove don't care. It is an impressive campus for an elementary school and a high school serving not quite 900 children between them. DAR contributions to KDS for the year ending April 1973, came to $78,000. (Part of that money went to pay off the new classroom building.)

Brooks Barfield, the mayor of Grant, calls KDS the nucleus from which the town as it is today developed. "Grant is now the bedroom community for Guntersville, Scottsboro, and other places," Barfield says. "Without the school as a spearhead, Grant would never have been more than a little community. I can't comment on the health program, because that was more in the old days, and I've only been here seven years. But KDS helped unite the people of the community and it has brought people into the community. It is noted for being well-run and progressive, with a disciplined student body. The teachers live in houses owned by the DAR. They only have to pay fifteen or twenty dollars a month for rent. Because we have more to offer, we get better teachers than other public schools, and the school is really a drawing card. Several families a year move here from Huntsville, people in the twenty to forty thousand dollar bracket, and they wouldn't come here if it weren't for the school. I was talking to people from a very large concern the other day. They're thinking of bringing a factory in here. Again, this will draw people in the higher income brackets. Schools here are one of their prime concerns. The people from the firm seemed very impressed with what I told them about KDS. I think they're going to come in here."

John Tyson is a tall man with a soft Alabama voice and a courtly manner. He has been at KDS on and off for a total of twenty years. He resigned as principal after six years to become executive secretary. After eight years in that job he left KDS and spent eight years as president of Snead Junior College in Boaz, Alabama. In 1967 he came back as executive secretary. A principal hired by Marshall County runs the school. Tyson's job is fund-raising and public relations. He is not an ordinary public-relations type. He seems to consider it within his bailiwick to correct the people who employ him if he feels they are carrying false impressions. He does this with the utmost courtesy, drawing himself up very tall so as to discourage argument but speaking so gently that no one could possibly accuse him of delivering a reprimand. For example, when Chick Anderson was visiting KDS once, Tyson began talking about the possibility of black families moving onto Gunter Mountain and black children coming to KDS. Tyson said he didn't think black students would pose any problems there, not for the DAR and not for the other children. Chick suggested that some local people would resent it. "Mrs. Anderson," said Tyson, in his courtly way, "I know some blacks I would rather eat with and work with than some whites." Chick said she thought that Negroes didn't want to come to white schools anyway. "Mrs. Anderson," said Tyson, looking down at her at very close range, "They want the right to come if they want to."

Because of Tyson's candor, his opinions carry a little more weight than those of an employee would otherwise. John Tyson says that things government and other institutions are doing today were pioneered by the DAR, such as work-study programs and the health program. "In recent years a number of schools have added nurses," he says. "The DAR has had a nurse here almost as long as it has had a history teacher. It has what I think may be the only high-school practice house in the country for home-economics students. Almost since the early Thirties the DAR has provided money for student 'work-ships.' All our graduates who want college and are college material and who need financial assistance may receive assistance from the money sent in by the DAR as college scholarships. Some of the nicer homes on the mountain belong to the KDS graduates."

Tyson says, "The DAR comes and says, 'These don't look like underprivileged children.' I say, 'They're wearing your clothes.' If a child doesn't have a coat, he gets one out of the rummage room. Many chapters send gifts at Christmas. The DAR pays me, Miss Kennamer—she's a secretary-typist—Mrs. Troup—she's a bookkeeper-secretary—three maintenance people, two full-time people in the old clothing store, and a full-time maid for the girls' rest-rooms and the chapel and the guest house. They also pay half the principal's salary and supplement the salaries of two or three teachers. The home-economics teacher is supplemented. She lives in the practice cottage, and that can be quite confining. The agriculture teacher is supplemented. [The teachers' cottages and apartments rent for $12.50 and $15.00 per month. This low rent is considered a supplement to their salary by the DAR Board of Trustees, and the low rent has helped secure and maintain a strong faculty.] The juniors pay for the nurse. Besides the buildings the DAR provides equipment and supplies—desks, audio-visual, books, mimeograph paper, crayons for poorer children, and a mid-morning lunch for the little-bitty people.

"The local people have been marvelous through all this. They did a tremendous amount of work on the athletic field, which used to be two hills and a valley. We have a number of men on the mountain who are heavy-machine operators. They would come in the evenings and on weekends and do thousands of dollars worth of work. That's a good example of how the local people have contributed."

Tyson says that most of the people on Gunter Mountain today are KDS graduates. He feels that they have been able to take advantage of the jobs that have become available since World War II because they have been healthy enough to do so and because they have the educational background to do so. Tyson believes that much of the credit goes to the Daughters of the American Revolution.

As far as John Tyson and Lincoln Jones know there has never been a black child at either Kate Duncan Smith or Tamassee DAR Schools. In the case of KDS, the explanation is very simple. Since there are no blacks on Gunter Mountain, and since the mountain is in essence a school district, there are no black children around to go to KDS.

The Daughters were apparently aware of the racial situation when they chose Gunter Mountain as the site for their school. In a large booklet called "The Kate Duncan Smith DAR School Story," published in 1962, the following passage appears:

"Here was a thickly settled mountain region, almost completely shut off from the rest of the world, that was inhabited by a pure strain of English people, descendants of soldiers of the American Revolution who had made their way southward through the Appalachians, generation after generation, until they had stopped in the foothills of the Cumberland Mountains. Here, isolated from the world, the Whitakers, Norrises, Coopers, Garretts, and Yorks (some directly related to Sgt. Alvin York) and many other families remained pure-bred, fair-skinned, with dark blond hair, a proud, independent people. There was not a single Negro or person of foreign descent on Gunter Mountain.

"However, the people were existing under the most primitive conditions . . ." and so on and so on.

If race was also a factor in the selection of the site for Tamassee, that is not mentioned in recent DAR schools materials. A 1969 booklet marking Tamassee's half century does point out that patriots who returned from the Revolutionary War to find their crops damaged and homes burned often decided to start west, and that a number of those who were delayed by illness or broken-down wagons settled in the upper Carolinas. Like KDS brochures, Tamassee brochures note the remoteness of the area at the time the schools were built. It is Jones's impression that while there are some descendants of the Revolutionary period in the area, the South Carolina Daughters' main concern was to put a school where there hadn't been one before. Jones says there aren't many "colored" people in the county today. There was once a black high school, but it was turned into a junior high. Its students were transferred into several of the other five high schools in Oconee County, primarily Seneca. There are no black students at Tamassee-Salem High School. "Of course if a child moves into the community he'll have to come here," Jones points out.

Tamassee has obligated itself to accept a black boarder if a child applies who is otherwise eligible. Like any other school receiving funds for the federal school lunch program, Tamassee may not discriminate on the basis of race, color, or national origin. Eleanor Spicer signed an agreement to that effect shortly after she took office. Jones feels if a black child were "qualified," by which he means worthy in character and record, and if the child showed himself to be serious about getting an education, the children of Tamassee "would very likely accept him without any reservation whatever."

Houseparent and cook Linda Chastain is somewhat less sanguine. She anticipates that there would be problems, caused not by the children but by the parents.

"The kids say 'nigger' without even thinking," Mrs. Chastain says. "That's all they ever say, because that's what their parents taught them."

Mr. Jones has told Mrs. Chastain and Mrs. Owen that he might have to get "colored" help in the kitchen. Mrs. Chastain and Mrs. Owen say they'd welcome it.

But, Linda says, stirring a pot of stew, "I'll tell you one thing. I'd hate to be the first black child here."

One of the special features of Continental Congress each year is the talks given by KDS and Tamassee students, usually seniors with good school citizenship records and an ability to speak in public. They are brought to Washington for that purpose by Mr. Tyson and Mr. Jones, and they see a little of the city when they aren't practicing what they are going to say to their benefactors. Congress delegates are often tempted to take an afternoon off to see the cherry blossoms or to browse in the shops on Connecticut Avenue. The afternoon they choose is usually not the one on which the children are scheduled to speak. That is the one time in the year given to the Daughters of the American Revolution to see the fruits of their efforts.

The children don't disappoint them. They stand at the podium looking like the kind of child any Daughter would be pleased to have as a member of her own family. They are scrubbed, dressed up, neatly groomed. The boys' hair is not too long. The girls aren't wearing too much makeup. The youngsters look sincere—not cynical, not sly, not wise, not calculating, only alert and open and scared. Speaking to one or two thousand people from the stage of a huge auditorium is an experience most of them have not had before, though they might have addressed fellow students or spoken at DAR chapter meetings. But though their voices occasionally skid, they handle the challenge with amazing assurance.

The Daughters love to hear what the children have to say. Mark Williams has graduated from Tamassee now, but the year he spoke at Congress he had the Daughters in the palm of his hand. Mark probably could have read from a Wheaties box and gotten applause. He is a basketball player, tall, with curly brown hair, and very handsome. He started right out by thanking the Daughters "for providing me a chance to grow in the understanding of what it means to be an American." He said he was convinced "that the democratic way of life taught at Tamassee is vital if true American life is to survive in America."

Mark went on to mention the beauty of the environment, the work he had learned to do, the social activities he enjoyed, the

attention Tamassee gave to spiritual needs, the recent improvements that had been made on campus, the schedule. He said,
"Tamassee DAR School stresses good citizenship and love of
country. We love the flag of the United States of America and we
practice patriotism in our daily living. We develop an understanding of the necessity of our country's law and order, and
respect of authority is of paramount importance in a teen-ager's
life."

At the end of his talk Mark Williams said he hoped to enter
college and become an architect or a lawyer. (Individual Daughters or chapters often give scholarship aid to Tamassee and KDS
students going on to college. About half of the KDS students go
on, and about a quarter of the Tamassee students.) "I have felt
by your example, Daughters of the American Revolution, that
real success comes from serving others and helping others. It is
my sincere hope that I can really help humanity. Tamassee has
truly been a Place of the Sunlight of God."

The Daughters have only to look at and listen to a boy like
Mark Williams to believe, as they frequently claim, that Tamassee and KDS are turning out "patriots" and fine, contributing
citizens. This to them is the reason the schools exist. According
to the most recent DAR Schools pamphlet, "The Society's educational programs offer students the opportunity to work, study,
and play together but, more important, to practice patriotism,
understand law and order, respect authority, love their Country
and its Flag, and thus become better citizens." The pamphlet
goes on to say, "The records achieved by students from DAR
Schools and those aided by DAR in the Approved Schools prove
beyond a doubt that DAR has invested wisely in youth."

The records may well prove just exactly that, but the fact is
that the Daughters don't really know what happens to the children once they leave Tamassee and KDS. Neither the DAR itself
nor anyone connected with either school has ever done a
follow-up study of any kind on even the graduates, much less the
children who attended without graduating. Of course some of
the Daughters may hear news of the more illustrious alumni,
such as the young man from KDS who went on to dental school
and is now the Mayor of Warrior, Alabama, as well as the dentist
there. The Daughters who go to KDS for Dedication Day and
partake of the legendary basket lunch prepared by the women of
Gunter Mountain must certainly hear from those women that
the KDS graduates who have settled on the mountain are doing

fine things, as undoubtedly many of them are. Tyson and Jones often know what such-and-such a student is doing in a nearby town and sometimes get letters from former students who have moved away. All this information is interesting. Much of it is pleasing to the DAR. But it is not proof of patriotism, nor does it begin to substantiate the blanket claims about the records of alumni.

The Daughters seem to believe that a patriot is an inevitable product of a patriotic education, and patriotic education, they feel, is the specialty of the house at KDS and Tamassee. This may be truer in theory than in fact. On one hand, John Tyson says that KDS has more to offer "patriotically" than any other school he has been in. "A number of things taken for granted in public school are emphasized here," he says. "They're required to learn the pledge of allegiance to the flag. A great deal of emphasis is placed on the history of the United States. There is an American flag in every schoolroom. You ordinarily find one in a school, or else a little one in the corner. During Armed Forces Week we would have an assembly. Now many schools have it, but that is a part of our overall program here where it's more emphasized. Some kids say the pledge of allegiance every day. We don't prescribe, but the teachers pretty well know what the DAR expects."

Students perceive efforts to inculcate patriotism slightly differently. Andy Lee, who served KDS as student-body president during the 1972/73 school year, and who won the DAR history contest in March, 1972, with an essay on U.S. involvement in Vietnam, writes:

"Most students realize that the goal of the DAR, in regard to us, is twofold—educational and patriotic. Patriotism, however, is not overly emphasized. Students are taught the basic ideals of patriotism in the lower grades, but in high school the individual forms his own opinion.

"I believe the history classes at KDS are comparable to those in other schools. [Lee attended several other schools before ending up at KDS.] Teachers are under no special pressure to emphasize patriotism, and students are free to determine for themselves how they feel regarding American involvement in the world. Discussions are often held on current events. We as students feel that it is up to us as individuals to stay enlightened on what is going on in the world around us."

In another letter Lee says, "An example of how a student's

views and opinions change is the Vietnam War. KDS students
are patriotic, respect the flag, love their country and, much like
the majority of the South, are conservative. We had a tendency
to support the war longer than most people in other areas of the
country. In retrospect, it is felt that America made a mistake in
entering the war. We are glad we were able to withdraw from
Vietnam with honor and get our POW's back. I hope this example shows how our views can change as we grow older."

If Andy Lee is any indication, what KDS students seem to be
getting in the way of patriotic education is a solid, thoughtful
public-school grounding in American principles, served up
without preachments and generally without efforts to either
interfere with or forcibly channel the students' own inclinations
or ideas.

At Tamassee Elementary School, principal Willard Johnson
also believes that the children in DAR schools get a better patriotic grounding than children in public schools with curricula
unadorned by DAR enrichments.

"The DAR presence is very much felt here, and it is because I
want it to be," Johnson says. "I may be the dominant factor. I feel
a dedication to the DAR and what they've done here, and I don't
let it die. Some of these things may be a little ritualistic, but you
can't get enough pledges to the flag and that sort of thing. We try
the best we can to have things we think are worthwhile
—respecting flag and country, the recognition of a Supreme
Being."

In terms of what goes on in the classroom, the DAR schools
exclusive of DAR enrichments seem to have all the potential
virtues and weaknesses of all other public schools. There are
good teachers and bad. In the 1972/73 school year it was possible
to sit in a classroom at Tamassee in the midst of near-total chaos
while an inexperienced teacher went around the room from one
small group to another as the youngsters stuck each other with
compasses, called to each other and to the teacher, sang, giggled,
made kissing noises, mocked the teacher's voice when she spoke,
and all in all were scarcely able to hear the teacher when she
hollered at them to put their desks back in order. She handled
the situation by ignoring most of it, hitting one child on the head
with a stack of papers, and telling another not to get smart. "I'll
get smart when I want to, fats," the boy replied.

It was also possible on the same day to sit in the first-grade class
of Anne Huey and be totally charmed by everything that went
on. Mrs. Huey was in complete and gentle command of every

child and of herself. She showed a movie called "Paddy Bear Learns About Christmas" and then had a little discussion with the children.

"Do you know why we celebrate Christmas?" she asked. "Theresa?"

"Because it's fun!" said Theresa happily.

Another child said, "Because the baby Jesus was born on Christmas."

Mrs. Huey nodded. "That's exactly right. The baby Jesus was born on December 25. We have a child in this room who was born on Christmas day."

A little girl raised her hand.

"No, not you," Mrs. Huey said smiling. "Your birthday's at Halloween."

Then Mrs. Huey, who was wearing a blue pantsuit and a prisoner-of-war bracelet, had the children make capital A's and lower case a's. After they finished, she let them take a rest. "Are you tired?" she asked. "Just be limp." The children seemed very experienced at being limp. When Mrs. Huey asked them to get their library books out, they stopped being limp almost immediately. One by one the children went to the front of the room, held up their books, showed their favorite pages, and explained why they liked them. One small boy said he liked a picture "because it has a pretty cow on it." Mrs. Huey looked delighted. "I knew you were goin' to say that!" she said. She reminded the class that this boy had some cows at home. "And he milks them every morning, remember him tellin' us about them?"

Comparing these two classrooms, an outsider can only conclude that a child in this public school has at least as good an opportunity for a solid, basic education as a child in any other. A child at Tamassee Elementary School, like a child at KDS, also has the extras. No one knows exactly what those extras do or don't add to education, but they are there, and the potential is there. A child at Tamassee Elementary School certainly has a better chance to learn arts and crafts than he would anywhere else in the county, because arts and crafts are not taught anywhere else in the county. But as far as patriotism is concerned, the various elements at work at Tamassee seem to add up to little more than the kind of patriotic education a child would receive if he went to any public school in the county, or, for that matter, the country.

Much of what the DAR would like the children at Tamassee

Elementary School to learn is available to them in the person of Willard Johnson. If the DAR took in honorary members, Willard Johnson would undoubtedly be one. His enthusiasm for DAR schooling rises strongly and directly out of his own experience. Johnson is a product of Tamassee. He grew up during the Depression in a family of fourteen children and has had "the unique experience of knowing what it's like to be hungry." ("The kids here know, but not to the extent they did then," Johnson says.) He didn't start school till he was ten and then had to walk three miles on a mountain trail to get there. Finally a school superintendent got three of the children into Tamassee as boarding students.

Johnson says now that if it hadn't been for Tamassee he would never have gotten an education. He would not have been forced to walk those six miles every day, and he wouldn't have walked them. Johnson managed to get himself expelled from Tamassee twice before he was through. "I took off in one of the school vehicles," he laughs. "It was with the owner's permission but not with the permission of the school!" He left to work in a Navy yard during the war. But he returned to Tamassee and graduated in 1947. Then he married, worked in a Detroit auto plant for seven years, went to college, got a master's degree, taught biology and social studies at Tamassee, and became principal of the elementary school in 1961. He is a balding man with a casual manner and a penchant for sport shirts who is as likely to be seen on a ladder replacing a bulb or burrowing into an ailing bus with a tool in each hand as he is to be sitting at his desk in a cluttered, dusty office. ("The janitor doesn't like dirt and doesn't see it," Johnson dryly explains.)

Johnson runs his school with care and sense. If the janitor puts his head into the office and announces that a child is outside singing a song of his own composition, Johnson is the kind of man who will drop what he's doing and go listen. When he felt that some children needed a certain kind of discipline, Johnson sent a note to all the parents notifying them that he intended to spank if he considered it useful. No one complained. "I don't know of any parent in the community that objects when we feel it's justified," he says. "It's the answer for some. It's not the answer for others. The teachers can spank, but in my office." Johnson says a third of the children in school would not hesitate to take money if it was lying around. He tries to impress upon the children that stealing is wrong, but he also cautions the teachers not to invite theft.

Willard Johnson, of course, is not a DAR enrichment. He is a county employee. But he went to Tamassee. Somewhere, out of a background that almost actively discouraged it, he got the notion that he should finish not only high school but college. However good a mechanic Johnson might be, the children of Tamassee Elementary School need him much more than Detroit does. It is almost certain that they never would have gotten him if he hadn't gone to Tamassee as a student—if, in other words, it hadn't been for the DAR.

If all or even many of the graduates of their schools are like Willard Johnson, the Daughters could be making even greater claims than they now do. In saying that their schools turn out contributing citizens with special feelings for America, the DAR may well have a point it can prove. But the Daughters won't be convincing till they do prove it.

Johnson himself says, "We don't know enough about our graduates. I'm president of the alumni association, and there are many that have a good deal of success in one way or another. I don't know whether it's in making moonshine or what."

When the first Tamassee supper bell rings at 5:30, the children who live on campus appear from everywhere and assemble outside the dining hall to wait for Mr. and Mrs. Jones. In their midst, a stranger sticks out like Tamassee Knob. The children don't let the stranger stand alone. Shyly but without hesitating, eight or ten little ones closely surround the foreign body as layers of pearl envelop a grain of sand in an oyster. They smile. They offer their names. The children would like to know what the visitor is doing at Tamassee. In exchange, if the visitor is un-schooled in cat's cradle or any of the other wonders that can be wrought with a circle of string, the children will reveal the secrets. If the visitor doesn't walk into the dining hall with both hands held firmly by children, it's the visitor's fault.

So many people come to see the children of Tamassee that after a while, Jones says, "there are no strangers." Most of the people are members of the DAR. The Daughters love to visit the schools. Any day of the year, a car could turn off Scenic Highway 11 bringing one or two or four women to Tamassee for their first or second or fourth look around campus. Tamassee board members—twenty-five of them—are at the school three times a year for a day or two at a time. Sometimes a busload will come in, and Founders' Day in October draws Daughters from all over the country.

The children have somewhat mixed feelings about the Daughters' visits. Some of them, more often than not the younger ones, have what they call a "DAR lady," a Daughter with whom they correspond and who may send them birthday and Christmas presents. These children eagerly look forward to seeing their DAR ladies.

For the older students, who are beginning to assess the situations in which they find themselves, encounters with Daughters may not be quite so uncomplicated. Some of these children look at the Daughters, and then at themselves, and they find themselves wanting, or feel that perhaps the Daughters do. Sitting one evening in the Texas guest cottage, three of the older girls tried to explain this feeling. They spoke sincerely, respectfully, not in the least petulantly. They weren't griping.

"Most of us here say the DAR have money, and this scares us because we don't," said blonde, bespectacled senior Pam Hamby, who was DAR Good Citizen at Tamassee-Salem. "The DAR, they *must* have money—they're puttin' us up, you know. And we feel like, oh, you know, the DAR are comin', we better move out of our beds, you know, be real good on the hall because we're gonna have a DAR stayin' up here. And we feel like they're so rich, and they wear beautiful clothes, and they're so proper. . . ."

"Mannerly," said junior Pat Meece, whose long dark hair covered her shoulders.

"Mannerly, you know," Pam agreed. "Well, how are we supposed to act, you know? And we just sit there and don't say anything because we think, 'Well, they're better than us.'"

"And like this cottage. Me and another girl, we clean the place. Anyway, after someone leaves, we're right down here, you know, get that bed made up, get clean linen on, get the lavatories clean and everything just right before the next DAR come in so they'll know that we do good. So we clean it each week. We respect the DAR, but. . . ."

"It's just that we do breathe a little sigh when they're gone," said eighth-grader Betty Sue Crane, a girl big for her age, with short, shiny brown hair cut like a boy's and rosy cheeks. "They just pop right in. You don't even know when they're gonna come, and the building is topsy-turvy and everything and the kids' cottage may have a little dust on it, and you really get scared. You say, 'Well, they're gonna say something to me if I don't get this thing cleaned out,' you know."

"And they usually do say something," Pat Meece said. "Like

one time this lavatory down here, it had just a little mud on it, and the next morning she comes into breakfast and reports it. And the first thing you know Mr. Jones. . . ."

Pam broke in apparently wanting to make sure both sides of the story were told. "You do hear quite a bit of comment, you know, some good, some bad," she said smoothly. "We usually hear the best ones. Mr. Jones compliments us."

Peace signs are not permitted at Tamassee, and the girls feel that policy resulted from the comments of DAR members visiting campus.

"Like last year I had a peace sign in my room, and it was toes, two toes, shooting the peace sign!" said Pam. "It was funny, but that's the way it was. And so my housemother walked in and said, 'Okay, girls, I've gotta break the news, you've gotta take the poster down,' and we look at her like 'What?' It's nothing but toes, you know. She says, 'But it's gotta come down. The DAR don't want this.' "

"And the necklaces and things," Betty Sue said. "Peace necklaces. We're not supposed to wear them. Or the patches. Some people do, I mean some people stick 'em under their blouses."

As the children understand it, the DAR doesn't like peace signs because they represent broken crosses. They don't represent broken crosses to the children.

"The peace sign to me," Pam started to say, "I've heard many versions of it. In fact I've done a research paper on this. Most pastors and other spiritual groups say, like, 'You know where that came from; now take it down. You know what that is, and the only reason you want to do it is just to be against us.'

"But that's not the reason *we* do it. The peace sign to us means peace. There's nothing today, really, that doesn't go back to the peace sign. Like all the children, we go around shooting peace signs. Everybody does it now. We don't understand why, really, the DAR's against this."

"And probably fifty percent of the people everywhere that have peace signs don't even know it means a broken cross," Pat said. "It just means peace to them."

The children mentioned another element in their relationship with the DAR that makes them a little uncomfortable. This subject arose when the three girls were talking about national junior chairman Susan Gonchar, who has two teen-age daughters of her own. In their book, Mrs. Gonchar is the greatest, and there are good reasons.

"Last time Mrs. Gonchar was here she came into the kitchen and I was trying to make candy apples," Pat said. "And something went wrong somewhere and they were just gooey, and all that stuff was rubbin' off, and I didn't know what to do. And she came down there and helped me fix 'em, and she ate one of them with us and got it all over her face!"

"She is the friendliest, and I would say she is the best we have met yet," said Pam with feeling.

"She's the best-loved DAR," Pat agreed.

"She's the best," Pam said. "I mean we all love her. I mean I don't know if she would like this to be revealed, but like she didn't want to dress fancy and stuff, you know. She wanted to be with us all the time, and she didn't brag about having so much. Immediately when she came, she said, 'I don't have anything. I'm not a big shot.' She says, 'I've come to Tamassee to be with you all.'"

"Well," Pat said, "she didn't look at us like, you know, 'You better be grateful.'"

"Grateful" is a word that comes up often when Daughters talk about the schools. "It's just wonderful to go down there and see how grateful those children are," women will say. Or they might say, "When you see the gratitude of those children, it just does your heart so good." The ideal time for an outsider to visit the schools, some Daughters believe, is Founders' Day at Tamassee and Dedication Day at KDS, because that's when it is possible to see how much the Daughters of the American Revolution are appreciated.

"Until you meet the people you'll never know how much they love the DAR," one Daughter says of Gunter Mountain residents. "Everybody on the mountain has had something to do with KDS. The women bring this beautiful basket lunch, and DAR members come from all over the U.S. Husbands come. Gifts by DAR members are dedicated. Older boys and girls act as guides. You've never seen such mannerly, lovely, patriotic children, because they're taught that. When the little ones stand up and sing 'DAR We Love You,' it's something, really it is. They do love us, and they should, because we do so much for them. Some of the best blood in the world is up there, and they don't even know it. The salt of the earth live up there. You can tell people up there you're a DAR, and they practically say Allah to you." A Daughter closely connected with Tamassee described Martha Ballew as "one of our most grateful students." Some Daughters seem to have the idea that the gratitude of the children is proof of the schools' success.

The message the children receive about gratitude may not be explicit. But while not all the Daughters put as much stock in it as some obviously do, it's understandable that their feelings would have somehow been conveyed. The children have only to look around them at the plaques on campus to see that something slightly different from ordinary building, ordinary gift-giving, is involved.

"I don't know the psychology of those plaques," Willard Johnson says. "It's not entirely the honor or the thought. A lot of it is that they do want credit, and I guess you can't blame them for that. The high-school kids thought it was kind of foolish, especially when they learned that plaques can cost forty dollars. One lady asked me to give her credit for the home-economics teacher at a board meeting. I did. Why not? To a great extent that's the way Tamassee operates—they will donate for something on which they can have a plaque, while the gutters on the building. . . ."

Some Daughters seem unaware that they inevitably perceive their gifts a little differently than the children perceive them. As the Daughters see it, the DAR has spent years and years building Tamassee. Members have invested large sums of money, some of which has come from women who were sacrificing to give it. They have raised that money not only to house and school children but to honor beloved presidents general or state regents or other favorite Daughters, some of whom are now dead. Their investment is at least as much emotional as it is financial. To some extent Tamassee is a monument to the DAR and a testimony to the women who helped build it.

To the children, on the other hand, Tamassee is a temporary place that isn't truly home. It may be a *nice* temporary place —and many or most of the children are extremely fond of Tamassee—but their primary emotional investment is somewhere else. The Daughters see Tamassee as a wonderful chance for the children. Jones says the children usually look back on it that way. But while they are there, the children have no way of knowing whether Tamassee is going to stand them in good stead or not, and with conditions at home to worry about, their thoughts are likely to be elsewhere anyway. "Everyone, in my opinion, wants to go home, no matter how humble it is," says Jones.

To compound these differing perceptions of the school, the Daughters and the children don't know each other very well. Mark Williams says that when the DAR ladies come to Founders's Day they only take pictures of the children and exchange "a word or two" with them. Johnson says Daughters rarely ask to visit a classroom. Undoubtedly this explains why some Daughters have very unrealistic notions of the children. They talk about them as if they were innocents. Jones says he often hears the term "poor little things." Some Daughters still seem to be under the romantic impression that the students at their schools are little hill children with a bush mentality. As Jones points out, "They're not backward. They're wiser to the ways of the world than some adults."

When the children give speeches to Daughters at Congress or chapter meetings they usually mention their unfortunate backgrounds. Jones says he edits the speeches in advance so they aren't sob stories, but he leaves some things in because, he says, the Daughters are interested in hearing them. Several of the children say that Daughters who visit Tamassee like to hear about their problems at home. In fact, the children are very open about bringing them up to any stranger, apparently assuming it is expected. Eleanor Spicer calls this a "macabre" interest on the Daughters' part. She feels that Jones hasn't always done enough editing on the children's speeches. "At Congress one year they had the kids get up and say they had come from poor homes, had prostitutes as mothers, and so forth," Mrs. Spicer says. "It was really awful. I put a stop to it immediately. Kids shouldn't be made to talk about their backgrounds that way."

But for some Daughters the information apparently serves a purpose. Daughters who feel that the children have nothing can also assume that they will be grateful for just about anything. A Daughter can give a little and feel she is giving a lot.

"Some pictures are hard to change," Jones says. "Some Daughters think of these poor little innocent children at Tamassee and they send a high-school boy a penknife they bought for fifty cents. Well, he wants a penknife for a dollar fifty, to be right up with the rest of them. Or a DAR will say, 'Well, this dress is outmoded. I think I'll send it to some poor little girl at Tamassee.' Well, that poor little girl at Tamassee wants the things she's seen in *Seventeen* Magazine this month."

The children of Tamassee are not staggering under the Daughters' expectations of gratefulness, certainly. But as the youngsters point out themselves, they are working long hours every week to maintain the campus. Jones has undoubtedly told the children, as he has told visitors, that while the school could not operate without the DAR, neither could it operate without the children. For that reason the children have difficulty appearing as appreciative as they think the DAR expects them to appear.

Despite these touchy areas, encounters between Daughters and the children of Tamassee can be the encounters of equals, rewarding to both sides. Sometimes the incident is humorous. A giggling Pat Meece told Pam and Betty Sue about something that happened in the dormitory one evening.

"It was after dinner," she said, "and we were upstairs, and Patsy was ridin' on my shoulders. And we were runnin' down the hall, and we didn't know there was a DAR lady comin'. We thought it was one of the girls in the kitchen. And Patsy yells, 'Hey, you got a cigarette?' And she starts comin' up the steps, and Patsy goes, 'Oh, no!'

"And I ran all the way down the hall with her on my shouldres. And we went and put the lights out in the TV room and lay on the couch. And you know when you look in a room and the couch is facing the back? And she couldn't see us. We were hiding there.

"Then Patsy started laughing real loud, and that lady comes in and looks over the chair, and she said, 'No, I haven't got a cigarette!' "

Some encounters are more serious. Pam told about a speech she had given at a DAR chapter recently. "And I was shakin' and scared to death, me and two other girls," Pam said. "We were sittin' there, all these ladies, I mean, we look at 'em, and they're so superior to us, we think. But then after we got up and looked around at all the people smilin' at us, lettin' us know that they were really interested in us and we weren't just there, you know, to make a show, it was easy to make that speech, to tell them just how it was like here. It was . . . I don't know, I guess that's as close as I've ever been to the DAR."

Then Pat Meece gave an interpretation of what the DAR is all about that the Daughters would have been very happy to hear. It was also an interpretation that indicates the Daughters are conveying several messages to the children of Tamassee, not just that they would like the children to be grateful.

"They've grown in this country so much," Pat said. "And they've seen it develop to just about its best. And it just doesn't go any further. I mean they just don't want it to be common. They want it to be something that everybody will appreciate."

Given the job, a lot of people would not run Tamassee as the DAR is running it. Psychologists or educators or parents who believe that children need unlimited freedom to express themselves and to make their own decisions would be horrified at what is going on down there off Scenic Highway 11.

But those who believe otherwise—who feel that children should be brought up on the straight and narrow, disciplined, taught to make their beds, required to tell the truth and speak nicely to adults, forced to learn what good sportsmanship and church are all about, and made to strive for rewards—would find Tamassee an impressive place indeed.

The Daughters' role in the running of Tamassee has apparently been to hire a business manager they trust and let him handle things as he thinks best. It would be hard to find a more committed child advocate than Lincoln Jones. Quite simply, he is first and last on the child's side. The children know it, and everybody on the staff knows it. If Jones is encouraged to do something he doesn't think is good for the children, he just refuses to do it. He says a Daughter objected to the children going to the canteen, saying if the children had money for the canteen they shouldn't be going to Tamassee. Jones told her that the children needed a canteen, just like her grandchildren did. If a child breaks a window through carelessness, he knows that Mr. Jones will make him work to pay for the replacement; if he breaks it accidentally, he knows Mr. Jones will forgive him. If a houseparent doesn't give a child what Jones calls a "fair deal," Jones talks to the houseparent and sets the matter to rights. If a drunken father storms up on campus demanding to take his child home, that child knows as well as she knows anything that Mr. Jones will not deliver her into her father's hands.

It is possible to take exception to some of Jones's attitudes. The Tamassee policy on peace symbols seems outlandish. Like many DAR members, Jones views the signs with suspicion. He feels that anybody who displays a peace symbol ought to be clear in his or her mind what it means. He says he isn't clear himself what it means, and he doesn't think the children of Tamassee are clear. But some of them, at least, have thought out what it means to them.

Jones does not seem wholly enlightened on the race issue. It is his opinion that the "colored" children in the South are very good athletes. (He says he doesn't know how it is up North.)

Were a black child to come to Tamassee to live, it is difficult to imagine Lincoln Jones preparing his staff, for example, as John Tyson might handle the job. Furthermore, Jones seems to view pregnancy out-of-wedlock somewhat more harshly than many other people do now.

Still and all, Jones is preparing the children of Tamassee to live in a social environment he knows extremely well. Jones grew up in South Carolina. (He used to do some courting at Tamassee.) As Eleanor Spicer says, "He really knows his mountain people." An illegitimate child presents a larger problem in a town the size of Salem than such a child might in New York, and the children of Tamassee have already had enough to worry about. However outmoded his notions of black athleticism, Lincoln Jones does not seem the kind of man who would hold dark skin against a child in trouble. If discipline is strict, his explanation is easy to understand.

"It's a big responsibility to have a hundred and fifty children that belong to someone else," he says simply.

Lincoln Jones's wife is a short woman who has whitish hair and wears glasses. She worries greatly about the children of Tamassee and supports her husband with what seem to be enormous respect and even deference. One evening while Jones was doing something with the lights inside the Tamassee chapel, Mrs. Jones sat in a back pew and told a visitor a story about Gerry White, he with the black-olive eyes, that went something like this:

"A photographer came to school and took some pictures of the children. The children received copies of the pictures which they were to buy or return. Gerry wanted to buy a big picture of himself to send to his mother. Someone mistakenly told him it would cost a dollar. He wrote home and got the dollar from his mother, and then he was told at the office that the picture was a dollar seventy-five.

"Gerry spent the dollar at the canteen. Instead of returning the pictures, he hid them.

"A child reported that to me at the library, and I called Gerry in. I told him I would pay for the pictures. I gave him the money to buy the big one and saw to it that he returned the others. I would have bought the picture anyway, if I knew he didn't have the money to pay for it. It was my gift. But also I was doing it to show him that if you do the honest thing, things work out. Of course some people would say, 'Why doesn't the DAR just buy all their pictures?' But that would make deadbeats out of all of them.'"

This is exactly the kind of lesson many Daughters hope the children who live at Tamassee are learning. It is a lesson informed with a toughness that some people might find distasteful. Some people might feel that children who have been through what the children of Tamassee have been through should be able to rest a little, should not have to confront rigors after surviving pain.

But it's impossible to visit Tamassee and come away thinking these thoughts. Something very good is going on down there. Children who have felt unsafe under the same roof with their own mothers and fathers sleep and eat without fear at Tamassee. High-school students whose parents have abandoned them know that if they have any trouble at Tamassee-Salem, the Tamassee students will stand up for them. Children who lived in shacks and received no Christmas presents now live in houses and know that they will have a package to open every year as long as they stay at Tamassee. Small wonder the children look healthy; they are being nourished. Small wonder they seem relaxed; they are relieved. There may be things going on at Tamassee that experts in one field or another would take issue with, but whatever is going on, the children are thriving on it. Somehow, children who have lived in unspeakable conditions and seen unspeakable things have been transformed into children who look like the treasures of the best families. A child new to Tamassee is conspicuous among them.

"You look at it one way and you say it's a great injustice to take a little child away from the parents," Jones said just before Christmas one year. "You look at it another way, the child is making its pattern. They just can't get a good start at home. They come back after Thanksgiving and hug the housemothers and say, 'We love you.' They love their parents—all children love their parents to a certain extent; they *want* to love them—but when they get to some of these homes that aren't properly heated. . . . One boy said he nearly froze to death at home over the holidays. Here they have good beds. TV.

"I heard of an eighth-grade girl who lived in a poor section of Walhalla. She would hide out in old buildings instead of going to school. She's shy and timid. I learned that the students were making fun of her. She came up here. It took her three weeks. She started working in the library and finished out the year. She requested that she be allowed to go back to school. She is in school. A child doesn't have to finish Tamassee to get some good out of it. She was here four months."

CHAPTER IX

At the Grass Roots: Independence Hall Chapter

On a sunny day in late fall, 1972, I met Dorothy Irwin for lunch at Les Amis, a restaurant in central Philadelphia. Miss Irwin was then regent of the DAR's Independence Hall chapter. When I had called her to ask if I could affiliate with her chapter for a while, Miss Irwin consented willingly. A tall, friendly woman of medium build, Dorothy Irwin appears to be in her fifties but is actually a decade older. Her hair is short, very dark, with only a little gray in it. She wears brown-rimmed glasses and, I was to learn over the next eight months, cheerful but not garish clothes.

Not tempted by steak tartare, Miss Irwin ordered a seafood crepe, which she tried to eat while trying to answer my questions about her and her chapter. Her voice is nasal; she speaks energetically.

"I'm a third-generation DAR," Dorothy Irwin said. "My mother was regent of Dr. Benjamin Rush chapter from 1927 to 1930. My great-aunt was also a Daughter, as was my father's sister. I went into the Dr. Benjamin Rush chapter in 1927. The work of putting the papers through was all done for me. Some years later I noticed that Independence Hall had a junior group, and I said to Mother, 'This is something I want to do.' There were twenty-five juniors at that time, in 1941. Many of us were teachers. I taught sixth grade until I retired in 1969. We met on Saturdays. It was a wonderful nucleus for later years. Our juniors now don't have a particular day.

"I became regent of Independence Hall chapter in 1971. I had been recording secretary of the chapter twice. Besides DAR, I push the hospitality cart at Abington Memorial Hospital every other Friday and also belong to the Daughters of American Colonists, which has more or less the same objectives as DAR. I have papers for Magna Charta and Order of the Crown, but I don't see the point, though I do think I'll join the Welcome Society. That's for people who came on the *Welcome*, William Penn's ship, in 1682. I live alone in an apartment in Abington township right outside Philadelphia.

"As of this month Independence Hall has one hundred ninety-three members. We strive for two hundred each administration, but we have older members and thus deaths. A number of our women are teachers or retired teachers. When Independence Hall was organized in 1898, a good many of its members lived in the city of Philadelphia. Now many of the members come into meetings from the suburbs." These women could join suburban chapters if they wished, Miss Irwin explained, but those with jobs find Saturdays convenient, and many of the older women have worked together for years and enjoy each other's company. I learned later that Independence Hall, like many older city chapters, is considered fairly traditional by Daughters familiar with it, apparently in part because of the stability of its membership.

Except on special occasions, Independence Hall holds its meetings in a small, private dining room on the sixth floor of the Strawbridge & Clothier department store. A hot lunch is served at 12:30. After lunch there is a program and then a business meeting. Daughters on the board—the ten elected officers —meet the morning of the same day in a corner of the Pickwick Dining Room, also on the sixth floor of S & C, where they discuss plans and decisions that are then presented at the regular meeting.

This format is followed closely only five months of the year. The chapter does not meet in June, July, or August. In September the members attend the Constitution Week luncheon at Philadelphia's Union League, and in December they hold a Charter Day luncheon at the Barclay Hotel on Rittenhouse Square. In April there is no meeting because of Continental Congress. In May the chapter has its annual outing.

In addition to these gatherings, Miss Irwin told me, there are two annual chapter events. The first, a recent innovation, is a reception for new citizens right after their naturalization ceremonies. The second is the card party in March, far and away the biggest event of the Independence Hall year. The card party usually nets about a thousand dollars for DAR schools. It requires a great deal of work. The Daughters are so fond of the schools that they do the work happily, according to their regent.

As we sipped second cups of coffee at Les Amis, Miss Irwin said she had just received some bad news about the card party. The Strawbridge & Clothier auditorium where it had always been held was being remodeled. The store would have to cancel.

"It was a terrific shock," the regent said. "Of course the Strawbridge auditorium is free, and you don't have to get your own fashion show. Everything is ready when we get in there. So we have taken the Academy of Music ballroom. We went from something nice—not ridiculous, but nice—to the sublime. We had to latch on to it quickly, but it will cost two hundred dollars. We want to clear one thousand dollars for scholarships."

Later in the day I read the Independence Hall yearbook Miss Irwin had given me at lunch. The yearbook, a small paper-

covered booklet, provides the names and addresses of members
and other information. According to the yearbook, Independence Hall chapter has had twenty-five regents in its lifetime, of
whom sixteen are no longer living. One member was currently
serving on a national DAR committee and three were on state
committees. Dues were $8.00 a year, the yearbook noted. The
application fee for a new member was $25.00, which included
chapter dues and a year's subscription to *DAR Magazine*.

When Dorothy Irwin took over as regent, the yearbook
showed, Independence Hall chapter had 192 members. Three-
quarters of them were married or widowed. Nineteen were
juniors. Six of the women had been members of the DAR for
fifty years or more. Seventy-one of the 192 lived in the city of
Philadelphia, eighty-four lived in Pennsylvania suburbs or small
towns farther out, nine lived over the river in New Jersey, one
lived in Pittsburgh, and five lived in Wilmington, Delaware. In
addition, four members of the chapter were living in New York,
four lived in Florida, and four lived in Massachusetts. There
were two each in Connecticut, California, and Maryland, one
each in Utah, Indiana, and Virginia, and one in Brussels, Bel-
gium. Some Daughters remain loyal to a chapter even though
they move far away.

On Wednesday, November 15, I went to the U.S. Court at
Ninth and Chestnut Streets in Philadelphia. There a delegation
of Daughters from Independence Hall chapter was to watch
naturalization ceremonies before the chapter's reception for
new citizens. The morning was cold with no sun, but inside
Courtroom 6 artificial light glowed in the polished paneling of
the walls, making them appear to beam. The room was full long
before ten o'clock, crammed with people who were about to
become U.S. citizens, accompanied by their friends and families.
Court officials darted around attending to last-minute business.
The new Americans chattered softly to each other. One or two
children sang to themselves. Miss Irwin sat in front looking
perky with her dark hair, a black coat, knee-high boots, and a
cherry red suit visible under the coat. Several other Daughters
joined her.

A large group of black teen-agers came in and took seats in a
kind of choir loft to one side of the judge's bench. They were
students at Germantown High School. A court official spoke to
them a moment, inviting them to the DAR reception. It was

10:05. People were becoming restive. The low noise became a little sharper.

Judge Daniel H. Huyett III came through the door at 10:10. He wished everybody good morning. He took his seat and looked down as a man in black-rimmed glasses announced, "We have sixty-seven petitions today—sixty-four adults and three children—representing thirty-one different nationalities."

"That's an unusually large number of nationalities," Judge Huyett said. "That's very interesting and very gratifying."

More delays. Finally the petitioners for citizenship were asked to raise their right hands. Every hand in the first four rows of the courtroom went up. The oath was read. The men and women said in chorus, "I do." The judge introduced Robert M. Landis, whom he said was "one of Philadelphia's most distinguished attorneys" and a "longtime friend." Landis did not rise. He gave a little talk, telling the new citizens that this was an occasion few would forget.

A new citizen, a short, gray-haired man, stood to speak. He was Reverend Flor Reyna from Cuba. "It is a time of joy, to be part of this nation," Reverend Reyna said. "We appreciate being granted this privilege, not merely because America is the largest or richest country but because it is at the same time the nation in which we have found the most sentiment of justice and the sentiment of mercy."

More than the native Americans who had preceded him, Reyna spoke from his soul. "To me the highest right is liberty —to worship, to make your own life, to find happiness, to find freedom from fear, from want, from everything that limits the image of God in every human being. We thank you for what we have had in the past. We thank you for what we are going to be able to do."

The judge asked the Germantown students to stand. Then he announced the DAR reception and asked the Daughters to stand. There were six, all in hats except Dorothy Irwin.

The second the ceremonies were over, the six women flew through the crowd, hurried a few hundred paces through a light snow to the Benjamin Franklin Hotel, and raced up to the ballroom on the second floor, where several dozen Daughters wearing insignia ribbons and buttons tersely labeled "Committee" waited to greet the guests.

The guests came. Their hands were grasped by Daughters at the door. Other Daughters took their coats and hung them on racks. Still others took the new Americans to a big buffet table where they chose miniature sweet rolls and received coffee or tea. Then the guests sat eight or ten to a table with a DAR hostess. The Germantown kids came, helped themselves to refreshments, and sat together. A Daughter went over and talked to them and to their teacher. Another Daughter took flash pictures of people lining up for coffee.

Standing at the podium, mustering a skill obviously acquired in her years as a teacher, Dorothy Irwin managed to get the attention of the crowd. "Your hostesses today are the members of the Independence Hall chapter, National Society Daughters of the American Revolution," she said. (Did the new citizens have any idea what that was?) "We are so happy to have you here, congratulating you as new citizens, and we extend best wishes to you. You have had a very serious morning. Our idea is to make this very informal. Would the new citizens raise their hands so we can give you a particular welcome?"

They did. Everyone else applauded. Miss Irwin introduced Ruth Lehr, her first vice regent and chairman of the reception.

"We are thrilled that you are here," said Mrs. Lehr, a blondish mother of two teen-agers. "Please feel free to linger as long as you would like, because this is the celebration end of a long, hard road." The guests clapped.

The Daughter with the camera took some pictures of the Germantown students and chatted with them a little. The kids went back for more food. "We had twenty extra people today," Mrs. Lehr told me, "but it's tremendous that youngsters come from these schools."

Mrs. Lehr went around and asked some of the new citizens if they had any plans to celebrate. Benjamin Fpatag, a Filipino teaching at Temple University Dental School, said he might go window-shopping that evening. "And," he said, "I might have a drink!" But the others said no, they had no plans to celebrate. Many of them left the reception early to go back to their jobs. Aside from the courtroom ceremony itself, the DAR party was, for most of the new citizens, the only way of marking their irrevocable decision to renounce their native countries and take on the troubles and privileges of a new one.

I had a roll and a cup of coffee with Mary Bierly. The reception was the only chapter function Mrs. Bierly was to attend all year. "I really take a beating for belonging to this organization," she said. "Of course I don't go around announcing that I'm a member. I'm a peasant, and there's no reason to believe I'll ever be anything different. But people say, 'Oh, the DAR, that's those society snobs.' There are just as many snobs outside. And I've met some very nice women. But Saturday, with the kids going in and out, is a bad day."

Three days later, while Mrs. Bierly and others stayed home, Independence Hall board members met for their November meeting. The Pickwick Room at Strawbridge & Clothier is a large dining room with tall windows looking out on other buildings. The draperies are cream, the carpet and the napkins and placemats are dark red. Members drew up chairs around a table for eight. The board meeting got going a little after 10:30. Dot Irwin had on a bright red dress and gold jewelry. Only she and a couple of other women wore DAR insignia. No one smoked. After a prayer and the reading of the minutes, Olive Cannon, a slim woman with blonde hair and glasses, handed out copies of a three-page printed treasurer's report. Chapter assets amounted to about $2,400. Items in the estimated 1972/73 budget of $3,000 included the following: Chaplain's expense account, $10. Public-relations chairman's expense account, $10. Scholarships, $625. Flag fund, $15. A Gift to the Nation, $200.00.

Corresponding secretary Ruth Styer said, "I'd like to present fifty dollars for Indians that I collected at my office. That will be my last fifty dollars, because of the Indians taking over the building in Washington and the pictures showing the damage. I've been asked not to collect for the Indians anymore. I'm sorry." Dorothy Irwin offered to send an acknowledgement for the money, but Ruth Styer said, "No. It's better to let sleeping dogs lie."

Doris Godfrey, a shy-looking woman with yellow-blonde hair, reported that Independence Hall now had 192 members and two associates. "We have had one death, and we have papers in Washington for Alexandra Lehr and one other," she said. Dorothy Irwin said it was fine to hear that membership was moving forward. Marjorie Lampe, the chaplain, said she had nothing new except Genevieve Sullivan's death. She gave details about survivors and date and place of burial.

Lillian Hemmerly, an older woman with short hair dyed reddish-brown, reported on plans for the Charter Day luncheon in December. The Daughters listened attentively. Lillian Hemmerly had never held a chapter office—she was speaking today merely as luncheon chairman—but she was known as a great behind-the-scenes worker who was willing even to type or file and whose job in town gave the chapter town contacts other members didn't have. Now Miss Hemmerly announced that the luncheon invitations had gone out. She described other arrangements and ended with a lament. "I haven't found anyone to play for the processional and singing of the national anthem," she said. Mrs. Lampe said she had a neighbor who played. Miss Hemmerly said she was hoping to find a member. The matter was not resolved.

The board agreed to submit the name of Ann Hawkes Hutton for the annual Gimbel Award, an event sponsored by Gimbel's in Philadelphia that gets some notice in the city each year. (It recognizes the efforts of women in all fields of service.) Miss Hutton, a Nixon appointee to the American Revolution Bicentennial Commission, is a Pennsylvanian and a member of the DAR. Then the talk turned to the February meeting, which Independence Hall members consider very special. That is the day they entertain the winners of the Good Citizens and Good Citizenship awards and their parents and school sponsors.

Miss Irwin said to her board, "I'm sure you feel the DAR book *In Washington* is good public relations for our Good Citizens and Good Citizenship winners in February. The paperback at a dollar twenty-five is gone. Last year we gave the red linen copy, which is two fifty. I see in the budget that we have allotted for that item twenty-five dollars. The books alone would be twenty-five dollars, and the allowance for pins is five dollars."

Mary Lou Henry, the chapter's national-defense chairman, said she thought pins would run to $15.00, including engraving.

A white-haired woman in glasses spoke up. "The parliamentarian is still a member of this chapter, isn't she?" Dorothy Irwin laughed and said, "Yes!" "Well, then," said Elsie Beatty, "this member thinks this is one of the important things we do all year, and I think we should pay for it." Everyone on the board agreed.

Dorothy Irwin looked at her watch. Then she briefly described the plans the DAR in Pennsylvania had for a Bicentennial project.

"As you know the Bell Tower at Valley Forge was started by the Pennsylvania Society and finished by the National Society," she said. "The project will be opened again as a sort of endowment. It will be a way to honor men in the Armed Forces, beginning with your ancestor, if you wish. You would submit the name and necessary information, and you would pay ten dollars for the name to be published in a book which will be located somewhere at the base of the Bell Tower. The money will be used for maintenance of the Tower."

The meeting adjourned a little before noon. It had gone very smoothly, with little discussion, no delays, and no arguments. The board members seemed to be in accord with their regent on almost everything. She had moved things along at a brisk pace, later described by one Daughter as "no-nonsense." The subjects discussed were important to the chapter but hardly cosmic in scale. Could this possibly be the same DAR that had so many enemies, that had a reputation for a sourpuss preoccupation with bloodlines and communist infiltration? The image and the reality seemed almost laughably at odds. Later meetings would tell.

As lunch was half an hour away, I sat in on a meeting of the card-party committee at a nearby table. It was chaired by Helen Eisenberg, a retired teacher with smooth cheeks and gray hair drawn back in a bun under her black-brimmed hat. Most of the meeting was taken up with the question of what to charge for tickets. Helen Eisenberg opened the discussion by suggesting $8.00. "Any comment?" she asked.

"Ouch!" a member said.

"Well, I've been thinking," said Miss Eisenberg. "I'm retired, and I don't think $8.00 is too bad."

Other comments: "We don't want to price ourselves out of business."

"You've got so many retired people."

"One chapter gets eight hundred dollars in contributions from the members. They have eight hundred dollars to start with. We don't have that kind of money in our chapter."

"We don't have that kind of membership."

The card-party committee agreed upon $8.00 for patronesses' tickets and $7.00 for ordinary tickets. But how much should people be charged who wanted to come to the party without reserving a place at a table? Suggestions were $2.00, $1.75 and $1.50. "I'd rather get two dollars out of my purse than one seventy-five," said one Daughter. "But I was thinking about people who come in from outside," said another. "We don't get that many," said a third. "This is a closed party. We don't want the public."

"All right," Helen Eisenberg said. "I'm hearing two dollars."

As 12:30 approached, members of Independence Hall drifted through the Lamps and Pillows Department into the smaller dining room where the regular meeting would be held. The windowless room is blue, decorated with mirrors, painted screens, and murals of Philadelphia. One of the first in was Martha Stevenson, a former regent who said she had been a school principal for thirty-seven years, until 1960. I talked with Adele Brant, a gray-haired lady in a maroon pillbox, who said she was a fifty-year member of Kappa Gamma sorority.

"I graduated from Boston University with a bachelor of business science and was secretary to the head of the Presser Foundation for thirty-eight years," Miss Brant said. "I retired in 1965 and live at the Plaza, that big white round high-rise in center city. I was never much of a joiner, but I'm the last one of my name in my family."

Anne Fulmer came over, and I asked the women about their ancestors. "My family goes back to 1711 right here in Philadelphia," said Miss Fulmer, a short woman with wavy, very black hair and heavy glasses. "My great-great-grandfather carried a message from George Washington to Lafayette at Brandywine."

Miss Brant said, "Mine was a sergeant, an aide to General Pulaski in the Battle of Germantown. When General Pulaski was wounded and fell off his horse, he delegated my ancestor to carry on in his place."

Miss Fulmer said, "I only proved one ancestor. My father was an SAR. He died when I was a teen-ager. He wanted me to be a DAR, and after I lost my mother, I joined. When I was younger I didn't have the time. I preferred Independence Hall chapter because it was centrally located. I'm city-oriented. I live in the city."

I sat at lunch with Anna McCaskey and Esther Jones, both grandmothers. Mrs. McCaskey was wearing a suit and a knitted hat. She had heard Anne Fulmer and Adele Brant talking ancestors. "My ancestor is honored at Allentown, at the Zion Reformed Church, the Liberty Bell shrine," Mrs. McCaskey said. "Outside the church is a big bronze thing that the DAR put to honor John Jacob Mickley about 1908. He furnished the wagons. They came into Philadelphia under cover of darkness with hay and manure in the wagons, and they got the Liberty Bell out, and the Christ Church bells, and took them through the British lines. The wagon broke down in front of the Moravian Church in Bethlehem. They got another wagon and took the bells on to Allentown. When the Liberty Bell is moved to the new tower, I think there should be a plaque to this man. Betsy Ross or any women at that time could have sewn a flag!"

Lunch was onion and chicken turnovers, broccoli, a salad of pineapple and grated cheese, chocolate sundaes, and coffee or tea. As the main course was being served, an envelope came around, and the Daughters put in it their contributions to the DAR Museum.

Esther Jones, a lady well along in years, seemed quiet. Soon she said that she had lost her husband five months earlier. "I'm a guide at the Bishop White House on Thursdays," she said. "I like to get there a little early. It's so peaceful." Mrs. Jones and Mrs. McCaskey began to talk about their daughters, and Mrs. Jones rested her fork.

"My daughter is a member, but you wouldn't know it," she said impatiently. "She pays her dues and that's it."

"My daughter lives in Wilmington," said Mrs. McCaskey. "She's a member of this chapter, but she's busy. Her children will be going into CAR."

"I'm sick of talking to Edith," Mrs. Jones said. "She said, 'But Mom, I don't have time.' I bite my tongue and take a walk. I had three kids, too, and I didn't have an automatic dishwasher, an automatic clothes washer, and an automatic clothes dryer." Mrs. Jones changed the subject. She reminisced a little about a recent trip to Europe sponsored by the Pennsylvania German Society. "We went to places where the Pennsylvania Dutch came from," she said.

During dessert Miss Irwin introduced guests. Following chapter custom, the program began with a prayer, the pledge of allegiance, the American's Creed, the reading of the president general's message from *DAR Magazine* and the national defense report. Mary Lou Henry held a copy of the *National Defender* in her hand. She read about the Russian wheat deal, mentioning "ecological roulette" and "gunboat diplomacy," and went on to Russian technology. At the end of the national defense report, the Daughters applauded Mary Lou Henry.

Dorothy Irwin introduced Mr. Stephen Uzzell, the speaker of the afternoon. Uzzell had not received much advance notice for his talk. Independence Hall had been planning another program for November, but Mary Lou Henry had suddenly realized that the chapter would need to have a national defense program before the end of the year in order to make the DAR honor roll.

Dorothy Irwin had sought suggestions from Archibald Woods, whose wife belongs to Independence Hall. Woods, a past state president of the SAR, suggested Uzzell, a graduate of the University of Pennsylvania, a member of both SAR and Sons of the Revolution, and husband of the first vice regent of the DAR's Philadelphia chapter. Miss Irwin did not know Uzzell, but she invited him on Woods's recommendation.

Stephen Uzzell wasted no time getting to the point. "Across the years I've spoken to a wide range of organizations," he said. "I've had people say to me afterwards, 'You frightened me to death.' I don't want to scare you, but I want to make you mad so you'll do something."

Uzzell spoke with great authority, and before he had finished three sentences everyone in the room had gone silent. There was no clatter of dessert dishes or coffee spoons. The women were very attentive.

"We are being lied to," Uzzell continued in a loud voice. "Lied to by our ministers in churches which have become nests of treason. Lied to by college teachers imprisoned in the left wing. Lied to by our own government. . . . A remorseless, relentless enemy is closing in for the kill on the United States."

Mr. Uzzell held his listeners spellbound for the better part of an hour. "Do you realize we're supporting Communist guerrilla action in Africa if you give to the Presbyterian or the Episcopal Church?" he asked sharply, looking around at each Daughter in turn. "How would you like a Soviet canal? We need a second canal, but you know what's going on in Washington right now? Secret negotiations to give the canal away, that's what's going on." Mr. Uzzell didn't offer a fragment of proof for anything he said, but he informed the Daughters later that everything in his speech could be documented. He said things like, "There's good reason to believe the missiles were never taken out of Cuba. The pictures in the paper were ash cans covered with tarpaulins, obviously. There has been a conspiracy, you know, to rewrite our history books. The British got into a multi-million-dollar conspiracy in this country to reorient this country for reentry into the British empire. Now let's stop going through rituals and repeating phrases we don't know the meaning of. You can't have a declaration of independence and a declaration of interdependence at the same time.

"The American Indian movement is a new Communist front. The Indians who took over the Bureau of Indian Affairs building in Washington had furniture and rugs soaked with gas, and that's Communist Chinese tactics. We've been asleep a long time, haven't we? The reason this country got where it did was young men knowing how to operate guns. Now they're trying to take guns away. If they register the guns they'll have a central record, and when the Reds take over, they'll get the guns and then begin the Red terror. Both parties are socialist today. They're controlled by the same source. If you want to wake up in a Communist state in ten years, play bridge."

The applause at the end of Mr. Uzzell's rousing speech was, if not rousing, at least solid. The Daughters applauded once during the speech when Uzzell called for an end to deficit spending. They laughed when he referred to "Senator Halfbright from Arkansas," and a few of them said "No" out loud in answer to his rhetorical questions. Some of the things he said seemed to upset some of the Daughters more than a little. Recording secretary Regina Sheehan in particular seemed disturbed. A few times she said "No" to Uzzell's questions in a sad, almost keening way.

Uzzell gave out *Reader's Digest* reprints of an article called, "Must Our Churches Finance Revolution?" Then he answered a few questions. One Daughter asked, "What can we do?" Uzzell told her to be on the offensive, to send Christian—not UNICEF—Christmas cards, and to utilize the prepaid envelopes in unsolicited mail. "Accumulate good literature and send it in those envelopes," he said.

After Uzzell had left, a woman at a nearby table said. "Boy, that was an earful." Anna McCaskey leaned over to me and whispered, "I'd like to tell you that not all of us agree with all the speakers have to say."

It was after 2:30 before the regular meeting opened. Ruth Lehr reported on the party for new citizens. "They are a positively fascinating group of people," she told the other Daughters. "The reception cost seventy-five cents a person. Dot got red, white and blue tablecloths. We also had twenty-one students from Germantown High School as part of a Title I project. [Title I of the 1965 Elementary and Secondary Education Act provides federal funds for enrichment programs at schools serving low-income families.] There were sixty-seven new citizens from thirty-one countries. What they know about our country—I think you'd be very impressed."

American Indians committee chairman Doris Snapp urged members to send their used clothing to the Indian schools.

Speaking on behalf of the DAR's conservation efforts, Dorothy Irwin got the members giggling by asking that each send her a postcard stating how many trees she had planted and how many pounds of seed she had fed the birds.

"What other wildlife did you feed?" Miss Irwin asked, smiling but serious. "Please make this very explicit on your postcards. How many trees, how many pounds of bird seed, how many skunks. . . !" Everyone laughed.

Betty Davy asked for volunteers to work at the veterans' hospital. Esther Jones was asked to give a public-relations report. "I don't exactly have a report," she said, "just the same old cry. What's the use of my sending things to the papers if I don't get any clippings back? There's a couple that do send, but that's all. And I send to eight papers and the state DAR bulletin." Mrs. Jones sat down and said to Anna McCaskey, "Every month I have to get up and cry, and I get a few!"

National defense chairman Mary Lou Henry stood up. "By a show of hands," she said, "do you know the names of your state and national legislators?" Some did. Others said no. Others said they were ashamed to say no.

"Do you contact them on important issues?" Miss Henry asked. About seven hands went up.

Adelaide Rice got up and talked a little about resolutions. "It's hard to find things that are really new after ten years," Mrs. Rice said. She talked mostly about the Pennsylvania state resolution that opposed the current plan of the National Park Service to move the Liberty Bell. The structure of Independence Hall has been weakened by the comings and goings of millions of tourists. Officials wanted to put the Bell in a new tower scheduled for construction near the Hall. Mrs. Rice asked the Daughters to write letters expressing the hope that wherever the Bell is displayed, it will be in a place in keeping with the colonial age.

After a few card-party announcements, the meeting adjourned. It was after 3:30. Some members would spend more than an hour getting back home.

On the way out, I was taken aside by Adele Brant, "I just want to put a flea in your ear," she said. "We don't necessarily agree with the speaker. He was too drastic. There's an old farm saying: 'If you want it to live, don't kick it.' "

On Saturday, December 9, dressed up and feeling in a holiday mood, some ninety members of the Independence Hall chapter and guests, including a few men, met for the Charter Day luncheon at the Barclay Hotel. There was a receiving line. As members went through, Dorothy Irwin, wearing a peach knit dress, a fur hat, and a white orchid, introduced them one by one to Bicentennial Commission member Ann Hawkes Hutton, who was going to speak that afternoon on 1976. Mrs. Hutton had come up from Washington especially for the luncheon. The Daughters were glad to see her. The high spirits and the Barclay's decorations made Christmas seem very close. There were pink cloths, red glasses, and a poinsettia plant on each table set for eight. The long head table was forested in greens.

I sat between Anna McCaskey and SAR Archibald Woods. We ate spinach soup, veal with mushroom sauce, sweet croquettes and green beans. When the tables were cleared, the dining room lights suddenly went out. A moment later the Barclay waiters came dancing in, literally dancing, carrying platters of pink and white ice cream and distributing them while a woman (Mrs. Lampe's neighbor?) played "The Battle Hymn of the Republic" on the piano. "We usually play 'Jingle Bells,' " said one Daughter aloud.

While members and guests were sipping coffee, Dorothy Irwin, looking happy, rose and began the program. She introduced seven past regents of Independence Hall, Brigadier General William Buchanan Gold from the Continental chapter, SAR, regents from four neighboring DAR chapters, and Mrs. Harold Saunders. "Mrs. Saunders received her fifty-year pin last year, and she's been coming to meetings ever since!" Dorothy Irwin said. "Today," the regent continued, "we celebrate the presentation of our charter on Wednesday morning, December 13, 1899, at 11:00 in the Supreme Court Room in Independence Hall." She spoke briefly about that ceremony and held up the framed charter for the guests to see.

A member of Independence Hall chapter, Edith Bailey Tofstad, sang two Christmas songs and "No Man Is an Island." She finished with "A for America," a song written for the Bicentennial by a member of the DAR. DAR leaders hope that Americans outside the DAR will take up "A for America," but it's even harder to sing than "The Star-Spangled Banner." "It makes me proud as a Daughter to be able to sing it for you," said Mrs. Tofstad.

Dorothy Irwin introduced the speaker. "She is chairman of the board of the Washington Crossing Foundation," said Miss

Irwin. "In 1960 she was the first woman to receive the Freedom Leadership Award from Freedoms Foundation. She was appointed by President Nixon in 1969 to the Bicentennial Commission. She is the author of numerous scripts and dramas on the Revolutionary period, and she has a number of honors from the DAR and the SAR."

Mrs. Hutton wore a fur-trimmed red suit and a pearl rope, and she kept her glasses on while she spoke. After giving her listeners several opportunities to laugh, Mrs. Hutton inspired some applause by complimenting President Nixon and Mayor Frank Rizzo for their service to America. Then, updating as necessary, she said essentially what she had told Continental Congress delegates earlier that year.

"At a meeting of the Bicentennial Commission recently, I listened to a severe lecture by a black," Mrs. Hutton said. "There are many blacks on the Commission who are doing a good job. This was an isolated case. He said, 'You don't understand what our problems are. Your people were over here in 1776. Ours were indentured servants.'

"I said, 'My ancestor came here as an indentured servant. That's how many people got here.'" Mrs. Hutton paused. "This was met with silence. No answer. These facts aren't being taught. I'm proud that my ancestor was an indentured servant. We got so excited in this discussion, talking about what you have to do for this group, for that group. Finally a student from West Chester College got up. He said, 'I'm tired of hearing people ask the Commission for money, asking, What can you do for my group? Don't you bring a gift to a birthday party?'"

The important thing about the Bicentennial, said Mrs. Hutton, was not where it was being held but that is was being held. "I think people are tired of being told what is wrong with America," she said. "I think they want to hear what is right with America. This is it, girls, This is almost the last chance. The battle is more subtle than the American Revolution. It's for men's minds."

The Daughters stood and gave Mrs. Hutton a warm ovation. Dorothy Irwin took the mike and said Mrs. Hutton would stay on for a few minutes to autograph copies of her book, Spirit of '76.

The Daughters and guests stood and sang one verse of "Silent Night." The mood in the room was very much like the mood around the fire on the last night at camp.

"May you all have a blessed Christmas, and a peaceful and happy New Year," Dorothy Irwin said.

As Daughters got into their coats and wished each other a merry Christmas, Anna McCaskey said very quietly to me, "I'm apprehensive about the new year. I just had some tests, and I may have to have surgery. I'll find out on Tuesday."

When the holidays were over, I called Helen Jensen, Independence Hall historian. I wanted to find out about plans for American History Month which the Daughters and a few other Americans observe in February.

Mrs. Jensen heads the math department at Philadelphia's Roxborough High School. She explained that the DAR gives American-history awards—bronze medals and certificates—to eighth and ninth-graders with either the best history grades or the best mark in a competitive exam devised by the principal. The awards are mailed to the schools and given to the children at the end of the school year.

The Daughters also sponsor an essay contest, or rather they try to. "With this I've always had difficulty," Mrs. Jensen said. "In public schools the program is often too full to permit essay-writing on the fifth-through-eighth-grade levels. I haven't found any schools in the area willing to take it on. The prize is something very insignificant—twenty-five dollars for the state winner, and for the national winner, not much more than that." The student is supposed to write five hundred words on a particular topic, but I don't know how much emphasis is being put on essays in public schools. It might be unrealistic to expect fifth-graders to write five-hundred-word essays. The essay contest is not aimed at appealing to a young person—not today's young person.

Helen Jensen has been a member of the DAR for only six years. "It was a matter of my having time to do it, my realizing that life had simplified itself," Mrs. Jensen said. "I put about two hours a month into DAR, aside from meetings. I'm not active in many things. I have elderly parents. Life is fairly full right now." She said she enjoys the DAR because meetings offer social contact and interesting speakers.

"You really learn something. A doctor of environmental science spoke two years ago on women's role in science and space. A beautiful woman, and young. She made us proud to be women. Also we had a man [Uzzell] who spoke last fall on national defense. He was very controversial but certainly very interesting. And the woman who spoke at the December luncheon, Mrs. Hutton—she made quite an impression on friends I brought in."

I called on Robert Stover, social-studies chairman at Indian Crest Junior High School, Souderton, Pennsylvania. Indian Crest is one of the schools offering students a history award from Independence Hall chapter. He said he was happy to be able to give it.

"I've always kind of made a big deal about it," he said. "This is one of the few national awards that we're giving. Most are local awards. I think the kids who receive it prize it, and I think the other kids look up to them.

"The good kids like an award that recognizes them in school citizenship or leadership. The others, it's hard to say what they like! Today you wouldn't be part of the 'in' crowd if you said you cherished an award!"

Later in January I called Dorothy Irwin and asked about juniors. So far Sara Knobelauch, Independence Hall's junior chairman, was the only junior I had seen at meetings. Miss Irwin said with concern, "Juniors are a problem for this chapter right now." She explained that most of those in the area were married and had small children, or were away at college, or had moved out of the area.

I asked Miss Irwin what reaction she had heard to Stephen Uzzell's national-defense speech in November. She said the reaction was generally good. She also passed along some kind words about her national-defense chairman.

"We're very proud of Mary Lou Henry," Miss Irwin said. "She gives a marvelous report every month."

When I hung up, I looked to see what I could find out about juniors in the Independence Hall yearbook. The yearbook doesn't show which girls are away at college or which women have children. It does show that eight of Independence Hall's nineteen juniors lived in other states, too far away to be active or even present, and that of the ten juniors in the Philadelphia area, only Sara Knobelauch and two others were single.

The January meeting was held on the twentieth. No lights were on in the S & C dining room. There was a decidedly post-holiday feel about the day. Board members drifted in and continued to drift in until 11:05, half an hour after the meeting started, until thirteen were present. Most wore knit suits or knit dresses.

"We have some very interesting correspondence," Miss Irwin said brightly after the opening formalities. "I thought you might like to see the Gimbel Award brochure which I received at the luncheon. This is one of the fringe benefits of being regent, you know!" The board members smiled, apparently unsaddened that their nominee, Ann Hawkes Hutton, had not won.

"The winner this year was very worthy," Miss Irwin said. "You have all been reading about Judge Lisa Richette. This is interesting, particularly to those who were teachers: She wanted to go to Girls High School, of course, but the counselor said, 'No, Italian girls don't go to high school.' Now imagine what we would have lost if that counselor had gone ahead with his ideas."

Miss Irwin said she was optimistic that Independence Hall would meet DAR honor-roll requirements. She showed the ad the chapter had helped buy in the January issue of the *DAR Magazine*, a line drawing of Independence Hall, the building, surrounded by chapter names. "Isn't this lovely?" she asked. Everyone agreed that it was. Lillian Hemmerly said, "It's in such good taste."

Two letters were read aloud. One was from Eleanor Spicer thanking the regent for her letter about the naturalization party. Miss Irwin seemed very pleased to have the letter. The other was from Ann Hawkes Hutton thanking the chapter for the fifty-dollar honorarium for Washington Crossing Foundation. "And this is her Christmas card, which you might like to see," said Miss Irwin.

The recording secretary read notes from two guests at the Charter Day luncheon, and the regent complimented the luncheon chairman. "No one gives as nice a party as Lillian Hemmerly," Dorothy Irwin said warmly. The board agreed.

Mary Lou Henry raised a question about her national-defense report for February, when the chapter would entertain the winners of the Good Citizen and Good Citizenship awards. "According to the honor-roll requirement," Miss Henry pointed out, "national-defense materials have to come from the national-defense committee mailings. But I used personal material once on what happened to the signers of the Declaration of Independence. It isn't from the *National Defender*, but I would like to have permission to use this material next month." Adele Brant made a motion that permission be granted.

"Well," said Dorothy Irwin, "I can't think that wouldn't be considered national defense. It also says this: that we devote at least five minutes at each meeting, and your reports are always longer. So we have two to three minutes left over, if anyone asks!"

Under new business Miss Irwin announced that the chapter had been asked to submit a nomination for Pennsylvania Distinguished Daughter, a service award made annually by Pennsylvania's governor. "As far as I know the DAR has not been asked to do this before, and other regents have said they haven't been asked," Miss Irwin told her board. She appeared pleased. She asked members to think about a candidate.

Dorothy Irwin then brought up the idea of presenting a DAR Americanism medal to Dr. Ling Tung. (Americanism medals go to naturalized adult citizens of outstanding ability.) A native of China, Dr. Tung is well respected in Philadelphia as conductor of the Philharmonia Orchestra. The board seemed to approve. The regent asked for volunteers to go to Continental Congress, either as delegates or alternates, and the meeting adjourned at 11:50.

Before lunch I spoke briefly with Mary Lou Henry in the small dining room. A teacher and one of the younger members of Independence Hall, Miss Henry is a tall, large-framed woman with brown curly hair and a deliberate way of talking.

"I've been on national defense five years now," she said. "I have to file a state and national report telling what I've done. Last month I asked how many had written to their congressmen. I also have to alert the chapter to make sure we have one meeting a year for national defense and make sure we donate to the Dollars for Defense program. You'll have to ask the treasurer what that money goes to. [It goes to the national-defense committee to help pay for "patriotic materials for schools, churches, libraries, and persons who appeal to the DAR for help," according to a statement by the national chairman. Independence Hall contributes $5.00 a year.]

"And I'm supposed to keep alert to the problems of national defense. For example, I was very interested in seeing if the defense budget is cut, and seeing about our relationships with foreign powers, like the recognition of Red China. Russia is building up; are we keeping up? We all know the Russians have been in Cuba for years, but I wonder how many realize their penetration techniques in other countries. Sometimes I suggest to members that they write to their congressmen on certain issues like Save the Seals or defense spending."

Miss Henry explained how she happened to be national-defense chairman. "When they asked if I'd serve on committees, I said yes and suggested that I was interested in national defense. I had been historian before, working with children. Also some people like to get up and talk! I guess I'm just a school teacher at heart."

While plates of meatball stroganoff and Mexican corn were being served, Miss Irwin gave a birdseed reminder and had Helen Eisenberg give a card-party announcement. Then the regent had everyone sing "Happy Birthday" to Miss Eisenberg. Not many women were present—January is always a small meeting, it seems—and the rendition was less than resounding. I sat and talked with Elsie Beatty, the parliamentarian, and Byrhl Plattenberger, the second vice regent. As the program that afternoon would be on conservation, the talk turned to living things.

Mrs. Beatty said, "I suppose most of us belong to the ASPCA and give money to it and have a membership at the zoo."

Mrs. Plattenberger said, "Feeding the birds is purely an individual matter, but it's encouraged by the National Society. We try to have one program a year on conservation."

Mrs. Beatty said she had been a member of Independence Hall chapter since 1931. "The quality of the membership has stayed pretty much the same," she told me. "I mean it's a working group. When I was regent we took in a woman with a list of ancestors as long as your arm, but she never went to high school, and one member said. 'We shouldn't take in anyone with such a plain background.'" Mrs. Beatty looked disgruntled as she remembered that remark. "I said, 'We shouldn't *not* take her.' She's here today. An excellent worker. I don't know whether such a protest would be made today. Chapters operate differently. Some chapters have dinner dances. It never occurred to us to. So I suppose we're plebeian."

Dessert was apple pie. Over coffee I chatted with chapter schools chairman Joann Kersch, who is Anna McCaskey's daughter. Mrs. McCaskey was not at the meeting. Joann, a Daughter not much over junior age, with dark hair tied back and amazingly rosy cheeks, said her mother would be having surgery with potentially serious results. She also talked a little about the chapter's involvement with the DAR schools.

"We have one child assigned to us in each school—Kate Duncan Smith, Tamassee, and Hillside," Joann said. "The school sends us the child's name but doesn't tell us much beyond that. I wrote and asked if my child could write to the youngsters we help, but the answer was, 'No, the children come from unscrupulous homes. They may get your address and ask for money.'

"We remember the children on their birthdays and at Christmas. We spent twenty-five or thirty dollars on a boy for birthday and Christmas last year. We always buy new things. The money comes from the card-party proceeds. Things have gone up so much that we've spent more this year. We also send used clothing to Tamassee. Tamassee does an evaluation and reports back, and we get credit for DAR honor roll."

Joann lives in Wilmington, an hour's drive from Philadelphia. She has no desire to transfer her membership. "I was a CAR with Independence Hall," she said. "I went to a couple of DAR meetings in Wilmington, but when I heard the treasurer's report—ten thousand dollars for this, ten thousand for that—I almost fell off the chair. They're snobby." However, her two daughters are in CAR in Wilmington. Her two sons, no. "One is in first grade," Joann said. "The one in sixth is shy."

When dessert dishes had been removed and the national defense report read, Mary Lou Henry asked to see the hands of those Daughters who had written to their congressmen recently. Arrah Lee Gaul, a tiny older woman wearing a dark blonde wig and a big black hat with velvet bows, raised her hand.

"Yes, I did," Miss Gaul announced to Miss Henry. "I was brazen enough to write to Senator Hugh Scott and say, 'We want Bibles back in the public schools; what can you do?' I didn't get an answer."

Some of the Daughters were amused. Anne Fulmer said she had written about retired federal employees. (Miss Fulmer is a retired purchasing agent of the Department of Defense.) Ruth Styer said, "I wrote, but it wouldn't interest you. It was on the railroads—our work, our jobs." (Mrs. Styer works for the Reading Railroad.)

For the program, Mr. Richard L. James, executive vice president of the Schuylkill Valley Nature Center, a young, balding man who seemed to think of himself as an entertainer, showed beautiful slides to accompany some fascinating information. "If you breathe regularly in Philadelphia, it's the equivalent of smoking one package of cigarettes a day," he said. (There was a sharp, surprised intake of breath around the room, where no one was smoking.) "Sixty percent of this city is under roads and parking lots—a way to handle cars. Possums no longer hang by their tails after eighteen months. Wrens and bluebirds compete for the same environment. The number of animals is decreasing, but their size in increasing. We will never really over crowd this planet; instead, we will pay prices."

Mr. James got warm applause.

"Is red sumac poisonous?" Adele Brant asked him.

"The only poison sumac is swamp sumac," said Mr. James. "It has little white berries on it, and you'd be up to your knees in water if you were anywhere near it."

After Richard James left Miss Irwin called on Joann Kersch for a schools report. "We haven't seen you in a while, Joann," Miss Irwin said.

Joann stood up, smiling, and said, "With the help of my friend Janet we did some shopping. The boy we had at Hillside is no longer there, and the school suggested Joe Aurelio. We got him a very nice watch for Christmas. At Tamassee we have a new child. Lisa Payne is not there now. We got Tommy Fowler a winter jacket, a pair of boot shoes and a wool hat. Since his birthday was in November, we combined the two. The girl we had at Kate Duncan Smith left, and she never got the coat we sent, but another girl, Joyce Bevel, got it. We found a sale coat, blue slacks. a purple sweater and a belt."

Lillian Hemmerly announced that $200 had been budgeted for the Charter Day luncheon but only $152 had been used. "No one else has such a nice party," Miss Irwin said again, and the Daughters clapped their appreciation for Miss Hemmerly. Elections were held for delegates to Congress.

"If there's anyone here this afternoon who can go to Washington and spend some time, don't hide your light under a bushel!" said Miss Irwin. Silence. Finally a couple of hands went up. In consultation with the parliamentarian, Miss Irwin decided to postpone the election of alternates until the next meeting.

Arrah Lee Gaul announced that she would be giving out books of chances—for complicated tax reasons the DAR calls them "voices"—after the meeting. Miss Gaul is a painter. She had donated one of her works to the chapter for the card party. Members would sell voices on the painting. "It's Tangiers," Miss Gaul explained. "The garden the Sultan used for his harem!"

Dorothy Irwin urged everyone to come to the February meeting. "Remember last February?" she asked. The Daughters laughed. They put on their coats talking about last year's snowstorm on Good Citizens day.

Just before the February meeting I spoke on the phone with retired sixth-grade teacher Elizabeth Fick, a grandmother who is probably smaller than some of her grandchildren. Mrs. Fick has iron-gray hair and wears bright colors. She is in her tenth year as chapter chairman of the DAR Good Citizens program, and when she gets going on the project her words tumble out like apples from an overturned basket.

"We sponsor five high schools," Mrs. Fick began. "The suggested procedure for the Good Citizen award is to have all the senior class vote and then to have the faculty suggest one from the top three. But I almost lost a wonderful school over that. Marple-Newtown said. 'We're too big. That would take a whole day.' I suggested they have a committee of students and faculty, and they agreed."

Mrs. Fick thought this procedure might work well in other large schools. She wrote to the state Good Citizens chairman with her suggestion and then, at the state chairman's urging, to the national chairman. That leader, according to Mrs. Fick, thought the idea was marvelous. But all that correspondence was during the last administration, before Mrs. Spicer. No changes have been made in the Good Citizens selection process.

"A lot of the top brass doesn't know what goes on in the schools," Mrs. Fick told me. "I'm a retired teacher and right here close to the schools. We teachers know how impossible it is to have these big schools vote. And the principal at Marple-Newton said, 'You know, Mrs. Fick, the children don't vote by patriotism. They vote for popularity.' I know the schools differ from our suggested procedures, but I'm not going to quibble over it.

"Marple-Newton has given us a lot of suggestions. We have this luncheon where we have a pin for the girls, and a gift, and then at the end of the year we give them a certificate. A man at Marple-Newton said he didn't like us giving the certificate at the end of the year because he had nothing to give the boys. There's no certificate with Good Citizenship. We decided to have a *chapter* certificate made up in old English, just like the other ones. We may be the only chapter in the whole United States doing that."

(For reasons DAR leaders are unable to explain, the Good Citizenship program is administered by the national-defense committee, and Good Citizens has its own committee. The criteria for selection are roughly the same, but the awards are different. Good Citizens is given only to girls; Good Citizenship used to be given only to boys. To make things less complicated, Independence Hall continues to give Good Citizenship awards only to boys.)

Independence Hall's innovation of certificates for boys pleases Mrs. Fick. "It's only because we had a suggestion from our sponsor and an accepting attitude in our regent," she says proudly. "Some might not have done it. But Martha Stevenson said, 'We don't have to ask permission to do that. We're not trying to get the whole DAR to do it. I don't think you have to ask permission for every little thing. We're not harming anybody, after all.'"

Mrs. Fick took a breath. "Last year we had a black judge as a speaker, Judge Charles Wright. When he went away, he said, 'I had no idea what DAR does.' He was kind of belligerent at first, but he said, 'I have found out many things today that I didn't know.' You see, it's a matter of p.r.

"We pay for the children's luncheons, and their families come at their own expense. One boy from Overbrook just asked me if he could bring seven people. I said to this boy—I think he's black; most from Overbrook are—I said, 'If you're that interested, I see no reason not to have seven people.' He sent me a money order for twenty-one dollars. So we have a whole table with just that family. I think it's wonderful."

I called Mary Lou Henry to find out if the national-defense chairman asked at every meeting how many Daughters had written to their congressmen. Miss Henry said she asked primarily when she had to fill out her report for the state Society.

"The three hands we got at the last meeting was a little low," she said. "Usually there are about a dozen members that do. I don't think they necessarily write about my national-defense reports. Many times it's their own personal things."

Again in answer to my question, Mary Lou Henry said the response to her national-defense reports was usually good. "At the meeting they'll come up to me and say, 'Gee, I wasn't aware of that.' They seem to be very much surprised that the Russians are infiltrating as much as they are."

Miss Henry teaches social studies, a discipline which many Daughters fear amounts to something more like socialist studies. But Mary Lou Henry doesn't necessarily think social-studies teachers are unsympathetic with the American way.

"I'm very much interested in America and American culture and not so much in the world angle," she said. "I know other people whose interests lie another way. They're not necessarily downing America. If you travel a lot, you get interested in other cultures."

Unlike some Daughters, Miss Henry sees no reason to be upset about either the books or the curricula in today's schools. "Someone says, 'My daughter is reading *Grapes of Wrath*, how horrible,' " Miss Henry said. "Now I probably wouldn't give that book to a twelve-year-old, but I don't believe in hiding things, no. They're exposed to it, so why not bring it out in the open? She's going to read it anyway. I have no qualms in talking about pornography, for example. We talk about abortion in connection with the Supreme Court. It was a perfect example, really. I didn't get all shaky, but I know people in and out of the DAR who would think that I shouldn't bring it up."

At the February executive meeting ten women were present. Five of them were in dresses of various blues, one was in red, and one was in pink. (Members of the DAR seem to wear shades of red or blue when they're together.) Three wore fur hats, two wore hats of black fabric, and Mary Lou Henry wore a rhinestone flag pin. Ruth Styer wore a green orchid. Dorothy Irwin commented on it. "It was a valentine," Ruth Styer said. "I got two. An embarrassment of riches."

Ruth Lehr was back, having recovered from a broken nose incurred when she tripped on a drain cover before the January meeting. "How's your nose?" asked Dorothy Irwin. "Ice is wonderful!" Mrs. Lehr replied.

Dorothy Irwin said right off, "They are extremely pleased with the results of Anna McCaskey's operation." She sent a get-well card around the table for the board members to sign. Then she passed around the honor-roll application for the board's information and color photographs of the reception for new citizens for the board's enjoyment.

"We're ready for the card party!" said Lillian Hemmerly. "That will be a shot in the arm, won't it?"

Someone noted that dues hadn't all been paid.

"About those dues," Elsie Beatty put in. "You don't write sassy letters like I do. I just blistered the mails. Got results too." Laughing, Dorothy Irwin asked Mrs. Beatty to bring in a sample of her blistering letter. Ruth Styer said she had sixty-three reservations for that day's luncheon. "We had fifty-eight reservations last year," Mrs. Styer said. "and forty-eight came in spite of the blizzard."

There was a fair amount of talk about delegates and alternates to Congress before that matter was settled. Miss Irwin said she and Adele Brant had found out a little more about Philharmonia conductor Dr. Ling Tung. They thought he would be an excellent candidate for the Americanism award.

The last part of the board meeting was given over to a very serious matter.

"For the last item I want your attention," Miss Irwin said gravely. "I am not going to bring this up at the meeting because nothing has to be done." She read a proposed amendment to the DAR bylaws, passed by the unanimous vote of the DAR national board of management, raising national dues from $3.00 to $7.00 a year.

"Oh boy."

"Good heavens."

Dorothy Irwin listened for a moment and then spoke. "Well, of course we're all thinking the same thing. The regents are concerned about it, but . . . it was passed unanimously. I feel sure that your instructions to the delegates would be to vote against. And what will happen in Washington I can't imagine."

"What do they need the money for?" asked Ruth Lehr.

"I think they should have said," said Elsie Beatty.

"That's a lot for ladies on social security," said Ruth Styer.

"We all feel the same," said Dorothy Irwin.

"It's because we lost the National Symphony," said Ruth Styer.

"There's also an amendment to raise the dues of the members-at-large from seven dollars to twelve dollars," said Dorothy Irwin. "Of course, the National Society has been wanting to eliminate members-at-large. There's no advantage for either the individual or for the Society. A person could say, 'I'm proud to be a DAR' without supporting the DAR."

"Well, if their goal is to eliminate the members-at-large, I think they've taken a very good path," said Elsie Beatty. The board members laughed, but when the meeting adjourned a few minutes later, at 11:40, they went off toward the dining room talking rather seriously among themselves.

There was a brief card-party meeting. By the time it was over, the small dining room on the other other side of Lamps and Pillows was overflowing with men, women, and children, black and white, all looking for seats. The Daughters had turned out in good numbers. Some greeted the guests. Others found chairs for themselves.

The feeling in the room was not totally comfortable at the beginning, but by the end of the afternoon, it was almost like

Christmas all over again. Daughters and parents sat together at tables for eight. Attractive and nicely gotten out (no straggly hair or jeans here), the five Good Citizen winners and five Good Citizenship Winners were seated boy-girl-boy-girl at one side of a long table along one wall, looking toward the room. Mrs. Fick sat at one end, Miss Henry sat at the other, and Dorothy Irwin and Mrs. Beatty sat in the middle. Two of the girls and one boy were black. The boy was Timothy Towler from Overbrook. Sure enough, there at a table with Helen Eisenberg were seven members of his family, beautifully dressed up. Dorothy Irwin gave a brief welcome. "Enjoy your lunch," she said smiling.

Lunch was chicken a la king, red Jell-O with fruit, lima beans, and hot-fudge sundaes. The kids talked to each other a little. The Daughters talked with the kids a little. Conversations began to get going at the smaller tables. Everyone seemed slightly relieved when the program started.

Mary Lou Henry gave her national defense report on the signers of the Declaration of Independence. She read with expression, and the kids seemed to listen.

"Have you ever wondered what happened to the signers?" Miss Henry read. "Five were captured by the British and tortured, two had their homes ransacked, nine fought and died, two lost sons . . . knowing full well that the penalty would be death. . . . These were not wide-eyed rabble-rousing ruffians but soft-spoken men of means. . . . They had security, but they valued liberty. They gave us an independent America. It is up to us to keep it."

A guest whispered, "That was very nice."

Dot Irwin asked Alexandra Lehr, Ruth Lehr's daughter, to come forward. Looking self-conscious, a girl with long, bright red hair made her way around the crowded tables and stood in front of the regent. Alexandra, a college freshman, was dressed in a mini-skirt and a blazer. Reading from the back of the DAR handbook, Miss Irwin installed her new member. "We are happy to welcome you as a Daughter of the American Revolution and as a member of Independence Hall chapter," Miss Irwin read. "Today, as you take your place in our ranks, let us pledge together our loyalty to our country and to our beloved Society, and our best efforts in behalf of its patriotic objects." Dorothy Irwin and Alexandra Lehr shook hands. Alexandra acknowledged the welcome shyly in words the guests could not hear.

Then Mrs. Fick stood up, welcomed everyone, said it was an

honor to have the guests present, described the DAR in a dozen sentences emphasizing schools and conservation, and told a story.

"I knew of a regent who went to Washington and couldn't find a parking place near DAR headquarters. A policeman asked her if she was a DAR. Upon learning that she was, he led her down to the end of a long line of cars and moved the No Parking sign one space so she could park." Mrs. Fick was smiling as she spoke. "He told her he had gotten a DAR award in junior-high school. The regent was a humorous person, and she said, 'That doesn't mean you can go around moving parking signs!' "

The tenseness had gone out of the room. People were enjoying themselves, although the kids still seemed a bit stiff. They appeared to be uneasy about the speeches the Daughters had asked them to give. Timothy Towler, a great strapping football player, said later that he was definitely nervous.

Mrs. Fick called the first Good Citizen to the microphone. She was Mary Winkler, a student at Collingdale High School. Dorothy Irwin attached a pin to Mary's dress and shook her hand. Mary faced the audience.

"Good afternoon, everybody," she began. She went on to tell about her activities and awards. "I got a ninth-grade award for all-around person. I'm in National Honor Society, Varsity Club, I'm a majorette, and copy editor of our yearbook. I really enjoy proofreading and looking over what things are about. I'm secretary of the principal's advisory committee, have been on the newspaper and in choir. I will go in for a secondary school teaching degree. I sent away to four colleges and was accepted at three. I want to go out for tennis. It keeps me in shape and gives me a good suntan!"

The Daughters applauded Mary Winkler, and she sat down. One by one, the other students rose to receive their awards and to tell the Daughters about the activities that contributed to their winning them.

"It is gratifying to be honored this afternoon and to be the recipient of such an outstanding award," said Timothy Towler. "I have two varsity letters in football, was nominated most valuable player in 1971 and 1972. I'm on the track team and in the National Honor Society. I applied to Columbia School of Engineering, Lafayette, the University of Pittsburgh, and Cornell. My number one preference is Columbia. I want to go into aeronautical engineering. A football player's life is mostly made up of significant moments. This afternoon is going to be one of the proudest moments I have." Mary Lou Henry introduced Timothy Towler's mother, grandfather, sister, aunt, niece, and two cousins. The applause was especially long.

"As I suggested," said Mrs. Fick, summing up after all the students had spoken, "they would be interesting and amazing, and I think you found them that."

Then Mrs. Fick introduced the speaker. The kids were startled. They looked at their watches or at their parents or at each other. It was clear they hadn't expected to hear a speech.

The Reverend Elliot Stabler did his darnedest, and he did it well enough to get the audience back. Speaking like a serious Music Man selling morality instead of brass bands, Mrs. Fick's Bible teacher did the kids the courtesy of assuming they not only paid attention to what was going on in the world but also had the intelligence and the interest to worry about it.

"Where are we headed?" Reverend Stabler asked them. "Why did McGovern change his position? Why did he drop Eagleton? Because he wanted to win. A man who started out as a sort of Mr. Clean became a do-what-you-have-to-do-to-win man. And Nixon sitting there in regal isolation saying hardly two words on issues while his surrogates flitted about the country saying what a good job they thought he had done, while going on was outright criminal activity. Once again, the name of the game is expedience. . . .

"We are ever so slowly and subtly being conned into giving up our spiritual beliefs. Less than half the people in this country attend church regularly. Precious few people believe in the Devil. He's a joke. But all I need to do is to look at the so-called 'amusement' page ads and the reviews of *Last Tango* to know that the Devil is alive and well. . . ."

A voice in the room growled softly, "Amen." It was Timothy Towler's grandfather.

"Do you wonder at the drug culture?" Stabler continued. "Do you wonder at the spread of VD, which is second only to the common cold in popularity?"

"But perhaps it's not too late to redeem our souls. . . . The opposite of courage is not cowardice; it is conformity. Do not conform to this world, but be transformed by the renewing of your mind. . . . Our future lies with the young and with older people who will seek the roots of our spiritual heritage, who will seek to love the land, to do good, to practice mercy. . . ."

"Amen," said Timothy Towler's grandfather aloud for the third or fourth time.

When the Reverend Stabler had finished, the Daughters wished their guests good-bye. White parents sought the hands of black parents, honorees thanked honorers, Daughters wanted to meet Timothy Towler's grandfather. The guests seemed reluctant to leave. The Daughters seemed reluctant to have them go. Guests and Daughters stood around the room for many minutes, talking to each other. When the guests did leave, there was a strong feeling of letdown in the room. About twenty-five Daughters stayed for the business meeting. It concluded with record speed, and at 3:30 the Daughters went home.

A few days later I called on the three black students honored by Independence Hall chapter. All were pleased with their awards. None had had second thoughts about being honored by an all-white group. All had heard of Marian Anderson, but only Timothy Towler had heard of Marian Anderson and the DAR.

"That's the only thing I knew about the DAR," Timothy said. "I heard on a radio show about black history that she was to sing in Washington and permission was denied. But I don't have any prejudice about anybody. There's things that I may not know about. Most blacks would just look back and say, 'It's just another thing that was happening at that time.' If it happened now, though, there'd be an uproar.

"I never thought about not accepting the award. DAR's just the name. The women aren't the same ones as back then. People are people. If they want to honor me, make an effort to come to me and honor me in public like that, I wouldn't turn it down. My family enjoyed it. This is the first time they have turned out for something like this."

To learn more about the woman whom Stephen Uzzell seemed to have upset with his dire warnings in November, I called recording secretary Regina Sheehan toward the end of February. Mrs. Sheehan is a medium-sized woman with glasses, who often wears a blouse and skirt and a multi-colored beret to DAR meetings. She is a relatively new member. Though she had wanted to join from the age of seventeen, she did not complete her papers until 1967. "I kept pushing it around for twenty years," Mrs. Sheehan said. "When my son got to be not too much trouble, about fourteen, I decided I needed a new interest. The DAR was *one* thing I wanted to do in life."

Mrs. Sheehan said she wasn't sorry that she had waited to join the DAR. "Now is when I need it." she said. "I didn't need it then. It's a family to me. I have no family here, except my husband's son. It fills a great need, for me, anyway. When I go to meetings, I feel like I'm going to a family reunion."

Regina Sheehan said she was particularly interested in the DAR's schools but also pays attention to the resolutions.

"I'm interested in what they say there, in the image they create," she said. "Some I don't agree with. I don't think they're representative of what the DAR stands for. That's what's disappointed me. We're patriotic and religious. The organization is dedicated to a high type of life. Some of the resolutions are, shall we say, picayune? If I were on the resolutions committee, I would think something should be said about keeping the Sabbath and not permitting it to be desecrated by the openings of supermarkets. The resolutions should be a little more timely.

"I do approve of the UN resolution. Long before I was in DAR my instinct told me it would be to the detriment of this country to become too much involved with other nations. My vocabulary isn't that good to explain it, but I would say they're definitely trying to get the upper hand. It gives them a sounding board, makes the smaller countries more important than they are. You do have to have something, but the UN may involve us too much."

On the third Monday of every month, Independence Hall member Betty Davy helps out at a veterans' hospital in Philadelphia in conjunction with the DAR's Service to Veteran Patients Committee. Mrs. Davy works in the Medical Ward. I spent her day with her in February. A large woman with upswept red hair and an easy manner, Mrs. Davy is not active in DAR. Her husband is retired, and they travel a good deal. Of the places they have been, she would most like to go back to India and Japan. The Davys have three married sons and twelve grandchildren. Their daughter, also a member of Independence Hall chapter, works in New York City as a secretary.

Mrs. Davy wore a blue smock over her dress, and low shoes. She began the day by going to the hospital canteen and buying some Kleenex and razor blades for a patient. "Nixon has cut back on Kleenex!" the patient told her when she returned his change.

Explaining that the hospital usually supplied tissues, Mrs.

Davy began collecting the styrofoam pitchers from each bedside table in her ward. She filled the pitchers with ice and water and returned them to the tables. Most of the beds were temporarily empty. Men were walking around in pajamas or sitting up in chairs reading the paper or playing cards.

"This is my third year coming here," Mrs. Davy said. "Dot Irwin asked me if I'd head the committee, so I started coming. I always start with the water and the bags. I may interrupt myself to take blood samples to the lab or take a patient to someplace. I used to play poker with a colored man in the afternoons when I had all my work done. We used matchsticks for poker chips. He used to get such a kick out of it when I called things wrong! Sure, I know how to play, but you know."

Kathryn Kilpatrick, chairman of the DAR Service to Veteran Patients Committee for the state of Pennsylvania, was back working at the hospital that day. She had been out for many weeks after suffering an embolism. If she guessed that she had only a few months to live, she didn't let on. She did say she was a widow with one daughter and three grandchildren in Virginia. "I've been there twice," she said. Something in the way she said it made it seem that twice was not often enough. Mrs. Kilpatrick had had a son, but he had died. A tiny woman with good teeth and pretty, gray hair, Kathryn Kilpatrick would spend six or eight hours a week sitting alone in a cold little corner of an operating supply room rolling stockinettes for surgery patients. She stopped only for lunch—a glass of skimmed milk—or to read the Bible to a patient if the chaplain asked her to.

"This is a labor of love," Mrs. Kilpatrick said. "Otherwise you wouldn't do it. It costs you money every time you come, and your time."

As she talked, Mrs. Kilpatrick rolled the stockinettes and wrapped them in a special way in faded greenish squares of cloth. "We keep records and send them to Washington. We put how many hours we put in and the value. You know the actual value of many things. Not this, what I'm doing, but the crocheted tracheotomy bibs we value at thirty cents, and we have given hearing aids for six hundred dollars, radio, TV, men's clothing, those artificial plants that are very expensive. I'm organizing a Flag Day celebration for every chapter of the DAR in the state."

Mrs. Kilpatrick said she was willing to come in spite of the expense because she got something out of the work. "The love of doing something. The satisfaction of doing something for somebody who needs it. You would never do this for a little tiny bit of praise. How much praise does anybody give you? You do it for God's sake. If you got paid, you'd do it for God's sake and your pay."

In the afternoon there was a program honoring all the volunteers in the hospital. Kathryn Kilpatrick got three certificates. Betty Davy didn't get any.

"You have enough hours," Mrs. Kilpatrick whispered loudly down the row.

Mrs. Davy shrugged. "I don't care," she whispered back.

"I do," Kathryn Kilpatrick said. "It's for the organization."

So later Betty Davy did turn in her hours. Earlier she had said, "The hundred hours, a lot of people like Kathryn like all that stuff, keeping records, getting recognition. To me it doesn't matter." By the time the Flag Day party was held at the hospital Kathryn Kilpatrick was in a coma. She died soon after.

I spoke with J.H. Kennedy, director of volunteers at the veterans' hospital. "The DAR requested wards," Kennedy said. "They took a six-hour course to work on the wards. I would say about eighty percent of all volunteers want to work directly with patients."

While Kennedy seemed happy to have help, he admitted that the DAR in his hospital was doing the minimum required of volunteers. "The DAR is on a one-day-a-month basis," he said. "Most volunteers work one day a week. Many come two days a week. Ten people work five days a week. One volunteer has put in twenty thousand hours since 1953. If they work anything less than one day a month, they automatically become inactive. No other organization has a specific assignment of one day a month. We gave that to them because that's what they offered."

The next day I called Lois Wilson, DAR director for southeastern Pennsylvania. Independence Hall chapter had no Junior American Citizens program, and I wondered whether any chapters in the area did. She said Philadelphia chapter was the only one that has been active. "In Pittsburgh it's very popular," Mrs. Wilson said. "I guess the chapters here are too busy with Good Citizens. Also maybe it's a more liberal clientele in this area. But my feeling is that no one has pushed it."

I told Mrs. Wilson I had spent the previous day at the hospital.

"Kathryn Kilpatrick is doing everything she can to get interest in veteran patients," Mrs. Wilson said. "But you know, it takes an awful thick skin to go down to that hospital. And it's in an awful bad place. Women aren't so brave about going into Philadelphia as they used to be, and there's no place to park."

A few days later I called Dorothy Irwin to find out about the March meeting. She was extremely upset.

"I'm doing something right now I wish I weren't doing," she said. "Lillian Hemmerly died suddenly yesterday. I'm calling some of the members to tell them. It was such a shock. I can't tell you what a shock it was."

I let a week go by and then telephoned Ruth Lehr, Independence Hall's first vice regent, a low-key, thoughtful woman who lives with her family in Wilmington. Like Dorothy Irwin, Mrs. Lehr had been stunned by news of Lillian Hemmerly's death.

"I've known her since the Forties," Mrs. Lehr said. "She's a very fine person. She worked for a cotton broker in Penn Center. Her boss retired, and she had been carrying on the business until a new one came, almost like the broker herself. They found her at the desk with the phone off the hook, as if she had been trying to dial. She hadn't even been sick."

Mrs. Lehr comes from a DAR family. She came up through CAR and paged at Congress regularly until she had her children. Now an Episcopalian, Ruth Lehr attended Quaker schools, then went to Wellesley and graduated from Temple. She talked with me about juniors and the chapter in general.

"In a sense juniors are a new problem to our particular chapter," Mrs. Lehr said. "At one time we had a junior group going strong. I was in it. But there's a tremendous amount of mobility in young people today. They don't tend to join things as quickly as they used to. They don't want to be pinned down.

"Do you know Mrs. Cupitt from our chapter? She's up in years now. She talked to me at length about the juniors recently. She said, 'When I got married, I started with four servants, and we were free.' That's not true anymore. Even when I was a junior, we had a number of women as young as forty who had not only beautiful homes but staffs. Most of the women in the chapter now aren't in that situation. If they have someone come in and clean once a week, they're lucky. It's hard to get a baby-sitter. And, too, many women are on a fixed income. We have half a dozen women with small children, and their husbands aren't too anxious to have them give up a Saturday and take care of the children themselves."

Even without a thriving junior group, Mrs. Lehr said, her

daughter, Alexandra, the newest member of Independence Hall, was still happy to belong to that chapter. "She likes the people. She subscribes to everything but national defense. She went to Quaker schools, so that makes a difference."

Mrs. Lehr belongs to a historical society, tutors children in reading, serves as a museum guide, and is active in church, but she does not belong to other patriotic hereditary organizations and does not plan to join any. "My son is in eleventh grade this year, and tuition is two thousand dollars, and we have a girl in college," she said. "We're not that rich. And I have more diverse interests. I like DAR, I enjoy it, but I don't know how much more I would want."

Independence Hall is only one of several DAR chapters Ruth Lehr has belonged to. She considers it a special one. She particularly remembers the chapter's buying bathrobes and slippers for every child in a Salvation Army orphanage and giving the children a Christmas party. "One year we gave them a jungle gym," Mrs. Lehr said. "We used to go out and play the piano and read stories to them on Sunday afternoons, because some of the children would go home or go visiting. We stayed with the ones who didn't go anywhere. The Salvation Army changed, its needs changed, and we moved on to something else.

"Like in a democracy, there's room for improvement in the DAR, but I get a great feeling of satisfaction that we achieve so much, oftentimes with very little money. We were always taught if you had a nickel more than anybody else, if you had time or money or energy more than anybody else, pitch in. For me, DAR has been an excellent outlet. I was a history major. I like things having to do with that. I like the Good Citizenship program because you're recognizing the good. I guess it's all self-satisfaction. That's very selfish, isn't it?"

Sara Knobelauch, Independence Hall's junior chairman, is a fifth-grade teacher in a Philadelphia public school. Her mother and sister joined the DAR together and got Sara in when she was eighteen. Sara describes herself as a political moderate and a rather inactive Daughter.

"I can't really get too active because maybe I can't believe wholeheartedly in everything they stand for," Sara told me one evening. "I think the work they do with Indians and the children in Appalachia is really great. But some of their ideas—did you hear the guy from the Birch Society in November? I don't know if he was a member of the Birch Society, but he sounded like a member I once heard at a singles club. He didn't come over very good for me. He sort of rankled me. I thought he was sort of dogmatic in his ideas.

"I've heard talks like that before in DAR. It seems when they get a national defense speaker, that's the way it goes. I'm not one of those people that think we should totally eliminate our defense program, but when the social programs are cut in favor of defense, that's a bit strong, especially since we're supposedly winding down our involvement."

Sara's sister, Carolyn, was Pennsylvania's outstanding junior member in 1972. Sara described Carolyn as "the exact opposite" of herself where DAR is concerned.

"In some respects I was the wrong person to be junior chairman," Sara admitted, "but there was no one else. I haven't devoted that much time to it. I became engaged over Christmas, and before that I was in some things, mostly social clubs. If I enjoyed the meetings, I'd be going more. It's something to do with age, something to do with the program. But DAR is a good way of making contacts. I've been looking for another job, and one of the members suggested somebody for me to contact. These women are well acquainted with what's going on in the city. And I enjoy the card party. I like to look at fashions. The juniors sell jewelry at meetings. That's fun. I like to watch people. Meeting them is what makes it interesting."

Part of Sara's lack of enthusiasm for the DAR seems to stem from an experience she had paging at the Pennsylvania DAR conference. "I paged once at national and three times at state," she said. "I enjoyed it till the last time. Then there was a hassle over dress. We were not allowed to march in the processional or carry a flag if we didn't have a long dress. This had never been an issue before. There was a girl in a pantsuit, and she wasn't allowed to march either, though she said she had marched in Washington in a pantsuit.

"I was very angry. I let it be known that I thought it was very trivial. I had always worn a short dress. It was all I had, and I wasn't about to go out and buy a new one on somebody's whim. We weren't told ahead of time. We were told evening dresses. But in this day and age, that can be a mini-skirt.

"The chairman came from a rural area. She said, 'Evening dresses means long dresses.' It was a lack of communication between the state chairman of juniors and the chapter chairmen.

I took office last year, and I have gotten nothing from her at all. I feel if this is how people feel about the organization, why should I bother?"

When board members gathered for the executive meeting in March, a heavy rain was beating against the windows in the Pickwick Room. The meeting began with a prayer for Lillian Hemmerly. The board members were subdued. Margaret Stevenson, sister of the former regent, had died March 8, and while she had been sick a long time, her loss was an added source of sadness. The meeting ended with a relatively long and serious discussion about starting a Lillian Hemmerly memorial fund.

"We're going to do this very slowly," Dorothy Irwin said. "There is no rush. We're going to do it right. Her family and friends know that Lillian was very interested in the schools, so I feel they'd like something in that area. I could talk with people in Washington about a specific tribute. It has been suggested that Mrs. Spicer is very interested in Hillside School—the DAR bus tour next fall will include it for the first time—and Lillian's sister Ruth Hemmerly was also very interested in Hillside when she was our chairman of schools. She wrote a boy there for quite a length of time, and visited, so the family name might be remembered there. We'll make no decision now. This is something you mull over in your mind."

All other matters were discussed much more briefly. The chapter had decided to nominate a conservationist as Pennsylvania's Distinguished Daughter. Ruth Lehr was absent because of a back problem. (She was considering acupuncture.) For their May outing Charles Dorman, curator at Independence Hall, would take chapter members on a tour of the second floor and explain how the DAR's money was being used. The women discussed American history awards.

"I also have a school interested in taking part in the essay contest next year, Merion Academy!" said Helen Jensen triumphantly.

Dorothy Irwin replied, also triumphantly, "Wonderful!"

The proposed amendment to increase dues was mentioned.

"You have two delegates to Congress, and I assume you would instruct them to vote against," said Dorothy Irwin. Her board made sounds of unhappy assent. The regent reminded the board that state DAR officers would be elected at the Pennsylvania state conference.

"That will be exciting!" Dorothy Irwin said.

"That's something new," said Elsie Beatty wryly. "Usually it's dull as dishwater."

Finally Dorothy Irwin named a replacement on the board for Lillian Hemmerly. "I'd like to suggest Helen Eisenberg so she can keep us abreast of card-party affairs," said Dorothy Irwin. The meeting adjourned at six minutes before noon.

Lunch was fish, broccoli, tossed salad, and strawberry sundaes. Sara Knobelauch was distressed because she had dropped her shopping bag full of DAR jewelry and note paper in a gutter on the way in. She talked about 4-H.

"I was in it ten years," she said. "I liked it better than Girl Scouts. That was so ceremonial."

After lunch the state schools chairman showed slides of Kate Duncan Smith and Tamassee and one or two other schools aided by the DAR. The Daughters always like to hear about the schools, and when the lights went on again, the members of Independence Hall chapter were smiling.

The business meeting was taken up mainly with card-party details and with questions and answers about whose names might be eligible for listing in the Bell Tower book. But as had been true that morning, the larger part of the meeting was devoted to the deceased members.

"This year Independence Hall has lost three members," said Dorothy Irwin. "Mrs. Hubert B. Sullivan died November 4, 1972. She was ill shortly after she joined, and we never got to know her. She descended from a signer of the Declaration of Independence.

"Miss Margaret Stevenson, March 8, 1973. We will remember Margaret as a dedicated worker serving in the capacity of registrar and as a very sweet, warm-hearted person. Sixteen went to the service, and a few went to the cemetery. We had a lovely basket of flowers.

"And on February 27, 1973, Miss Lillian M. Hemmerly. We have not gotten over the shock of losing our beloved Lillian. A loyal, dedicated member of the National Society, a devoted member of Independence Hall chapter, she gave of herself, her time, her energy way beyond the call of duty, with dedication and interest and a vivacious personality. She will be remembered by this chapter for a long time."

By the time Dorothy Irwin finished, she was near tears. Marjorie Lampe gave a short memorial service. "Heal all the hurt places in our lives," she read softly.

The Academy of Music, home of the Philadelphia Orchestra, is one of the finest old buildings in a city that has tried hard to keep its old buildings. The ballroom on the second floor is a huge space walled in mirrors, hung with long draperies in pale gold, carpeted in beige print, and lit by two large crystal chandeliers. If the room costs more than the S&C auditorium, it also makes events seem more important. And no event is more important to the Independence Hall chapter than the card party.

March 31 was a damp day but warm. The Daughters broke out their spring dresses and came in spring moods. The ballroom was full of excitement. The Daughter selling candy had been at the Academy of Music since 10:00 and was doing a land-office business in homemade fudge, chocolate and white, with or without nuts. Serious cardplaying wasn't due to begin until 1 P.M., but serious cardplayers—among them a number of men—came earlier. While they shuffled and dealt and bid at tables with white paper cloths and African violets as centerpieces, Daughters and guests bought goodies or chances. For two dollars the Daughters could buy a book of voices on Arrah Lee Gaul's oil painting. For one dollar they could buy five chances on tombola table prizes—a watch, a round black tray decorated with a Liberty Bell, a felt hat stuck with a couple of dozen pleated dollar bills, a clock, a decorated Easter egg. They could buy mystery packages for fifty cents or a dollar, homemade cakes and breads at various prices, or secondhand books—a quarter for hardbound, a dime for paperback.

In a black mini-dress and white boots, Sara Knobelauch circulated among the card tables selling voices for the painting. Joann Kersch's daughter Missy, and Missy's friend Paula, both seventh-graders, manned the cake and cookie table. Mrs. Fick showed off some color photos of the February Good Citizen luncheon. By 1:00 every table was full, and the big room was noisy with the sounds of cards slapping and cardplayers chatting.

"I was going to wear this suit to Europe, but I think it might be too hot."

"Were you tempted to go to five diamonds?"

"I felt piggish to be going because I know you girls had something going between you, but. . . ."

". . . three eights. . . ."

". . . . she'da had one, I'da had one."

"Well, you have to take a chance, girls."

"That's what I was doing, and I lost."

There was a fashion show courtesy of The Carriage Trade, a suburban shop. A bright blonde in bright yellow narrated. Models from the Independence Hall chapter walked up and down a long platform to the admiration of their friends. Doris Godfrey's husband took flash pictures of her whenever she reached the end of the platform. Cardplayers continued to play cards and to chatter in low voices. One foursome chattered loudly. Behind the cookie table at the back of the room, Missy Kersch, a miniature Joann with glasses and lighter hair, talked about CAR.

"Girl Scouts is livelier," Missy said. "CAR isn't any different than I expected. The kids meet on the fourth Sunday at the home of the organizers. It's hard to have a program to interest everybody, because the kids are four to eighteen. Some of the kids at school kick the Scouts around, but very few know anything about the CAR. More could join, but I guess they're not interested in history."

The fashion show was over at 2:15, and Dorothy Irwin welcomed the guests. Some of the women headed back to do some last-minute buying. A few inspected the door prizes, some of which had been purchased with trading stamps. It took nearly an hour to give all the prizes away. About 3:10 guests began to drift toward the elevator. Helen Eisenberg, card-party chairman, expressed her pleasure at the turnout and the apparent success of the event. "I'm going to be a bad girl tomorrow and not go to church," she said. At 3:15 the remaining candy and the remaining cakes and cookies were put on one table, and Missy Kersch tried to sell them off.

By 3:45 most of the card-party guests had left. A few were still playing cards. Daughters were packing boxes and getting ready to go home. Missy Kersch was still selling. Most of the books had been sold. The ballroom finally emptied out around 4:30.

Helen Eisenberg later reported that despite the increased expenses of ballroom rental, the Independence Hall card party made a profit of $1,214.59.

Continental Congress was to be held in Washington April 16-19. Dorothy Irwin and Edna Weber would be delegates. Miss Irwin was looking forward to going but said that Congress in the two years between the election of national officers is fairly calm.

"If not for the dues discussion, I would have nothing on my mind," Miss Irwin said on the phone one evening. "No explanation came with the notice of the proposed change in the bylaws, but in the *DAR Magazine* Mrs. Spicer explained very clearly that the money is most necessary. I know that they need it. There's no question about that. But what will the chapters do? The magazine says we must not give up any of our programs for youth, and we feel that way. My chapter and others could probably afford a few more dollars, but I'm thinking of around the country. I don't want to hear an angry discussion, but I would like to hear the facts. I hope we can agree on five dollars. I'll vote down the seven dollars."

Dorothy Irwin said she expected to have a good time in Washington. "Sure!"

In April each year the juniors in Pennsylvania hold a luncheon to raise money for junior projects, and I ran into Dorothy Irwin there when she had returned from Congress. She had had a lovely time in Washington. "Of course we all voted for the raise in dues," she said. "It was so beautifully explained. What else could we do? There's one hundred percent money, but the operating expenses are one hundred eleven percent, and seventy-two percent of that is salaries. I doubt if there were twelve women standing against. Every regent in this room thought there would be a compromise, but we all voted for."

Dorothy Irwin said she worried about the women on fixed incomes. She also expressed impatience with women who wanted to belong to the organization but not support it.

"Some people are proud of being a DAR, period," she said. "We never see them. At the time of the card party we send them a note saying, 'This is your chance to give something.' Many of them pass up the privilege."

The next time I talked to Dorothy Irwin, she was spluttering with indignation over an article she had read in *The Philadelphia Evening Bulletin*. Writing about General James, the black keynote speaker at the 1973 Congress, columnist Nick Thimmesch had mentioned the DAR refusal to let Marian Anderson sing. He referred to the Daughters, Dorothy Irwin said, as having "blue-veined hands" and "crepe-y throats."

Laughing a little, but clearly dismayed, Dorothy Irwin said. "I wrote him a letter! And we'll get each of the delegates to send a Marian Anderson brochure to him. Crepe-y throats and blue-veined hands indeed! I never wrote a letter to a newspaper before in my life. I said, 'Time to get with it, Mr. Thimmesch!' "

Miss Irwin herself had enjoyed and admired General James very much. She thought his speech was excellent. She couldn't believe that when James said his presence in Constitution Hall was evidence of progress, he was referring to Marian Anderson. She assumed he meant the general progress of blacks in white America. Surely a guest in the Hall would not insult his hostesses.

Dorothy Irwin also had happy news. "I've just come from a luncheon where I got Dr. Tung!" she said. "He can come in November. It's too bad he can't come in December, when we'll be at the Barclay, but we can decorate the room at Strawbridge so it looks nice."

Dorothy Irwin said she was winding up her second of three years as regent with mixed feelings. A lot of work was involved in the job, but also some fringe benefits. "I've gone to everything I've gotten an invitation to," she said. "Last week I went to the Miss Armed Forces Contest!"

Miss Irwin said she had no interest in high DAR office. "I won't live long enough!" she laughed. "Maybe there'll be a state chairmanship, but I don't know whether I want to feel obliged to run around the state. It depends on the chairmanship."

The outing and final meeting of the Independence Hall year were scheduled for May 8. The Daughters could not have had a more perfect day. The women gathered outside Independence Hall for their guided tour luxuriated in sun and bracing breezes, and as if the weather weren't enough to ensure a good day, Anna McCaskey came back, nearly recovered from surgery. She walked slowly, leaning on her daughter's arm, and she looked as though she had been through an ordeal, but as she came toward the steps of Independence Hall, she smiled. The Daughters were very glad to see her.

Mr. Dorman, the curator, is a big, square-faced man who wears his hair slicked back. Making no effort to hide his fascination with his job, he gave a delightful tour of the second floor. The Daughters were very attentive, pleased to learn how their money was being used. "We want this whole building to come alive again," said Charles Dorman. He talked about the difficulty of finding certain pieces of silver and furniture. "History gives up its secrets rather reluctantly. One of the hardest things to find is a set of twelve chairs. Under this green cloth is a series of trestles and plywood. We haven't found a table in England or America, but we're hopeful."

In the Governor's Council Chamber Dorman noted that

whenever the state or proprietary governor wanted to impress some constituents in warm weather, he invited them for a picnic on his yacht on the river. He offered them plenty of refreshment. They responded by getting drunk and heaving the governor's pewter plates and mugs over the rail. Martha Stevenson whispered. "Maybe we should stop teaching our children history!"

When the tour was over, the Daughters walked at a leisurely pace the few blocks to the Holiday Inn. Before lunch Miss Irwin gathered her board. Members agreed that in view of the increase in national dues, chapter dues, through which national dues are paid, should go up to $15.00 a year. None of the Daughters on the board could think of anyone in Independence Hall chapter who would resign because of the increase.

They talked about the Lillian Hemmerly Memorial Fund. Dorothy Irwin said she had talked at Congress to the head of Hillside School. He had indeed recognized the name of Hemmerly. He had suggested a high-school scholarship for promising boys leaving eighth grade. Lillian Hemmerly's sisters had liked the idea very much. The man from Hillside had offered to come to Philadelphia and speak to Independence Hall and any other interested chapter. The board thought the chapter should go ahead with those plans.

Forty-four Daughters met for lunch in a small, windowless blue room at the Holiday Inn. They ate fruit cocktail, bluefish with lemon, roasted potatoes, green beans with almonds, and chocolate-cherry parfaits. They talked about the Watergate hearings which had begun that week. The Daughters seemed to feel that President Nixon had not played a part in the break-in but shouldn't have waited so long to find out who had. They expressed sympathy for his wife.

There was a national-defense report with a little more comment than usual from the regent. Dorothy Irwin mentioned the Atlantic Union. "Of course, we never see any of these articles in the newspapers," she said. "I'm very much afraid it has been passed by the House. We will all watch the newspapers for more on this." (According to a national-defense committee pamphlet, the Atlantic Union would transform NATO nations from an alliance into a federation in which each nation would be the equivalent of a state.)

After installing a new member, the regent talked for nearly ten minutes on the proposed dues increase. She had been worried about how the members would react. At the board meeting she had said she would raise the subject before the Daughters got too tired. But she had corrected herself. "No," she said, "before *I* get too tired!"

Miss Irwin was careful to explain that the dues had not been raised since 1960, and that they had been raised only three times in eighty-two years. She reminded the Daughters of the privileges of membership. "You belong to a prestigious Society and a prestigious chapter," she said seriously. "Independence Hall chapter has a tradition. You hear it in the state, and you hear it in the nation." There was silence. "Are you ready to discuss this problem?"

There was almost no discussion. Marjorie Lampe got up and said, "I don't think there's a question in anybody's mind. We have to do it, so let's do it."

Sounds of assent filled the room. Adele Brant moved to raise chapter dues to $15.00. Every woman in the room voted yes.

Miss Irwin described plans for the Lillian Hemmerly Memorial Fund. The Daughters liked the idea of a scholarship very much. They voted for it with no discussion. There were elections for delegates and alternates to the Pennsylvania state conference in October. Then officers and committee chairmen gave annual reports which included the following details: in 1972/73 the Independence Hall chapter had contributed $812.39 to the DAR's educational endeavors (as compared to $104.75 for patriotic and $36.00 for historic endeavors), had balanced its books, had sent fifty-eight pounds of clothing to St. Mary's Indian School, had donated $49.00 to the DAR Museum, and had given $5.00 to Betty Davy for the Flag Day party at the veterans' hospital.

The Daughters were beginning to fidget. Some left. Nevertheless, Dorothy Irwin and two other women gave reports on Congress, briefly describing the meetings and such functions as the national-defense luncheon, the tour of the White House Rose Garden, and the Pennsylvania luncheon. "And that, I think, is enough to let you know that we were there and conscientious!" said Dorothy Irwin.

The meeting adjourned at 3:40. Virginia Rumbarger asked Dorothy Irwin for a copy of the resolutions passed at Congress. The Daughters of Independence Hall scattered into the late-afternoon sun talking of travel plans and wishing each other a happy summer.

CHAPTER X

At the Helm: The President General

It is a cold, rainy November evening at the end of a long, rather harrying day, and the small group of Daughters who have gathered in the big revolving restaurant atop the Trenton Holiday Inn seem happy for the opportunity to relax. They have been in and out of cars all day—first to Jersey City to mark the grave of their first state regent, then to Trenton for lunch, then out to a tea at Watson House, a museum they maintain. More important, they have been responsible for the safety and comfort of a very special guest. Eleanor Spicer has been with them since early morning. She will speak tomorrow morning when the New Jersey DAR opens its annual two-day state meeting here in the hotel. Tonight the state's top officers are entertaining their president general at dinner.

Eleanor Spicer looks a lot better than she feels. A relatively small woman (five feet four inches tall, a size twelve or sometimes ten), she is wearing a lovely suit of pink and silver brocade, and her gray hair curls softly around her face. She is close to seventy but seems younger; only a slight paleness and heaviness to her eyes hint that she is not in perfect health. Mrs. Spicer has a bad cold for the second time this year. While the other Daughters enjoyed a drink together in the state regent's suite after they dressed for dinner, the president general rested in her room until the last minute. The Daughters were a little concerned, feeling they might have tired her with too heavy a schedule. But now Mrs. Spicer sits talking and listening with interest to the women sitting around her. Her frequent smile sets worried minds at ease.

Rainy Wednesday nights in November inspire few people to go out on the town, and aside from the women at the DAR table, the Top of Trenton is rather sparsely populated. There is only light applause when Raquel and her partner come out onto the dance floor to entertain. The two don't exactly look handpicked for the DAR. Raquel is obviously wearing no bra under her long, slinky, pale green V-neck dress. With thick black hair, clamorous makeup, and a Marilyn Monroe whisper, she comes on like a floozy. Her sidekick has a beard, a Western twang, and a Western vest. He sits down at the piano and picks out a few chords. Raquel stands at a microphone and gets ready to sing. Her partner tosses a comment at her. She tosses one back. They banter. They are very corny. The Daughters listen politely and a little uncertainly.

Suddenly Raquel says, "I've heard the word 'patriotic' mentioned here tonight." She must have heard it from the Inn managers, because the subject has not come up at the DAR table. Raquel looks at the Daughters and smiles. They look at her. They are not comfortable. Raquel says she likes the word. She talks about it a little. Is she putting them on?

"I'm going to sing something for a very pretty lady named Eleanor," Raquel purrs into the microphone.

She says again, "This is for you, Eleanor." She smiles.

Everybody at the DAR table knows that Raquel must now be acknowledged.

"Why, thank you," Mrs. Spicer says, giving a little bow with her head and returning the smile. The Daughters begin to breathe.

Raquel announces that she is going to sing "I Left My Horse in San Francisco" because Eleanor Spicer is from California. The other people in the room seem to enjoy this version of the title, but the Daughters' laugh is strained. Raquel seems to be baiting the president general. But Raquel corrects the title and finally sings. The Daughters join in the applause. Raquel and their partner return to their corny banter. The Daughters begin to talk among themselves, feeling relieved.

But not for long. The male singer goes after Mrs. Spicer's attention again. He seems determined to draw her into the act. Everyone in the room stops talking to listen. "I thought I married a California peach," he laments to her, "and I found I got a Georgia lemon!" The laughter is scant and reserved. "Lots more zest, isn't there?" Eleanor Spicer retorts. This time the laughter is full and appreciative. Raquel begins to talk about the DAR. She says she would like to learn more about it. "Next time you're in Washington, come into our buildings," the president general says. "I'll take you around."

After another song, Raquel's partner says, "You know, Eleanor, people all over the room are telling secrets about you."

The New Jersey Daughters stiffen.

Mrs. Spicer says, "Really? I didn't know anybody knew them!" She laughs. Everyone laughs. The singer says, "I understand you're descended from George Washington."

"No," Mrs. Spicer says. "He didn't have any children. From his sister."

"I'm very glad to know that."

"I'm very proud of it."

After a few more songs and a little more badinage between

themselves, the entertainers retire. A waitress comes over to the DAR table carrying a tray of champagne glasses. The Daughters are puzzled. They have not ordered champagne. The waitress smiles. She passes out the glasses. In a moment or two, Raquel comes to the table bringing an open bottle of champagne wrapped in a white towel. She is smiling. "This is from me, Eleanor," she says. She goes around the table, pouring champagne for every Daughter there. When the bottle is empty, she goes away and returns with another.

Looking back on New Jersey a week or two later, Eleanor Spicer reflected, "I enjoy these meetings. I really get a kick out of them. Invariably something happens that never happened before. And I think I must have an awful lot of ham actor in me because no matter how miserable I feel, how exhausted I may be, I seem to rise to the occasion. I'm like a firehorse when the bell goes off!"

Most DAR members probably did not know they were choosing a ham actor to lead them when they elected Eleanor Spicer to office in 1971. What they needed was a woman with the ability to steer the nation's largest hereditary patriotic organization through what they regard as the crucial Bicentennial planning years. Daughters who saw Mrs. Spicer on the campaign trail —and a fair number did, because in her role of historian general she accepted invitations to speak in thirty-eight states—got a glimpse of an unimposing lady who spoke sincerely but not dynamically from the platform and who smiled directly—and usually up—into the eyes of every person who shook her hand in the receiving line. She sounded sensible; she seemed approachable. Those who didn't see her must have been impressed by the experience she offered them. In the little brown and beige booklet Mrs. Spicer sent out describing her slate, the Daughters could read that as chapter regent in California she had built up her chapter to meet DAR honor-roll standards. They could also read that during her two-year term as California state regent ten new chapters had sprouted to life. They could learn that she took her job as historian general seriously enough to give up her own home in Coronado and move to Washington.

They also learned that Eleanor Spicer had been born into a Marine Corps family, had married a Marine officer, and had lived in many countries, including the Philippines and the Virgin Islands. Mrs. Spicer's brochure noted that while her husband was a prisoner of the Japanese for forty-five months during World War II, she had headed a department of seventy handling classified information at the San Diego Naval Air Station, a job for which she had received the United States Navy Meritorious Award for Civilian Service. The brochure further informed the Daughters that Eleanor Spicer had been active in the Episcopal church and in other organizations besides the DAR, among them the Red Cross and the Mayflower Society. Finally, the Daughters could read that Mrs. Spicer was a widow with three sons, a DAR daughter, and ten grandchildren.

The DAR does not operate on a two-party system. Every president general is bound to uphold the organization's historic, patriotic, and educational objectives, and the work of the national committees remains basically the same no matter who is in office. Elections, therefore, are won or lost not on issues but on personal qualifications, and on the geographical support a given slate of officers can secure.

Eleanor Spicer had geography on her side. Not only was she a Californian, but she was the first Daughter ever to run for president general from the West. There was some feeling in the Society that it was the West's turn. Furthermore, the Spicer ticket included women from New York, Pennsylvania, Illinois, Ohio, New Jersey, and Texas. Her opponent, Elizabeth Barnes, had on her ticket women from only two big states, Pennsylvania and New York.

Mrs. Barnes had been no pushover as a candidate. As organizing secretary general, Elizabeth Barnes had seen to the foundation of seventy-five new DAR chapters. In her three-year term as state regent of Maryland, Mrs. Barnes had supervised the development of fifteen new chapters, at that time a DAR record. She had inaugurated the *National Defender.* She had graduated cum laude from both Bryn Mawr and from the University of Maryland Law School and was a member of the bar in Maryland.

"They were both tremendously qualified," said a Midwest junior who had seen both candidates in person. "You're deciding between two images. Mrs. Barnes presented the image of a buxom, straight-faced lady lawyer. It's not the image we would like to present today." A woman who thought that Mrs. Barnes ought to have the job because of her educational qualifications felt that Eleanor Spicer was the more appealing candidate. "When Mrs. Barnes spoke at our state meeting, she never smiled once," this Daughter recalls.

The delegates to the 1971 Continental Congress cast 945 votes for Elizabeth Barnes and 1,347 for Eleanor Spicer. While geography played a large role in her victory, many Daughters would agree with three young Illinois women who felt that Mrs. Spicer's personal assets were also an important factor.

"She's a wonderfully warm woman," says Linda Lee. "Her experience is incredible."

"Her personality, that's what it comes down to," says Phyllis Whitmore.'

"I think Mrs. Spicer was foremost in our thoughts because we had somebody on her ticket, Mrs. Wakelee Rawson Smith, and everybody in Illinois loves her," says Karen Kiser, "But I got to know Eleanor Spicer when she was at state conference. She had broken her leg, and I wheeled her around for three days. The only word I can think of is charisma. I compare Eleanor Spicer with Adele Sullivan [PG from 1965-1968], and I thought she was great. They're *human*."

It is a cloudy, dark afternoon in January. Eleanor Spicer is sitting in bed wearing a pale pink robe with ruffles on the collar and cuffs. The bed takes up most of the space in the living room of her tiny apartment on the third floor of the Mayflower Hotel. Folded up, the bed is a brocade sofa in fall colors, but it is usually open because Eleanor Spicer uses it as a second office. Since the birth of her youngest child, she has had phlebitis, and while she has little pain from it, her left leg swells. She is conscious of its appearance when she stands in a receiving line wearing street clothes, so she stays off her feet whenever possible, spending many evenings and many hours of the weekends propped up against pillows with a white bed desk pulled over her knees, working on the mail that demands a substantial portion of a president general's time.

She goes through letters that await her signature, describing them to a visitor. "Here's one from the Freedoms Foundation. They want to give an award to *DAR Magazine* at the October board dinner. I've written a letter to confirm.

"Here's a letter from the state historian of the New York DAR who wants help in working out some details of doing a composite on the graves of signers of the Declaration of Independence, listing location, condition, who marked, and so on. Here's a letter from somebody who wants us to consider having a motion picture made about the DAR. He's not the first one. We have gone as far as getting bids.

"Here, somebody has found a grave marker of a Real Daughter in an antique shop, a Real Daughter being an actual daughter of a Revolutionary War soldier and a DAR. This marker had no identification. I suggested what she should do if she finds such a grave.

"Mrs. Russell, the Pennsylvania state regent, wants information on a motion picture which is going to be shown at state conference, *Only the Strong*. It's about the growth of Russia's strength and the lack of growth—to put it mildly—of ours.

"The state regent of Arkansas wants to have a Bicentennial project to commemorate the Coburn Expedition. He went up the Mississippi to Arkansas. They want a diorama at twelve or fifteen thousand dollars. Showing that the Revolution did go west of the Mississippi is extremely important. I'm going to protect that baby!

"Somebody wants to know how to convince the daughter of a deceased Daughter to come into the DAR. There are other letters on insurance. We now have full medical insurance, group, so you have to keep your membership to keep it. They brought it to us, of course—a damned good salesman."

A phone rings. There are two, a beige Princess and a black hotel phone, on a small metal table on wheels next to the bed. Mrs. Spicer pulls the table to her. She likes the idea that people feel they can call her at the Mayflower, and she sometimes gets several calls an hour relating to DAR business. Eleanor Spicer has a quiet, thoughtful voice a little above middle register. When she is exercised, it develops a slightly citric quality.

The Mayflower is one of the best hotels in Washington, but it is still a hotel. From her home in Coronado, Eleanor Spicer could look out the window and see the ocean and the Mexican mountains. Sitting on her bed at the Mayflower, she can see women cleaning the offices across the street. There is a decidedly temporary feeling about her apartment. A few touches are hers. Photographs of her grandchildren stand on a bureau; near the bureau there is a tiny table with a colonial flag emblazoned on the surface (a gift of New York state regent "J. O." Baylies), and on the kitchen door there is a prickly symbol of Eleanor Spicer's campaign, an eagle with hazardous feathers fashioned from tin cans, another gift. But aside from the flag table, all the furniture belongs to the hotel. The television set belongs to the hotel. The big watercolor over the bed belongs to the hotel. "What we give up for the DAR!" Mrs. Spicer once said, looking around at the apartment. "But it's repaid in full. You bet it is."

Eleanor Spicer put her furniture in storage, rented her home, and moved to Washington shortly after she became historian general in 1968. She is one of the few women ever to take up full-time residence in Washington for the express purpose of doing a DAR job. Sally Jones, also a widow, moved from Wisconsin to Washington's Fairfax Hotel when she first became national-defense chairman in 1962 and is still there. Pennsylvanian Ruth Ziesmer, Eleanor Spicer's treasurer general, rented an apartment in Washington because she wanted to personally oversee the DAR's conversion to computer, but this is a unique situation. Mrs. Ziesmer does not feel that her successor will need to live in the District as the conversion will be complete. However, Mrs. Spicer believes strongly that the increasingly complex job of president general can best be done by someone on the scene all the time.

"Good land save the country!" The president general draws her phone conversation to a close and talks about her schedule.

"The alarm goes off at six-fifteen. I crawl out about six-thirty, put my breakfast on a tray, go back to bed and watch the news for an hour. I bathe, dress, and go to the office by taxi a little past nine.

"I'm a brownbagger, I make all my sandwiches on Sunday and put them in the freezer, then take them one at a time. When I'm in Washington, I spend all day at the office. I travel a third of my time. I'll be out six weeks in the spring, attending conferences in eleven states. Nothing in the bylaws says the PG has to travel, but it's custom, and the states want it. Then I will go to board meetings in May and June at our schools.

"When I'm in Washington, I leave the office about four-fifteen. Usually the girls—Jean Jacobs and Marie Yochim —bring me back because getting a taxi at that hour is not very easy. Sometimes they come up for a drink and a chat. If they don't, I generally crawl out of my clothes and onto the bed and start working. I work a while, watch TV a while, correct and sign mail. I fix myself a tray and watch TV while I eat dinner, if I'm not interrupted. The phone rings often. I get an awful lot done on the phone. I rarely put out the light before one. And I do have to keep in touch with the children and do things for myself, like income tax.

"Weekends are the same as evenings, though there's an occasional chapter event I go to. I have no church affiliation here. I have my old-fashioned prayer book and have my own little service by myself. I love the cathedral, and once in a while I get up early and go over there. In the evenings good friends may come and take me out to dinner. I combine business and pleasure, so I don't have much time for my non-DAR friends."

One of her DAR friends describes Eleanor Spicer as a loner and she admits that the description is not a bad one. "I've always been very good company for myself," she says. "I could do a great deal more than I do in the way of accepting invitations, but my time and my strength are limited. Some PGs have made the rounds of the embassies and so on. I don't want to do that alone, and I don't want the follow-up of entertaining. Being a social butterfly as part of a couple and being that as a single, older woman are quite different. And I've had all that.

"But I'm not a martyr. I'm exactly what I want to be. I'm doing the job just the way I want to do it."

Eleanor Spicer is the first service wife to serve the DAR as its president general. Her nomadic life began in Key West, Florida. The oldest of three children, she went to grade schools in Pennsylvania, Virginia, and the state of Washington and then to high school in a French convent in the Virgin Islands. Much of her childhood education was provided by her paternal grandmother. "She had a home with us from the day I was born," Mrs. Spicer says. "She was unusually well-educated. She told us fairy tales in French—I learned to read French almost as soon as I learned to read English. She used to make up games with the multiplication tables, and we played games of naming the rivers of the world and drawing every continent. My grandmother was vital and alive. She read constantly, had an insatiable curiosity, and was an exquisite needlewoman. I spent hours working on a doll's quilt and had her rip it out. The stitches could not show."

Eleanor Spicer never formally graduated from high school. Before she could her family left the Virgin Islands and moved back to Virginia. But because her grandmother had wanted to go to Vassar, Eleanor Sullivan had made up her mind that she would go to Vassar in the fall.

"But then," she says, "I met Don Spicer. And that was the end of it. I was seventeen when I met him. We were living in Fredericksburg. My family didn't think I could pass the exams for Vassar. I thought I could.

"Then I went to a dance one night, and Don Spicer saw me dancing. He was just recovering from a broken love affair and had sworn off women for life. He asked the man next to him if he knew me, and I think he described me as dark-haired and pretty. The man on the other side said, 'I know her. I've known her all my life. In fact she's my date.' Don said, 'I warn you, she may be your date, but she's going to be my wife.'

"We were dancing a Paul Jones, where you dance with one for a while and then mix. He pulled me out of the line and was dancing with me and said, 'You don't know me, but you're going to be my wife!' I was engaged to another man at the time, or thought I was. I said, 'Would you mind telling me what my name will be?' He told me, and I said, 'Uh-uh. I've spent a lot of time teasing my grandmother, because her mother's maiden name was Spicer, and I think it's a funny name.'

"We had a Saturday-night date. On Sunday afternoon we went on a picnic with a group on the Potomac, and we were engaged Sunday night. We weren't married for nearly a year. My mother said, 'Nothing doing. Not at your age.' We would have waited a full year, but he got his orders to Haiti, so we were married at the end of May, 1922, and I went to Haiti with him."

Until December of 1941, Eleanor Spicer occupied herself primarily with being a mother to her four children and a wife to her husband. Then Don Spicer was taken prisoner on Guam. To support her family and the war effort, Mrs. Spicer went to work at the North Island Naval Air Station in Coronado. Two of her children were at school in the East; two were home. She had never held a job in her life. She started as a file clerk and worked up.

In September of 1945 Donald Spicer came home. "He was in the last prison camp to be found," his widow says. "When the first big bomb was dropped we got word that he and other prisoners had been killed. I couldn't believe it. I just had this feeling of serenity about it, that he was not dead. It was a good twelve days before we found out he was alive. I think that was the happiest day of my life."

The Spicers were living in Atlanta when Don Spicer retired from active duty in 1949. In 1950 their son-in-law was killed in Korea. They and their widowed daughter, Nancy, moved to California in 1953. Eleanor Spicer had fewer responsibilities those years than she had ever had, but she was not eager to spend much time away from her husband. "When I got him back, I wasn't going to let him have any absences that would prevent us from doing things together," she says.

Don Spicer died in 1960. Only then did his wife, who had

joined the Daughters of the American Revolution in 1938, begin to let the DAR absorb her.

During the fall of 1972, when the airwaves were crackling with political spot announcements for Presidential candidates, Eleanor Spicer turned on her television set one day just in time to witness an appeal for votes by the Communist Party registered in America. She was extremely distressed by what she saw. Yet she did nothing about it, either as a private citizen or as head of the Daughters of the American Revolution. She knew quite well that in a democracy communists have a legal right to advertise on television.

"The only thing I could have done to vent my ire would have been to throw something at the television," she said later. "And that wasn't very practical. If I'm going to buy a set I'd just as soon buy one that's in working condition!"

Eleanor Spicer does not take communism lightly. She views with dismay the inroads she feels it is gaining in American churches, encouraged by ministers who take it upon themselves to preach sociology instead of religion. She is fully convinced that once Americans leave Southeast Asia the communists will take over, and that prospect makes her very unhappy. At the same time, she is not ready to spring into action whenever the shadow of communism happens to fall between her and the sun. When Eleanor Spicer looks behind the draperies, she sees a wall or a window. When she talks about the work of the DAR, she rarely mentions communism.

A criticism some Daughters made of Eleanor Spicer during her campaign was that she was weak on national defense. Mrs. Spicer insists this is not true. "Nobody could be stronger for national defense than I am," she says. "But I see our work in the schools as national defense.

"Of course we need national defense to keep us alert and educated, but there are those who want it to be the total concept of the Society, who work only for national defense and the resolutions. I think every DAR is strong in national defense, but each has her own concept of what it means."

Like many other Daughters, Mrs. Spicer opposes amnesty, favors military preparedness, and hopes the Equal Rights Amendment will not be ratified. That the head of a large women's organization would object to the ERA might seem surprising, but many conservatives believe the amendment would nullify existing laws which protect women and thus could be detrimental to family life. Eleanor Spicer shares that view.

"Mothers have the right to stay home with their little babies and be protected and cared for and supported while they do, if that is their wish and their husbands' wish," she argues. "Now the husband is required by law to support his wife and his children. But if the ERA goes through it will depend on whether the husband is willing to do this. Under this amendment she's required to put up half of the support, regardless of the fact that she's got dependent babies that she can't leave. And maybe she can't afford a baby-sitter, maybe she doesn't have somebody who's willing to stay with those children while she goes out and earns her money, and maybe she can't find a way to earn money at home, and maybe she doesn't want to put her child in a public day-care center. I wouldn't." (Proponents of the ERA say there are no laws requiring husbands to support wives and claim further that if the amendment is ratified, support obligations will depend on the earning power of each spouse.)

Mrs. Spicer feels that although men don't realize it, they are being cheated by the system that leaves child care primarily up to women. Still, she believes that the decision open to the husband should be not whether he wants to provide for his wife but to what extent he wants to participate in raising the children. Now and then Eleanor Spicer sounds more like women's liberationist Betty Friedan than like ERA opponent Phyllis Schlafly. But she does not sympathize with radical feminists and believes that, as DAR leaders all along have proven, women with the ability and desire to make contributions to society beyond the home will do so.

"I think that women are as much liberated as they want to be and are capable of being," she says. "Any sense of restriction is basically what we put on ourselves."

Along with other conservatives, Eleanor Spicer deeply resents Americans who fail to show proper faith in their country or its government. Speaking before the so-called peace agreement in Vietnam, she said of participants in the peace movement, "If they're demonstrating peacefully, and they're not carrying the North Vietnam flag, I think they have a perfect right to express their opinion as long as they don't interfere with the rights of others. I can see that it's possible that someone who would do that might be acting according to his conscience, feeling like a patriot, though his definition may differ from mine. In other words, he can feel patriotic without having the conviction that

'It's my country; right or wrong, I still love it.' But he doesn't want to love it unless it's right according to his notion. I love it anyway.

"On the other hand, I think these people who have carried the Viet Cong flag, desecrated their own flag, vilified everybody in our country in authority and extolled everybody in North Vietnam are traitors. I do. But remember, when I'm talking I can't divorce myself from my service background. And a serviceman in the old school did not criticize his commander-in-chief.

"When I think of what just the men in my family alone have been through, and what they've done because it was their duty to do it—and never a scream of protest. And they weren't dumb. Or what their families put up with. The things we did without. The places we lived in at times. And it was just part of the game."

For the most part Eleanor Spicer supports the stands the DAR has taken on various national issues. However, the United Nations resolution gives her a little trouble. Though she believes the original concept had grandeur, the president general views with dismay the course the UN has taken. But unlike some Daughters, Eleanor Spicer doesn't view U.S. withdrawal as a solution.

"I believe firmly that it should either change and go back to its charter, which the UN itself violated, or it should cease to exist," she says. "I feel that as long as it exists we ought to stay in and try to swing it."

While Eleanor Spicer is firmly conservative, she is not necessarily an evangelist for conservatism, or even for her own position. In discussing almost any issue she is careful to point out that her views are inescapably formed by her background, particularly its military aspects. "All my thinking is so much a part of that military life and atmosphere that I was brought up in that it's hard for me sometimes to disorient myself from it, or try to," she says. Still, she tries to make clear that she knows different backgrounds might produce different views.

Her feelings about race are a good illustration of this. She believes that some young people "made a fetish" of their support of blacks; she can understand people who object to romantic liaisons between men and women of different races; she still feels, though less than she used to, that the child of mixed blood is "tragic." But she acknowledges that her associations with blacks are limited. "I've always had black servants living in my house," Eleanor Spicer says. "I delivered a baby for one. One family stayed with me sixteen years. There wasn't anything I wouldn't have done for those people. It was a very close relationship. But they did not sit at my table."

Hearing how Lucille Fryxell had stood up in a room full of Illinois college students and expressed her determination never to be unkind to any person, black or white, Eleanor Spicer said, "I think I'm in her class, I will admit to you. She's a very good representative of Southern gentlefolk who have always felt just as she did. They were never unkind to their servants. They made them part of the family. It's a paternalism, I grant you. It's hard to get away from that. People have a hard time getting away from the way they were brought up."

Mrs. Spicer says she doesn't know how she would have handled the Marian Anderson situation if she had been president general in 1939. She notes that PG Sally Robert was on a train and therefore difficult to reach. She thinks a moment but finally says only, "It's easy to look back and say, 'I would have done this or that.'"

It is a mild winter afternoon two days before Richard Nixon's second inauguration. The sunlight coming through the myriad panes of glass in the president general's office is tentative and reserved. Large, carpeted, full of rich woods and lovely fabric, accented with brass and crystal, decorated tastefully with antiques, the office looks like a room in a museum or an elegant private home. The last PG to redecorate the room was Adele Sullivan, a redhead. The grayish-aqua and gold she chose are as becoming to the room as they must have been to her. "The job of DAR president is so difficult that it's just incredible that you have to work to get it," says a woman who has run for the top job, but the president general's office could probably tempt many people to try.

Eleanor Spicer is sitting at the desk stirring some orange powdered gelatin into a glass of water. She occasionally has lunch at the Army-Navy Club but usually refuses luncheon invitations even on quiet days, as she says this one is. Letting a thawed sandwich warm up on a paper towel, the president general contemplates her calendar.

"This afternoon I'm expecting a Mrs. John Fluor from Santa Ana. She's here for the inauguration, a very close friend of the Nixons. She's bringing in a friend to see the building and me. I didn't know till this morning that she was coming. She's going to collect signatures from the descendants of signers. The signatures will be placed in Independence Hall as part of our Gift to the Nation."

Mrs. Spicer reflects on the DAR's project in Independence Hall. She considers the refurbishing of the two rooms there her chief accomplishment as president general.

"The Gift to the Nation fits all of our objectives, and it is completely unselfish," she says. "I have been criticized by someone who says that we shouldn't be putting our money into something that doesn't belong to us. Well, my answer is that Independence Hall belongs to us as much as it does to anybody. My happiest moment as PG was when Congress passed that gift."

Continental Congress has only once failed to approve a president general's project, but in this case approval was not a foregone conclusion. The money raised would not be going to DAR programs. Only twice before had the Daughters spent their money on outside projects. Early in this century they placed twelve "Madonnna of the Trail" statues along the National Old Trails Road from Maryland to California. Memorials to pioneer mothers, the statues cost a total of $12,000, a fraction of what Eleanor Spicer was asking the Daughters to spend on furnishings. After World War II Congress delegates gave the go-ahead for a bell tower in Valley Forge, but in essence the National Society was bailing out the Pennsylvania DAR. Pennsylvania Daughters started the tower as a state project in 1941. When postwar building costs soared, they were unable to complete it. By the time the tower was finished in 1953, the DAR had spent half a million dollars on it, far more than they would ever have planned to invest. Some were still smarting from the experience nine years later when the incoming PG proposed that the Daughters build a Patriots' Lobby at the Freedoms Foundation at Valley Forge. Congress delegates said no.

When her turn came, Eleanor Spicer mustered all her forces. She thought the vote might go her way if the DAR had somebody on the national American Revolution Bicentennial Commission. Mrs. Spicer says she asked her congressman, Bob Wilson, "to see that the patriotic societies were represented" on the Commission. Wilson says he was "pushing" to get Mrs. Spicer on it. In a letter to Wilson explaining why the PG was not offered an appointment, a Commission staff member noted that a bill introduced by Maryland Senator Charles Mathias required Commission membership to include representatives of youth, minorities, and ethnic groups. As there were only eight slots open, the staff member pointed out, everyone could not be satisfied. However, Mrs. Spicer would be asked to be part of a special advisory council.

Six months later, sipping her orange gelatin, Eleanor Spicer muses on the outcome of her efforts. "So those spaces were filled by people because they were ethnic groups, not necessarily knowing anything about. . ."

The PG thinks better of finishing her sentence. "Well, I don't have that much information on them," she says. "The Commission wasn't doing much even before that. I would have liked to get on the Commission, but not now. The *Post* said I had *tried* to get on but settled for a lesser appointment. I have yet to see the lesser appointment! There are two DAR's on the Commission, but not by virtue of their being DAR. SAR should be there, and they're not. Of course SAR changes their president every year. So does CAR."

If the Commission did not need Eleanor Spicer's services, neither, it turned out, did she need the Commission appointment. Delegates to the 1972 Congress expressed overwhelming support for the project in Independence Hall. A handful cast votes against. If any Daughters still opppose Gift to the Nation, they aren't saying so very loudly. The regent of an Eastern state says that some of the women in her state grumbled about the project at first, but finally they chartered a bus and went and saw it for themselves. They returned home with high praise for their leader. "Independence Hall is just the epitome of what the DAR should be doing," says Illinois Daughter Phyllis Whitmore, and it seems that most Daughters agree.

Mrs. Spicer finishes her sandwich and glances at some clippings her secretary has placed on her desk. "I've always read a paper," she says, "but I just don't have time now. I subscribe to *U.S. News* and *Human Events*. Sometimes I leaf through them, sometimes I read them cover to cover. The other night between eleven-thirty and one A.M. I signed one hundred certificates recognizing chapter contributions for Independence Hall and then signed, corrected, and sealed the mail. The project is over the top now. We have one hundred eleven thousand dollars."

The president general takes a phone call. It is from Kendrick Holle, the administrator of Constitution Hall. "Mr. Holle is often on the phone," Mrs. Spicer says, replacing the receiver after a brief conversation. "We're working on Congress scheduling.

We're cutting Congress a day this year because it's Holy Week. The other day I spent almost all day with personnel because there was a fight among the maids. We had to tread very carefully. Fair employment practices are very strict. You can't fire somebody as easily as you could. And I like to hear both sides of the story. That takes time."

The DAR has been in the process of computerizing, and Mrs. Spicer decides to see how things are coming along. In a room down the hall, she finds four or five women working very hard to update membership information. Eleanor Spicer walks over to treasurer general Ruth Ziesmer and rests her hand on Mrs. Ziesmer's shoulder, offering a few words of encouragement. She doesn't stay long because the women are obviously rushed. On the way out, Eleanor Spicer runs into a middle-aged man in white overalls holding a paintbrush and a can of paint.

"Hello, Mr. Booth," she says, stopping in front of him and smiling. Mr. Booth greets her looking slightly troubled. He seems to want to say something to her. She waits.

"Did you like the paint job in the Connecticut Board Room?" he asks in a hurt voice.

"I *did*," the president general says.

"You haven't complimented me on it yet. You haven't said anything."

Mrs. Spicer looks up into his face. "Why, I thought I had, Mr. Booth, I'm so sorry. The room looks just lovely."

"What about the stars? Did you like the stars?"

"I think they're just what the room needed."

Mr. Booth looks happier. He goes on about his business. Eleanor Spicer walks back toward her office with her visitor in tow. After a few steps she looks behind her. Mr. Booth is nowhere to be seen.

"Did you hear my hesitation?" she asks. "I haven't seen the stars! I don't even know where they are!"

The PG continues along the hall. "I like to take little walks through the building," she says after a moment. "I like to talk to people in the halls, like Mr. Booth. It keeps me from getting tired. I get cooperation that way. I'm stimulated by the way people respond to me. It's my stock in trade." Mrs. Spicer beams.

Eleanor Spicer likes to shatter conceptions about what manner of person might be expected to head the DAR. She feels the misconceptions exist inside the Society as well as outside.

"One of the sad things is that some Daughters think the PG should be austere," she says. "I try to break that feeling down. When I get through at a conference, I feel like they get over the notion, because I can have fun, too.

"I suppose we have some aspects of a monarchy in DAR. People approach me reverently. They're even a little frightened. The PG *is* treated much like a queen, I suppose. I think this is true of any organization head. I don't feel that I'm treated that way in my office, and I don't want to be. I like the free and easy aspect of my relationship with the girls. I have taken a very motherly interest in them. I don't ask anything of them I wouldn't do myself.

"I'm very careful about not having the pages do anything for me physically except to zip me up, maybe, which I'd ask any friend. As personal pages they are up there to see to it that I don't have to fumble for my glasses or a pen, the papers and medals and so on. It's their responsibility to see that I have what I need when I need it. It's not just carrying a handkerchief for me.

"As for reverence, I appreciate the fact that it's reverence for the office and not for me. The average DAR appreciates to some degree the responsibility and load the PG carries. That's what their reverence is for. At Congress, that's their opportunity to tell her they appreciate it. And they do."

Out of more than half a million women who have joined the DAR since its founding, scarcely three score have wanted to be president general badly enough to actually run for the job.

There are good reasons. For one thing, it is expensive to be PG. Women who have held the office are reluctant to say just how expensive, but Mrs. Spicer says the top officers can spend at least as much as a state regent on her office. The president general does receive a travel stipend of $10,000. Still, the woman who becomes PG must be willing and able to invest fairly large sums during her term for clothes, travel not covered by the stipend, entertaining, and the incidentals—from Christmas cards to dry cleaning—that eat into the budget of any organization head.

Recent leaders have also provided themselves with residences in Washington. Until the last twenty years or so, presidents general ran the DAR from their own homes. They went to Washington only every so often. But as the Society has grown larger and its administration increasingly complex, its top leaders have been spending more and more time at headquarters. The last five presidents general took apartments in Washington during their terms.

(Four lived part-time in their own homes as well. Eleanor Spicer lives full-time at the Mayflower. That is her decision, not a requirement of the office. Being an organization of volunteers, the DAR has not demanded that its leaders change their lives in order to serve. In that respect the Daughters differ from the General Federation of Women's Clubs, also headquartered in Washington, which does require its president to live in the District. The GFWC, however, provides the residence. Eleanor Spicer does not foresee that the DAR will ever to be able to provide one. If she is right, the apartment precedent that has been established could affect future DAR elections. Women seeking top office must be able either to pay for a Washington residence or to explain to the satisfaction of voters why the job does not require one.)

Besides being expensive, the job of president general is time-consuming. The PG must preside at every meeting of the National Society, the Executive Committee, and the National Board of Management. She is a member of the boards of the DAR schools, an ex officio member of all DAR committees, and the Society's only official spokesman. She oversees all programs, all finances, all real estate, all paid personnel at headquarters, and Constitution Hall.

These duties are required by the bylaws. Tradition makes further demands. It requires the PG to visit every state once during her three-year term of office. Also according to tradition each president general devises, convinces Congress delegates to pass, and then sees to the execution of her own special project usually involving, like Gift to the Nation, tens of thousands of dollars. The PG is not required to put in a five-day week and a fifty-two-week year as Eleanor Spicer has done, but there is no question that the DAR's top office can absorb all the time a woman is willing to give it. If she does the job conscientiously, she can do little else. She becomes, temporarily, a stranger to her friends and even to her family.

Furthermore, though the job has its rewards, they don't come free. The PG has responsibilities which are increasingly demanding of scope and skill. In 1968, for example, Adele Sullivan had to decide whether to convene Continental Congress while the city of Washington still smoldered from the riots following

Martin Luther King's assassination. Though many organizations canceled their meetings in the District that spring, Mrs. Sullivan did convene Congress, a decision for which Mayor Walter Washington has expressed his gratitude to the Daughters at every Continental Congress since. Adele Sullivan also had to worry about the effect of the proposed Kennedy Center on Constitution Hall revenues. In part to make the Hall competitive with the Center, she convinced the Daughters to spend $400,000 to air-condition their auditorium.

Betty Seimes, Adele Sullivan's successor, faced both a rising District wage scale, patterned largely after the civil service, and an ever-larger DAR membership. More members meant more paperwork. Instead of hiring more people to do that work, Mrs. Seimes chose to install a computer, committing every administrative operation possible to the machine.

The completed Kennedy Center posed a whole series of problems for the Spicer administration. When the National Symphony decided not to renew its contract with the Daughters, Eleanor Spicer had to seek other programs for Constitution Hall—in the age of acid rock and young audiences. She scheduled some rock programs, and the Hall was vandalized. The DAR had to pay for some of the damage, file claims for the rest, and buy burglar bars for all the first-floor windows. The president general cut out hard-rock concerts. That put an end to both the vandalism and the income. These problems took too much of the PG's time away from DAR business. She therefore had to redefine the job of Constitution Hall administrator and find and hire someone to fill it.

The large headquarters and Constitution Hall set the DAR apart from all other voluntary organizations, but even if these facilities did not exist, running the DAR would not be like running any other club. A unique handicap compounds virtually all of the president general's responsibilities—the DAR's poor public image.

No president general has attacked that problem head-on. Every president general has tried in her own way to improve the image, but these efforts have been largely cosmetic. The Daughters have tried to make the DAR look better while failing to squarely confront what makes it look bad—its resolutions and its equivocal racial stance. Rather than solving these problems, the DAR has attempted to compensate for them.

Eleanor Spicer's administration has been a classic illustration of this approach. Fully aware that the DAR is viewed as racist, Mrs. Spicer invited a black to address Continental Congress, wished that a black child could win the DAR's history scholarship, issued a revised statement on Marian Anderson, and, out of the misconceptions she shares with most Daughters about what 1939 really signified, toyed with the idea of writing to Miss Anderson and asking her to help the DAR set the record straight. Mrs. Spicer did not undertake to find out why the Daughters are still being held accountable for 1939. She did not organize a campaign to recruit black members. She did not take any public steps that would show that the DAR favors equal rights for all Americans.

Despite the continued tendency of outsiders to view the DAR as reactionary, Mrs. Spicer appointed two of the organization's staunchest old-guard national defenders to head the resolutions and national-defense committees. She did not ask those committees to show cause why they should continue to function in a way that has repeatedly made trouble for the Society. Though all indications are that the DAR badly needs an aggressive public-relations campaign, Eleanor Spicer's approach to public relations has been rather passive. She has been criticized for not promoting the Society vigorously enough, and she is aware of her own limitations in this regard. "I'm not that kind of person," she has said. "I don't think I can do the Society a whole lot of good unless the papers come to me first." Nevertheless, recognizing her limitations, Mrs. Spicer fired the one person on her staff with public-relations experience and did not replace her.

Shortly after she took office, Eleanor Spicer told a reporter that as she saw it, her mission was to make the DAR's good works known and to make the DAR understood "on issues where we have been grossly misunderstood." Asked how she hoped to do that, Mrs. Spicer expressed a belief that the project in Independence Hall would help. The project undoubtedly will help somewhat. But two rooms of furniture, however rare and valuable the pieces, will not make Americans stop viewing the DAR as reactionary or racist. To let those furnishings substitute for modifications where needed and a coherent, imaginative, and forceful public-relations policy is to invite the American public to go on thinking of the DAR as it always has. It's a little like giving a boy a bicycle when his dog dies. The bicycle may distract the child, but it won't make him forget the dog.

Nevertheless, Mrs. Spicer's handling of the DAR's toughest

problem must be viewed in perspective. She is only the latest in a long line of presidents general who have failed to come up with an alternative to the bicycle approach. Inviting General James to Congress and issuing a gentle statement on Constitution Hall may be small steps in the direction of racial understanding, but they're bigger steps than any other president general has taken. As for old-guard appointments, the women who end up in national chairmanships are not necessarily the women the PG wants most. The ones she wants most may turn her down. While she has not said whether Genevieve Morse and Sally Jones were her first choices for the resolutions and national-defense committees, Eleanor Spicer has commented of the latter appointment that there was no one else who knew as much as Mrs. Jones did "who wasn't so radical that we were scared to death of her." (The PG added, scowling, "You can be as radical on the right as you can be on the left, and just as dangerous.")

In her lack of public-relations expertise Eleanor Spicer is like most of her predecessors, and she also shares with many amateurs in and out of the DAR a certain doubtfulness about the propriety of professionally promoting oneself or one's causes. Furthermore, money was a factor in her dismissal of public-relations aide Aileen Jordan. It wasn't the only factor, but the dues increase was not to take effect until after Eleanor Spicer left office, and as her administration drew to a close, she was cutting corners wherever possible. Mrs. Jordan was not the only casualty.

Actually Eleanor Spicer has done more in behalf of a better image for the DAR than have a number of her predecessors. Again and again a president general has chosen as her project the construction of a building at KDS or Tamassee, a building which, when finished, bears her name. The buildings serve a useful purpose, some less useful than others, but from the point of view of image they all suffer a common drawback: no one but the DAR ever sees them. Eleanor Spicer showed more imagination. Her name does not appear on the plaque at Independence Hall, but the DAR is named, and if public goodwill was not the major objective of the project, it certainly promises to be a fringe benefit. As the Bicentennial draws nearer, the Gift to the Nation can't help but redound to the Daughters' credit.

Furthermore, Mrs. Spicer has been better with the press than some other PG's. She can be faulted for not reopening the resolutions sessions her predecessor closed and for waiting too long to authorize the resolutions chairman to speak to reporters. On the other hand, DAR relations with the press were at a low point when she took office, and at least one Washington reporter feels Mrs. Spicer improved those relations immediately: She let reporters see that she understood their wish to be present while the resolutions were being discussed, and she was courteous and thoughtful in explaining the DAR's position. It is a measure of Mrs. Spicer's success with the press that she has rarely been unhappy with the way reporters have treated her in print. This can be attributed in large part to her accessibility and openness. Some DAR leaders are guided by mistrust, but Eleanor Spicer willingly makes herself available to reporters and answers questions forthrightly and fully. She knows the value of exposing her organization to the light of day, its warts notwithstanding. (Some Daughters counseled Mrs. Spicer not to cooperate with the author of this book, but she told them, "The author is a journalist. If she finds a story, she's going to write it. Wouldn't you rather she hear it from us?")

Eleanor Spicer is also an excellent spokesman for the DAR. She is no liberal and does not talk like one, and she has not renovated her organization, but she represents it very well to outsiders. For one thing, she doesn't sound holier than all the rest of us. "We don't feel we have any special rights in the field of patriotism," she once told a reporter. "We have an obligation in the field. That doesn't mean I think I'm any more patriotic than you, but I think it's my responsibility, as a DAR or as a patriotic American, to help you understand if you don't. That if you're not patriotic because you don't understand what's involved, it's my responsibility to show you what's involved. If you'll let me."

She is also thoughtful. Asked what she thought America should be, Mrs. Spicer's answer included the following comments: "Of course I haven't touched on godliness, but that's written into the Constitution, and there just has to be something wrong when one woman can take the right to pray away from all schoolchildren. But I also feel that the child who is told at home not to pray would be confused by being forced to do so in school. So it should be expected but not demanded."

Many Daughters, asked what the DAR has accomplished, give back a kind of shorthand which presumes that the activity is the effect. "Schools," they say. "Conservation. Indian scholarships." Eleanor Spicer weighs the question carefully. "There are truly so many accomplishments," she says at last, "but I think probably the greatest single general accomplishment is proving, beginning at the time that women were just beginning to prove themselves, that women can act independently, can achieve what they set their minds to achieve, can function as a group, efficiently, effectively . . . that they can, and do, set aside personal ambitions for the good of the whole, that they can use their talents and abilities and physical strength for both home and country without neglecting either . . . that they have imagination and initiative, and that they can accomplish these things in the face of criticism and ridicule without being fazed by it. We've gone ahead and done the things we've planned to do. Each succeeding generation of us, each succeeding administration, has set its own goals and achieved them for the good of the whole Society."

Finally, Eleanor Spicer exhibits none of the stuffiness outsiders believe to be characteristic of DAR members. She was sixty-eight years old when she went to see *Jesus Christ Superstar*, and she went because some Daughters had criticized her sharply for letting *Superstar* appear in Constitution Hall, but the PG liked the production and said so aloud.

"I was told I'd be horrified by the libretto," she said later. "I was told I'd see proof of an illicit relationship between Mary Magdalene and Christ. I didn't see it. And I looked. But she had a grandmother's dress on down to here. The only time she touched Him was when she held His face in her hands, like this. There was not a kiss exchanged. Now I don't know what they did in New York.

"The positive evidence I'd been warned of that Christ was a drug addict and a weakling. . . . The only place I think that someone might have gotten that idea was when Christ was beaten. As the music came across, 'Crucify Him! Crucify Him!'—the music came across as a whiplash, and his body moved. Was that an indication that he was going cold turkey? So what was wrong with the play?

"At the end it was dark. Completely dark. For two minutes you just sat there and held your breath. And then this galaxy of stars broke out. All over the whole ceiling. The walls. And if that didn't spell eternity, I don't know how better they could have said it. There was not a sound, except a gasp."

For all these reasons, Eleanor Spicer has made the DAR look better than it has looked in some other administrations. To the extent that she has had contact with outsiders, Mrs. Spicer has almost certainly prompted revised notions about the organization. But because she is not an aggressive blower of the DAR's horn or her own, that contact has been limited. She will not leave office as the president general who has given the DAR image its biggest boost. That honor belongs to the woman who headed the Society from 1965 to 1968: Adele Erb Sullivan.

Adele Sullivan is almost legendary in the DAR. She is a presence. She is relatively young. She is something of a character. She has been criticized for extravagance, but the Daughters admire her anyway. She reversed the downward trend in membership, but that isn't why the Daughters like her. On opening night of her first Congress as president general Adele Sullivan swept into Constitution Hall wearing a Hattie Carnegie gown. Adele Sullivan was interviewed by *McCall's* and *The New York Times*, and her picture in *The Times* was not a picture of the DAR member in the traditional image. Adele Sullivan went to Vietnam (on her own money) to find out for herself what was going on over there. When the troops yelled, "Hi, Mom!" she laughed. She went on the David Susskind show and "won" a grilling he gave her, securing for the DAR some of its best publicity in recent memory. "Adele Sullivan is the best thing that ever happened to the DAR," a Washington reporter has said, and many Daughters agree. Adele Sullivan made the DAR look like the Daughters want it to look. They reward her by speaking of her as the most popular president general the DAR has ever had.

Unfortunately for the Society, Adele Sullivan's gifts left office when she did. Her contributions to the DAR's image were transient because they were almost exclusively a function of her own personality. The DAR appeared to be a different organization when she was president general, but that was an illusion. When Adele Sullivan's term was over, Americans who were aware of her saw that the DAR was the same organization it had always been. Most reverted to thinking about it as they always had—the DAR still has image problems. That would not be true if Adele Sullivan had made changes that permitted the improved image to stand without her, but she made no such changes.

In all fairness, no president general has made substantial changes in the DAR. No president general has unlimited power to do so. A PG may serve only one term, and three years is not a long time to learn the job and set wheels in motion when the wheels are all impelled by volunteers. As minimum demands of the highest office have been interpreted, the

PG doesn't have a great deal of time to formulate and pursue new ways of doing things. Perhaps more than members of other organizations, women who serve at the top levels of the DAR are exceedingly reluctant to appear to impugn the efforts of their predecessors. A change which is seen as necessary may actually be put off until a powerful Daughter who would be hurt by the move has died. Changes which carry the possibility of widespread disapproval, such as an increase in dues, may be left for succeeding administrations to tackle. Daughters who oppose certain changes may just drag their heels until the next administration moves in with different ideas. Furthermore, any leader is inevitably limited by her own experience, ability, and orientation.

For all these reasons, presidents general have not been known for the new directions in which they have turned the DAR. The president general who becomes popular among the members is the woman who has the personality and the vision to inspire the Daughters, who engages them in projects that catch their imagination, and who does them proud when she carries their banner into the world.

It has befallen the presidents general in recent memory to be compared to the twenty-fifth. Eleanor Spicer is the twenty-seventh. She is not Adele Sullivan. She is older. Her hair is gray. She has neither the dash nor the flamboyance of the lady from Scarsdale, and where Adele Sullivan speaks with extravagance, Eleanor Spicer speaks with caution. Adele Sullivan is active in the Republican Party in New York and has been known to bop over to see Jeanne Dixon or Maurice Stans when she is in Washington. In general she conducts her life like a confirmed extrovert. Although Eleanor Spicer is charismatic in company, she is quieter than Mrs. Sullivan, more contemplative, happy alone.

Still, the two women have much in common. They are attractive, approachable people who look upon life with enthusiasm. Both have all the ego they need to run a large organization with the DAR's reputation, but neither is overbearing. Their loyalty to America and to the DAR shows no marks of silliness or extremism. Both seem more attuned to the gentler aspects of their organization than to the sharp exhortations for which the DAR has become known. As Mrs. Spicer's administration drew to a close, it was not uncommon to hear Daughters speak of her and Adele Sullivan in the same breath, and with the same admiration.

All indications are that the women in the DAR will look back with approval and respect on the leader who helped them plan for the Bicentennial. Eleanor Spicer is a woman of considerable charm and warmth—fun to be with, dignified when dignity is called for, and, Daughters say over and over, gracious. Her administration has been marked by no storms of bad publicity. She has kept and attracted members: in each of her first two years in office the increases in DAR enrollment were greater than they had been in any year since 1956. In proposing a dues hike of unprecedented proportions, Eleanor Spicer showed herself willing to put the Society's welfare ahead of her own popularity, and in convincing initially reluctant Congress delegates to vote every dollar she requested, Mrs. Spicer relieved the financial burden on the Society without making program cuts. She hoped she could inspire the Daughters to spend their money outside the organization, and she gauged them, and herself, correctly. To the extent that the Daughters feel proud of their contributions to Independence Hall, they are likely to be grateful to the woman responsible. In all these ways Eleanor Spicer has been good for the DAR.

But because she failed to change it, the stamp she has given her organization is not permanent, any more than Adele Sullivan's stamp was permanent. Eleanor Spicer's gifts, too, are destined to stay in the president general's office only until she leaves it. As long as the Daughters permit the troublesome aspects of their reputation to fester, as long as the organization remains unchanged, the burden of refuting the DAR's poor image will fall almost exclusively on the person of the president general. To the extent that she is like Eleanor Spicer or Adele Sullivan, the DAR will profit—temporarily. To the extent that she is weak where they are strong, the organization is bound to suffer.

CHAPTER XI

Remaking The Image

If the Daughters of the American Revolution are ever to prove to the other inhabitants of this nation that they are not doddering old dowagers waving the flag and worshipping their ancestors, they may never have a better opportunity than in the last quarter of the twentieth century.

In 1976 America will celebrate her two-hundredth birthday. In 1990 the DAR will celebrate its own centennial. Two years later the country will observe the five-hundredth anniversary of Christopher Columbus' landing. Eight years after that the world will enter into a new age, and while the Daughters aren't talking about A.D. 2000 as yet, it is inconceivable that an organization which exists in part to mark historic events will ignore that one. Over the next two and a half decades Americans might be unusually receptive to just the kind of activities at which the DAR is expert and for which it has often been scorned: looking for significance in the past, marking the efforts of citizens now dead who tried to help America become its best self, preserving what can be preserved of the culture that preceded and spawned Americans alive today, observing or commemorating important moments with ceremony. The Daughters have a good chance, perhaps unprecedented in recent times, for good press. For that reason, now is an ideal time for them to give some thought to how they will—and how they want to—appear. And no question is more important for them to answer than the question of what is to become of Susan Guisbert Hammett.

Susan Hammett is young, slender, attractive, and chic, the kind of woman most Daughters would be delighted to have represent them in a newspaper photograph, and an asset as well in substantive ways. She is willing to work and does so with efficiency and aplomb. She deals smoothly with the press. She is proud of the DAR. When she hears other juniors say they are reluctant to admit they are members, Susan tells them, "You shouldn't apologize for being a DAR, just as you wouldn't for being a Presbyterian, though it's not as important as religion. Other people can be as bigoted as they say we are."

Someone with these attributes at the age of twenty-four could give much to the Daughters of the American Revolution in the course of a lifetime. Although she has begun a career in banking, belongs to Young Republicans, and thinks about going into politics, Susan expects to remain an active Daughter. While she says she has no political aspirations in the Society, she might consider assuming responsibilities beyond chapter offices.

However, Susan Hammett's future in the DAR is not solely up to Susan Hammett. It also hinges on how willing other Daughters are to be led by someone who thinks the organization may die unless it changes. Susan objects to many things that go on in the DAR and says so. She views the United Nations as nothing more than a big international cocktail party and can't understand why the Daughters fuss about it. She doesn't see, either, why Daughters get upset about entertainment groups such as the Rolling Stones coming to America and allegedly violating U.S. narcotics laws. "What's it got to do with the DAR?" Susan demands. "Why should the DAR take a stand on something like that?"

Unlike many Daughters, Susan feels that the DAR itself may be responsible for some of its image problems, "I think the image of the DAR has a lot to do with what it comes down on," she says. "That resolution about rock music—the DAR drew a parallel between rock music and the drug culture. I thought it was a bad move p.r.-wise. Rock music is a cultural development, and that resolution makes the DAR look like an anachronism. It makes it look reactionary. The one on the quota system—it sounded as though the DAR wanted America for the WASPs. I'm thinking of what's on the Statue of Liberty. I say to myself, you know, does this negate what's written there?"

In Susan's opinion, the Daughters haven't tried hard enough to divest Americans of the notion that the DAR is elitist. She feels that where prospective members are concerned, "personal acceptability" far too often means social acceptability. "The basic reason for being in DAR is a common genealogical background," Susan protests. "Why is it that to become a member of a chapter you have to have so many people supporting you? Why aren't your papers enough?"

Aside from these heresies, Susan has not yet made up her mind on some things other Daughters take for granted. "Like what is patriotism?" she muses. "Some people demonstrating against the war, to them it's an expression of patriotism. You're idealistic in supporting the war, and they're idealistic in being against it. I haven't worked out a definition for myself. So DAR promoting patriotism—what kind of patriotism? Patriotism on the the right, which is power to the United States, its ideals, its Constitution, its power structure; or patriotism of the left, which is power to the people? Everything's so relative. This is why I'm rather concerned about the DAR taking definite stands on things that perhaps will never relate to the mainstream of

American thinking. Members say events have proven that we had great foresight, but if what we have to say is true, why is it that people don't listen to it and regard it as the truth?"

Susan Hammett poses a dilemma for the DAR. On one hand she exhibits qualities any Daughter would consider beneficial to the organization. On the other hand, she has ideas in her head that many Daughters neither share nor sympathize with. If she got into a leadership role, her approach might make some Daughters very unhappy. But if she were squelched, the organization could lose her skills and could even lose her as a member.

Susan Hammett is young. In ten years she might be more orthodox. But if she isn't, the DAR will have to decide what to do about her, as it must decide about others like her—talented women and good Daughters who are outspoken in their belief that the DAR must change. If the majority of members resists change and discourages those who want to make them, the DAR meeting the opportunities of the last quarter of this century will be essentially the DAR about which many Americans, rightly or wrongly, have long since drawn their conclusions. For that reason, Susan Hammett's future in the DAR could have a lot to do with what is to become of the DAR in America.

The challenge confronting the DAR is not how to survive. It need not change just to do that. Staying basically the same, the DAR has continued to add more members so that today, after more than eighty years of life, it claims the loyalty of more women than at any other time in its history. Among them are many talented, intelligent women who see a meeting place between their interests and the DAR's objectives, and who are ready and willing to support the organization with enormous amounts of time and money and energy.

But surviving is not the same as thriving. There is no guarantee that the DAR's membership will continue to increase. Women's organizations today are operating in a seller's market. Under the influence of women's liberation, American females are taking a second look at themselves and becoming more selective in deciding how they will spend their time and talents. As one Daughter puts it, "Women are no longer sitting around wondering what meeting they're going to attend today." Even if the DAR proved able to continue growing in size, there is no reason to suppose that it would grow accordingly in the affections of other Americans. A good reputation has nothing to do with size: The DAR is already one of the biggest organizations in the country, yet it has very little influence. Not all members acknowledge that. But a good many say quite readily that the DAR has considerably less influence than they would like it to have.

Image thus becomes the crucial factor in the future of the DAR. However worthwhile the organization's programs might be, if a woman has little by which to judge the organization but a reputation she considers poor, she is not going to cast her lot with the Daughters. The DAR has managed to grow without changing, but it has failed to win the esteem of its countrymen. The implication is clear. If the organization wants a better image and the admiration and influence that go with it, changes must be made.

This is a stern challenge because there is no precedent for real change in the DAR. Perhaps the main reason is that the Daughters are basically proud of the organization as it is. A few months after Eleanor Spicer took office she told a reporter that in trying to make the DAR understood she wanted to change not the organization itself but the public conception of it. As the Constitution has served the United States for two hundred years, the DAR's original historic, patriotic, and educational objectives have held up well, too, Daughters believe. Furthermore, since the DAR is by nature devoted to tradition, it naturally appeals to conservative people, interested in tradition, and people interested in tradition are rarely advocates of doing things differently. The DAR's philosophical atmosphere provides plenty of nourishment for the status quo.

But philosophy is not the only hurdle confronting the Susan Hammetts in the DAR. There are also some very concrete institutional obstacles.

One of these is the code of acceptable behavior. In the DAR as in other institutions, certain behavior is acceptable and certain behavior is frowned upon, but in the DAR the frowns seem to form rather easily. An older Daughter tells a story about a junior in her chapter, a woman who had been named the outstanding junior in the state. After the junior went to state conference for the first time, the chapter members asked her how she had liked it. The young woman replied that she had found the evening when every chapter regent gave a report the most boring thing she had ever sat through. The Daughter telling the story, a national committee vice-chairman, was in total agreement. "But," she said, "that girl hasn't been given a thing to do in that chapter all year."

A Daughter needn't be a junior to ruffle feathers. Eunice Haden, who could be a junior's grandmother, upset some of her colleagues simply because she took literally something she read in the DAR Handbook—that any member could make a suggestion.

"I suggested rewriting the objective of the conservation committee or dropping the committee, because we had fulfilled the objective," Miss Haden later told a visitor to her Washington apartment. "People around here went to pieces over it. They said I was new. I said, 'I've worked in government. We all get crackpot letters. The thing you should have done was to write me a note thanking me for my interest and then thrown my letter in the wastebasket.' But people went to pieces. Now there the DAR had a method, and this was a weakness of the person, not of the method." But, Miss Haden added, "They dropped that item from the Handbook about any member making suggestions!"

The code of acceptable behavior extends to the president general. Before the 1972 Congress delegates voted on Eleanor Spicer's Gift to the Nation, they were given an opportunity to learn about the project in detail from two National Park Service officials involved in the administration of Independence Hall. The men made a trip to Washington to show the Daughters some slides and to answer their questions. Since Congress votes are always cast on Thursday, this program took place Wednesday evening. That entailed a change in the Congress schedule, because Wednesday evening is usually set aside for state regents' reports. But some of the state regents were candidates for vice president general. The schedule change meant that the state reports would take place after the voting, putting several women in the position of standing up in front of the assembly after they had lost. Some Daughters were not a bit pleased with the change, and Eleanor Spicer was criticized for making it.

Given the reactions to these minor incidents of boat-rocking, it is difficult to be optimistic about what would happen if a Susan Hammett reached high office in the DAR and then urged the Daughters to drop "personal acceptability" as a requirement of membership, for example.

There is even less cause for optimism about whether Susan Hammett could ever reach high office. The route to decision-making echelons in the DAR is steep and long, well marked with signs saying "Wait your turn" and "Don't go too fast." A Daughter with the desire and ambition to serve the Society at high levels is expected to follow that route faithfully. She must hold certain positions in a certain order. Members in small states can take short-cuts on lower levels, where competition for offices is not so stiff, but in larger states there aren't many short-cuts. A Daughter in New York who joins the Society at eighteen with the fixed idea of becoming president general can expect to spend thirty years at an absolute minimum working her way up through various levels of the chapter, state, and national hierarchy until she can run. A few states now have two-year terms of office, which cuts the duration of the climb down a few years. But most states, like the National Society, operate on the basis of three-year terms.

The prescribed process for getting into the DAR hierarchy assures that a junior will not reach a position of influence in the Society until she is long past junior age. It virtually assures that Daughters who are impatient for change will never get far enough to implement it, since only a rare activist would care to spend thirty years going up an institutional ladder.

The established route to PG obviously permits a Daughter to learn the ropes. But if a man in his forties can run the United States, as John Kennedy did for a brief time, it seems odd that an apprenticeship of thirty years is considered necessary to run an organization of 197,000 members. The two youngest women ever to become president general were in their late forties when they took office. Eleanor Spicer believes the right junior could handle the job of PG. Seven of the eleven Daughters who have held national outstanding junior honors agree. But even the women who support that view—and many do not—are unanimous in their belief that as things presently operate, a junior could not possibly get the job.

As things presently operate, it is difficult to see where the impetus for change in the DAR might originate. Recognized problems seem to inspire no concerted attempts at solution. For example, many Daughters feel that the organization needs to be completely restructured. These women are convinced that the Society is unwieldy and that too much time and money is wasted in overlapping efforts. As they see it, the committees should be winnowed and combined where possible. (No one denies that overlap exists—the DAR long ago gave up trying to classify its committees according to the organization's three objectives, because few committees clearly belong in one category or another.) Some view winnowing as an opportunity to "dump" national defense. The issue is somewhat complex, because streamlining *could* mean cutting out some of the DAR's programs.

While some Daughters favor this course of action, believing that the DAR is spreading itself too thin, others would vehemently oppose it. Many women feel the variety of activities is one of the DAR's greatest strengths, enabling a woman to work in her field of interest whatever it might be. Furthermore, national committee chairmanships are viewed as a training ground for women interested in higher office. A move to cut activities, or to eliminate or consolidate committees, would undoubtedly be met with strong resistance in some quarters.

Nevertheless, restructuring is not a brand-new idea in the DAR, and it is an idea that is favored, according to one national board member, by forty-nine out of fifty state regents. But everybody seems to be waiting for somebody else to take the initiative. Any president general has good reason to avoid the task. For one thing, committee chairmanships are patronage jobs, and if there were fewer committees, a PG could reward fewer women for supporting her candidacy. For another thing, as one Daughter in DAR politics points out, "Each PG has it in mind to outshine her predecessors. For that reason she's better off adding a committee than subtracting any."

Even if these obstacles could be overcome, the PG is not free to act on her own. According to one Daughter close to the inner workings of the Society, "The executive board would stop her from doing anything radical."

Eleanor Spicer has said she would be glad to cut out committees if someone could point out to her which ones could be cut without adversely affecting the Society's programs. She has also expressed herself willing to preside at board meetings of extended length if board members wanted to discuss restructuring. In other words, the responsibility for raising the matter belonged, in Eleanor Spicer's view, to her board.

Her board in turn apparently felt it belonged to her. "Restructuring could be the best thing that could happen to this organization, but it must come from the top down," says one of the youngest state regents. "It's just somebody getting up the nerve to say this is what we'd like."

Why any nerve should be required if forty-nine out of fifty state regents support streamlining is a mystery that perhaps only DAR members can fathom. In any case, the state regents as a group aren't grappling with issues that touch on the organization's effectiveness, restructuring or any other.

"I'd love to come down here and see the state regent's meet-ings set up so we'd be able to ask, 'What did you do, how did you achieve it, where did the idea come from?' " says the state regent who mentioned nerve. "Instead we tend to get social. People are more willing to talk about themselves and their honors than about methods of improvement."

The DAR's elected officers might be more aggressive about making changes in the Society if they felt themselves under pressure to do so, but they are prodded very little by the mem-bership. Most Daughters are not professional DAR members: They attend meetings once a month or even less frequently; they are concerned only with what goes on in their own chapters; they have a million other things on their minds. Those who disagree mildly with certain policies or certain aspects of the National Society's modus operandi can circumvent or ignore the sources of their irritation fairly easily. Women who disagree violently are more likely to quit than to go to the trouble of trying to reform the DAR according to their notions. Some Daughters would not presume to suggest improvements to the Society. Others who have thoughts on the subject would not dream of trying to organize support on their own, viewing such a tactic as an affront to the duly elected officers. Members sometimes express their views in letters to the president general, but such letters are more likely to oppose change than support it. As DAR public-relations consultant Paul Wagner puts it, "There's a lot of pressure on the officers, by a very small group, when they do anything moder-ate, or anything that looks left-wingish."

It is logical to suppose that the younger Daughters might constitute a healthy threat to the status quo, but actually the juniors seem no more ready than other members to agitate for change in the DAR. This should not be surprising, since the process of natural selection operates the same way for the juniors as for everyone else: women who have serious differ-ences with the organization don't join it, or if they belong for sentimental reasons, out of deference to a mother or a grand-mother, they remain inactive. Active juniors, like active mem-bers who are older, tend to support the DAR's conservative philosophy. As conservatives, they approach change with cau-tion and reject the idea of trying to effect it outside of normal channels. As young conservatives, they tend to feel that decisions about the DAR should be made by people who know it well, and that the people who know it best are those who have belonged the longest—the older Daughters.

A few juniors feel much differently. There is more than one Susan Hammett in the DAR. But even the juniors whose views would be shared by most Daughters have very limited influence in the DAR power structure—and thus on the Society. To let New York state regent "J.O." Baylies speak for many, "The role of juniors has not yet reached its potential in the DAR."

As of April, 1972, the last year for which figures are available, only sixty-nine of nearly three thousand chapters in the country were headed by juniors. (These figures are not complete because some chapters and states did not report the pertinent statistics to the national junior chairman.) There has never been a junior among the top twelve DAR officers. There aren't even many juniors who hold state offices. In 1972 there were twelve in the whole country, according to figures available.

While juniors could conceivably be elected to the regency of some of the smaller states—regent Ada Helmbreck thinks it's quite possible in Maine, for example—leaders can recall only one woman who became state regent while she was still a junior, Suzanne Cameron of Arizona. Many Daughters believe that former president general Marion Duncan became state regent of Virginia before she turned thirty-six, but in fact Mrs. Duncan was three months beyond junior age when she took office. Even on lower levels juniors in leadership positions are rarely found. A chapter in Illinois with three out of ten elected officers of junior age is something for the regent to boast about, as Karen Kiser does.

Counting chairmanships and offices on all levels, there are more than 100,000 leadership positions available in the DAR. A 1973 survey showed that juniors held about 3,000 of them. Since figures did not come in from all states, national junior chairman Susan Gonchar believes that estimate is on the low side. But even if it were tripled, juniors would still hold fewer than ten percent of the posts available. Although juniors are unquestionably assuming responsibilities within the organization, the DAR is still run almost exclusively by older women.

That is not at all a blanket indictment of the older women. Any number of Daughters, including national leaders, would be delighted to have juniors take a more active role in the Society. Some chapters push the younger women as fast as the younger women are willing to go. But juniors are often unwilling to go very fast. Positions of responsibility involve time and money that many younger women with careers or children or both are unable or unwilling to spend. Very often older women fill the DAR jobs simply because if they did not, no one would.

Furthermore, a woman seeking to influence the power structure from within needs to know the system before she can use it. Most juniors have not had time to become organizational experts. Even those who are giving the DAR their full attention aren't necessarily capable of taking responsibilities. As Susan Gonchar says, "Often the older ones don't want to yield, but on the other side, they may give a job to a junior and she won't follow through." A junior isn't necessarily effective just because she's a junior.

There is no question, however, that juniors are kept down in some chapters and some states. A classic example is the case of Sue Barr. A former social worker from Bethlehem, Pennsylvania, Mrs. Barr was named the DAR's national outstanding junior in 1971. That same year Eleanor Spicer appointed her to the second spot on the junior-membership committee, making Sue Barr one of the four or five highest-ranking juniors in the DAR. The year before, Mrs. Barr had become the youngest woman ever to be appointed to the board of Kate Duncan Smith DAR School. But despite her standing nationally, Sue Barr, now thirty-seven, has not yet been elected regent of her own chapter. She is serving the third year of her second term as first vice regent, and she almost didn't have a second term.

As one Pennsylvania Daughter puts it, "Sue Barr was cut down in her own chapter." The apparent explanation is that Mrs. Barr displeased a powerful woman in the Pennsylvania Society by refusing to organize "Juniors for Barnes" in the 1971 election campaign for president general. Mrs. Barr supported the Spicer ticket because a former Pennsylvania state regent was on it. "I feel that Pennsylvania should have someone on the national board," Mrs. Barr said later. "It's the second [now third] largest DAR state in the country." While Mrs. Barr cannot prove that what happened to her in her own chapter resulted directly from her refusal to lead "Juniors for Barnes," she points out that the head of the chapter nominating committee was a known supporter of the powerful Pennsylvania Daughter whose "lieutenants" had asked Mrs. Barr to organize the juniors in the first place.

Sue Barr categorically denies that she is interested in running for president general. However, she is in principle quite willing to serve in posts loftier than that of chapter regent. She is an inventive woman of enormous energy and is, in the opinion of many members of the DAR, a good Daughter. Enough like other DAR members to be quite acceptable to the Daughters in the mainstream—she abhors Jane Fonda—Sue is also independent enough—the guests at her wedding included a number of good friends who were black—to challenge assumptions. In keeping her out of the regency of her chapter, the organization set itself back three years in terms of the contributions Mrs. Barr could have made to the DAR and has discouraged her, at least temporarily, from making them.

"I will work hard for my chapter whether I ever become regent or not," Mrs. Barr says. "But I have a lot of other things to fulfill my life. If the DAR were my overriding love, that might have really hurt very badly. I can see it from the side of the elderly woman who has worked for years, but I can also see it from the young person's point of view. I have been kept at bay in my own community. I still feel the people in Pennsylvania try in every possible way to negate moves made by juniors."

The difficulties Sue Barr has encountered did not necessarily stem from the fact that she was a junior. In another chapter or another state she might have had clear sailing. Her case, however, is not unique. DAR politics are such that a powerful woman can affect the futures of other Daughters, young or old. This, of course, obtains in national politics as well. But an organization with an old-fogy image is courting trouble when it impedes the progress of its talented young. If a junior with national standing is vulnerable, ordinary juniors are doubly vulnerable.

Sue Barr's experience and that of other women who have held national outstanding junior honors are a significant gauge of what is likely to happen to the Susan Hammetts in the DAR. The national outstanding junior contest was inaugurated in 1963 as a way of recognizing young and talented women and encouraging them to keep the faith. At the time they are honored, the winners are institutionally acceptable, or they wouldn't have been candidates. They are also considered among the Society's most promising members. Perhaps in future years some of them will become stars in the DAR's crown. (More than half of those who have been honored are still under forty.) But so far, at least, their promise has not been realized. In some cases it probably never will be.

Eleven women have held the title of national outstanding junior. Eight have been chapter regents, and six now hold chapter offices. None holds a state office. Only one, Suzanne Cameron of Arizona, has ever risen to the rank of state regent. None of the eleven has held national office. As for appointive positions, five of the women chair chapter committees, three chair state committees, and one chairs a national committee. Two others hold vice chairmanships of national committees. One is both a member of a national committee and a vice chairman of a Continental Congress committee.

What do these figures actually mean in terms of gains and losses to the DAR? In view of the fact that seven of the women have children (though not all at home), that six of the eleven hold full-time jobs, and that one is a full-time student, the former (and current) outstanding juniors are rendering a fair amount of service to the DAR. Only two of the eleven hold no offices or chairmanships. None has dropped out of the organization; seven are very enthusiastic members who seem, for the most part, bright and thoughtful people with much to offer the DAR.

On the other hand, of the eleven former outstanding juniors, only one, Mary Pierce, would like to be president general. Three would not like to serve as national officers. Five say they are less active in DAR today than they were the year they were national outstanding junior. Three have never even been regents of their own chapters. This is not a record the DAR can be particularly proud of.

Again, statistics tell only part of the story. The former outstanding junior who would like to be PG is a woman many Daughters, perhaps a majority, would be pleased to have at the helm of the National Society. Mary Pierce is attractive, she dresses well, she has the financial resources the top job requires, she has the connections in high places—Melvin Laird is her cousin—and she has worked for the DAR (though some Daughters are convinced she currently holds a national committee chairmanship because she is the niece of national-defense committee chairman Sally Jones).

Furthermore, Mrs. Pierce thinks as many DAR members think. She views crime, drugs, inflation, "lack of respect for law and order, and complacency of 'educated' middle and upper strata" as America's most serious problems. When asked what the DAR is doing or can and should do about these problems, Mary Pierce replies that the education of members is "a strong point" of the DAR generally and of the national-defense committee in particular. "Members are encouraged to study, to learn, to be active in the community as individuals," Mrs. Pierce says. "The NSDAR position is one of upholding the Constitution, abiding by the Law of the Land. If all 197,000 members were catalysts in their communities, perhaps there would be less complacency."

Mrs. Pierce considers organizational growth the DAR's biggest challenge in the next decade. Like many Daughters, she feels the DAR has too many committees. Unlike some, she feels that juniors have as strong a voice in the Society as they should have. Describing the DAR as "an organization of dignity and protocol" where a member must "learn the ropes," Mrs. Pierce says rather pointedly, "Actions speak louder than words, and the DAR juniors' achievements are well known in DAR. Juniors don't need 'a strong voice.' As future leaders they should listen and learn while working on the chapter, state, and national levels."

These are the thoughts of the former national outstanding junior who puts the greatest amount of effort into the DAR today and who is most likely to lead the DAR in the future. The two women who are least active speak quite differently. In fact, among DAR members their views are downright unorthodox.

One of these women believes the biggest challenge to the DAR in the next decade is "to open doors to black Americans eligible to membership." She feels the DAR's weakness is that it is "not taking an active role in the social issues of the day."

The other inactive former outstanding junior believes that the DAR should concentrate its energies in fewer areas, and she seriously questions several of the Daughters' favorite programs. For example, she feels the National Society should "get rid" of KDS and Tamassee.

"The time and effort put into the mountain schools certainly is rewarding but benefits only a limited few," she says. "It also focuses work in education elsewhere than in the community in which a chapter exists. Projects closer to home or at least within the state would seem to me to be of more benefit in the public-relations job DAR needs. The states in which the schools are located could continue looking after them."

This woman would also consider dropping the designation "junior." "I'm against age discrimination," she says. "I feel it has no place in any organization. This goes for discussion of elderly members as well—we all know that DAR's are stereotyped as being elderly. I think everybody looks on 'juniors' as a curiosity, and the term connotes other than full membership."

It may only be happenstance that the two former outstanding juniors least active in the DAR today are those with the least conventional views. (Both have careers, one has children, neither seems to bear the DAR a grudge.) But whatever the explanation, the former outstanding junior who devotes the most effort to the organization conforms closely to organizational norms while the former outstanding juniors with the most unusual ideas are no longer making their services available to the DAR.

The issues these two women raise about DAR policies and programs are issues the Daughters should be discussing. But the Daughters are under no pressure to consider such ideas as long as those proposing them are neither inside the power structure nor concerned enough about the organization to pose a direct challenge to the power structure. The organization that does not seek to retain the services of potentially influential members with extraordinary ideas is divesting itself of the pressure to change.

These factors combine to produce an environment that seems distinctly unfavorable for the Susan Hammetts in the DAR. The fate of the national outstanding juniors in particular is a bad sign. If the DAR cannot even command the commitment of its most acceptable, most promising young Daughters, can it possibly keep those women who challenge the institution? In light of these considerations, it is difficult to imagine that Susan Hammett can be either happy or important in the organization if both she and it remain the same.

But there is a positive side to the DAR forecast. While it is true that the pressures against change in the DAR are considerably stronger than the pressures for it, there is also evidence that the organizational status quo is not sacrosanct. For one thing, the Daughters are not operating under the illusion that their organization is perfect. Virtually any criticism an outsider could think to make of the DAR has almost certainly been made earlier within. Lots of Daughters are giving thought to the necessity for improvements and aren't afraid, at least, to talk about it. For example, at a cocktail party one evening after a DAR board meeting, talk arose about Margaret Gibbs' book *The DAR*. Written by an author who claimed to be eligible for membership but didn't care to join, the book is a brisk and unflinching history of the organization, and some of the Daughters thought it was terrible. Curator general Sarah King was not one of them. After the cocktail party and the evening program were over, she said later, "I kept eight national officers and one state regent up till one o'clock in the morning while I read them parts of that book. I think every DAR member should read it and learn from it."

That Sarah King should even be in Washington to read bedtime stories to other DAR bigwigs is further proof that tradition does not have quite the force of law in the Society. Mrs. King, in her early fifties, is the youngest woman on Eleanor Spicer's executive committee. She became state regent of Tennessee after she had been a member of the DAR for only seven years. Similarly, Wisconsin state regent Barbara Janikowsky bypassed a number of steps ordinarily considered de rigueur for a woman who wants to attain the highest state post. True, these two women rose to power in small DAR states, but their experiences show that under the right circumstances, individual Daughters can prevail over the system, however well entrenched that system may be.

Developments in the career of Georgie Anderson show that and more. Aside from being a very hardworking Pennsylvania Daughter, Georgie Anderson is one of the most outspoken women in the DAR—a Susan Hammett with much more experience and much more at stake. To put it mildly, as Sue Barr does, "Georgie in essence tells it like it is, and where it falls, it falls." Mrs. Barr continues, "All right. I would say that a good two-thirds of the women in the DAR can't tolerate that in an individual." Sue Barr is an admirer of Georgie's. Her observation of how people react to a critic in their midst need not have been limited to the DAR. A Georgie Anderson could provoke two-thirds of the members of almost any organization.

But Georgie Anderson is being tolerated by any number of Daughters in Pennsylvania—by so many, in fact, that it seemed logical to the 1973 state nominating committee to select her for first vice regent of the state. Unless matters go very much awry, or Mrs. Anderson decides for some reason not to go on, she will become state regent in 1976. Her future in the National Society is a matter of pure speculation, but there are women in Pennsylvania and beyond who believe quite firmly that in the head of the lady with the college-girl prettiness and the mischievous grin smolders a very serious plan to run for president general. Georgie does not deny that she would like to be PG. Pennsylvania is the third largest DAR state. Its regents are almost always asked to run on a national ticket. If she wanted to, Mrs. Anderson could conceivably become a candidate for PG in 1983. She has the means. She will have had the experience. She will still be only fifty-seven, which would make her one of the youngest women ever to run for that office. She is a character, and there are Daughters who believe that a character as PG would do the DAR a world of good. Her outspokenness would inevitably be a factor in the voting. Whether the Daughters would decide to put themselves in her hands, and what would happen if they did, are intriguing questions. Only time will answer them. But some of the highest hurdles are already behind her. Georgie Anderson's career thus far offers strong proof that the DAR is not wholly unreceptive to mavericks.

Nor has it been wholly unreceptive to change. Certain leaders have shown themselves willing to break with tradition and have discovered members more than willing to go along. Eleanor Spicer found this out when she got the Daughters to agree to spend their money outside the DAR, which was a significant innovation for the organization. When Marion Duncan was president general, she instituted a resolutions forum at which delegates could discuss the resolutions and ask questions about them in advance of the actual voting session. The forum was very well attended. Members apparently welcomed the opportunity to apprise themselves of the issues involved. When Wisconsin state regent Barbara Janikowsky took it upon herself to ignore DAR protocol and alter the customary seating arrangements at state conferences, mixing officers in among members, she found the reaction very encouraging. "People responded beautifully," she says. "I got letters saying, 'This was the happiest state conference I've ever been to.' The people I had been warned wouldn't like it have been very helpful."

These departures from tradition are hopeful signs for the DAR. True, most are very small signs. Substantive changes are difficult to make in an organization as large and as old and as conservative as this one. So far the status quo has been challenged only in the most minimal way, and not always successfully—experiments may founder even if they work. Marion Duncan's successor did not continue the resolutions forum and, though Eleanor Spicer ran one, the forum has not become a permanent item on the Congress agenda. Without constant shepherding, it probably won't.

Nevertheless, the status quo has its opponents in the DAR,

which means that new ideas have potential supporters. How many potential supporters? Every chapter committee chairman who ever felt dissatisfied with the instructions or materials sent her by her national chairman. Every chapter regent who feels there is too much paperwork connected with her office. Every state regent who feels there is too much travel connected with her office. Every leader who objects to learning nothing at meetings of leaders. Every Daughter who might like to serve as a state or national officer if getting there didn't take so much time and money. Every Daughter who disagrees with some of the resolutions, who objects to national defense, who favors streamlining, who wishes the DAR's efforts might benefit more people, who wishes that leaders would devote less time to politics and more to programs. Every Daughter who thinks the DAR should have more influence. Every Daughter who is reluctant to admit to outsiders that she belongs to the DAR.

If one were to count all the members who at some time took issue with things as they are, one might very well discover that the number of Daughters of the American Revolution who are theoretically open to new ideas constitutes the majority of the Society. A leader interested in making changes would have every reason to hope for considerable backing from members who already believe that changes are necessary.

But what changes *are* necessary, and where would the changes start?

The Daughters need to think first and hardest about the most troublesome aspects of their organization's image—its racial and reactionary overtones. Those more than anything else are the elements separating the DAR from a position of respectability in America. The Daughters have to do something to convince outsiders that they stand for racial equality. What they can do that would not appear contrived is a difficult problem and one that should probably be ignored. Their first steps will undoubtedly seem contrived no matter what they are. The Daughters might be better off just accepting this in advance and simply preparing themselves for inevitable accusations of insincerity.

Once they have done that, a number of avenues are open to them. Five thousand blacks fought in America's War for Independence. Most were racially anonymous, but not all. As the DAR is charged with finding and marking the graves of Revolutionary War soldiers, there is no reason why it could not begin to concentrate on the graves of black patriots. The Daughters could also begin to seek out, mark, and restore any buildings or landmarks significant for their relationship to the blacks who helped win the war. The conservation committee could direct some of its efforts to planting trees in the inner city. The student loan and scholarship committee could designate scholarships for inner-city students or make scholarships available to black colleges and universities. The American heritage committee could develop local exhibits of black art and crafts. Chapter genealogists could set up seminars for blacks in their communities as a means both of identifying potential members and of lending expertise in a realm that is becoming increasingly important to blacks. Experts in black genealogy could hold workshops during Continental Congress for Daughters working in the local seminars.

Such activities would fall quite naturally into the DAR's current programs. The Daughters could also invent new programs within the context of their three objectives that would benefit blacks in particular—why not make materials available to schools on blacks in the Revolution, for example? Perhaps most important, they could devise appropriate ways of expressing opposition to discrimination. Translated into the terms of the DAR's own third objective, this means simply that the Daughters must show that they are truly dedicated to the proposition that all mankind should enjoy all of the blessings of liberty. Some of the members may not be so dedicated, but the good of the organization and the justness of the cause must take precedence over reluctance on the part of individual Daughters.

No one of these steps would cause the DAR's racist image to evaporate. A single step would be ridiculed as tokenism. But if the Daughters acknowledge the rights and humanity of blacks in a variety of ways, so that the acknowledgement becomes a pattern, it is difficult to believe that they could continue to be charged with racism.

While countermeasures are in order with regard to the racist aspect of the DAR's reputation, the reactionary aspect could conceivably die a natural death if Americans weren't reminded of it once a year by the resolutions. The Daughters should give some serious thought to dropping the resolutions altogether. However, they could keep them and still eliminate some of the trouble they cause. The resolutions could be drastically cut, which would lessen the possibility that they would appear unofficially condensed in a newspaper. The Daughters could vote on the resolutions at the end of Continental Congress instead of almost at the beginning. That would give delegates more time to think about them and would avoid the appearance of rubber-stamping. Procedures could be changed so that the resolutions reflect the views of the entire membership, not just those of the national defenders. The American Association of University Women manages to send its resolutions out in advance for consideration by members; Daughters could investigate that system and make a determined effort to apply it in the DAR.

At the very least these matters should be aired so that the Daughters continue the resolutions, if that is their desire, as a calculated risk rather than because they've always had resolutions.

All DAR programs would profit from this kind of reevaluation. Pointed questions should be asked and answered about every activity in which the organization is involved: Why does this program exist? How does it relate to the DAR's three objectives? What is its purpose? What techniques are being used to achieve that purpose; which are successful and why, which are not and why not? What has the program accomplished? How many people does it benefit, and how does it benefit them? Is it worth what it costs in time and effort and money? How could it be improved? Why should it be continued? Is it the most effective means of achieving the goals of the organization? While the DAR might well end up with fewer programs after this kind of analysis, they would almost inevitably be very sound programs.

The Daughters could also explore new directions with juniors in mind. Given the organization's historical orientation, the DAR will probably never appeal to a majority of young women, but in order to appeal to as many as possible, current juniors could be asked to suggest new activities which might attract new members thirty-five and under.

Changes in organizational operations and procedures also suggest themselves. The Daughters desperately need a full-time, tenured public-relations professional on their staff, at least until their image has begun to improve substantially, and that professional needs free access to information and the full support of the national officers. Campaign reforms are in order; they have been discussed but not implemented on an institution-wide basis. Visits by state regents to chapters and by presidents general to states could be curtailed or cut out altogether. These visits are nice for the members, and they help leaders keep in touch with the grass-roots, but they also absorb an enormous amount of time which leaders could better spend on organizational improvements.

Resignations could be investigated. The National Society receives figures from the states but no explanations. Forms could go out to women who drop their membership; the responses of juniors in particular should be given careful attention by the national board. Members should be begged for suggestions. The DAR is full of women with ideas the organization could use, and this resource has been too little utilized. The invitation to members to make suggestions should be restored to the DAR Handbook in a place of prominence. With perhaps a few exceptions, the organization's voluminous reports could be filed, not delivered orally, from the platform so that the time at state conferences and Continental Congress could be devoted to a real exchange of ideas. Leaders should very firmly discourage traditions which seem to put the interests of individual Daughters or groups of Daughters ahead of the interests of the organization as a whole, such as the practice followed by some chapters of limiting membership to a certain number or to women of a certain ancestry or social standing.

Leaders should also do everything in their power to make clear that the chapter or state which holds juniors back is guilty not of a minor mistake but of a very serious offense. As for the juniors themselves, absolutely nothing but tradition prevents them from deciding to get up their own slate of women to run for national office. Imagine how the Daughters' image would be transformed if the president general turned out to be thirty-five.

These suggestions represent only the most obvious modifications that could be made in the DAR. The list is by no means intended to be comprehensive, and some of the items on it may be found to be unworkable. But if tradition is not permitted to stand in the way, the remodeling possibilities are almost endless, and there is no better source of ideas for them than the Daughters themselves.

The remodeling possibilities are endless within certain parameters, of course. The DAR is never going to become something other than itself. It will remain a conservative organization with conservative members and conservative programs. If it had different objectives, it would be a different organization. Whatever changes the DAR might choose to undergo would be geared only to enable the Society to do more effectively a job that is defined by the Daughters' own conceptions of it, and by their own capabilities. The Daughters may undertake only such activities as fall under one of the DAR's three objectives. Granted that "historical, educational, and patriotic endeavor" is rather broad in scope, it doesn't include everything. As Eleanor Spicer points out, "We are not a welfare organization." Furthermore, the DAR is under no obligation to anyone to be other than it is.

Many outsiders believe that the DAR should change to become more "relevant." The days of Lady Bountiful are over, they say; the DAR should get with it and start dealing with the problems of today. This may seem like a better idea than it is. To most of the women who belong, the DAR is a diversion. Even the women who serve full-time at the upper echelons are professionals only in the very broad sense that they have a great deal of organizational experience. They are neither trained nor paid to be expert administrators in the fields of history, education, and patriotism. This is not to underestimate their abilities in these fields; it is only to say that in a strict sense the Daughters as Daughters are all amateurs. But today's problems—crime, poverty, the economy, drugs, racial tension, the justice system, unemployment, corruption and credibility in government— confound experts. Untrained amateurs can be useful in their solution only to a limited extent.

Not that the Daughters haven't given some thought to how they could ease America's current plight. Adele Sullivan wished the DAR could get into drug education, and Eleanor Spicer has thought about whether the DAR might be useful in rehabilitating ex-convicts and ex-addicts. But Mrs. Sullivan felt the Daughters didn't have the expertise for drug education, and Mrs. Sullivan was right. Eleanor Spicer wonders if there is a place for amateurs in rehabilitation, and the question is legitimate. It is much more commendable for the Daughters to stay out of areas they have no special aptitude for than to jump on a bandwagon just to be modern. While the DAR might possibly find a place for itself in drug education or rehabilitation, leaders are wise not to rush headlong into programs of such delicacy.

Skills aren't the only consideration. There is also the matter of orientation. Speaking one day to an outsider, a black minister who runs an inner-city settlement house where a DAR chapter started a Junior American Citizens club had this to say about the Daughters: "They don't have a good understanding of poverty or kids brought up in the drug scene. They live on the Main Line or somewhere in Jenkintown, and they look at our kids and say, 'These people are failures. Why can't they do more for themselves?' This is all so strange to them." But a few minutes later the minister said, "It would be nice if the women gave a little more of themselves instead of just running in and out."

His listener replied. "If they have the attitudes you say they have, how in the world would you utilize them in your program?"

The minister agreed that it would be difficult.

There is truth in the observation that the DAR is playing a Lady Bountiful role. The classic illustration for that kind of giving is, of course, the dowager who goes in her chauffeured car to the home of some poor family and stops just long enough to drop off a Thanksgiving basket. She is there long enough to reap the gratitude but not to face that family's real problems. This kind of giving has gotten a very bad reputation of late, but there are two ways to look at it. One is that the giver wants to receive credit or to salve her conscience as much as she wants to help. The other is that a Thanksgiving basket is more than that family might have had otherwise.

Helping people in need is an incredibly complex science involving all kinds of psychological factors on both sides. Experts have yet to work out satisfactory formulas—the federal poverty program scarcely made a dent in poverty—and the efforts of amateur do-gooders are tolerated with increasingly less patience—if at all—by those on the receiving end. The Daughters may have once had the option of working in the ghetto, but they really don't have it any longer.

Their kind of assistance is of a different order. They are providing scholarships to Indians who need money for education. They are providing a life for the children of Tamassee. Raising and giving money may be playing Lady Bountiful, but money can be helpful to people who lack it. The Daughters' work in conservation and restoration is useful to all Americans—not crucial, but certainly not insignificant. Giving away flags and honoring students are gestures the world could certainly live without, but if those gestures hurt no one and make some people feel good, they have their value. Making newcomers feel welcome is steering very clear of solving America's most serious problems. But naturalization is an important event for the people relinquishing their homelands. It deserves special emphasis. Because Independence Hall chapter threw a party, Benjamin Fpatag did not have to celebrate his new status by window-shopping. This is irrelevant to current crises, but directly relevant to certain human needs.

Because it is serving some useful purposes in America, the DAR doesn't have to start from scratch in remaking its image. If the Daughters worked to perfect the organization's strengths and to shed the paraphernalia that prevent outsiders from seeing them clearly, the greater part of the job would very likely have been accomplished.

But to be done well, the job would be exceedingly difficult. The concept of the Daughters as doddering dowagers waving the flag and worshipping their ancestors is deeply rooted in America. The Daughters' attachment to tradition is strong. The responsibility of initiating reform would have to be borne primarily by the president general, and even a PG who was determined to make the necessary changes would be up against formidable obstacles. She would have to begin by redesigning her own office in order to free herself of the traditional travel, the constant worries of Constitution Hall, and the many lesser demands to which presidents general in the past have customarily given—and wanted to give—their personal attention. Then she would have to figure out some way for national officers who are volunteering their services and paying their own expenses to spend enough time together to make plans and carry them out. She might have to convince some of the officers that plans were necessary. She would have to devise ways for the members to participate in the renovation, which would mean establishing channels through which women accustomed to leaving things to their leaders would submit their own criticisms and suggestions.

She would probably have to do all these things in the face of opposition from Daughters who won't like what she is doing for a hundred reasons of their own. A PG would have to be very dedicated to change to go through all that. She would have to be very secure as a person and very tactful as a leader, and she would have to be inspiring besides. She could be less gifted herself if she was backed by a superb set of officers, and in order to put a slate like that together she would have to pay an enormous amount of attention to qualifications and no attention at all to whose turn it was. If the best-qualified Daughters lacked financial resources to serve, the woman heading the ticket would have to think of some solution. If the best-qualified Daughters were not from the large states, the slate might lose—unless the reform candidates ran a smashing campaign and struck just the right chord in the membership. Even so, the winners would probably start out with enemies.

But the winners start out with enemies now. The Daughters

are not strangers to unpleasant politics. The prospect of unpleasant politics would seem the most minor of obstacles to a woman who believed that the organization could profit from her leadership.

In fact, none of the obstacles to change in the DAR seems overwhelming. Putting together the right slate would be the most difficult part of the task, because women who have spent years going up through the ranks cannot be expected to take kindly to being bypassed just as they are about to achieve their goal. But the problem does not seem incapable of solution. These women would in essence be waiting a little longer to run; they would not necessarily be losing their chance at high office altogether.

Balancing the obstacles to change are the organization's substantial resources. The DAR has the people. Three of the last four presidents general could probably have spearheaded reform in the DAR if they had put their minds to it. Any number of Daughters are imaginative enough to come up with suggestions for improvement. Any number from chapters on up have the necessary competence to implement the changes.

Furthermore, there is a lot of motivation waiting to be tapped. The Daughters' desire to be thought of in positive terms is very strong. It might be strong enough to power even sweeping renovations.

Finally, there is potential in the belief of many Daughters that improvements are necessary. Among most members the belief doesn't even approach being a fierce conviction, but it could conceivably be turned in that direction under the right circumstances.

The odds are high against all these rather radical changes taking place. But it seems at least possible that the DAR is capable of revising itself sufficiently to restore the organization to a position of respect in America. The reason such renovations have not been made before is that the Daughters have never thought seriously enough about making them. Assailed by frequent attacks, they have concentrated on protecting the organization and reassuring themselves.

That is understandable. But it has been clear for some time that the attacks will not stop of their own accord. The Daughters themselves must take steps. The right president general could probably convince them that the surest way to protect the DAR is to change it. The single missing element is commitment.

CHAPTER XII

Afterthoughts

In October of 1971, when I was working as a feature writer for *The Philadelphia Inquirer*, I was assigned to do a story on the DAR. The Pennsylvania Daughters were getting together at the Sheraton Hotel for their annual conference, and the president general was coming to town for the occasion. I was mildly curious. Although I grew up in a half-WASP, half-Swedish Protestant Republican suburban home, I had never knowingly met a DAR member, even during the five years I lived and worked in Washington. With the other members of my car pool, I had ogled the women in town for Congress every April with something less than reverence, but I learned nothing about the DAR's activities, and what little I knew of its reputation was based entirely on hearsay. The president general in my preconception was the Daughter in the myth. However, when I was asked to interview Mrs. Spicer, my curiosity was tempered with slight annoyance. The interview was scheduled for a Sunday evening. I would have to come back early from New York.

My annoyance didn't last. I liked Eleanor Spicer immediately. She was easy to talk to, and the interview went well. When I left her, I had good feelings about the DAR. In the next couple of days I read the *Inquirer*'s files on the DAR with amazement. I was astonished that anyone would think to oppose the Peace Corps and UNICEF Christmas cards and dismayed to learn about Marian Anderson.

My editor had counseled me to write a fair article, and I tried to do that, but it was difficult to mention the resolutions and the Constitution Hall incident in a way that didn't appear to be dumping on the DAR. The piece appeared on a Sunday. A journalist friend who was in town for the weekend took one look at the story and said, "Oh, my God." I asked, "What's wrong?" I was informed that there was a serious typographical error. The date for the Marian Anderson incident was given as 1959.

It wasn't a typographical error. Somehow I had misread the clips. I had written 1959 myself. What did I know? In 1939 I was less than a year old. My editor hadn't even been born. The desk man who processed the story was a Norwegian who knows more about America than most Americans, but he didn't know about Marian Anderson. I spent Sunday wondering how I would explain to the irate Daughters I knew would call me on Monday.

No one called. On Monday afternoon my editor and I each received a dozen red roses from the DAR. Six Daughters wrote thank-you notes the week after the story appeared, and I received a lovely letter from Eleanor Spicer.

That reaction interested me. That the Daughters were willing to forgive a rather serious breach of truth in light of what they apparently considered to be a favorable article put them into a different category from some of the people a reporter has to contend with. For some, such an error in even a less sensitive area would have ruined the story, confirming the notion many hold that journalists are not to be trusted. The DAR had every right to be upset about the mistake. If any member was, she didn't say so to me. Furthermore, the Daughters I had met and those I heard from didn't seem at all the kind of people who would view UNICEF Christmas cards as public enemies. I found that I wanted to know more about the women so many Americans, myself included, had ignored or written off.

I did not begin my research in a good mood. Although Eleanor Spicer gave her permission for me to associate with a chapter, and although Independence Hall regent Dorothy Irwin was willing, a snag developed. On October 21, 1972, I walked the streets of Philadelphia with a fellow journalist and tried to calm down while the members of Independence Hall chapter lunched at Strawbridge & Clothier and held their first meeting of the fall in my absence. It seemed apparent that some Daughter who mattered wasn't satisfied with the arrangements that had been made. I could understand the Daughters' suspicion of reporters, but since I had approval from both the president general and the chapter regent, I couldn't understand why further negotiations were necessary. The situation was complicated by the fact that Eleanor Spicer was on tour and unreachable except in an emergency. Since her permission had been given to me in writing, I thought that should have sufficed. I felt the first meeting of the year was important, and I felt rather uncharitable about missing it. I griped at length to my companion that sunny Saturday afternoon, and he finally tried to put the matter in perspective by saying, "Peggy, they're housewives."

His words were meant to explain, not to disparage. But women's liberation had begun to have its effects, and even though I was feeling less than kindly toward the Daughters at that moment, I bristled.

Still, reflecting upon the statement later, I decided that the point is an important one. The Daughters *are* mostly housewives. When Adele Sullivan analyzed her membership survey, she added up the twenty-three percent of Daughters who held full-time jobs and the sixteen percent of Daughters who served on community boards and concluded that thirty-nine percent of DAR members were "a very alert and busy group of women, interested in the professions and civic affairs of their communities." This kind of arithmetic is highly questionable, since the woman who does both is counted twice, once in each category. But even assuming that the categories are mutually exclusive, one point the figures make is that at least sixty-one percent of the Daughters *neither* work full-time *nor* serve on community boards. They are, in other words, women whose primary affiliation is with the home.

What's important about that? Two things. First, that a group of housewives should raise the money the Daughters have raised and could take on the projects the Daughters have taken on is fine testimony to the capabilities of housewives.

Second, that the Daughters are mostly housewives means that they should be judged as housewives. The DAR has been generally viewed as a kind of political party or pressure group bursting with zealots bent on peddling their particular ideology, but in fact its membership is composed largely of women who like to dress up and get out of the house, associate with friends, and do a little work on behalf of a good cause. The DAR is not a lobby. It never has been. The organization did not form to work for American retention of the Panama Canal, and it does not exist for such purposes. It is inherently limited as to the role it can play on the American political scene. If the DAR began to push for implementation of its views, it would lose its status as an educational institution. The moment that happened, the Daughters would be liable for income taxes on the full value of their buildings. (The DAR is registered with IRS under category 501 C3, a public charity. All property is tax-exempt by statute for real and personal-property tax, but to the extent that Constitution Hall is rented to outside organizations, it is subject to real-estate taxes which by agreement with the city of Washington are a flat eleven percent of gross rents.) Dues and contributions to DAR projects would no longer be tax-deductible. The Daughters say they couldn't afford to maintain their buildings under those circumstances. They would have to give them up, which they profoundly don't want to do. The buildings give the DAR a special identity. Without them the organization would be just like every other hereditary patriotic association in the country, distinguishable from the others only in size. The Daughters want to retain their programs as much as they want to keep their buildings. So the DAR's incentive is very strong indeed not to back up its public stands with pressure on the public. The Society is powerless almost by definition.

However it may appear to outsiders, the DAR considers itself, and is, a service organization. It does not ask outsiders for contributions; it is not operating on public funds; it is not run by a professional staff. The DAR operates on its own money. The services it renders are free. The work it does is done by volunteers. It does not owe the public an account of itself in the way that a political party or a private or government agency owes one, and it should not be expected to meet the objectives of some other kind of institution. The DAR is a women's club, no more and no less.

Having never belonged to a women's club, I can find nothing comparable to the DAR in my experience. I can only give my impressions of this particular organization as I have seen it operate. My strongest impression is that the DAR at its most authentic is the DAR at the local level. Chapter work is mainly what the Society is all about. Yeoman service is the chief characteristic of membership for the vast majority of Daughters.

In Independence Hall chapter I saw that service rendered with enthusiasm, efficiency, and a noticeable absence of flap. I didn't hear a woman raise her voice either at the executive meetings or at the board meetings. I saw nothing remotely approaching a heated argument. The women almost never interrupted each other. While Dorothy Irwin was clearly in charge, no one deferred to her except out of ordinary courtesy. When there was something to discuss, it was discussed briefly and dispensed with quickly. Compared to other discussions I have been in or observed, the discussions at Independence Hall were marked by little if any spouting for the sake of being heard.

The fact is that the issues didn't warrant much argument. The women were not deciding whether to be for or against the United Nations. They were trying to judge whether it would be best to charge $1.50 or $2.00 for the card party benefiting DAR schools. I don't say this at all to belittle the chapter's efforts. I say it because I think it indicates how little resemblance the real DAR bears to most people's ideas of it.

Aside from the meeting at which they were read, the resolutions were mentioned just once—and briefly—during the year. The women spent most of their energies those nine months trying to raise a thousand dollars for education. They made plans to honor children and a historian and a conservationist and an orchestra conductor. The highlights of their year were the day the students came to lunch, their Christmas meeting at the Barclay, and the card party. They enjoyed the conservation speaker and the slides of DAR schools. They felt deeply the death of one of their members and spent a good deal of time thinking on what kind of project they could best express their affection for her. While Independence Hall's activities would not appeal to everyone, they are scarcely harmful to America.

Chapters are a good place to judge the DAR; Continental Congress is a good place to misjudge it. The annual meeting has often been assessed—and found wanting—as a work session, which is why reporters usually point out how little consideration the delegates give the resolutions. But Congress isn't really a work session. The primary function of the delegates is to ratify, not to devise or to hammer out. Most of the work connected with Congress is done by the leadership beforehand. The leadership proposes; the delegates express themselves if they care to and then vote. Aside from decisions about the resolutions, fiscal matters, and bylaw changes which are usually minor, the delegates have no responsibilities except to elect national officers every three years and to attend sessions as dictated by their interests and their conscience. The purpose of these sessions is not for the Daughters to figure out better ways of achieving their goals (though perhaps it should be). It is to give leaders the opportunity to stand up and boast a little about what their efforts have yielded over the past year, and it is to inspire members, by the sheer volume of the statistics they hear in reports, to go back to their chapters and do what they are already doing with greater diligence.

Anyone can see at a glance that the real source of inspiration at Congress is the pageantry. For most women the appeal of Washington lies in opening night. The music, the procession, the flag, the formal dress, the sight of Constitution Hall filled to the rafters with sisters from every state in the union—the emotion in the Hall that night is so powerful as to be almost palpable. A Daughter who could stand there without feeling happy, proud to be an American, and determined to recommit herself to her organization and its goals could probably read a book at her son's wedding. Most of the business of Congress would be dispensed with and its major function would still be served. For officers and members alike, Congress is a reward.

The reward is not the same for delegates as for leaders. Members get to see old friends, go to parties, meet the Society's officers, and sit in the audience on opening night. Leaders get to parade, and to sit on the stage, and to speak to a captive audience. Furthermore, they get very special treatment. Members stand in long lines to greet them. Applause compliments them throughout the week. And the pages await their bidding.

Congress is a very special occasion. Receiving respects as they are paid that week in April is a fringe benefit of hard jobs done voluntarily, and most leaders have undoubtedly earned the acknowledgement they get. All the same, the treatment of leaders sometimes approaches a sort of glorification that can make an outsider a little uncomfortable. I can see the necessity for pages to do errands and to escort the president general, who would be inundated with well-wishers otherwise. I can't see why pages should stand like sentinels through the president general's remarks to the assembly or arrange someone's fur stole on a chair or accompany someone who isn't infirm to the powder room. I can't conceive of myself or any of my friends in that role. I can't conceive of my mother or any of her friends in the role of recipient of such attentions. While on occasion the pages have been encouraged by someone on the page committee to remember that they are members, not maids, pages say leaders rarely take advantage of the assistance. But to me there's something unequal about that relationship between page and leader. I don't see what such a relationship accomplishes.

On the other hand, though I was out of the country at the time John Kennedy was assassinated, I remember reading a great deal about Jackie's "majesty" during those grim days. "Maybe America would really like to have a queen," people said. Well, perhaps the president general fulfills that wish for the Daughters. Perhaps the willingness of the young to honor their officers as a kind of royalty, and the willingness of the officers to be so honored, is an acknowledgement of instincts to which other Americans do not admit. If both sides profit from the arrangement, why quibble about it?

("Do you think they're lesbians?" several people have asked me of the Daughters. I put the question a little differently to a professor at the University of Pennsylvania, a young mother who teaches feminist history, Dr. Carroll Smith-Rosenberg.

"Why do you think women dress up formally when there are no men around; do you think they're dressing up for each other?" I asked her. Dr. Smith-Rosenberg saw the point immediately and dismissed it. "I think they're saying, 'Even *though* there aren't any men around, we're important, and we're going to look good,'" she replied.)

Having said that the DAR should be judged as a women's club, I don't mean to suggest that the organization's weaknesses should simply be written off as the foibles of amateurs. The DAR is old enough to have learned from experience, to have refined its operations, to know what it's doing and what it wants to do. It deserves to be assessed seriously.

In that light, I think the Daughters must be held responsible for the fact that the DAR's biggest problem has not yet been solved: the organization is still burdened by 1939. Leaders have explained the story so many ways that even they are confused. It is unlikely that a DAR leader would knowingly pass on demonstrably false information, but the point is that the Daughters have been less than scrupulous about tell their side of the story. That is probably why Americans have never accepted it.

At one meeting of Independence Hall chapter, I found myself in a conversation about 1939 with parliamentarian Elsie Beatty, a woman well on in years with a ready wit and a democratic spirit her forebears would admire. She brought the subject up. I don't recall her exact comments, but they were words to the effect that if someone would take the trouble to look into the records, that person would learn that Marian Anderson had sung in the Hall prior to 1939, which information would certainly clear up any misunderstandings of how the DAR stood on race. By the time I had this conversation with Mrs. Beatty, I had already learned a good deal about the policies and practices of Constitution Hall in those days. I knew that her information was wrong. It occurred to me that if I had been a newspaper reporter interviewing her for a story, and if I had been enterprising enough to check what she told me, I would have found out it was wrong, and perhaps I would have said in my story that a DAR member had given me false information.

That is not very pleasant journalism, but it is journalism. I would not have liked to see that happen to Elsie Beatty. She has served the DAR for many years. She is a loyal Daughter and a nice person. She was speaking to me in good faith. She believed what she was saying because the truth had not been impressed upon her. Quite aside from the fact that conveying false information can do the organizational image no conceivable good, I find it unforgiveable that Mrs. Beatty's leaders would have put her in such a vulnerable position. Elsie Beatty can take the truth, and she deserves to have it. I met few if any women in the DAR I would consider incapable of facing the facts if they knew them.

I further think the DAR has been remiss in letting its bad image fester for so long without making a serious, institutional assessment of the resolutions. While I can appreciate the belief of Susan Barr and others that the DAR should take stands on important issues, it seems to me that the stands the organization has taken have been nowhere near worth what they have cost. True, the American Association of University Women has resolutions, and the League of Women Voters takes stands. But AAUW also has study committees made up of women with expertise in a particular field (not in writing resolutions). The LWV is fundamentally a study organization—it lobbies, but it studies first. In both cases the positions the organization takes relate to a program in which the members participate. For these reasons the positions of AAUW and LWV are far more credible than the DAR's resolutions, which does not necessarily mean they serve the organizations' best interests. The AAUW is itself reevaluating its resolutions to determine just what their function is and should be. The DAR badly needs to do the same.

The Daughters' failure to deal head-on with these problems arises out of the organization's major weakness: its neglect of self-analysis. Of course there is such a thing as too much contemplation of navels. But the Daughters ask themselves "Why?" far too seldom. They are much more inclined to take their own version of things on faith. They have convinced themselves that a third of their members are juniors, and the fact that virtually no DAR gatherings show any evidence of that doesn't seem to register. They assume their schools are turning out patriots when no one really knows just what the schools are turning out. They say the resolutions have proven to be correct, but they don't seem to wonder why so few of them have come to pass. They have accepted each other's versions of 1939 without ever once attempting to investigate the inconsistencies in those versions.

The general failure to question is not a determined effort on the part of the Daughters to avoid learning the truth. In part it is an institutional characteristic which developed naturally out of a personal characteristic shared by a good many of the Society's members. These women are simply unaccustomed to thinking critically. A number come from military backgrounds; those who don't are nevertheless just as likely to hail from the so-called old school where criticizing the commander-in-chief or almost anyone else in authority was definitely not encouraged. While no one knows just how many Daughters have college degrees, the chances are that most do not, and although a college education guarantees nothing in the way of discerning powers, it does ordinarily provide practice in weighing evidence that may make a graduate somewhat more skeptical about information than she might have been otherwise. Like many people outside the DAR, many Daughters underestimate themselves. They are conscious of their limited knowledge and believe that those reputed to have a great deal of knowledge can be trusted to know what they're talking about. Many of these women have common sense in very respectable proportions but lack the confidence to apply it outside their own particular bailiwicks.

The Daughters often assume their leaders know best. Even members who have questions don't necessarily voice them where it counts: challenging authority face-to-face is an awkward business for anyone. Leaders accept the members' assumption as a matter of practicality as much as anything. A president general doesn't really have time to conduct institutional evaluations if she observes the traditional demands of her post.

In part the Daughters just don't want to hurt each other's feelings. Leaders bend over backward to avoid casting aspersions on previous administrations, and for any Daughter to point out flaws in a program or policy could be to seem to reproach those responsible for it. Most Daughters would be reluctant to do that, feeling that, after all, DAR members are just volunteers doing the best they can; they deserve support or, barring support, silence.

This is a nice instinct. Nevertheless, the Daughters would profit from a more critical attitude toward the status quo and each other's assumptions. Though harmless in themselves, the deceptions that result from failure to question give the Daughters a false sense of security that isn't good for the organization. As long as the DAR is convinced of the unassailability of its accomplishments, it has no cause to reevaluate its policies and try to improve them. The Daughter who believes that a third of the DAR's members are juniors has got to be less diligent about finding new junior members than she would be if she knew that the actual figure is closer to ten or twenty percent.

It is difficult to assess the overall accomplishments of the DAR, at least in terms of the organization's three objectives. Who can say whether the Daughters have—or haven't—succeeded in fostering true patriotism, developing an enlightened public opinion, or perpetuating the memory and spirit of the men and women who achieved American Independence? The DAR has most certainly cherished the institutions of American freedom; whether it has extended them or not is something else again. It has most certainly promoted education. Through its schools and its scholarships it has afforded untold numbers of children the chance to be better off, the access to personal development. Being a bit abstract, however, the educational and patriotic achievements don't lend themselves well to appraisal.

But some of the DAR's achievements under its first objective are concrete, and they are very easily appraised. To state it simply, the Daughters have preserved a part of early America. The buildings they have saved, the papers they have collected, the accoutrements of everyday life they have discovered or hunted up and put on display in their museum, the sites they have marked all serve to provide Americans living and Americans yet to be born with an insight into their origins. The DAR is not the only provider, of course. But the insight that is available to Americans from a variety of sources has been greatly enriched by the Daughters' efforts.

Beyond these contributions, the DAR has established itself as a sort of watchdog over America's traditions. This role sometimes takes on humorous overtones, as when the gentleman wrote to Eleanor Spicer asking her to protest the musical 1776, and at other times seems misguided, as when Daughters in the South worked to rewrite textbooks to suit their own notions of how American history ought to be taught. But the role has its solemn aspects which could be of value to a large segment of the American people.

"I think," says Sarah Casey, a political liberal and an inactive Daughter, "That if they ever try to tear down Independence Hall, the DAR is who's going to stop them." I think Sarah Casey is absolutely right. The Daughters probably wouldn't be the only Americans to cast their bodies in front of the bulldozers, but they would quite likely be the first there and the last to leave.

The DAR has rendered services to America. It has services yet to offer. But the Society's contributions to the general population are limited by the relative size of the organization, the resources of the members, and the amount of power a women's club is able to wield.

In fact, the Society's most important service has not been rendered to the American public. It has been rendered to the Daughters themselves. The DAR has had its most profound effect on its own members.

According to Dr. Smith-Rosenberg, women's clubs developed because such organizations gave women contact with the outside world. "There's a lot of indication that subconsciously women were looking to get out of the home," she says. "Their letters talk about it in terms of mental health, fighting depression. The organizations had newspapers, and women wrote letters to the newspapers saying the highlight of their month would be receiving this newspaper.

"These were not radical feminist organizations. But middle-class women, at least, suffered isolation, so they sought ways to get out of the home, meet other women, give something to their lives. I can see why. They would spend the whole day making calls on each other. I think they found this tedious after awhile They were bored. It was much more interesting to go into the prisons and pray with the prisoners."

Clubs not only made life more interesting but gave women an opportunity to discover talents and to exercise powers they had little use for in the home. According to assistant professor of sociology Ann Beuf, who teaches women's studies at the University of Pennsylvania, "Clubs were one of the legitimate ways for women to get together and develop organizational skills."

It is interesting to speculate where women's clubs would be today if women had always felt as free to pursue their own careers as they do now. Dr. Smith-Rosenberg thinks it quite possible that women sought the kind of stimulation and fulfillment in clubs that many are currently finding in jobs. She also believes that one effect of women's liberation could be to actually strengthen women's organizations, since women are rediscovering themselves as individuals and feeling much less than they used to that personal worth derives from being accepted into traditionally male domains.

For women who prefer not to devote their energies strictly to the home or to employment outside the home, clubs continue to fill a variety of needs: the need to spice up routine, the need to make friends, the need to be acknowledged, the need to be identified with something larger than one's own family, the need to use one's talents, the need to fulfill one's obligations as a citizen of a nation and a member of the human race. The DAR has provided these kinds of opportunities and satisfactions for tens of thousands of women for more than eight decades.

Duffie Bruning is an Illinois housewife in her forties and a third-generation Daughter. Her mother had been a member of the DAR, but Mrs. Bruning put off joining. "Mother had been trying to get me interested for quite a few years," she says, "but I knew everyone at home, you know. I grew up there. I was so used to them. Then I went away to school, you know, so forget it, Mom!

"Then when I moved to Arlington Heights, they were just starting a chapter. I was invited. I went to the first meeting, and I was very impressed with the caliber of the women who were there. I was just in the time of babies and diapers and everything, and really, it was just very interesting to me to get into this group. Most of them are very talented women. Some of them are very career-minded and very civic-minded. I got very interested. I came up here and just got into my own little world, you know. It was fun to get out of it once in a while. And that's when I decided they really had a lot to offer."

Phyllis Whitmore also lives in Illinois. She is younger than Duffie Bruning, and she makes a point of saying she is not a "love-it-or-leave-it American." One thing Phyllis Whitmore has gotten out of the DAR, she says, is the knowledge that "you can't sit around and criticize without doing anything." Mrs. Whitmore is spending one day a week at Hines Hospital near Chicago, where she gives all the help she can to veteran patients. Mrs. Whitmore feels she profits at least as much as the patients do.

"You can live with yourself," she says. "You can go to bed at night. I came home one night after being there one Wednesday, and I said to my husband, Jim, 'You know, I can really come home from there and say I have had a good day.' *I've* had a good day. *Me*."

The DAR made life a little more pleasant for Duffie Bruning at a time when she needed to be reminded that the world had something to offer besides soiled diapers. The DAR has shown Phyllis Whitmore a little more of herself than she might other-wise have seen. Many thousands of women over the years have been able to come home saying, "I've had a good day" because of the DAR. In a sense, and to an extent varying from person to person, the organization has liberated these women. That is important. It may be more important than anything else the DAR has ever done or ever will do.

Too, the DAR is a little like the old benevolent societies that sprang up among the immigrants to this country. Those societies gave their members the chance to put aside the strains of coping with life and to relax with friends from the homeland, but they also provided for members who became sick, and they saw to it that a member who died got a decent burial. The people who belonged could count on support for occasions happy or sad. Belonging to the DAR has similar advantages. The DAR as an organization provides the means to associate; the Daughters supply the concern. When Dorothy Irwin, who lives alone, went into the hospital for tests, she got phone call after phone call from Daughters offering help and letting her know they cared what happened to her. When Sara Knobelauch became engaged, that fact was announced by a smiling Dorothy Irwin from the head table, and the members of Independence Hall applauded their pleasure. Regina Sheehan, who has few kin in the North, looks upon chapter meetings as reunions of a family —her family. Lillian Hemmerly's sisters have the comfort of knowing that the pain of their loss is shared by the Daughters of Independence Hall. When a woman is widowed, she does not need to be alone. In fact, she can start life over in the DAR, as Eleanor Spicer did when her husband died in 1960.

Just knowing there are real people opening mail at headquarters is a help to some Daughters. No one knows that better than *DAR Magazine* editor Rose Hall. Miss Hall gets lots of mail, and some of it has very little to do with *DAR Magazine*.

"I hear from people about their subscriptions," Miss Hall says, "and all they want to do is renew or note a change of address or say they didn't get their last issue. But I get three-page letters in which they say, 'My son is dying of cancer, my husband was operated on.' They have nobody else to write to. If the National Society serves that purpose, that's good."

Furthermore, the DAR is an ego-booster. It is an organization that puts a great deal of stock in giving credit where credit is due and in recognizing status. For example, certificates could easily have been mailed out to chapters completing their contributions to the refurbishing project in Independence Hall. Instead, where possible, Eleanor Spicer delivered the certificates in person from the podium when she visited state conferences. At the 1973 New York meeting, that system enabled each chapter regent to come to the front of the room, shake Mrs. Spicer's hand, receive the applause of the assembly, and have her picture taken with the president general. Women who have risen to positions of consequence in the DAR wear sashes which make them immediately identifiable. The wider the sash, the more important the woman who wears it. (The office of vice president general exists essentially to accord recognition to Daughters who have held high leadership posts but hold none currently. There are twenty-one VPG's all together, and though a PG may call on any of them for special tasks, the position carries no specific responsibilities. Mainly a vice president general has the right to wear a sash and to sit on the stage at Continental Congress.) Pins are available for every conceivable contribution to DAR efforts, from holding chapter office to making donations of a certain size to DAR schools. The more contributions a Daughter makes, the more pins she may display on her insignia ribbon.

The concern over credit—the attendant bragging is sometimes voiced and sometimes merely implicit—can be rather offputting. *DAR Magazine* editor Rose Hall says she gets "bugged" by some Daughters' desire for credit, and some of the efforts at recognition don't seem to be a very good use of resources. For example, Daughters in one large state recently spent a thousand dollars to erect and maintain a plaque at one of the DAR schools to honor their regent. That thousand could have supported a child at Tamassee for a year. Most Daughters don't actively seek this kind of recognition, however, and some definitely discourage it.

At a small informal gathering at the Mayflower Hotel one evening, Mississippi state regent Stacia Peaster was describing what she gets out of the DAR. Toward the end of her comments she said, "It's quite a thrill to go to a town and have your name on the marquee. They did that for this lowly state regent. I spoke at Columbus in early fall, and I was just shocked to see it at the motel when I arrived: 'Welcome Mrs. Dixon Peaster, State Regent DAR.'"

Stacia Peaster told this story without apology, which is exactly how she should have told it. Though many would not have the grace to admit it, lots of people, perhaps most, would respond exactly as she did to seeing their own names on a marquee. Stacia Peaster did not join the DAR to be recognized by the Holiday Inn. She does not continue to belong in the hope that she will be recognized again. But the incident raised her spirits a little. DAR membership is full of opportunities for raised spirits. They do not accrue only to leaders. The DAR enables the Daughters to feel good about themselves. It embraces its members with warmth, helps them to develop, rewards them when they do. It is creating a sense of belonging for nearly 200,000 American women.

And who are these women? When the trappings of the myth have been all shorn away, who are the real Daughters of the American Revolution?

They are for the most part older women whose families are grown and whose careers, if they had careers, are behind them. They are women who have elected to get out and do something instead of wandering from room to room dabbing at a day's dust. I have met very few complainers in the DAR, and very few women looking for sympathy. Most Daughters don't seem to have time for that sort of activity. They are busy and enjoy being busy. There are certainly some layabouts in the DAR, but most of the women I met gave the impression of being people who like to be up and out by eight or nine in the morning, ready to spend the day tending to personal chores, exploring personal interests, and doing what they consider to be their part as citizens.

The average Daughters are average Americans. They are neither the rich nor the poor, neither intellectuals nor troglodytes. Most seem to be part of the middle class, with more at the bottom end of it than at the top. Many came from working families. Some came from struggling families. The older Daughters were young mothers during the Depression; they know what it's like to go through an earthquake and discover that solid ground can never again be assumed. Some who can afford it go to the Caribbean on vacation, and some go to Europe, and a few go around the world, but it's more common to hear the younger Daughters talk of such trips. A good many of the older women, and of the younger ones, too, seem happy to stay in familiar surroundings, philosophically as well as physically. Like most other Americans, most members of the DAR are interested primarily in their own families, their own friends, and their own communities. They set store by the "old" virtues—honesty, hard work, respect for others, responsibility for oneself. Of course, there are hypocrites among them.

The Daughters love their country and feel a responsibility to it. Most of them are no more rabid about communism or about national sovereignty than they are about parsnips. Right-wing watcher Wesley McCune calls the DAR the "day-in, day-out right," and although there are of course exceptions, Daughters who are liberal or ultra-conservative, this may be as good a description of the Daughters' politics as any. From what I could tell, there is an aversion to the radical right among most members, and an aversion to being linked with the radical right.

When Clarence Manion spoke at Congress one year, he was publicized by the DAR as being a former Notre Dame law school dean, and Wesley McCune took it upon himself to write a letter to *The Washington Post* pointing out that Manion's more recent position was on the John Birch Society board. McCune says he got a phone call from a DAR leader—he thinks it was Adele Sullivan—thanking him for calling attention to Manion's position. She hadn't known Manion was a Bircher, she said. She told McCune that the DAR was eager to steer clear of such associations. Except for certain resolutions, speakers, and national-defense committee materials, the Daughters seem to be giving the Birch camp a wide berth.

It doesn't appear that many members are in that camp. Gerald Schomp, a former Birch recruiter who quit the organization and wrote an exposé, did not mention the DAR in his book. He says that in his experience there was little if any contact between the two organizations. Schomp also wrote in a letter to me, "In all the Florida cities where I represented the Birch Society, only in St. Petersburg was I aware of any Birch members who were also active in the DAR. And the relationship there was strictly coincidental and somewhat natural: patriotic-minded ladies getting involved in super-patriotic right-wing activities. Frankly, I'm somewhat surprised that there hasn't been more overlapping between the two memberships." Schomp believes that for the most part the Daughters and the Birchers "just aren't the same kind of people," which he explains by saying, "If the [Birch] Society ever gave much thought to the DAR, and I doubt if they did, I imagine they were inclined to write them off as relatively useless for really active right-wing work."

Although I didn't always keep it, I made it a rule never to become involved in discussing politics with the Daughters. One reason was that I thought a known McGovern supporter might scare the Daughters off. I would have answered a direct question honestly, but the subject rarely came up. Most Daughters seemed to assume that if I was writing a book on the DAR I must be supporting the conservative candidate. At a DAR tea I attended right after the 1972 election, one Daughter told me that she had relatives in Massachusetts, and hastened to add, "But you'll be happy to know they voted for Nixon."

Finally I began to feel burdened by the possibility that I was operating under false pretenses. A day or two after a phone interview with Eleanor Spicer, I found I needed answers to a few more questions, so I wrote the president general a letter which I ended by saying, "Do you realize you're talking to a liberal?" At the end of her reply she wrote, "Analyze 'liberal' and 'conservative' for me as opposed to open-mindedness with leanings." There were times during my research when I thought it would be fascinating to gather ten Daughters and ten members of Students for a Democratic Society, say, into a room with plenty of time and plenty of refreshment, just to see how long it would take them to discover how many things they could agree on.

I am certainly not saying that all Americans could share all the DAR's views of America. Many Daughters feel that freedom of speech was not intended as permission for citizens to criticize their country. Many believe that America is truly qualified to be a moral leader in the world. "America first" seems to mean to many Daughters exactly what it seems to mean to Richard Nixon—America owes it to posterity to be better than every other nation. Although they exhibit profound faith in the American system, many Daughters show very little faith in the ability of that system to speak for itself. This explains why some think the uglier aspects of America's history ought to be downplayed for school children. It also explains the dismay some Daughters feel about certain college courses in social studies. If students graduate with what the Daughters view as leftist leanings, the reason is that they've had socialist professors, not that other political systems may have merit. In the opinion of some Daughters, anyone who doesn't think the American system is far superior to any other is simply incapable of thinking very clearly.

Although these notions would find no support in some quarters, many Americans who laugh at the DAR or consider it harmful may be overlooking the things they have in common with the DAR. Daughters believe America is the best place in the world to live, and so do most of the people living here. Daughters grieve over America's failure to live up to its potential; so do other Americans. Like other Americans, Daughters consider it important for children to be raised respecting themselves, their origins, and their rights and obligations as citizens. Like people who aren't in the DAR, Daughters believe that Americans should vote, express their views to their Congressmen, and make amends to American Indians. Daughters of the American Revolution would cringe if they saw someone burning or sullying an American flag, and so, with very few exceptions, would the rest of us.

Daughters may also be closer to many other white Americans on the subject of race than many white Americans have chosen to acknowledge.

When General James spoke at Congress in 1973, someone sitting in the press section commented that James was just the kind of black the Daughters could be expected to like. I found him so solidly Establishment as to be almost obsequious in several of his statements. But I don't think the DAR should have invited Huey Newton. Very few people are converted to any cause by militants. I imagine that some of the delegates had their eyes opened by Chappie James. He spoke to them on their terms. He challenged them, but he did not insult them. If he didn't convert them, he certainly didn't make them vow never to be converted.

The Daughters in general don't seem to me to be any more unenlightened on race than a good many other white Americans. The suburbs are crowded with citizens who were impelled to move away from the cities because blacks were moving in. Betsy Campaigne is right when she says some Daughters have a long way to go, but I have met DAR members who have already traveled a good distance along that road. Some of the Daughters are trying hard to shed old notions. Others have largely done so. Some can't themselves but respect those who make the attempt.

Almost every Daughter I talked with—not all—expressed her opposition to intermarriage. My impression is that that view places the Daughters squarely in the mainstream. I never discussed race with a Daughter who said she opposed equal rights. Of course she might not have said so to me (though some Daughters didn't see anything untoward about pointing out to me that I live in an integrated neighborhood). Assuming these women were sincere, it is legitimate to wonder what they are doing in support of the cause, and I don't think many of them are doing very much. That, too, places the Daughters among the majority of white Americans.

It is not easy to define a racist. Is a racist someone who believes blacks are inferior or somehow different, who supports equal rights in principle, who does nothing to support the cause, and who is determined to never knowingly be unkind to blacks? Is a racist someone who cannot shed feelings of bigotry even though he may not behave in a bigoted fashion? Then lots of Daughters are racists, and they have lots of company.

The Daughters of the American Revolution are not a distinct breed of Americans. They are our neighbors. Some like a cocktail or two before dinner; others wouldn't dream of having one at any time, and some, like some outsiders, drink too much. Like many other Americans, some Daughters use plastic flower arrangements as centerpieces, go barefoot when the spirit moves them, pray in a crisis, swear in a traffic jam, criticize friends behind their backs, make casseroles for bereaved neighbors, read when possible, flirt with other people's spouses, interrupt their guests, worry about their waistlines, postpone dental appointments, dream, remain silent when they should speak up, divulge information they ought to keep secret, take forty first-graders to the zoo on Tuesday afternoon, forget the birthdays of relatives, burn dinners, gossip, and, when the occasion calls for it, admit their mistakes. In most respects most members of the DAR resemble most of the rest of us.

In some ways they don't much resemble each other. I spent weeks in the company of Daughters and heard no kind words for Eleanor Roosevelt, but the minute I concluded that the DAR didn't like Eleanor Roosevelt, Janet Shay told me she had the highest regard for Mrs. Roosevelt and considered her a humanitarian of the first water. Then Ruth Lehr mused that perhaps Eleanor Roosevelt resigned from the DAR because she had outgrown it. Recently Eleanor Spicer told me she thought Mrs. Roosevelt was a remarkable woman. The DAR has gone on record again and again against world government, but when I spoke with a Maryland councilman who had been an official of the World Federalists in the Pacific Northwest, he told me he had found some of the Daughters there very helpful in promoting the one-world cause. So much for generalizations.

In the two years that have passed since I first interviewed Eleanor Spicer in Philadelphia, I have rarely met a Daughter who fit the description of the Daughter in the myth. I'm not saying more don't exist. No one was steering me to them, obviously. But I looked, and although I met plenty of women who exhibit one or more characteristics of the image—smugness in particular—I only ran across one or two who precisely match it.

A good number of the Daughters I interviewed I found to be interesting women who talk thoughtfully and go about their business sensibly. They resent the notion that the DAR is a club for society matrons with nothing to do. They work hard but not fanatically for what they believe in. Some of those who are deeply involved in community affairs proudly showed me improvements in their towns that they had had something to do with or buildings they had helped to save. They know what the local conservation issues are. They know who their congressmen are. They are capable people who can laugh at themselves and see other points of view. They are fun to be with. I like to think that some of them will become my friends. I have had some very interesting conversations with DAR members and some very good times in their company. On occasion I have sensed that some Daughters did not altogether trust my enjoyment. "Well," they say after a cocktail or two, "have you found out that we're not just a bunch of old ladies in tennis shoes?"

They ask lightly, but they wait for an answer.

My answer is that I have found that out.

Bibliography

CHAPTER I

Books
Gibbs, Margaret, *The DAR*, New York: Holt, Rinehart and Winston, Inc., 1969.

Periodicals
Bailie, Helen Tufts, "Dishonoring the DAR," *The Nation*, September 25, 1929.
"Blacklist Party," *The Nation*, May 23, 1928.
Somerville, Mollie, "Service to the Nation," *DAR Magazine*, October 1965.
Smith, Helena Huntington, "Mrs. Brosseau and the DAR," *Outlook and Independent*, March 20, 1929.
"What is Behind the DAR Blacklists?" *The Literary Digest*, April 14, 1928.

CHAPTER II

Books
Social Register Locator, 1973 edition, New York: The Social Register Association.

Proceedings
Proceedings, NSDAR Continental Congress, 1960-1973, Washington, D.C.

CHAPTER III

Books
Britt, Albert, *The Hungry War*, Barre, Massachusetts, 1961.
Davies, Wallace Evan, *Patriotism on Parade*, Cambridge: Harvard University Press, 1965.
In Washington, Washington: National Society Daughters of the American Revolution, 1965.
Montross, Lynn, *Rag, Tag and Bobtail*, New York: Harper, 1952.
Spirit of Seventy-Six, Henry Steele Commager and Richard B. Morris, editors, New York: The Bobbs-Merrill Co., Inc., 1958.

Periodicals
Aikman, Lonnelle, "The DAR Story," *National Geographic*, November 1951.
"Colonial Dames of America," *Woman's Home Companion*, March 1904.
"Early History of the NSDAR," Excerpts of *The National Historical Magazine*, October 1940, and from The Act of Incorporation.

CHAPTER IV

Books
Nelson, Jack, and Gene Roberts, Jr., *The Censors and the Schools*, Boston: Little, Brown and Co., 1963.

Periodicals
Jones, Sara R., "United Nations Resolutions, DAR Endorsement to Repudia-
tion, 1946-63," *DAR Magazine*, March 1964.

Proceedings
Proceedings, NSDAR Continental Congress, 1971-2.

CHAPTER V

Books
Anderson, Marian, *My Lord, What a Morning*, New York: The Viking Press,
1956.
Gibbs, *op cit*.
Green, Constance McLaughlin, *The Secret City*, Princeton University Press,
1967.
Haynes, George E., and Sterling Brown, *The Negro in Detroit and Washington*, for
Federal Writers Project, 1938.
Hughes, Langston, *Fight for Freedom*, New York: W. W. Norton, 1962.
Hurok, Sol, with Ruthe Goode, *Impresario*, New York: Random House, 1946.
Lash, Joseph P., *Eleanor and Franklin*, New York: W. W. Norton, 1971.
Myrdal, Gunner, *An American Dilemma*, New York: Harper and Row, published
1944, revised 1961.

Periodicals and Pamphlets
"Civil Rights in the Nation's Capital: A Report on a Decade of Progress,"
Commission on Civil Rights, National Association of Inter-Group Rela-
tions Officials, 1959.
Minutes, D.C. Board of Education, February through May 1939.
"Segregation in Washington," A Report of the National Committee on Segre-
gation in the Nation's Capital, published by the Committee, Chicago,
1948.
Smith, Carlton, "Roulades and Cadenzas," *Esquire*, July 1939.
Stokes, Anson Phelps, *Art and the Color Line*, Printed for the Consideration of
the Executive Committee of the DAR at their meeting, October 23, and for
the Marian Anderson Committee, Washington, October 1939.

Sources supporting information on black productions in Washington
1.   Charles Gilpin in *The Emperor Jones*, Belasco Theater, some time prior to
1927.
    —Jones, William H., *Recreation and Amusements Among Negroes in
Washington*, D.C., Howard University Press, 1927.
2.   Armstrong High School (black), "On the Slopes of Calvary," Belasco, May
1, 1927.
    —*The Washington Star*, May 2, 1927.
3.   *Lew Leslie's Blackbirds*, Belasco, 1929.
    —Program on file in Lincoln Center theater library.
5.   Marian Anderson recital, Belasco, April 19, 1931.
    —*The Washington Star*, April 20, 1931.

4. Ethel Waters in *Rhapsody in Black*, Belasco, April 18, 1931.
    —*The Washington Star*, April 19, 1931.
    —Reference verified by theater librarian, Free Library of Philadelphia.
    —Waters, Ethel, *His Eye is on the Sparrow*, New York: Doubleday, 1951.
6. *Green Pastures*, National Theater, February 1933.
    —Green, Constance, *The Secret City, op cit.*
    —Johnson, Haynes, *Dusk at the Mountain*, New York: Doubleday, 1963.
    —*Literary Digest*, March 9, 1935.
    —*The New York Times*, February 10, 1933; March 17, 1936.
7. Todd, Duncan in *Porgy and Bess*, National, March 1936.
    —Mrs. Todd Duncan
    —Green, Abel, and Joe Laurie, Jr., *Show Biz*, New York: Henry Holt & Co., 1951.
    —Stern, Arlene, "Todd Duncan: Summertime at 66," Potomac Magazine, *The Washington Post*, April 24, 1969.
    —*The New York Times*, March 17, 1936.
    —*The Washington Post*, March 17, 1936.
8. Ethel Waters in *As Thousands Cheered*, National, 1936 or 1937.
    —Brown, Sterling, *The Negro in American Culture: Section D, the Negro on Stage*, unpublished, prepared for a 1940 study on blacks in Washington.
    —Mrs. Todd Duncan
    —Stern, *op. cit.*
9. Abby Mitchell in *Mulatto*, Belasco, February 1937.
    —Bond, Frederick W., The Negro and The Drama, The Associated Publishers, 1940.
    —Dorothy Porter, former head of Howard University's Moorland Collection.
    —*The Washington Tribune*, February 20, 1937.
10. Marian Anderson recital, Rialto, 1938.
    —Stokes, *op. cit.*
    —Minutes, D.C. Board of Education, *op. cit.*

CHAPTER VII

Proceedings
Proceedings, NSDAR Continental Congress, 1970.

CHAPTER VIII

Pamphlets
Calhoun, Grace Ward, *Tamassee's Half Century*, 1919-69, South Carolina, 1969.
The Kate Duncan Smith Story, Grant, Alabama, 1962.
"Scholarships for American Indians," U.S. Bureau of Indian Affairs, Branch of Higher Education, Albuquerque, N.M.

Proceedings
Proceedings, NSDAR Continental Congress, 1973.

INDEX